D0065868

MARY RICHARDSON WALKER
From her earliest known picture, taken
about 1855. Courtesy of the Oregon
Historical Society.

MYRA FAIRBANKS EELLS
From Myron Eells, *Father Eells*, 1894.

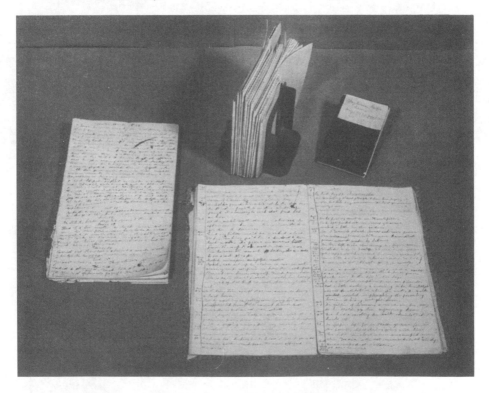

THE DIARIES OF MARY WALKER
This complete set of notebooks containing the diary for May 9, 1837 to November 11,
1848, is in the Huntington Library, San Marino, California. The diary on the left
begins with the entry of April 9, 1846; the central double page begins with March 15,
1844; and the closed book begins with May 9, 1837. The other thirteen notebooks
are within the folders shown in the upper part of the picture.

ON TO OREGON

The Diaries of Mary Walker and Myra Eells

Introductions and Editorial Notes by
Clifford Merrill Drury

Introduction to the Bison Books Editon by
Mina Carson

UNIVERSITY OF NEBRASKA PRESS

LINCOLN AND LONDON

⊗ The paper in this book meets the minimum requirements of American National Standard for Information Sciences—Permanence of Paper for Printed Library Materials, ANSI Z39.48-1984.

First Bison Books printing: 1998
Most recent printing indicated by the last digit below:
10   9   8   7   6   5   4   3   2   1

Library of Congress Cataloging-in-Publication Data
Walker, Mary Richardson, 1811–1897.
On to Oregon: the diaries of Mary Walker and Myra Eells / introductions and editorial notes by Clifford Merrill Drury; introduction to the Bison Books edition by Mina J. Carson.
p.   cm.
Originally published as v. 2 of: First white women over the Rockies, Glendale, Calif.: A. H. Clark, 1963.
Includes bibliographical references and index.
ISBN 0-8032-6613-8 (pbk.: alk. paper)
1. Women pioneers—Northwestern States—Diaries.   2. Women pioneers—Northwestern States—Correspondence.   3. Women missionaries—Northwestern States—Diaries.   4. Women missionaries—Northwestern States—Correspondence.   5. Overland journeys to the Pacific.   6. Oregon—History—To 1859.
7. Missions—Oregon.   8. Eells, Myra Fairbanks, 1805–1878—Diaries.
9. Indians of North America—Missions—Oregon.   10. Walker, Mary Richardson, 1811–1897—Diaries.   I. Eells, Myra Fairbanks, 1805–1878.
II. Drury, Clifford Merrill, 1897–   III. First white women over the Rockies. Volume 2.   IV. Title.
F587.W35   1998
979.5'03—dc21
97-50202   CIP

Originally published in 1963 as volume 2 of *First White Women over the Rockies: Diaries, Letters, and Biographical Sketches of the Six Women of the Oregon Mission Who Made the Overland Journey in 1836 and 1838* (2 vols.). Reprinted from the original edition by the Arthur H. Clark Company, Glendale, California.

Introduction to the Bison Books Edition

Mina Carson

An intimate insight into the struggles, passions, and very dailiness of family life lived under duress a century and a half ago: this is the incomparable gift of these diaries, yielded by personal archives lovingly preserved. These two women, Mary Richardson Walker and her less voluble friend and colleague Myra Fairbanks Eells, offer a view from inside the Protestant mission to the Northwest Indians in the 1840s. Written primarily for family members, these reflections on their experiences as women, wives, tourists, mothers, teachers, and missionaries create a larger sympathetic audience, even among those today who recognize the ambiguous and often destructive cultural legacy of Euro-American religious enthusiasts on American Indian communities in the eighteenth and nineteenth centuries.

Several things distinguish the overland journey of the Walker and Eells families from the 350,000 similar stories over the next decade. First, these couples were among the very first white Americans to undertake this arduous journey with the intention of settling on the West Coast and raising families. In the mid-1830s, the white presence in the Oregon Territory consisted largely of men connected with the fur trade. (In fact, the small band of missionary wives to which Mary Richardson Walker and Myra Eells belonged was cited by at least one emigration promoter as proof that women could not only survive but flourish on the overland trail.)[1]

Secondly, these emigrants went out as Protestant missionaries. They saw the American Indians *primarily* as subjects for religious conversion rather than *primarily* as impediments to appropriating and developing the rich resources of the Northwest. As many of us read these intimate documents today, we sometimes wince at the missionaries' assumptions of cultural superiority and their presumptuous intervention in the Indians' habits and traditions of living. We recognize, too, the unique, if labored, closeness and familiarity these white families cultivated with their indigenous neighbors, as well as their raw dependence on the Indians' knowledge of the area and continued good will toward these interlopers. The massacre of the Whitmans and their cohorts at the Waiilatpu mission—the Walkers' sister mission—in 1848 brought this era to an end as it offered bloody testimony to the explosive tensions fostered by white pressures on Northwest Indian lands and cultures.

Their religious mission was the context for other unique aspects of the material, social, and emotional experiences of the Walker and Eells families, particularly the women. We know from the work of previous scholars that the impulse to migrate westward was often the man's, with the woman acquiescing from her subordinate position in the family structure and then doing much of the social and emotional work of parting from friends and relatives.[2] By contrast, Mary Richardson and Myra Fairbanks were both unmarried when they developed an interest in missionary work, and we see in these pages that Mary Richardson actively sought assignment as a single woman to a post in a Protestant foreign mission. Initially turned down because of her unmarried status, she was introduced by mission advocates to the young minister Elkanah Walker, an earnest, gangly, socially awkward graduate of the Bangor (Maine) Theological Seminary. The pragmatic quest of both for a spouse who shared their ideology of evangelical service grounded their stable forty-year marriage. Similarly, Myra Fairbanks, a thirty-year-old, seminary-educated teacher, responded enthusiastically when her suitor, Cushing Eells, asked her to become a missionary's wife. In fact, she returned to the seminary for further preparation before their marriage and cross-country trek.

Though both Mary Walker and Myra Eells brought conviction and adventurousness, as well as duty, to their choice of mates, both marriages were ruled by conventional gender ideas that gave the husband primary responsibility for work outside the home, while the wife managed household and children. (This would be true also in a frontier or rural setting if the husband were a professional of some description: minister, physician, attorney.) Periodically, Mary Walker lodges a poignant complaint (in a journal regularly read, we note, by her husband) that "Mr. W." does not take her seriously or honor her as a conversational partner. Newly pregnant as their daunting overland journey began, she, along with her female traveling companions, found herself in an intensive tutorial on the roles and activities expected of a mid-nineteenth-century wife and mother. The Walkers and the Eellses, destined to be intimate companions and coworkers for the next decade, joined two more couples at their rendezvous with the American Fur Company caravan that would lead them from Missouri, their jumping-off point, to the Oregon Territory. After a stage, rail, and steamer journey from New York to Independence, variously fascinating, uncomfortable, and distressing—their arrangements required travel on Sunday, to them a violation of the Biblical commandment—the missionaries faced the nineteen-hundred-mile horseback ride from Missouri to the Pacific.

For the women, jolting for hours sidesaddle over the plains and mountains was punctuated by preparing and cleaning up after meals, scrubbing clothes in streams, and mending the party's garments as well as the crude tents they slept in with scant protection from the intrusions of weather, predators, or each other. "We dressed in our night dresses for washing, built a fire almost in the center of the creek on some stones, warmed some water, commenced washing in the kettles because we had nothing else to supply the place of wash-tubs," wrote Myra Eells in the travel journal kept for her family back East. Add to these challenges the hazards of the trail and the bodily discomforts and alarms of the first trimester of a first pregnancy, and again we pause over the determination of these voluntary migrants and the energy that allowed them to comment on the glories of the scenery along with the dangers and discomforts of travel.

The men, educated scions of the settled East, fared little better. Elkanah Walker later registered a protest that the overland missionaries seemed to be treated less well than those who traveled by ship and were served rather than expected to fend for themselves. The women's diaries suggest that the men were sick or weakened by unaccustomed activities at least as often as the women. What they enjoyed over the women was authority. They might not influence the executive decisions of the caravan, but they could regulate their wives, and sometimes the other men's wives, as well. "Mr. Smith undertook to help Mr. W. correct me for dictating to Mr. Gray. I think the reproof quite unmerited. Feel so tried with Mr. W. I know not what to do," wrote Mary Walker in her diary, in one of the earliest laments at Walker's seeming insensitivity and ready criticism of her. "He seems to think more of Mrs. Smith than of me. Spends a great deal more time in her society than in mine. Do I deserve all this, or is not my dear W. to blame. I feel that I am cruelly neglected."

Elkanah Walker had married a spirited woman—resourceful, practical, passionate, physically strong, and resilient. Lacking his account of the marriage, we have only indirect evidence of Walker's feelings about his spouse, but there is little room to doubt that Mary Walker genuinely loved her husband and preferred his company and aid to anyone else's. Her sense of the requirements of a companionate marriage—the style of marriage that became more common in the American middle classes as the century passed—is clearly delineated: intimacy, loyalty, companionship, intellectual respect, as well as basic decency. Because Elkanah Walker's work often drew him away for long periods of time to other missions and white outposts, Mary Walker punctuates her journal with patient laments for her absent husband. While he was gone, she communed with the Eellses and with the Spokanes, maintained the household in crude conditions and all weathers, taught English and religion, and birthed and reared her children.

"Fear I shall be sick before a room is ready for me," she wrote on November 21, 1838, at their first Oregon home, the Whitman-Spalding Waiilatpu mission. Two weeks later she bore her first son, Cyrus, in her new room, without complications but also without her husband, away at Walla Walla. To be "sick" was her term for labor and childbirth, which she survived eight times between 1838 and 1852, bearing seven sons and one daughter. All eight lived, though a baby adopted in 1848 died shortly afterward. Though Mary Walker rarely minced words about her emotional states, it is in keeping with her culture that she recorded the births of her children tersely, with little detail, even of the attendants. However, she gave intimate accounts of postpartum difficulties and the early development of her children. Nursing Cyrus brought terrible pain to her nipples, and she frankly recorded her anguish and the remedies and makeshifts attempted. Her journal also became a place to reflect on the right discipline of young children and to speculate about the appropriateness of different regimens at different ages. Though she and Elkanah Walker used corporal punishment (she mentions slapping and whipping) in the matter-of-fact manner of many nineteenth-century parents, she paused several times to wonder whether the punishment had truly fit the crime. Her entries suggest her sensitivity to the struggles as well as pleasures of sibling relations. When Cyrus complained that his sister, Abigail, had hit him, she proposed to whip the little girl; when Abigail hid and threatened to run away, Cyrus asked his mother please not to whip her. "I told him as it was him she hurt, if he did not want her punished, he might go & tell her." Remarkably, given her chauvinism toward the Spokanes and other Indians among whom they lived and to whom they had come to evangelize, Mary Walker was content to let her children play freely among the Indian families. Thus at least the oldest four, born in the first seven years of the Walkers' almost ten years among the Indians, would have had a protracted intimate exposure to tribal languages, practices, and individuals.

Thus we return to the rich complexity and ambiguity of these white families' relations with their Indian neighbors, the subjects of their attention and the purpose of their transcontinental migration. We witness Mary Walker's almost humorous struggle with her conscience as she (and her husband) procrastinate in learning the Spokane language—which they must do in order to work effectively as Christian evangelists. We shudder as they develop degrading nicknames for individuals they meet: Mufflehead, Simpleton, the Old Fool. We watch the Walkers care about, negotiate over, and grow exasperated with the young Spokane women they took on as household servants or nannies. Over and over, Mary Walker's diary reflects what strikes us as a fundamental disrespect for the cultural integrity of the Spokanes—a posture entirely congruent with the Walkers' own cultural heritage as well as their religious mission. Their struggle with the Spokanes over traditional medicine versus the European remedies the Walkers hoped to substitute captures beautifully the larger contest for command of Indian cultures and politics the missionaries had undertaken. We also see the Walkers mourning the loss of their friendships in the Indian community when they end the mission at Tshimakain, and we come to believe in the grief some of these Spokanes expressed at their departure.

A final comment on the painstakingly detailed editing of this volume by Clifford Merrill Drury for its first publication in 1963: the reader of this 1998 edition will note Drury's tacit acceptance of the missionaries' ambitions and practices, as well as their assessments of the Spokanes and other Indians. In other words, Drury's work, like ours, reflects its moment. The shining strengths of Drury's research and editing are legion; the deficit in terms of a critical cultural perspective on his subjects we must as responsible readers attempt to supply ourselves.

NOTES

1. John Mack Faragher, *Women and Men on the Overland Trail* (New Haven: Yale University Press, 1979), 6.

2. Lillian Schlissel, *Women's Diaries of the Westward Journey* (New York: Schocken Books, 1982), 20–22.

Contents

8

Illustrations

Persons and Places Mentioned in the Text

Since Mary Walker mentioned so many people in her diary covering her ten years' residence in the upper Columbia River country, 1838-48, a brief identification of each is here given. This identification is needed especially when we meet with the names of the natives. The following list does not include the names of colleagues of the Walkers in the Oregon Mission of the American Board or of the independent missionaries who migrated to Oregon in 1839 and 1840. These have been sufficiently identified in volume I of this work and in the author's *The Diaries of Spalding and Smith*. The names of the Walker and Eells children, with their birthdays, will be given. A few names, which have been identified in the text or in footnotes, will not be listed.

I. WHITE PEOPLE, MIXED BREEDS, AND HAWAIIANS

ABERNATHY, GEORGE. Member of the Methodist Mission in Oregon, arriving on the "Lausanne" in 1840. Was elected the first governor of the Provisional Government of Oregon in 1845.

ADAMS. Mountain man who worked for Walker for a short time during the summer of 1843. His native wife was the mother of Peter Skeene Ogden's eldest son.

ARMSTRONG, DR. WILLIAM J. Presbyterian minister; secretary of the American Board. It was he who first suggested that Elkanah call on Mary Richardson. He lost his life in a shipwreck on November 27, 1840, while en route from Boston to New York.

BINGHAM, REV. HIRAM. Founder of the Sandwich Islands Mission and pastor of the Honolulu church for natives.

BLACK, SAMUEL. Chief Factor of the Hudson's Bay Company in charge of Fort Kamloop, junction of the Fraser and Thompson rivers. Killed by natives in February, 1841.

BRIDGER, JAMES. Famous mountain man who met the missionaries at the Rendezvous. Had a native wife and a daughter, Mary Ann, who was placed in the Whitman home in the summer of 1841.

CAMPBELL. Worked for Walker in the summer of 1843, during which time he had much trouble with his native wives.

COMPO, CHARLES. French-Canadian mountain man who with a native wife settled on a farm near the Whitman station in the spring of 1838. Often served as an interpreter.

CONNER, JAMES. Mountain man with a native wife, who was hired by the reinforcement of 1838 at the Rendezvous to assist them. He joined the mission church on November 29, 1839, but was excommunicated February 4, 1843.

CRAIG, WILLIAM. Mountain man with a Nez Perce wife, who settled in the vicinity of Lapwai in November, 1839.

DESMET, PIERRE JEAN. Jesuit missionary, native of Belgium, who, beginning in 1841, made several trips from St. Louis into the Rocky Mountain and Oregon country. Visited the Spokane country in the fall of 1844.

DORION, BAPTISTE. Son of Pierre Dorion who was with the Lewis and Clark party and a Nez Perce woman.

DUMONT. Half-breed who settled about midway between Tshimakain and Fort Colville in 1847.

EELLS CHILDREN. Born at Tshimakain: Edwin, July 27, 1841; and Myron, October 7, 1843.

EMERSON, REV. NOAH. The Congregational minister at Baldwin, Maine, who married Elkanah and Mary.

ERMATINGER, FRANK or FRANCIS. In the employ of the Hudson's Bay Company, who escorted the reinforcement of 1838 from the Rendezvous to Waiilatpu. A frequent visitor at Tshimakain.

FINLEYS. Two half-breeds who settled about 1845 on the road connecting Tshimakain with Fort Colville. A brother, Nicholas Finley, was one of the ringleaders in the Whitman massacre.

FRASER (or FRAZER), SIMON. Hudson's Bay official who had a native wife, and who was an occasional visitor at Tshimakain during 1842-48.

GEYER, CHARLES (or KARL) AUGUSTUS. German botanist, who spent much of the first six months of 1844 at Tshimakain.

GILPIN, MAJOR W. Went out to Oregon in 1843 with Fremont. Was appointed first Governor of Colorado by President Lincoln in 1861.

GOUDY (or GOUDIE). Blacksmith at Fort Colville, married to a native woman. Their daughter, Sarah, lived for several years with the Eells family beginning in May, 1840. She was at the Whitman mission school in June, 1846.

GREENE, DAVID. Secretary of the American Board, in charge of the Oregon Mission.

HALE, H. Member of Wilkes Expedition, who visited Tshimakain in September, 1841.

HAMLIN, REV. CYRUS. Classmate of Elkanah Walker's, in Seminary. Missionary to Turkey and founder of Robert College. The Walker's first son was named after him.

HINMAN, ALANSON. An Oregon immigrant of 1844, who was hired by Whitman to be the schoolteacher at Waiilatpu. In the summer of 1847 Hinman took the Mission press to the Willamette Valley.

HOBSON, EMMA. Two motherless girls, Emma and Ann, ages six and thirteen, were left at the Whitman station in the fall of 1843. The Walkers took Emma in May, 1844, and kept her until May, 1845.

JACK. Hawaiian who was working for the Whitmans in the fall of 1838, and who later worked for the A. B. Smiths at Kamiah.

JOHNSON, LT. ROBERT E. A member of the Wilkes Expedition, who visited Tshimakain in June, 1841.

KANE, PAUL. Canadian artist who visited Tshimakain in the fall of 1847.

LEWES (or LEWIS), JOHN LEE. Succeeded Archibald McDonald as Chief Factor of Fort Colville in the fall of 1844. The missionaries at Tshimakain turned to Lewes for protection following the Whitman massacre. Had a daughter, Nancy.

LOVEJOY, ASA L. Accompanied Dr. Whitman on his ride East during the winter of 1842-43, as far as Bent's Fort.

LOW, THOMAS. Hudson's Bay man in charge of Montreal express, westward bound, spring, 1847 and 1848.

MAKI, MARIA. Wife of Joseph. The two Hawaiians, members of the Mission church in Honolulu, entered Whitman's employ in June, 1838. Joseph died August 8, 1840. Maria returned to the Islands in 1841.

MALIN, DAVID. Half-breed boy, who had a Spanish father, whom the Whitmans took into their home in March, 1842, when he was three or four years old. Narcissa named him after an old schoolmate friend of hers, a Presbyterian minister.

MARQUIS, MRS. Arrived at Tshimakain on October 15, 1847, to help Mrs. Walker. Left with the Walkers in June, 1848, when they were escorted by soldiers out of the Spokane country.

McDONALD, ANGUS. A son of Archibald, whom Mary Walker reported as having died on June 5, 1843. Another Angus, a nephew of Archibald, was placed in charge of Fort Colville in 1852.

McDONALD, ARCHIBALD. In charge of Fort Colville, 1836-44. His second wife, Jane Klyne, a half-breed, was a very capable woman. The McDonalds were friendly with the mission families at Tshimakain.

McKAY, (or McCay as Mary spelt it), THOMAS. Half-breed son of Alexander McKay, of the Hudson's Bay Company. Often in charge of the Company's pack trains. His daughter, Margaret, was left with the Whitmans in March, 1838, when she was in her early teens. She remained there for at least a year.

McKENZIE. Hudson's Bay man who frequently visited Tshimakain during 1843-46. Perhaps a courier.

McKINLAY, ARCHIBALD. Scotch Presbyterian who succeeded Pambrun in charge of Fort Walla Walla in 1841. He remained there until 1847. Very friendly to the missionaries.

McLEAN. Hudson's Bay employee stationed at Fort Colville. His half-breed daughter, Elizabeth, was received into the Walker home in April, 1841, where she remained for nearly a year.

McLOUGHLIN, DR. JOHN. Chief Factor, Hudson's Bay Company, Fort Vancouver, 1824-45.

McPHERSON. Hudson's Bay man who was a frequent visitor at Tshimakain. He was married to a native woman called Charlotte, in the Walker home on April 1, 1843.

McTAVISH. Hudson's Bay man who visited Tshimakain in April of 1844 and 1845.

MEVWAY, MUNGO. Half-Hawaiian, half-native lad who was received by the Whitmans into their home in December, 1837, when he was twelve or thirteen years old. He spent the winter of 1841-42 with the Walkers, where he took for his wife the daughter of a native called Teacher. A baby was born on August 2, 1843.

OGDEN, PETER SKEENE. Hudson's Bay Factor in charge of the New Caledonia post on the Fraser River, 1830-45. Succeeded Dr. McLoughlin at Vancouver in 1845. Was in charge of the operations which rescued the survivors of the Whitman massacre. Visited Tshimakain several times after June, 1842.

OVERTON. Mountain man who helped Walker build a house during September and October, 1841.

PAMBRUN, PIERRE C. Hudson's Bay Factor in charge of Fort Walla Walla, 1832-41.

PELLY. Possibly SIR JOHN HENRY, Governor of the Hudson's Bay Company, 1822-52. Visited Tshimakain in January and February, 1846.

PEONE, BAPTISTE. Quarter-breed employee at Fort Colville.

PERKINS, MRS. H.K.W. Wife of a Methodist missionary living at the Dalles. She was the former Elvira Johnson, a schoolmate of Mary's at Kent's Hill.

RODGERS, ANDREW. Migrated to Oregon in 1845 and was hired by Whitman to teach school at Waiilatpu, for white children. Killed in the Whitman massacre.

ROY, THOMAS. Hudson's Bay man employed at Fort Colville.

SAGER, CATHERINE. One of the Sager children adopted by the Whitmans. Visited Tshimakain with Mrs. Whitman in May, 1847.

SIMPSON. Hudson's Bay man who called at Tshimakain in April, 1848.

SINCLAIR. Leader of a colony of about one hundred and twenty-five Canadian immigrants who arrived at Fort Colville in September, 1841.

STANLEY, JOHN MIX. Artist. Spent a month at Tshimakain in fall of 1847. Narrowly escaped Whitman massacre and sent first word of the tragedy to Tshimakain. Painted portraits of Elkanah and Abigail Walker.

STEARNS, S. ALBERT. Member of Wilkes Expedition who visited Tshimakain in June, 1841.

WALKER CHILDREN. Born at Waiilatpu: Cyrus Hamlin, December 7, 1838. Born at Tshimakain: Abigail Boutwell, May 24, 1840; Marcus Whitman, March 16, 1842; Joseph Elkanah, February 10, 1844; Jeremiah, March 7, 1846; and John Richardson, December 31, 1847. Born at Forest Grove, Oregon: Levi Chamberlain, February 8, 1850; and Samuel Thompson, May 2, 1852.

WHITE, DR. ELIJAH. Former Methodist missionary in Oregon who became first U.S. agent for Oregon Indians in fall of 1842.

WHITMAN, PERRIN. A nephew of Dr. Whitman who, at the age of thirteen, went to Oregon with his uncle in 1843.

WHITNEY, MRS. SAMUEL (MERCY). A missionary stationed at Waimea, Kauai, Sandwich Islands. Although the two never met, she and Mary Walker corresponded for years. Some of Mrs. Whitney's letters are in Coll. WN.

II. NATIVES

In a few instances names of Indians mentioned only once in Mary's diary are included in eliminated passages. Often both Mary and Elkanah used varied spellings of the same Indian name in their respective diaries. In order to avoid confusion and to give uniformity, the author has selected that form which appears most often and then has changed the variant spellings to make them conform.

BIG HEAD. See Cornelius and Old Chief.

BIG STAR. One of the lesser Spokane chiefs. Principal medicine man of the band that lived in the vicinity of Tshimakain.

CHARLES. Sometimes assisted Walker.

CORNELIUS. Name given by Spalding to the principal Spokane chief who lived in the vicinity of Tshimakain. See Old Chief.

ELLIS. First Head Chief of the Nez Perces. See entry for April 6, 1848.

FOOL. Sometimes called Old Fool. Lived on the road between Tshimakain and Fort Colville.

GARRY. See Spokane Garry.

KANTEKEN. See entry for June 15, 1847.

KWANTEPETSER. The first native girl to help Mary in her house work. Died June 8, 1844, and was succeeded by Shoshenamalt.

LAWYER. Prominent chief who was half-Nez Perce and half-Spokane. His Indian name was Hol-lol-sote-tote or Ish-hol-hol-hoats-hoats. Mary referred to him as Hull Hull.

MUFFLEHEAD. Sometimes worked for the Walkers.

OLD CHIEF. Also called Big Head and Cornelius. The most prominent Spokane chief who lived in the vicinity of Tshimakain. J. M. Stanley gave his Indian name as Se-lim-coom-clu-lock.

OLD QUEEN. Possibly a wife of Big Star and probably the mother of Soshenamalt.

SHOSHENAMALT. Began working for Mary in February, 1842, and is frequently mentioned in Mary's diary.

SILLAPAL. Sometimes helped Mary in her house work.

SIMPLETON. Sometimes worked for the Walkers.

SOLOMON. One of the most reliable of the natives who worked for the Walkers. It was he who carried the news of the Whitman massacre to the families at Tshimakain. See his picture on page 167 of this volume.

SPOKANE GARRY. The best known of the Spokane Indian chiefs. He was sent as a fourteen-year-old boy to the Red River Mission School in Canada; returned on a visit to his people in 1829 with a Bible from which he read to his people; returned again to the school and came back in 1831. For a time he was active in promoting the white man's ways among his people. Sensitive to criticism, Garry soon lost his enthusiasm. He was a frequent visitor at Tshimakain after 1841 but failed to cooperate much with the missionaries. He had two wives, Lucy and Nina.

TEACHER. Helped Walker in the study of the Spokane language after January, 1842.

THREEMOUNTAINS. An Indian lad whom the Walkers took into their home for a short time in 1839-40, and whom Mary called "my boy." Later became one of the lesser Spokane chiefs. He was baptized by Spalding in 1873 and was one of the main leaders in the Presbyterian Church organized at Deep Creek in 1880. For further references to him see Drury, A Teepee in his Front Yard.

TIMOTHY. One of Spalding's first converts.

TORTESER. Sometimes employed as a messenger.

III. PLACES

BARRIER. A fish weir, probably made out of a series of wattled enclosures, which the Indians placed in the Spokane River for the annual run of salmon which began in May or June of each year. The main barrier was about ten miles from Tshimakain.

BAY. A part of Pend Oreille Lake, perhaps in the vicinity of what is now Sandpoint, Idaho. Both Walker and Eells made frequent itinerating trips to visit the Ponderay Indians living there. The Bay was a long day's ride over a mountain from Tshimakain.

KETTLE FALLS. Located about two miles below Fort Colville. These were the highest falls in the Columbia River. The total descent was about fifty feet, although the perpendicular fall in no place exceeded fifteen feet. The site is now covered by waters backed up by Coulee Dam.

KI-HA-KILIN. Also spelt Kaihakailu. A camping site on the Palouse River, about midway between Waiilatpu and Tshimakain.

LAPWAI. The site of Spalding's mission on the banks of the Clearwater River at the mouth of Lapwai Creek. The name is a corruption of Nez Perce words meaning "Butterfly Valley."

PALOUSE RIVER. A tributary of the Snake River coming in from the north. The river has a falls with a drop of 198 feet.

SEAKWAKIN. Also spelt Seerkwatum, and Seerwakum. A favorite camas grounds along Tshimakain Creek, about a dozen miles to the north of Tshimakain.

SPOKAN. The site of Spokane Falls where the city of Spokane, Washington, is now located. The Indian name of Sinhumanish was also used for the Falls. In the early day the word was pronounced with a long "a".

TOUCHET. A tributary of the Columbia River coming in from the south. Mary sometimes spelt it Tusha.

TSHIMAKAIN. The site of the Walker-Eells mission on what is now called Walker's Prairie, about twenty-five miles as the crow flies, northwest of Spokane. The name means "the place of springs" or "the head of waters." According to a poem that Mary wrote, the last syllable rhymed with "fine." Today the pronunciation would make the last syllable rhyme with "lane."

WAIILATPU. The site of Whitman's mission on the Walla Walla River. According to the late Dr. Stephen B. L. Penrose, former president of Whitman College, Myron and Edwin Eells, sons of Cushing and Myra Eells, differed as to the correct pronunciation. One placed the accent on the second syllable and the other on the third. It means "the place of the rye grass."

WASCOPAN. Or The Dalles, a site on the Columbia River where the Methodists had established a mission.

Mrs. Elkanah Walker

The Diary of Mary Richardson Walker

One of the most valuable documents to come out of the early history of Old Oregon is the diary of Mary Richardson Walker. The first entry of the oldest extant portion of her diary is dated January 1, 1833, more than five years before she was married. She was then twenty-two years old, was teaching school, and living with her parents at East Baldwin, Maine. On the first page of this part of her diary she wrote: [1]

> These lines are pened that in after life should my life be spared I may have the opportunity of comparing myself with myself, & of calling to mind many events which might be forgotten. By looking over this I am reminded of the different situations in which I have been placed & the kind of thoughts I then had. It is intended exclusively for my own use & many things are mentioned which to any one but myself must appear extremly trifling; yet they are linncked with associations which to me are interesting.
>
> As life is uncertain I write this page that should I be taken away sudenly, this book may not be seen except by a sister or some very near and intimate friend, & I hope that my friend will have the compassion to burn it immediately. Should it by chance fall into the hand of any other, pray be so good as not to read it. [2]

Once, after her arrival in Old Oregon, Mary discovered that her husband was surreptitiously reading her diary. Instead of verbally approving or disapproving his action, she inserted a letter in her diary under date of July 26, 1839, formally addressed to "Elkanah Walker, My Dear Husband." She wrote:

> I find it in vain to expect my journal will escape your eyes & indeed why should I wish to have it? . . . I have therefore determined to address my journal to you. I shall at all times address you with the unrestrained freedom of a fond & confiding wife. When therefore you have leisure & inclination to know my heart, you may here find it ready for converse.

---

[1] See "Sources and Acknowledgments," vol. i for an account of the Walker diaries.

[2] As a rule, the original spelling and punctuation are retained. A few changes have been made for the sake of clarity. The earlier portions of Mary's diary contain more misspelled words than do the latter sections.

In her later years, Mary was willing to let others read her diary. We find evidence of this in the following entry in her Autograph Album dated Forest Grove, Oregon, September 11, 1885:

DEAR "GRANDMA" I shall never forget the delightful hours spent in the "oldest house in town," in talking with the dear old lady who is the only surviving woman of the brave missionary band, and in poring over the old trunk of journals and letters. The memory will always be very precious to

Your loving make-believe Daughter   LUCY A. M. BOSWORTH [3]

Mary wrote for her own personal satisfaction. This is the secret of the sparkle and content of this intensely human document. In the early entries we see revealed the restless spirit of an active, alert young woman who was eager to do something worth while with her life. She was ambitious. Once she dreamed of being a doctor but was told that such an idea was preposterous and contrary to accepted standards. In her generation, besides being a housewife and mother, the only respectable calling open to a young woman was that of schoolteacher. Mary was always aspiring to something bigger than the lot circumstances forced upon her in her little home community. This in part accounts for her courage in offering to go as a foreign missionary to the heathen.[4]

Mary was far more faithful in keeping her diary during her connection with the Oregon Mission than any other members. The ten-year period beginning with her marriage on March 5, 1838, and continuing until July 3, 1848, when the Walker family left Tshimakain following the Whitman massacre, contains about one hundred and ten thousand words. While writing his *Elkanah and Mary Walker, Pioneers among the Spokanes,* the author used an imperfect transcription of the diary which had been made by a member of the family.[5] In the preparation of the present volume, he has made a new transcription direct from a microfilm of the original manuscript. Mary's writing is sometimes extremely difficult to read. In a few instances an undecipherable word renders a whole sentence meaningless. In such cases the three-dot ellipsis (. . .) will be used to indicate the elimination of a few words or a sentence.

An imperfect copy of Mary's diary, from June 10 to December 21, 1838, appeared in the Montana *Frontier* for March, 1931. Some extracts from the 1896 transcription were included in Ruth Karr McKee's volume about her grandmother, *Mary Richardson Walker: Her Book,*

---

[3] From Mary's Autograph Album, Coll. WN.

[4] The word heathen was used by New England Protestants of Mary's generation as a synonym for non-Christian.

[5] Notebook 16 of Mary's diary carries a statement by J. E. Walker, one of her sons, to the effect that he had copied all or part of the diary in 1896. Mrs. Ruth Karr McKee claimed that she had spent eighteen months deciphering and copying her grandmother's diary. The author believes that it was this copy he used.

published in 1945. Now, however, for the first time, the major portion of the diary, carefully transcribed, covering the full time Mary was associated with the Mission, is given to the public. Because of the necessity to compress the diary within the limits of this volume, repetitious entries and certain passages dealing with incidental items will be eliminated. Such omissions will also be indicated by the three-dot ellipsis.

Mary's diary for these ten years, 1838-48, has a fourfold value. In the first place, we here get a glimpse into the mind and heart of a most unusual woman. No one can read this document without having a great admiration for her spirit, her abounding energy, and her unfaltering loyalty to her religious commitment. Here we see unfolded that high religious idealism which moved her to offer herself as a missionary to the American Board. It is impossible to account for the daring of the six women who crossed the Rockies in 1836 and 1838, and who performed what Mrs. Marcus Whitman once described as an "unheard-of journey for females," apart from their religious motivation. Mary's diary throws considerable light upon the religious convictions of herself and her associates. To modern ears her religious terminology may sound somewhat pious and some may dismiss certain words and phrases as outworn clichés, yet these expressions were meaningful for that generation.

In the second place, Mary's diary gives an unrivalled description of pioneer life in the untamed wilderness of the Spokane country before the white settlers came. With the exception of the Reverend and Mrs. Cushing Eells, who shared with the Walkers their life at Tshimakain during the nine years, 1839-48, their nearest white neighbors were the Hudson's Bay men at Fort Colville, seventy miles to the north. Mary's first-born, Cyrus, arrived three months after the Walkers reached the Whitman station at Waiilatpu in the fall of 1838. Five more children were born to them at Tshimakain. When we remember that the Walkers never had a cook stove during their nine years' residence at Tshimakain, we marvel that Mary was able to do all of her cooking and baking in a fireplace. In addition to the necessary duties within the home, we read that she milked the cows, tended the garden, dipped candles, made soap and cheese, and sewed clothing and moccasins. Sometimes on a Sunday she found a little time to read. Occasionally her scientific interests led her to collect plants or to stuff the skins of birds. She often bemoaned her lack of opportunity to study the language or to do more for the natives. Her first duty was to her family and in this diary we get intimate glimpses, as through a window, into the Walker home at Tshimakain.

Mary's diary is invaluable, in the third place, because of the detailed information it gives of the life and work of the entire Mission. With characteristic frankness, Mary penned her likes and dislikes. She did not hesitate to write criticisms of her fellow-workers. Consequently we see this small band of missionaries as being rather ordinary people who displayed some of the same weaknesses which appear among people of this generation. Being missionaries did not prevent them from having sharp disagreements among themselves. Mary is often heartsick over the unhappy situations which developed. Through the pages of this diary we are able to obtain a sympathetic understanding of the difficult conditions under which the little band of missionaries were living. After reading of the difficulties they faced and the hardships they suffered, we can ask ourselves the question: "Could any have done any better under those same conditions?" Far removed from the sources of friction at Waiilatpu and Lapwai, the Walkers and the Eells exercised a moderating influence especially during the critical years of 1838-42. All this is revealed in Mary's running narrative.

And finally, Mary's diary is a commentary on the world that flowed around her during the years she lived at Tshimakain. Her diary is peopled not only with members of her family and of the Mission, but also with mountain men, Hudson's Bay men, United States Navy officers, explorers, scientists, artists, independent missionaries, Roman Catholic priests, Oregon immigrants, half-breeds, and natives from several tribes. Here is a major source of information regarding the life and customs of the Spokane Indians. Mary made many penetrating comments on passing events. Students for generations to come will find this an invaluable source document.

Mary continued writing in her diary after she and her family settled at Forest Grove, Oregon, in the fall of 1848. However, as the years passed the entries became more and more irregular. Sometimes long intervals elapsed between notations. The last entry was made in 1890, when Mary was nearly eighty years old. Thus the diary which began on January 1, 1833, covers a span of about fifty-seven years. No other diary of similar length and detail is known to have come out of the early history of Old Oregon. Herein is presented a magnificent self-portrayal of a remarkable woman.

THE EARLY LIFE OF MARY RICHARDSON

Mary, the daughter of Joseph and Charlotte Richardson, was born on a farm near West Baldwin, Maine, on April 1, 1811. An older sister died in infancy. Following Mary came six boys and three girls. Thus Mary grew up as the eldest in a family of ten. In 1832 the Richardson family moved to East Baldwin, where they occupied a story-and-a-half house which stood about three hundred yards from the Congregational Church. This house was still standing when visited by the author in the summer of 1938.

Life was rugged and money was scarce in the Richardson home at both West and East Baldwin. True to the New England manner of life then prevailing, Joseph and Charlotte Richardson made their home largely self-sustaining. There Mary learned the basic skills of a pioneer home, an invaluable preparation for her later life in Old Oregon.

Mary's parents were once schoolteachers and realized the importance of giving their children as good an education as possible. Two of Mary's brothers were graduated from Bowdoin College. Another became a doctor in Baldwin. Mary and two of her sisters, Charlotte and Phebe, at different times attended the Maine Wesleyan Seminary at Kents Hill, Readfield, Kennebec County, located about twenty-five miles north of East Baldwin. There the Richardson girls had relatives. A sister of their mother, Mrs. Dudley Moody, was the wife of the man who ran the local inn. For many years Moody was also connected in some official capacity with the Seminary. In all probability the Richardson girls lived with their uncle and aunt, perhaps working for their board and room in the inn, while attending the Seminary.

Mary enrolled in the Seminary in the fall of 1830 when she was nineteen, but her education was interrupted with periods of school teaching. The Seminary's records list her as a student in the spring and fall terms of 1832, and again in the fall of 1834. When Mary entered the Seminary in 1830, she found that the principal was an attractive young man, five years her senior, by the name of Merritt Caldwell.[6] Available information does not indicate whether or not Caldwell was married during any or all of the time she studied at Kents Hill. This we do know, a warm friendship grew up between Professor Caldwell and Mary Richardson which led to an exchange of long letters during the years that Mary lived at Tshimakain. Caldwell accepted a call to a position on the faculty of Dickinson College, Carlisle, Pennsylvania, in 1834.[7]

While at the Seminary, Mary developed a strong love for the sciences. According to a family tradition, she once asked Professor Caldwell about her grade after taking an examination with some young men. The professor is reported to have replied: "Mary, I say it to your shame, your paper was better than any turned in by the boys."

Among Mary's schoolmates was a girl, Elvira Johnson, who later married the Reverend H. K. W. Perkins.[8] The two went out to Oregon under the Methodist Board and were stationed at The Dalles. There they entertained Mrs. Whitman during the winter of 1842-43, when

---

[6] The Presbyterian Historical Society, Philadelphia, has a 23-page pamphlet entitled *An Address delivered before the Readfield Temperance Society at their first Anniversary, July 4, 1832*, by Merritt Caldwell. (Hallowell, Maine, 1832). Undoubtedly Mary was present on that occasion.

[7] An oil portrait of Caldwell hangs in the chapel building of Dickinson College.

[8] Under date of Oct. 19, 1849, Perkins in a letter to Jane Prentiss, a sister of Mrs. Whitman's, wrote a penetrating analysis of the Whitmans. The full text of this letter is given in Drury, *Whitman*, pp. 458 ff. See index.

her husband was on his famous journey East. Although we have no evidence to indicate that Mary and Elvira ever saw each other in Oregon, we do know that they corresponded.

The Maine Wesleyan Seminary was under the sponsorship of the Methodists. During the fall of 1830, when Mary was enrolled at the school, the Methodists conducted a revival and she was converted. As will be noted later, Mary was somewhat embarrassed when, in her first letter to the American Board, she found it necessary to explain this experience. There would have been no question if her religious awakening had come in a Presbyterian or a Congregational Church where Calvinistic theology was preached, but it was different when such an experience came in a Methodist Church where the Arminian doctrine was dominant.

The diary contains frequent references to school teaching during 1833 and 1834. For the January 27, 1833, entry, she wrote:

> I have now been teaching school three weeks. I like the employment very well. I think I shall prefer schoolkeeping to any thing else for geting a living. It affords me more time for study. I think we should not be guided by selfishness, but seek the glory of God in all we do. . . Guided by this principal I have continued my school on the sabbath in order to give my schollars some religious instruction. I find them very ignorant in this respect.

VOLUNTEERS TO GO AS A MISSIONARY

Mary Richardson was blessed with abounding vitality and good health. An entry in her diary for October 20, 1835, speaks for itself.

> We have now about 20 in the family. I am able to do nearly all the cooking besides keeping school. My health is very good. My school pleasant, more so than any I have taught before. Five of the girls board with us.

In fact, Mary's days were so full during the winter of 1835-36 that she found little time to write in her diary. On Thursday, May 5, 1836, she mentions the presence of "Mr. Thayer, Sunday School Agent," who with another guest was in her home for dinner. Mary and her sister Charlotte helped Thayer raise ten dollars for the Sunday School cause, an accomplishment which undoubtedly made a great impression upon him. As will be noted, William Thayer's visit to East Baldwin had far-reaching consequences for Mary.

Her love affairs were much affected by her religious views and her dreams of having a cultured, educated gentleman for a husband. No doubt, consciously or unconsciously, such an one as Merritt Caldwell was the ideal. As early as January 12, 1833, Mary noted in her diary: "If ever I have a husband, may God give me a christian." And again on August 7 of that year: "I see very few men that are perfect enough to please me." Mary's opportunities for meeting cultured and educated young men in such a small frontier community as East Baldwin were limited. However, among her suitors was Joshua Goodwin, a young farmer, to whom Mary seems to have made reference in a diary entry of May 12, 1834. "Hear very often that Mr. G. is attentive to me. I know not as it is so. I think it would be next to impossible for me to love him." On Sunday, May 14, 1836, she wrote:

> My attention has been called of late to the subject of matrimony. . . I have had a fair sort of an offer, dont know whether I ought to think of accepting it or not. Did he possess knowledge and piety I should like him. But I fear he lacks a kindred soul. Could I inspire in his bosom the sentiments that expand my own, but alas I fear it is impossible. Ought I to bid adieu to all of my cherished hopes and unite my destiny with that of a mear farmer with little education and no refinement. In a word shall I to escape the horrors of perpetual celibacy settle down with the vulgar. I cannot do it.

Thayer was a theological student at the Congregational Seminary located at Bangor, Maine, about eighty miles as the crow flies, northeast of East Baldwin. He returned to East Baldwin in the following September and again saw Mary. Since Thayer seems to have had a lady friend at that time, his interest in Mary was purely platonic. He was enthusiastic for the cause of foreign missions and evidently transferred some of his convictions on this subject to the susceptible Mary. It is altogether possible that her interest in becoming a foreign missionary was an alternative to the unattractive prospect of becoming the wife of a rude, uneducated farmer. On September 8, 1836, Mary noted in her diary:

> Being greatly perplexed, ventured to adress my Father on a subject I never did before. Dont feel much better satisfied than I did before. Think about it, cry about it, pray about [it,] get no satisfaction. I wish I knew what to do.

On Sunday, September 18, she continued the discussion of her problem:

> My mind very much excited, dont know what to do, have always harbored the design of going on a mission. If [I] listen to the proposals of G. then farewell to the design.
> MONDAY MORNING. Declare to Mr. T[hayer] my thought of offering myself to the A.B.C.F.M. He rather approves and very kindly offers me all the friendly instruction I need. And now Oh! God direct my decision, lead me in the path of duty.

THURSDAY, 22. By night and by [day] I scarcely think of any thing but becoming a missionary. I think I feel more engaged in religion than I have ever before. At least I have more freedom in prayer.

Mary talked with her pastor, the Reverend Noah Emerson, and he gave her encouragement. On October 24, she wrote to her friend, Professor Merritt Caldwell, asking for his advice. Caldwell replied on November 4, giving his wholehearted endorsement to the idea and on the same day wrote a strong letter of recommendation to the Board which contained the following:

To an apparent firmness of physical constitution, (which should not be lost sight of in the selection of candidates for a Foreign Mission) there is added in her case a vigorous intellect, and the power of persevering and successful industry. Her literary improvement, during the time she was under my tuition, was unusually good. . . I have no hesitation in saying that in my opinion she possesses a rare combination of those qualities which would be called for in such a station as that for which she proposes to offer herself.

Mary wrote to several friends for testimonials, all of whom commended her in the highest terms. Miss Phebe Payne, one of Mary's teachers at Readfield, wrote on November 28:

Her intellectual acquirements are more than respectable. She has a strong love for natural science and mathematics, in which her attainments are valuable. She is a chemist and practical botanist. . .
The powers of her mind are strong and masculine, quick for observation and fond of investigation. Her moral courage is conspicuous from which has grown out real independence of character, which combined with energy, perseverance, industry, and a robust physical constitution admirably qualify her to meet the exigences and bear the trials and privations of a missionary life.

This was an excellent analysis. Having received the testimonial letters requested, Mary on December 5, 1836, addressed a letter of application to the American Board in Boston for an appointment as a missionary. Of the six missionary women who made the transcontinental journey to Old Oregon in 1836 and 1838, only Narcissa Prentiss and Mary Richardson made application to the American Board for appointment before their engagements to their respective husbands. At the time each applied, the whole foreign missionary movement in the United States was still in its infancy. The fact that each seriously considered such a calling as a single person speaks eloquently both for the depth of their religious convictions and for their venturesome spirit. At the time Mary was writing, Narcissa Whitman was waiting at Fort Walla Walla for her husband to complete building that first home at Waiilaptu. But of course, Mary Richardson in Baldwin, Maine, knew nothing of that. In all probability Mary had read about the Whitmans and the Spaldings going out to Oregon in the columns of the *Missionary Herald,* the official organ of the American Board, but if so, this made no perceptible impression upon her mind. Her letter of application, somewhat abbreviated, follows:

REV. AND DEAR SIRS   By the certificates that accompany this you will perceive that I design to place myself at your disposal to be employed in a Foreign Mission, provided you wish to employ me. I have no particular station in view, but wish to leave it entirely with you to assign my destination. Yet I would confess that owing to some prejudice, perhaps an ill founded one, I feel less interest in the African than other races. I think however I have no prejudice I could not easily overcome or predilection that I could not easily transfer.

I wish to devote myself as a Missionary for life or so long as I can be useful. With me the field is the world, and I think I feel willing to be placed in that station where I can do the most good.

At the age of nine or ten my mind first became interested in the cause of missions and I determined if ever it were in my power I would become a missionary. I fixed on the age of nineteen as the time when I would engage in the work. This determination I never forgot. But when arrived at the proposed age, as I was without hope in Christ, I deemed it a sufficient reason why I should relinquish the design. It was the following autumn while attending school at Readfield that I first indulged a hope. . .

While I was at R, there was something of a revival in the Seminary and my mind was called seriously to the subject. I felt the time had come when I must attend to it or never. Life and death seemed set before me. I felt confident the decision I made would be for eternity. The idea of being converted among Methodists seemed exceedingly humiliating. But I felt that it must be so, or the Holy Spirit would leave me forever. Thanks be to God, thro the assistance of his grace, I trust I was enabled to lay down the weapons of my rebellion, to renounce my idols and find peace in believing.

My evidence at first was not clear. Surrounded by an atmosphere of Methodism, I feared I was deluded, and that my experience would not stand the test of orthodoxy. But after returning home and passing several months, my hopes were confirmed and I united with the Congregational Church in B[aldwin]. . .

I am the eldest of a numerous family, and as such I have ever felt that a fearful responsibility rested upon me. My example good or bad exerts an influence [that] many others cannot counter-act. . . In wishing to become a missionary I [have] endeav-oured to consider well the importance of the undertaking. It is not personal ease or temporal comfort that I hope to attain. I feel that a life of usefulness alone can render me truely happy. . .

I wish to be employed as a Teacher or in any capacity you may see fit. If I were sent among Savages I could teach them to put their hands to the spindle and hold the distaff, . . .

Mary referred to the sealed letters of testimonials she was sending with her application: "I know not what my friends may have written but fear they have given a higher character than I can support." The letter was folded, according to the custom of that day, so that part of the back of the last page was used for the address. Here she wrote: "Secretaries of the A.B.C.F.M., Missionary Rooms, 28 Cornhill, Boston, Mass." A portion of this same page bears the notation: "Dated Bald-win Me Dec. 5, 1836. Received Dec. 10th. Offer of service. Wrote Dec. 16th. Appointed May 2. Wrote to Mr. Walker informing him of his appt. May 3." This notation by one of the Secretaries shows that Mary was not actually appointed until after the Board had learned of her engagement to Elkanah Walker the following spring.

Secretary William J. Armstrong, in his reply, after commenting upon the highly favorable nature of her letters of recommendation, wrote: "You are not probably aware what difficulties exist in regard to the employment of unmarried females in our missions abroad." He sug-gested, however, that she might be used as a teacher of missionary children in Bangkok, Siam, or at Constantinople, Turkey. "What would you think of employment of that kind?" he asked.

Mary noted in her diary for December 21 that she was "much pleased with the reception and reply my proposals to the A.B. have received." She wrote to the Board on that day signifying her willing-ness to be a teacher of missionary children should such an opening arise. In this letter she penned the following frank self-appraisal:

I feel a great delicacy in refering to my domestick habits in an address to a stranger. Yet I think it would be very well for you to know a little information on this subject. I uniformly enjoy more than an ordinary share of good health; and have succeeded in combining the intellectual and domestic in a greater degree than I ever knew any one else to attempt. Ever inured to household labor and care it is to me rather pleasant than irksome. I feel myself perfectly at home in the schoolroom, nursery, kitchen, or washroom or employed with the needle. I am wont the "lowliest duties on myself to lay", the public good not private interest to consult. I am aware that I possess an aspiring mind. But I have endeavoured and I hope with some success to cultivate a spirit of humility; to be willing to do nothing and be nothing if duty required. I have endeavoured to resign myself wholly into the hands of Providence and say "choose thou mine inheritance for me."

She added that her hope of becoming a missionary had prevented her "from forming strong local attachments." In other words, she was not engaged to be married.

After waiting impatiently for several weeks for a reply, Mary addressed a third letter to the American Board on February 25, 1837. She wanted a yes or no reply to her offer. "I hope if they [i.e., the members of the Board] think I had better remain at home," she commented, "they will not hesitate to tell me so. . . Altho I have set my mind on going, yet I can bear disappointment." Armstrong replied on March 2, passing on the bad news: "But at present," he wrote, "I do not know of any station in the missions of the Board abroad to which the Committee think of sending unmarried females." And there the matter rested for the time being.[9]

ENTER ELKANAH WALKER [10]

In the meantime other events had taken place. On September 1, 1836, William Thayer wrote to the American Board suggesting the appointment of his fellow classmate at Bangor Theological Seminary, Elkanah Walker, to the Zulu Mission in Africa. During this same month of September, Thayer returned to East Baldwin where he talked with Mary Richardson about the possibility of her becoming a missionary under the auspices of the American Board. In his bubbling enthusiasm for the foreign missionary cause, it is possible that Thayer told Mary about that classmate of his at Bangor who happened to be thinking of the same general field of service. If so, then the name of Elkanah Walker was just a name to Mary. But to return to Thayer's letter of September 1 to the Board. In it Thayer gave the following brief biographical summary of Walker:

> Native N. Yarmouth, 31 yrs age. Professed religion in 1828, in a revival of religion. Began education in 1831. Prepared for College, then entered the Sem. Has been here two years. Means to stay another. Good health — a farmer. Can turn his hand to mechanic arts. No debts. No matrimonial engagements. Would do for Zoolak Mission.

[9] A more detailed account of the early life of Mary Richardson Walker may be found in the author's *Elkanah and Mary Walker*.

[10] This is a Hebrew name found in the Old Testament. The family accented the first syllable although correct Hebrew pronunciation calls for the accent to fall on the second.

Elkanah, the sixth child of Jeremiah and Jane Walker, was born on August 7, 1805. His parents lived on a farm and were members of a Congregational church at Pownal near North Yarmouth. As a youth his educational opportunities were limited to the local grade schools. He had a religious experience when he was twenty-three which induced him to study for the ministry. Records show that Elkanah joined the Congregational Church of Pownal on May 8, 1829, on confession of faith. He entered Kimball Union Academy in 1832 when he was twenty-seven years old. By nature Elkanah was shy and diffident. The fact that he was five or more years older than other youths at the Academy may have contributed to a feeling of inferiority. At the Academy, Elkanah was encouraged to continue his studies for the ministry by the principal, Israel Newell, who saw latent possibilities in the tall, awkward farmer from North Yarmouth.

After two years' work at the Kimball Union Academy, Elkanah entered Bangor Theological Seminary without having taken the four-year college preparatory work usually required in the Congregational Church of its theological candidates. There Elkanah took the full three-year theological course and was graduated in 1837. Among his classmates were two with whom he became very friendly, William W. Thayer, already mentioned, and Cyrus Hamlin, who later went as a missionary to Turkey.[11] Hamlin became the founder of Robert College in Constantinople.

On January 9, 1837, Elkanah wrote his first letter to the American Board for an appointment. He expressed his willingness to go anywhere the Board might wish to send him but expressed a preference for South Africa. The Board acted favorably on his application and on February 1, Secretary Rufus Anderson informed him of his appointment. Elkanah was told that in all probability he would be sent to his field "at the close of next summer or the beginning of autumn."

On March 16 Elkanah wrote a second time to the Board. This was no doubt the most important letter of his life. Looking forward to his coming departure for his missionary field overseas, he asked a number of questions regarding his outfit. He also inquired: "Is it advisable for me to go out without a companion [i.e., a wife]. This is rather a delicate question to ask, but as I view it of much importance, it will plead its own apology." The letter was referred to Secretary Armstrong to answer. It was he who had written to Mary Richardson a few days earlier saying that the Board could not appoint her because she was an "unmarried female."

Imagination must here supply what documented facts fail to explain. It is possible that Armstrong, remembering Mary's application, took her letter from the file and laid it alongside the one he had just re-

---

[11] Hannibal Hamlin, a brother of Cyrus, was Vice-President of the United States 1861-65.

ceived from Elkanah Walker. And possibly he said to himself: "If the two only knew each other!" He took his pen and under date of March 20, wrote to Elkanah. All of his questions were answered. The most important of all, that regarding a companion, was saved until the last. Then Armstrong wrote: "You ought by all means to have a good, healthy, patient, well informed, devotedly pious wife. There is a Miss Mary Richardson of Baldwin, Maine, who has offered herself to the Board, but we can not send her single. From her testimonials, I should think her a good girl. If you have no body in view, you might inquire about her. May the Lord direct & bless you."

If Armstrong had only known how very shy Elkanah Walker was, perhaps he would never have dropped such a suggestion to such a person. We have evidence which leads us to believe that Elkanah was somewhat astounded at the idea. What did the Board expect him to do? Was he to rush down to Baldwin and propose to a girl he had never heard of before? He showed Armstrong's letter to his classmate, William Thayer. Here again imagination must fill in the details. No doubt Thayer slapped Walker on the back and shouted: "Wonderful! Just the girl for you!" And of course Thayer could say much about the "good, healthy, patient, well informed, and devotedly pious" Mary. But the hesitant Elkanah was full of objections. "How do I know but that she has someone else in view?" he asked. "I'll write and find out," replied Thayer.

So under date of March 23, Thayer wrote a four-page, foolscap size, letter to Mary. Thayer was tactful. He began by inquiring about her interest in the foreign mission enterprise. He discussed items the two had talked about when they were together the previous September. And then came the crucial question: "Suppose Providence should bring to your hand a good-hearted mission-spirited companion — not the strangest supposition in the world, after all. . . Yield yourself to the guidance of God's Providence & you cannot err or fail of the right course."

Mary in her diary for March 29 mentions the fact that two days earlier she had closed her school of "from 25 to 40 scolars," and added: "The day before I closed my school I received a letter from W. W. Thayer. . . T. wishes to learn what has become of me." [12] Of course Mary did not know the urgency which lay behind Thayer's letter. She was, therefore, somewhat slow in replying. Finally she wrote on April 11. While all of the other letters relating to this incident have been saved, it seems that Mary's letter to Thayer has been lost. We can only surmise that Mary gave a diplomatic and favorable answer to Thayer's hint regarding the designs of Providence.

However, even though Mary was not engaged, the bashful Elkanah

---

[12] Mary saved the letters she received from W. W. Thayer and from Elkanah. These are now in Coll. WN.

was far from being convinced that he should endeavor to win the heart and hand of this girl whom his classmate so highly praised. Moreover, time was getting short. Thayer urged the importance of immediate action. It was he who planned the strategy of attack. As good fortune would have it, there was a small Congregational church at Sebago, about seven miles from East Baldwin, which had no pastor. Students from the seminary had been supplying the pulpit. It was very simple to arrange a Sunday supply for Elkanah. Being in the vicinity of the Richardson home, Elkanah could then pay a casual call and meet Mary. Cautious Elkanah was far from being convinced that the plan would work but finally consented. So on April 15, the day after he had received Mary's reply, Thayer wrote the letter of introduction that Elkanah was to carry. "As good fortune would have it," he wrote with tongue in cheek, "I have learnt today of an opportunity to send a line near you at least by the bearer Mr. Walker & perhaps he will pass through Baldwin, in which case I have invited him to call at your Father's on my account."

Still Elkanah was not convinced. Suppose that he were able to gain a graceful entry into the Richardson home and suppose Mary did make a favorable impression upon him, how could he make love and propose on such short notice? Time was short. He was supposed to be ready to sail for Africa in about four or five months. Two days were spent in discussing such questions. Then on April 17 the resourceful Thayer wrote a third letter to Mary.

Here I am writing again at a date of only two days later than my last. Perhaps this "respectful distance" between the two will be maintained in the reception of them but I should not wonder if this treads within six hours of its predecessor's heels.

This, by the way is a sort of "corps de reserve" to be brought into action if the case requires. If you ever receive it, you will receive it as an introduction of the bearer — Mr. E. Walker to your kind regards, as a suitor for your heart and hand. Should he thus present himself to you, the act will not be so hasty on his part as might at first seem — he has not been wholly unacquainted with you for some length of time past — though personally unknown. . .

Thayer then began to extol the virtues of his classmate. He was under appointment of the American Board to go to the "Zoolak Mission" in South Africa. Had Thayer known that Mary had specifically mentioned her disinclination to go to Africa, he might not have mentioned this fact. He continued:

That his character is a worthy one needs not . . . a more satisfactory evidence than that afforded by the fact that upon the weight of sufficient testimonials he has been accepted & appointed by the Board. Of his *disposition* something more can be said. Without flattery or puffing I number it among the kindest. . .

Of his talents I cannot predicate any thing more than respectability. He is not brilliant, but he is exceedingly tormented with diffidence & therefore his first appearance speaks less for him than after-acquaintance would justify. In short, he is one of those men who *must be known* in order to be justly appreciated.

As for his manners — look for yourself. If you can put up with somewhat of the uncultivated — If you can get by that obtrusive awkwardness which he will no doubt "lug in" directly in front of him when paying his addresses to you — If you find nothing insufferable in these . . . I think you can love the man. But you must judge for yourself. A husband is a husband notwithstanding the fact he may be a missionary.

According to a postscript which Thayer added, Elkanah had no knowledge of the exact contents of this last letter; only in general did he know that it would favor his suit should he decide to press it. This then was the strategy of the hesitant suitor's approach. Elkanah would carry two letters from Thayer, an unsealed letter of introduction and the sealed letter of near-proposal to be presented only if he deemed the opportunity propitious.

A FORTY-EIGHT HOUR COURTSHIP

On Saturday, April 22, 1837, Mary drew a line across the page of her diary on which she had already written a brief entry of the day's happenings. That line was her continental divide separating everything that had happened to her before she met Elkanah Walker from everything that came after. She even repeated the date as she began another entry for the same day.

APR 22, 1837, P.M.   Along some time about 3 o'clock perhaps, I was folding away some old news papers and looked out and saw two gentlemen approaching. Gazed a moment, concluded one was Dr. Whitney, could not tell who the other was. Thought it might be some one coming to see father on some business. Continued my work without hardly stoping to take a second look. They rapped, sister P[hebe] received them at the door. Dr. W. entered & introduced a tall and rather awkward gentleman. . . Query: is not the hand of Thayer with him in all this. . .

Elkanah presented Thayer's letter of introduction. Mary's alert mind immediately suspected some collusion — hence the reference to "the hand of Thayer." She noted that Elkanah was tall. He stood six feet

and four inches. She was short. In the summer of 1938 the author
called on Samuel, the youngest son of Elkanah and Mary Walker, who
was then living at the old Walker home in Forest Grove, Oregon.
Samuel described how his mother could stand under his father's out-
reached arm.

Elkanah returned to the Richardson home that evening with the
Reverend Noah Emerson, pastor of the Baldwin Congregational
Church. Mary was somewhat puzzled over the reason for the second
call but, according to a notation in her diary, concluded that it was for
the purpose of making arrangements for a meeting to be held in the
Richardson home on Sunday evening. Before retiring on Sunday evening, Mary took time to write some three hundred words in her diary
regarding her impressions of their visitor.

> His remarks were good. But not delivered in a style the most
> energetic. . . After meeting instead of shaking hands in a kind
> of free cordial kind of a way as I was anticipating, his attention
> seemed rather taken up in some other way . . . I thought he
> took more interest in getting acquainted with me than the rest of
> the family. . .

Elkanah was a guest in the Richardson home that night. Monday
was the BIG day in Mary's life. She devoted about one thousand words
to a description of the events of the day. This was by far the longest
entry in her entire diary. She confessed that she awoke early in the
morning and was unable "to compose myself to sleep" because of
thinking about "that man," and added: "I however prayed for resignation and thought perhaps he might be after all more than he seemed."

When Mary went downstairs to assist in getting breakfast, she found
herself the object of some teasing on the part of her sisters. Phebe
asked: "Are you going to ketch him?" "Me ketch him," replied Mary
according to her diary entry, "No sister, never." "Phebe ketch him,"
was the reply. For some unexplained reason, Mary's old suitor, Joshua
Goodwin, was present. In Mary's diary we read:

> I never was so disappointed in my life, said J. Goodwin, Why?
> said I. I thought, said he, I was going to hear something last night,
> & I nevr heard any one make out less. If he should preach till he
> is grey, he will nevr get half up with Mr. Emerson. There is no
> kind of life to him.

Before breakfast was ready, Mary found Elkanah reading his Bible
in the living room. He was alone. "Finding all the folks in the house
were busy but me and that W. & I were like to be left alone, I began
to feel a little embarrassed." Elkanah laid aside his Bible and the two
began to talk about the missionary enterprise. "As good fortune would

have it," wrote Mary, "I happened just that moment to think that very likely he would like to read my letter from Armstrong." She handed him the letter and "seating myself at a respectful distance, pleased with the fortune of the moment, began composedly to knit. As he read, I remarked that they seemed to object to me very much on account of my being unmarried." Elkanah rose to the occasion and without further delay presented the sealed letter that Thayer had written. Mary's diary entry continues:

> A little confused he proceeded, I am going to surprise you. I may as well do my errand first as last. As I have no one engaged to go with me, I have come with the intention of offering myself to you. You have been recommended to me by Mr. Armstrong, & here is another letter from Thayer.
>
> Blushing, agitated & confused, I took the letter, confessed my surprise and retiring to the ferthrest corner of the room & attempted to read. It was with difficulty I could raise my hands sufficiently to read.

Just at that inopportune moment, Mary's mother called them to morning prayers. Breakfast followed. Excusing herself from the "first table," Mary withdrew to the privacy of her "attic chamber" where she read and reread Thayer's amazing letter. She is tantalizingly silent on just how or when she said "Yes." But this we know, sometime that day, within forty-eight hours after she looked out of the living-room window and first saw him coming down the road toward her home, Mary accepted. The one primary factor which induced the two to pledge their troth to each other on such short acquaintance was their mutual conviction that the "hand of Providence" had indeed brought them together. However, even on the afternoon of the fateful Monday, Mary had some qualms on the subject. This she confessed in her diary:

> For a few hours after it was divulged, the conflict was rather severe. The hand of Providence appeared so plain that I could not but feel that there was something like duty about it, and yet how to go to work to feel satisfied and love him, I hardly knew. But concluded the path of duty must prove the path of peace.

That afternoon the newly-engaged couple called on Dr. Whitney and took tea with the Emersons. Among those who saw them was Mary's rejected suitor, Joshua Goodwin, who was quoted by Mary in her entry for the twenty-ninth as saying: "I would rather have seen you pass on a bier than in a chaise with W." Before returning to Bangor, Elkanah found an opportunity on Monday evening to speak to Mary's parents. Of this she wrote: "He asked their approbation of his design. And I guess went to bed rather satisfied with his days work."

A YEAR'S INTERLUDE

Elkanah started back to his Seminary on Tuesday morning, April 25, eager to inform Thayer of the success of his venture. Shortly after his return, Elkanah notified Armstrong of his engagement. Armstrong replied on May 3 and, after expressing his pleasure upon hearing the news, wrote: "Miss Richardson was last evening appointed an assistant Miss. of the Board on condition that she goes out as your wife." He also reported that the state of the Board's finances was such that there was some doubt if the two could be sent to their field that fall. Armstrong advised against marriage until the eve of their departure.

Instead of falling in love and then becoming engaged, Elkanah and Mary reversed the ordinary procedure. They became engaged and then fell in love. The story of this deepening affection is revealed in Mary's diary and in their love letters which are still extant. The courtship which followed their engagement climaxed in their marriage a year later on March 5, 1838, on the eve of their departure for Oregon.

With but few exceptions, Mary never referred to Elkanah by his first name, not even after years of married life. Almost always it was the respectful "Mr. Walker" or sometimes "Husband." Once Elkanah wrote to her saying: "I wish you would make as free with my name Elkanah in your letters as I do. It is a wretched name but the bearer of it is the same as though he had the prettiest name in all Christendom." Mary's letters and diary show that at times she was apprehensive over their sudden engagement. On June 8 she mentioned in her diary a talk she had had with Joshua Goodwin and on the twelfth commented in her letter to Elkanah: "I wish he were in another town. It is painful to pity when it is not in one's power to relieve. May I ever have it in my power to make you as happy as I have made him miserable." The following entry in her diary for November 22 reveals the persistence of the rejected but still hopeful Joshua. "Mr. G. called. Query: Shall I not be sorry I did not have him. He will probably be rich & I & mine poor. Answer, I have done what I thought best . . . I do not repent my decision."

Elkanah was notified in July by one of the secretaries of the Board that the outlook was discouraging for their appointment. In addition to financial difficulties, a tribal war had broken out in that region in Africa to which the Board was thinking of sending them. Elkanah was graduated from the Bangor Theological Seminary on August 30. Mary was unable to be present because of "pinching times." Shortly after his graduation, Elkanah paid another visit to Mary. On this visit she learned that her lover was sometimes subject to moody spells, during which he would be supersensitive to the remarks and attitudes of those about him. Mary wrote in her diary on September 14:

Feel very unhappy. Know not how to feel or act. I feel sad, sad, sad. I fear my courtship with W. will amount to nothing but trouble. Surely I thought my trials in love were over. I feel sick and discouraged. . . If W. leaves me what shall I do. I have endeavored to seek relief by prayer.

And on Sunday, September 17, Mary wrote: "The state of my mind has resembled the weather in time of thunder showers." She had been weeping. However, a letter from Elkanah when he was in a better mood brought relief to her mind. The following from Mary's letter of October 2 to Elkanah shows that he had wanted to get married in spite of the recommendation of the Board:

There was another respect in which I felt that I was culpable & this was in respect to be so little disappointed that we were not to be married this fall & also what I said about Ministers marrying while in debt. O Elkanah what a desolate being should I be if you should forsake. It seems to me I could never have the least courage or wish to have any one again.

As the year 1837 drew to its close, the hand of Providence was shaping events which began to bear upon the lives of Elkanah and Mary in what was to them a surprising manner. Accompanying the Whitman Spalding party to Oregon in 1836 was a single man, listed as a mechanic, William Henry Gray. The missionaries were given such an enthusiastic reception by the natives, especially by the Nez Perces, that Gray decided to return and seek reinforcements. The fact that he was engaged and wanted to take his bride to Oregon was also a motivating factor for his return. Somewhat to the surprise of the Board, Gray reported his return to the States in a letter to Greene, written from St. Louis on September 15, 1837. Gray gave such a favorable picture of the opportunities in Oregon that the Board decided to send out a party with him the following spring.

The Prudential Committee of the American Board met in Boston on December 5, 1837, and voted to send at least two couples who had been designated for South Africa. They were Elkanah Walker and Mary Richardson, and Cushing Eells and Myra Fairbanks. Letters of inquiry were sent to Walker and Eells to find out if such a change of designation would be agreeable. Elkanah received his letter at North Yarmouth on December 12 and wrote at once to Mary for her opinion. Elkanah was glad to make the change. He was no sailor, as the short voyages along the Maine coast had proved. He had secretly dreaded "the unpleassentness of a sea voyage." In his letter to Mary he said: "It seems to me that I can trace the hand of Providence in thus keeping me. . . But now I rejoice that I have been thus detained. . . I hope you will consent to the change."

Mary wrote in her diary on December 17:

> Had a letter from Walker last night. The Board wish him to go beyond the Rocky Mountains. The proposal strikes me favorable. They wish us to be ready to start in April. I hope we shall be able to go. . . My mind is full of tender thoughts on bid[ding] adieu to home. It is indeed trying.

Going out to a foreign mission field in those days was a far more momentous act that it is today. Nothing was said about furloughs. An appointment was usually made for life or for as long as health permitted. As early as June 21, Mary commented in her diary on this aspect of the undertaking: "Getting ready to go on a mission is like preparing to bury all my friends, to die myself and to live many years."

Elkanah arrived at Mary's home on December 28 for a few days' visit. He was invited to preach in the local church and did so. Mary wrote that day in her diary: "Heard Mr. W. preach to day. Was much gratified with him. . . My only fear in respect to him is that I shall be vain of being his wife. I do not know why Providence should deal so kindly with me." The young people, including Mary's sisters, sat up to see "the old year expire & the new one come in."

After Elkanah returned to his home, he wrote a letter to Mary which contained some criticisms. Evidently one of his moody spells had gripped him. On January 20, 1838, Mary confided to her diary:

> Recd. a letter from my dear W. It contained such severe criticism as I allmost feel as if I could not bear it. It is extremely mortifying for me to meet such reproof. . . I will, therefore, bear it patiently and determine never to let any one have occasion to notice a repetition of the same. I will however retaliate a little by just letting him know that I have noticed a thing or two in him as well. . .
>
> I have some distressing fears that Elkanah Walker does not love me or never will. If this be the case, dark & mysterious indeed must be that Providence that brought us where we are.

Mary visited Elkanah and his relatives during the last week of January. She was most cordially received and evidently the little tiff of the previous week was forgotten for she was supremely happy. "It is wonderful," she wrote in her diary, "that among so many more brilliant than myself, I should have power to please. Surely the Providence of God was in it. But I am determined if possible that Mr. W. shall never have reason to repent his choice."

One of the big subjects for discussion was the mode of travel to Oregon. Were they to go by land or by sea? Elkanah at first assumed that it would be by land, but later some question arose. How would women be able to stand the long horseback journey? The fact that Mrs. Whitman and Mrs. Spalding had accomplished the feat was reassuring. Gray, writing to Walker from Fairfield, New York, on December 18, assumed that they would travel by land. He stressed the necessity of keeping their baggage to a minimum.

A change of clothes is all we want. Buckskin drawers are the best for riding on horse back — our ladies should also have drawers to prevent being chafted in riding. We should carry no baggage excepting such as we want to wear or use on the journey. . . All the baggage we carry will cost us one dollar per pound.

Gray said that he was to proceed in advance of the others to Independence, Missouri, in order to buy the necessary animals and supplies. He told of the great eagerness of the Oregon Indians for missionaries and added: "I think you will never regret the day you are permitted to enter the Columbia as a Missionary to those Natives." Elkanah wrote to Secretary Greene of the American Board on January 3, asking for definite information as to whether they were to go by land or by sea. Greene replied on the eleventh, saying that the Board favored the overland route. By this time the Reverend Samuel Parker, who had gone out to the Rockies with Dr. Whitman in 1835 and who had made an exploration of the Pacific Northwest, had returned to his home in Ithaca, New York. He had gone to Oregon by land and had returned by sea around South America. No one, therefore, could speak about the relative merits of the two routes with as much authority as he. Greene, in his letter of the eleventh to Walker, reported that Parker recommended the land route.

On January 8, before he had heard from Greene, Walker wrote to Gray and asked a number of questions regarding the overland route. Gray happened to be visiting Parker in Ithaca when he received Walker's letter so he referred the inquiry to Parker. On February 19 Parker wrote to Walker saying:

By all means go across the continent by land. I had rather go across the continent three times than around the Cape once, and probably it would not take more time, nor be attended with half the dangers and hardships, as to go by water. . . A lady can go with far more comfort by land than by water.

Elkanah Walker was ordained to the gospel ministry in the First Congregational Church of Brewer, Maine, on Wednesday, February 14, 1838. Mary was unable to be present. They were informed by the Board to be ready to leave by March 20, so tentative plans were made to have their wedding about the middle of that month. There were so many things that needed to be done and the time was so short! Mary refers to the many tokens of affection shown to her during these days by her relatives and friends.

MARRIED AND ON THEIR WAY

On Saturday, March 3, Mary was at Gorham, a village about fifteen miles from her home. Elkanah, who was to conduct services in the Congregational Church of that place on the following Sunday, was due to arrive on the third. Mary looked for him most of the day. Finally he came at nine-thirty that evening with the startling news that they were to be married as soon as possible so as to be in Boston by the following Thursday. Mary wrote in her diary:

> We passed the Sabbath at Gorham. W. preached in the A.M. In the evening gave some account of our mission. They took up a contribution of 22 dollars. . . After evening meeting we rode home. The evening mild & delightful. Reached home about 12, called up brothers & sisters, did not go to bed.

The whole Richardson family was aroused and told the news. Plans were hastily made for the wedding to be performed the next morning. Mary's wedding was even more precipitous than her engagement. A few friends were invited and the Reverend Noah Emerson was asked to officiate. Mary must have been almost physically exhausted as she had had but little sleep on Saturday night and none on Sunday night. At times Mary's practical, matter-of-fact temperament becomes apparent in her diary. Such is the case in the following tantalizingly brief account of her wedding:

> Called on Aunt Pierce. Came home, looked around a little. Dressed & at eleven was married. . . All went pleasantly. At half past two P.M., took leave of friends. About nine reached Father W's.

Elkanah was then in his thirty-third year and Mary was nearly twenty-seven. What should have been one of the happiest days of her life was tempered with the sadness of parting. Years later Mary told her children that her wedding day was like a funeral. When she said goodby to her parents and to her brothers and sisters, she knew and they knew that in all probability most of them would never see each other again in this world. And such was the case. Thirty-three years later, or in 1871, after the completion of the transcontinental railroad, Elkanah and Mary returned to Maine for their first visit. Only a few were living who remembered the events of March 5, 1838, when Mary Richardson became Mrs. Elkanah Walker.

One of Mary's brothers drove the bridal couple to Elkanah's home at North Yarmouth. She confessed in her diary that after their six-hour buggy ride, she was "very sleepy." Tuesday was spent in saying their farewells to members of Elkanah's family. On Wednesday morning, the bridal couple left for Boston, the beginning of the long journey to Oregon which was to take nearly six months. They spent Wednesday night in Portland, Maine. Mary's account of the next day's travels is likewise brief and business-like:

> Took the stage at 5 in the morning. Took breakfast at Saco and soon left the State of Maine behind. Dined at Portsmouth. Took tea at Salem, reached Boston at ½ past 8. Found the traveling much better than we expected, not at all fatigued. Could not have imagined one could travel 120 miles on wheels & feel so little fatigued as I do.

Mary endured the rigors of their travels better than her husband who found it necessary to take to his bed on Sunday. In her first letter home after her marriage, dated from Boston on March 12, Mary showed one of her characteristic flashes of insight: "My health is as good as ever. I hope Mr. Walker will get well again soon. But I suspect it takes less to upset him than it does me." She also mused:

> Nothing gives me such a solitery feeling as to be called Mrs. Walker. It would sound so sweet to have some one now & then call me Mary or by mistake say Miss Richardson. But that one expression, Mrs. W., seems at once to indicate a change unlike all other changes. My father, my mother, my brothers, my sisters all answer to the name Richardson. The name W. seems to me to imply a severed branch. Such I feel to be. . .

And she signed her name "Your Pilgrim sister Mary W."

While in Boston, Elkanah received his official commission from the American Board, dated March 13, 1838, and probably at the same time his "passport" from the United States War Department, dated March 9, which granted permission for him "to pass through the Indian country to the Columbia River, with his family." The Walkers spent a week in Boston during which time they became acquainted with several of the secretaries of the American Board including Dr. David Greene,[13] with whom they were to correspond from their field, and the Reverend William J. Armstrong who was the one who suggested to Elkanah that he call on "a Miss Mary Richardson of Baldwin."

On Thursday, March 15, the Walkers left for New York City. They first "took the cars for Providence," which was undoubtedly the first

---

[13] Greene supervised the Board's missionary activities among the American Indians. All of the correspondence to and from the members of the Oregon Mission passed over his desk. His letters reveal a kindly considerate man of fine judgment.

time either had ridden on a railroad, and then took a steamer for New York. Mary wrote in her diary: "This is the first time I have been on the water. I enjoy it much. Wonder if the folks at home think of me to-night."

New and stirring experiences awaited the couple in New York where a number of church people who were keenly interested in missions did all in their power to make them welcome. One of the city's merchants, William W. Chester, took them to his store and then to "the University." Some of the ladies took Mary shopping. On Saturday evening, March 17, the Walkers met for the first time Cushing and Myra Eells, who were also designated for the Oregon Mission. By an interesting coincidence the Eells couple had also been married on March 5. Mary wrote in her diary: "Hope we shall like one another. But it seems to me I could not like to exchange husbands & I think Mr. Walker would not like to exchange wives." Little did any of the four imagine how closely their lives would be intertwined for the next ten years.

Mrs. Cushing Fells

Myra Fairbanks Eells

Myra Fairbanks, who on March 5, 1838, became Mrs. Cushing Eells, was born at Holden, Massachusetts, on May 26, 1805. She was the eldest daughter of Deacon Joshua and Sally Fairbanks and the oldest of their eight children. Myra joined the Congregational Church when she was thirteen. Judging from scattered references in her writings, and from other circumstantial evidence, it may be assumed that Myra came out of a home of more wealth and culture than happened to be the case with any of her associates in the Oregon Mission.[1]

Myra attended a female seminary at Wethersfield, Connecticut, and received a teacher's certificate in 1828. There is evidence that she alternated her studies with teaching. We find also that she received special training in sewing and dressmaking. In later years, although doubtful of her abilities in other respects, she was always sure of herself with the needle. In 1823 she joined a "Gentlemen's and Ladies' Missionary Association" which her pastor, a returned missionary from India, had organized. In all probability Myra's interest in missions began at this time.

Just when a young ministerial student by the name of Cushing Eells came into her life is not known. Cushing was born at Blanford, Massachusetts, on February 16, 1810, and was, therefore, about five years younger than Myra. He was graduated from Williams College in 1834, from Hartford Theological Seminary in 1837, and was ordained a Congregational minister on October 25, 1837. During the time he was pursuing his theological studies in Connecticut, he taught school during vacation periods. On one of these occasions he taught in Holden where Myra Fairbanks lived. A common interest in foreign missions probably helped to draw them together. When Cushing proposed marriage, he asked whether she would be willing to join him in the life of a foreign missionary. Myra is reported to have replied: "I doubt that you could have asked anyone who would be more willing."

---

[1] Eells, *Whitman,* carries in the Appendix short biographical sketches of the men connected with the Oregon Mission of the American Board. Some biographical material regarding the wives of these men is also to be found in these sketches. For the Eells sketch see pp. 327 ff. See also Myron Eells, *Father Eells,* and the article about Mrs. Myra F. Eells in *T.O.P.A.,* 1880, pp. 79 ff. Although this article is unsigned, it was probably written by her son, Myron.

Hartford Theological Seminary was then located at East Windsor, Connecticut, only fifty miles from Holden. The proximity of the two localities gave opportunity for occasional visits. Myra returned to the seminary in Wethersfield in 1835 when she was thirty years old in order to prepare herself the better for the life of a missionary. Since Wethersfield is a suburb of Hartford, Cushing and Myra were able to see each other rather frequently while pursuing their studies. In the spring of 1837 the two were appointed by the American Board to go as missionaries to the Zulus in southeastern Africa. The Board recommended that they postpone marriage until the eve of their departure, which was expected to be sometime that fall. However, as has been stated, a tribal war necessitated a change of plans and on December 5, 1837, Cushing was asked by the Board if he and his fiancée would be willing to go to Oregon. After consulting with Myra, Cushing sent an affirmative reply.

Even as Gray had advised Walker to take only the minimum baggage on the overland journey, so he advised Cushing Eells. Gray was positive that they could buy everything needed for their homes and their mission at one of the Hudson's Bay forts. However, both the Walkers and the Eells decided to send some household goods and personal belongings to Oregon by sea. It took eighteen months for the shipment to reach Fort Walla Walla after leaving Boston.

Myra was informed that all of the personal effects she wished to take on the overland journey would have to be compressed into a trunk which measured no more than 26 x 15 x 14 inches. A trunk was constructed to these dimensions of heavy leather over a wood frame and a brass plate fastened to the top with the inscription: "M. F. EELLS, COLA. RIVER, OREGON TERRY." [2] Writing to a sister from Waiilatpu on October 4, 1838, she has the following to say about the trunk:

> Were I in the states and to prepare another outfit for the missionary, it would be in some respects different from the one I prepared without any experience of a Missionary's wants. If any should want to know what is necessary for the journey over the mountains, tell them in the first place to have a leather trunk with no wood in it, or a leather vallice. Trunks like ours are too heavy and hard to pack on the animals. They should have a comfortable outfit sufficient to last them one year after they reach here.[3]

Like Elkanah and Mary, Cushing and Myra planned to be married

---

[2] The trunk is owned by a member of the Eells family. Mrs. Walker's trunk, now in Coll. WN., measures 24 x 19 x 9½ inches. See picture in Drury, *Walker*, p. 77.

[3] Original letter in Coll. WN.

about the middle of March so as to be on the western frontier by the end of April, in order to join the caravan of the American Fur Company for the journey across the plains through the hostile Indian country. Then word came, probably from Gray who, with his bride, had gone on to St. Louis in advance of the other members of the reinforcement, that they should be ready to leave the frontier by April 15. So with the same precipitous haste which caused Elkanah and Mary to set forward their wedding day, Cushing and Myra likewise made plans to have their marriage performed on March 5.

Myra Eells began a diary that same day which she faithfully kept until September 2, after she and her husband had completed their transcontinental journey.[4] Unlike Mary Walker, who wrote only for herself, Myra wrote for her family. Whereas Mary felt free to insert personal opinions about others and to give her reflections on passing events, Myra contented herself with a more factual account of events. Myra began her diary with the following:

March 5th — My affectionate parents. However uninteresting such a memorandum may be to others it may sometimes give you satisfaction to read a few hasty sketches from an absent and far distant daughter; to you, therefore, they are most cheerfully devoted. You will often find much that is dull and monotonous. They are the notes of every-day occurances, always written in the most unfavorable circumstances, being fatigued and worn out with journeying and with no accommodations for writing.

6th.   Left home, Father, Mother, Brothers & Sisters, and all near and dear by the ties of nature and affection, with the expectation of never seeing them again in this world. . .[5]

Cushing and Myra took a week to go by stage from Myra's home in Holden, Massachusetts, to New Haven, Connecticut. They went by way of East Windsor and Hartford, where farewells were said to their many friends. Myra was near-sighted and this explains the following entry in her diary for March 15 when they were at Hartford: "Purchased two pair of spectacles, one pair of Silver bows. . ." On the sixteenth they left Hartford for New Haven. Myra wrote: "Rode all day, the roads are very bad, rode through Wethersfield . . . but could not stop. At night much fatigued, but in good health and spirits."

---

[4] The original copy of this diary was lost when the Eells home, which had been erected in 1860 on Whitman's mission site at Waiilatpu, burned on May 28, 1872. Fortunately her son Myron had made a copy. A copy of this copy is now on deposit in the Oregon Historical Society in Portland, from which the text was taken for publication in *T.O.P.A.* of 1889.

[5] Mrs. Eells never returned to her old home in the East. Her husband, after her death in 1878, was able to make one visit.

FINAL INSTRUCTIONS

At six o'clock on Saturday morning, the seventeenth, they took passage on a steamboat for New York and arrived there about one p.m. That afternoon for the first time Cushing and Myra Eells met Elkanah and Mary Walker. Circumstances were such that the American Board had had no opportunity to hold any commissioning and farewell service for the Whitmans and the Spaldings who were sent out in 1836. Now, however, the situation was different. The presence of two newly-weded couples about to depart on their long and hazardous overland journey to Oregon gave the Board an excellent opportunity for some much-needed publicity for their Oregon Mission. The idea of women making the nineteen hundred-mile horseback journey from the western frontier over the Rocky Mountains to the Columbia River was still such a novelty as to excite public interest. A meeting was therefore arranged for Sunday evening, March 18, in the Brick Presbyterian Church of New York City, at which time the two couples would receive their final instructions from Dr. Greene. The event was considered to have been of such importance that at least five thousand words of Greene's speech were later printed in the July, 1838, issue of the *Missionary Herald.*

Greene warned the missionaries of some of the difficulties which lay before them.

> You will commence a pilgrimage, which, for three or four months, and through a distance of from 2,000 to 2,500 miles, will subject you to an untried, and in some respects, an unpleasant mode of life. The shelter, and the quiet apartments of a comfortable house, either by night or day, you must temporarily forego; you must look for no well furnished table, no permanent resting place, and none of the security and retirement of home.

In his description of South Pass and the Wind River Mountains, Greene drew upon the writings of Washington Irving, whose *Adventures of Captain Bonneville* and *Astoria* had appeared a year or so previous, for some of the following amazing statements:

> . . . while passing through the grand defile, you are supposed to be about 10,000 feet above the ocean level, while you look up on either hand to snow-capped peaks rising 8,000 to 10,000 feet above you. Indeed some of the peaks near this pass are estimated by scientific men (Prof. Renwick of Columbia College) to be not less than 25,000 feet above the ocean level, and thus surpassing all other mountains on the globe, except the highest points of the Himmalayah's chain in Central Asia.[6]

---

[6] Irving, *The Adventures of Captain Bonneville*, 219: ". . . the same measured by Mr. Thompson, surveyor to the Northwest Company; who, by the joint

Such a public statement as this reveals the colossal ignorance of informed people regarding the Rocky Mountains. If such a description of the Rockies were true, even the boldest adventurer would have hesitated before attempting such a crossing. However, in their complete ignorance of mountains, both the Walkers and the Eells seemed to have accepted the prospect without a qualm. The most frightening descriptions of the hazards which faced them were tempered by the knowledge that the Whitmans and the Spaldings had already made the journey. What had been done once could be done again.

On Monday Asa and Sarah Smith arrived, just a few hours too late to be present for the commissioning service. Mary noted in her diary: "Mr. Smith arrived. His wife, she is a 'little dear'." In the afternoon the women went shopping. According to Mary, a friend furnished them "a supply of needles, scissors, thimbles, etc." There was always room for such small but important items to be tucked into the corner of their trunks. And there was sight-seeing. Myra referred to the scenes which were "of uncommon interest to us who are so little accustomed to be in the city." And Mary wrote that evening: "Think I have been rather off my guard, quite too cheerful, have not been as careful as ought to maintain a prayerful spirit. Try to do better tomorrow."

NEW YORK TO PITTSBURGH

On Tuesday, the twentieth, the three couples left New York for Philadelphia. A party of friends, including some of the secretaries of the Board, saw them off at the pier about five o'clock in the afternoon. The railroad connecting New York and Philadelphia had not yet been completed. The steamer took the missionaries about thirty miles down the New Jersey coast, where they landed in the night and took the "railroad cars" for Philadelphia. They arrived at their destination between one and two o'clock in the morning, and had little time for sleep as they had to board a train leaving for Chambersburg at seven the next morning. Thus they began a gruelling five days' travel with the hope of reaching Pittsburgh by Saturday night, so they would not have to break the Sabbath.

The railroad to Chambersburg, one hundred and fifty miles from Philadelphia, was still not completed. Once the passengers had to leave the train, walk around a place where a tunnel was being dug, and board another train. As the train slowly wound its way westward,

means of the barometer and trigonometric measurement, ascertained it to be twenty-five thousand feet above the level of the sea; an elevation only inferior to that of the Himalayas." Greene's reference to Prof. Renwick is to a letter he wrote dated February 23, 1836, which Irving included in the appendix of his *Astoria*. Renwick claimed that there were other mountains "of nearly the same height in the vicinity." The highest peak in the Wind River Range, Mt. Fremont, is only 13,730 feet high.

Mary suddenly became aware that they would be passing through Carlisle where her dear friend, Professor Caldwell, was teaching. But there was no stopping. "I have not felt worse in leaving any place or any friends," wrote Mary in her diary, "than I did to be obliged to pass by Carlisle, to see the buildings where the instructor of my youth was teaching & not be able to just call."

The train arrived at Chambersburg at ten o'clock that night, having taken twenty-seven hours to go one hundred and fifty miles. And yet Myra wrote in her diary: "In the day time we seemed to be flying rather than riding." Included in the schedule was the time taken at Lancaster for lunch. At Chambersburg the missionaries were able to get a fair night's rest. The last half of their journey from Philadelphia to Pittsburgh was to be by stage. Before them rose several ranges of low mountains, including the Tuscaroras and the Alleghanies. Mary's diary for Thursday, March 22, tells us that they

> Left Chambersburg about ten. Crossed the Tuscarora Mts. in the stage. Four miles in ascending the heights & four in descending. I suffered more from timidity than I ever did before, being confined closely in the coach. The scenery much of the way sublime. Did not dine. Took supper in the evening, rode all night. Felt less fear in the dark than by day.

To all members of the mission party, travelling on the Sabbath was a mortal sin. They had carefully planned their journey with the full expectation of reaching Pittsburgh by Saturday afternoon but they had not allowed enough time to make the slow tortuous crossing of the mountains. Their willingness to push themselves to the limit of physical endurance attests to the depth of their convictions regarding keeping the Sabbath. We turn now to Myra's diary.

> 23d. Much fatigued, rode all night — stoped one hour to take breakfast and change horses again. Ride until night, change horses once during the day. Take supper and change horses, pack ourselves into the stage for another night's ride.
> 24. Rode all night. Change horses once. Took breakfast at what is called an Inn, but not much like the taverns in New England. Our only alternative now is to ride. My feet are badly swollen. Think it is in consequence of losing my sleep. Think it doubtful whether we arrive in Pitsburg to-day, owing to the unsettled state of the roads. Crossed the Aleghany Mountains last night. Nine o'clock, pack ourselves into the stage again, much refreshed by breakfast and rest. Ride all night, not within thirty miles of Pitsburg where we have letters of introduction and expected to spend the Sabbath.

Now the question is, Shall we ride on and thus encroach on the duties of the Sabbath, or shall we stop and spend the Sabbath here. If we stop, we must pay a large bill for accommodations, if we go our expenses will be free. Every meal we have eaten since we left New York has cost half a dollar.

All were agreed that they must stop when they reached Greensburg that evening except a Methodist gentleman and his wife, who wanted to proceed to Pittsburgh about fifteen miles distant. The missionaries, being in the majority, made the decision. Myra noted in her diary that they had to pay the expenses of the gentleman and his wife over the Sabbath day "to appease his anger with them for stoping." She also wrote: "Never were we so thankful for rest as now. I have not slept any of consequence since Tuesday night. My feet are so swollen that I can scarcely walk." [7]

On Sunday the party attended the Presbyterian Church of Greensburg three times — morning, afternoon, and evening. That is, all except Sarah Smith, whose frail health was not equal to such rigorous travelling. She spent most of the day in bed. Early Monday morning they were on their way again and reached Pittsburgh between two and three o'clock in the afternoon, where they were given a cordial welcome by the Rev. D. H. Riddle, pastor of one of the leading Presbyterian churches of the city. [8] With his assistance, passage was engaged for the party on the steamboat "Norfolk," due to depart down the Ohio River for St. Louis the next morning. In those days, before the arrival of the railroads, the rivers were the great liquid highways of the middle west.

PITTSBURGH TO INDEPENDENCE

The fare for the members of the mission party from Pittsburgh to St. Louis was twenty-five dollars each, including board. Since the steamboat was not due to leave until late in the morning of Tuesday, March 27, the three couples were free to accept an invitation to take breakfast with the Riddles. A social hour followed, when a number who were interested in missions were invited in to meet the Oregon-bound missionaries. Myra's entry for the twenty-seventh follows:

[7] See Drury, *The Diaries of Spalding and Smith,* 40-50, for another account of the experiences of the missionaries in their travels from New York to Westport. Because of this earlier printed account, the present narrative for this part of the journey will be abbreviated.

[8] Although all members of the 1838 reinforcement were Congregationalists except the Grays, who were Presbyterians, they felt perfectly free to establish Presbyterian contacts along the way of their travel, as the Presbyterians then cooperated with the Congregationalists in the support of the American Board. Dr. Riddle had welcomed the Spaldings on their way to Oregon two years previous.

Ten o'clock our friends, though strangers, accompany us to the boat, bid us God Speed and an affectionate farewell. Half past ten, rapidly passing down the Ohio; easy and quick riding compared with riding in the stage. We have each of us a handsome berth and the boat well furnished with everything for our comfort.

The boat tied up that night at Wheeling, West Virginia, about fifty miles from Pittsburgh as the crow flies, but several times longer as the river flows. They arrived at Cincinnati on Thursday, March 29, where they disembarked. Here they found letters from Gray advising them to tarry a few days as the caravan would not be ready to leave the frontier before the last of April. The missionaries called on Dr. George L. Weed, the agent for the American Board in Cincinnati, who immediately made them welcome.[9] Accommodations were found for the three couples in church homes in the city. Dr. and Mrs. Weed entertained the Walkers.

On Friday following their arrival, the missionaries met Cornelius Rogers, twenty-three years old, who became so interested in their projected mission that by the next Tuesday he had decided to go with them. Myra wrote in her diary: "He has no wife and goes on his own responsibility for support, though he has the promise of some personal friends that will help him to funds." Rogers never received an official appointment from the Board although he undoubtedly had the approval of Dr. Weed. Thus the reinforcement of 1838, counting the Grays, was increased to nine.

The missionaries spent the days at Cincinnati sight-seeing, meeting people, and tending to incidental needs. A brief comment in Myra's diary for March 29 tells us much about her inherent timidity. She wrote: "Cincinnati is a large city, so thickly settled that I do not dare go out alone lest I should get lost." Among the people they met was Dr. Lyman Beecher, President of Lane Theological Seminary located at Walnut Hills, a suburb of the city. It was there that Henry Harmon Spalding had studied for the two years, 1833-35. One of the party posed the question to Dr. Beecher as to what should be the proper course to pursue, when crossing the plains, with the ungodly men of the caravan who did not observe the Sabbath. If the party observed Sunday by remaining in camp, the caravan would move on leaving them unprotected perhaps in hostile Indian territory. If the party continued with the caravan on Sunday, it meant breaking one of the ten commandments. It was a case of caution versus conscience. "Well," replied the practical-minded theologian, "if I were crossing the Atlantic, I certainly would not jump overboard when Saturday night came." [10]

[9] Dr. Weed entertained Dr. Whitman when the latter was on his famous trip East in 1843. A son of Dr. Weed's wrote his memories of that event for the November 1897 issue of the Ladies Home Journal.
[10] Eells, Father Eells, 39.

Mary Walker celebrated her twenty-seventh birthday on Sunday, April 1. "What a year of mercy has the past been to me," she wrote in her diary. "I have now a good husband, better perhaps than I deserve, & am about to realize I trust what I have so long desired, the privilege of becoming a missionary." On Tuesday following, she went to the dentist "& got my teeth repaired. Gratis." In the meantime Eells had been taken ill and on Monday was confined to his bed. "A great favor we are not obliged to travel," wrote Myra. Another letter from Gray arrived on the second, urging them to proceed "with all possible speed." Passage was engaged on a steamboat scheduled to leave on the third. For that day Myra wrote:

3rd. Husband a little better, though he does not sit up much, on account of weakness. About 2 o'clock afternoon go to boat, have a good stateroom and are as comfortable as we can expect to be to travel. Feel as though we were fast hastening away from the land of our birth to a land we know not of.[11]

Actually the vessel did not leave Cincinnati until Wednesday, the fourth, which meant that she did not arrive at St. Louis until early Monday morning, the ninth. The missionaries hoped that they would be able to disembark at some town on Saturday and spend the Sabbath ashore and then proceed on the next vessel that might pass. Of this Myra wrote:

7th. SAT. Ride all day without coming to one convenient place to spend the Sabbath, or one regular stopping place for boats.
8th. Sabbath. Obliged to travel most of the day sorely against our wishes and principles. Kept our stateroom most of the day. Tried to get some good from books, but cannot feel reconciled to our manner of spending the Sabbath. Have witnessed enough to-day to convince us of the deficiency and wants of the Great West.

Mary, who often comments in her diary on the scenery, refers to the passing of the boat from the Ohio into the Mississippi on Saturday. The entry in her diary for that day includes the following: "Wish I knew whether [W] is satisfied with me or not. Sometimes I think I will try and get along one day without displeasing, but the first thing I know, I do something worse than ever. Still I am determined not to give up trying."

The missionaries had only a day to spend in St. Louis. This was their last good opportunity to buy supplies. Again interested church people, who were strangers, entertained them. Boat fare from St. Louis up the Missouri to Independence amounted to fifteen dollars each. While in

---

[11] Like Mary Walker, Myra Eells rarely if ever referred to her husband by his first name. Usually it was "Husband" or "Mr. Eells."

St. Louis Walker wrote to Greene saying, in part: "I think it was quite fortunate that Mr. Smith was enabled to join us. I do not know how we should have succeeded without him. I have much more confidence in him than in brother Eells." This initial favorable impression which Walker entertained of Smith probably accounted for the fact that when the time came for the four couples to divide into two groups to occupy the two tents taken for the overland journey, the Walkers elected to camp with the Smiths.

The "Knickerbocker," carrying the missionaries, left St. Louis for Independence at five p.m. on Monday, April 9. For the first time the New Englanders came into close contact with slavery. Their chambermaid was a slave owned by the Captain. Myra wrote on the eleventh: "To-day have my feelings moved almost to indignation on account of the wretchedness of slavery." Mary, however, has nothing to say on this subject. Instead she was concerned about keeping her sensitive husband from being too critical. "Feel some dark foreboding in contemplating this journey through the wilderness," she wrote. "Tomorrow I will not, if I can possibly avoid it, do anything that will displease my dear. I wish he would try to make me at ease instead of embarrasssing me by continual watchfulness."

The trip up the Missouri occupied six days and was spiced with excitement. On Wednesday a fire broke out in one of the staterooms on the "Knickerbocker." That afternoon there was a race between the "Knickerbocker" and the "Howard" during which the two boats collided, somewhat to the consternation of some of the passengers. On Thursday the captain of the "Knickerbocker," having discharged some of his passengers and freight along the way, decided to transfer the remainder of the passengers and of his freight to the "Howard" and return to St. Louis. The members of the mission party found that they had rather miserable accommodations on the second vessel. Mary wrote of the noise and confusion. On the thirteenth she noted: "The poor children on deck cried all night."

Again to the dismay of the missionaries, they found it necessary to travel on Sunday. Myra wrote:

> 15th. I can hardly suppress my feelings when I think of the many precious seasons spent at my own happy home. I now realize some of the privileges I once enjoyed; but I am happy in the choice I have made in relation to spending the remainder of my days among the heathen. I love to feel that I am making a little sacrifice, if such it may be called, for the cause of Christ. If I am but the means of bringing one soul into the Kingdom of Christ I shall be abundantly paid for all my privations.
>
> Noon. One of the wheels break so that we are obliged to stop for four or five hours to have it repaired. Never before did I hear

so much profanity and see so much wickedness on the Sabbath.

Night. Seven o'clock arrive at Independence landing about four miles from the village. We inquired if we could find lodging here; one man said "O, yes, if you have blankets." He then directed us to a small log house, for there are no others here, where three separate families live. They invited us to tea with them, but we had taken the precaution to get our supper on the boat. Mr. Rogers went immediately to the village in search of Mr. Gray. Our husbands busy in removing their baggage from the boat; in the meantime we are expecting to camp together on the floor for the night.

About nine o'clock Rogers returned with Gray and three couples met him for the first time. On short notice the two men had been able to secure only four horses. Each of the women had a mount and perhaps the fourth horse was used to transport the most necessary baggage. Gray insisted that all must go to the village that night. Myra's account continues:

Accordingly, we ladies mounted our strange horses and went to the village. I confess I was a little bit frightened, it being dark and not at all accustomed to riding, and besides, no lady had ever been on my animal's back before. We went up a steep hill and through deep mud, Mr. Eells walking by the side of me, sunk in mud and water over the top of his boots, but we reached Independence in good spirits about ten o'clock.

Many years later Eells commented as follows in his "Reminiscences" on the experiences of that evening: "The question was more readily asked than answered, can those unaccustomed to the use of the saddle ride by night on horse back over a road of Mo. mud and ruts in the month of Apr. With a footman holding the rein in close proximity to the mouth of the steed, the gentle riders made the first stage of a journey of near 2,000 miles in the saddle." Eells added that the three horses were "appropriately caparisoned for the use of females," which no doubt implies that they bore sidesaddles. Thus were the three women initiated into the rigors of what was to be an almost four-month horseback journey to Oregon.

Upon their arrival at Independence, the three couples met Mary Gray, and at last all members of the 1838 reinforcement were assembled. The party found that only limited accommodations were available. Of this Myra wrote:

We commited our way to God and retired, though I think none of us slept much. We had two rooms and two beds, consequently four of us must occupy one room and five the other. Mrs. Gray and myself take the bed, our husbands and Mr. Rogers the floor.

Mary, in the privacy of her diary, added a portentous note: "Mr. Gray did not like Mr. Smith's movements & considering it was the first time, we came very near having some unpleasant feelings." Gone for the duration of the journey, except for a few nights spent at one of the forts along the way or at the Rendezvous, was the privacy of separate sleeping accommodations for any of the four bridal couples. The pairing off of the couples at Independence, the Walkers with the Smiths, and the Eells with the Grays, set the pattern for the use of the two tents on the overland journey.

THE DAYS OF FINAL PREPARATION

The mission party had only a week after their arrival at Independence to complete their outfit before leaving with the fur company's caravan on the long trek across the prairies to the Rockies. The men bought twenty-five horses and mules, nine yearling heifers and four fresh milch cows, a dog named King, and a light wagon. On Monday, Tuesday, and Wednesday the women were busy sewing their tents which Myra described as being "made of thin duck." On Wednesday, the eighteenth, Myra wrote: "Finish our tents, made some bags, cover some books, etc. Ride a little way to try our horses; do not know how I shall succeed in riding."

The missionaries planned to take enough food with them to last for four weeks, by which time they expected to be in the buffalo country. According to a letter Myra wrote from the Rendezvous in July, they laid in a supply of "a hundred and sixty pounds of flour, fifty-seven pounds of rice, twenty or twenty-five pounds of sugar, a little pepper and salt." [12] After reaching the buffalo range, the missionaries planned to subsist on an almost exclusive meat diet supplemented with milk from their cows.

While at Independence a number of interesting people called to meet the little band of intrepid missionaries. Among them was the Hon. Lilburn W. Boggs, Governor of Missouri. Of him Mary wrote: "He is said to be a benevolent public spirited man. Thinks we will have a railroad over the mountains one of these days." Most of the members of the mission party lived to see that prophecy come true and five of them made the return journey by rail to the East for a visit. They were the Grays in 1870, the Walkers in 1871, and Cushing Eells in 1883.

On Friday afternoon, the twentieth, the party moved twelve miles to Westport where the American Fur Company, under the direction of Captain Andrew Drips, was assembling a caravan of about two hundred horses and mules, seventeen carts and wagons, and about sixty men. Describing their first experiences on the trail, Myra wrote: "Our

---

[12] Eells, *Father Eells*, 59.

horses, mules & cattle being unaccustomed to traveling make us much trouble. Mr. Rogers drives the wagon. . . The roads are so bad that he breaks the wagon and we are obliged to leave it two or three miles this side of Westport, it now being quite dark. About 9 o'clock reached Westport." There they met Dr. J. Andrew Chute,[13] a native of Maine, whom Eells described as being "a graduate of Yale,, an excellent Christian gentleman," who helped them find suitable accommodations for the night. The Walkers and the Grays were entertained in the home of the Reverend and Mrs. Isaac McCoy, former Baptist missionaries to the western Indians. All were tired. The next day Myra wrote: "Feel the fatigue of yesterday. . . Suppose this is but the beginning of hardships."

Saturday was the last opportunity the women had to do their washing before leaving the frontier. Of this Mary wrote:

APR. 21. We, Mrs. Gray & myself busy washing & ironing. Mrs. S[mith] & E[ells] chose to hire theirs done. So Mrs. McCoy, her niece, & myself & Mrs. Gray did it for them. I had a severe cold, though I was about sick, but I walked over to the village & back, then washed & ironed till nine in the evening without sitting down to rest. So I think I am not sick yet.[14]

At noon on the following day, Sunday, the Fur Company's caravan left for the Rendezvous which was to be held that year at the junction of the Popo Agie and Wind Rivers, on the east side of the Wind River Mountains. The mission party decided to tarry for one more day in order to avoid traveling on Sunday and also to enjoy another opportunity of going to church. Myra wrote:

Go to church; a Methodist minister, missionary among the Kansas Indians, preaches in the morning. Feel it is a privilege to find a few Christian brethren and an unfinished log Church here in this part of the country. Mr. Eells preaches in the afternoon. The truth the same here as in a civilized land. This is probably the last Sabbath this side of the Rocky Mts. where we can have public worship. Am I prepared to live without the ordinances of the Gospel?

---

[13] On March 9, 1836, Greene wrote to Whitman: "We have lately received letters from a Dr. J. A. Chute, of Westport, expressive of a deep interest in religious and missionary affairs." Mrs. Eells, in her diary for April 20, states that he was "a missionary," but no record has been discovered to indicate any connection with any missionary board. So far as is known, Dr. Chute did not make contact with the Whitman-Spalding party but he was of great service to the reinforcement of 1838. Recently the author has located a series of nearly forty letters Dr. Chute wrote which were published in the *Christian Mirror* of Portland, Maine, during 1836-8. His death is reported in the Nov. 1, 1838 issue of this paper as having occurred the previous October 1 at the age of 27.

[14] The strict formality of the times demanded that even the women should refer to each other by their married names.

As Mary contemplated the long journey which lay before them, her mind was haunted with forebodings due no doubt in part to suspected pregnancy. On this Sunday, April 22nd, she wrote:

Took some medicine last night which, I suppose makes me feel rather poorly today. I dread very much the thought of the journey before us. Almost fear we shall labor in vain & spend our strength for naught. Still I am inclined to hope that God will prosper & bless us. Thus far we seem to have prospered abundantly on our way. When I look back to N.E. it seems very dear, still I could not think to return. I regret not as yet the course on which I have determined. Yet I see some dark hours. When all the streams fail, may I not forget to go to the fountain.

The Overland Journey

Combining the Diaries of Myra Eells and
Mary Walker, April to September 1838

The Overland Journey

NINETEEN HUNDRED MILES ON A SIDESADDLE

The overland journey of the 1838 reinforcement of the American Board for its Oregon Mission is one of the most remarkable in the entire history of western travel. This is because the party included four brides, the second group of white American women ever to cross the Continental Divide, and also because we have such a wealth of original source material written by members of the party. At least five diaries were written by members of this 1838 reinforcement which cover all or part of the westward journey. These include those of both Elkanah and Mary Walker, Myra Eells, W. H. Gray, and A. B. Smith.[1] The author's *Diaries of Spalding and Smith* contains Mr. Smith's diary together with a detailed map of the route of the party.[2]

Both Myra Eells and Asa B. Smith kept a daily mileage record. Just how the actual mileage was calculated is not known. Since the American Fur Company had taken wheeled vehicles to the Rendezvous prior to 1838 and had wagons in the caravan of that year, it is possible that odometers attached to the wagon wheels were used to measure the distance traveled each day. Also, the actual time spent in riding could be used as an estimate. Possibly the members of the caravan discussed at the end of each day's ride the estimate of the approximate distance covered. A comparison of the figures given by Myra Eells with those given by Smith show general agreement although Myra was inclined to favor a slightly larger figure. We have no evidence to indicate that either of these two knew that the other was keeping the daily mileage record.

After leaving the Rendezvous, the missionaries would not have had

---

[1] Drury, *The Diaries of Spalding and Smith,* 39-40, gives more details regarding these documents. In addition many letters from members of this party are extant.

[2] *Op. cit.,* p. 222. The trail taken by the 1838 caravan and missionary party followed the Kansas River to the Little Blue; up the Little Blue and over a divide to the Platte River; then along the Platte to the Sweetwater; from the Sweetwater north to the Rendezvous on the Popo Agie and Wind Rivers. After leaving the Rendezvous, the mission party returned to the Sweetwater; then through South Pass to the Green River; then to Fort Hall and along the south bank of the Snake River to Burnt River; then over the Blue Mountains into the Columbia River Valley.

the benefit of a wagon meter if such had been available on the first part of their journey. However, they then traveled with a small company of Hudson's Bay men who knew the trail well and no doubt were able to give a fairly accurate estimate of each day's accomplishment. Only twice did Myra fail to indicate in her diary the daily distance traveled — April 28 and June 13. Smith's figures for these days, five and sixteen miles respectively, have been used to complete Myra's records.

A general comparison of distances as compiled by Myra Eells and Asa Smith follows:

	EELLS	SMITH
Westport, Missouri, to Fort Laramie April 23 — May 30, 1838	776	740
Fort Laramie to the Rendezvous June 2 — 21	315	294
Rendezvous to Fort Hall July 12 — 28	309	327
Fort Hall to Waiilatpu July 31 — August 30	532	498
	1,932	1,859

Thus Myra's estimate was only seventy-three miles more than that of Smith's.[3] The mission party left the frontier on April 23 and the Walkers and the Eells arrived at the Whitman mission on August 29. The Grays arrived a few days earlier and the Smiths with Rogers reached the station on August 30. Of the one hundred and twenty-nine days spent on the trail, the Walkers and the Eells spent ninety-one days traveling. The other thirty-eight days were spent in camp either at one of the forts along the way, at the Rendezvous, or occasionally along the trail. The average distance covered per day was about twenty-one miles. After leaving the Rendezvous, as may be seen in the chart facing this page, the mission party traveled as much as forty miles a day and once made a record of forty-five miles.

What an amazing journey for a party of greenhorns! All except Gray were complete strangers to the rigors of overland travel that were so suddenly thrust upon them as soon as they left the frontier. These were young men and young women of education and culture who had come out of comfortable homes, even though such homes might be considered modest and even primitive by modern standards. The three

---

[3] Spalding was more generous in his estimates. He figured the distance traveled by the mission party of 1836 from Liberty, Missouri, to Fort Walla Walla at 2,300 miles. See Drury, *Spalding*, pp. 142 and 162. More credence should be given to the estimates of Mrs. Eells and Smith than to that given by Spalding, as he is not known to have kept a daily record.

CHART OF MILEAGE TRAVELED
As recorded by Myra Eells
May – August, 1838

Sun	Mon	Tue	Wed	Thu	Fri	Sat
MAY 1838						
		1-12	2-17	3-14	4-21	5-15
6-27	7-26	8-16	9-21	10-25	11-13	12-27
13-25	14-25	15-27	16-16	17-14	18-27	19-27
20-21	21-22	22-27	23-25	24-27	25-25	26-30
27-30	28-25	29-24	Fort Laramie			
JUNE 1838						
					1-(L)	2-12
3-28	4-25	5-12	6- 23	7-20	8-25	9-(C)
10-(C)	11-(C)	12-12	13-15	14-28	15-20	16-20
17-21	18-10	19-20	20-12	21-12	Rendezvous –	
– – – – – At Rendezvous through July 11 – – – – – –						
JULY 1838						
– – – – – – – Rendezvous – – –				12-22	13-16	14-27
15-20	16-45	17-8	18-20	19-24	20-13	21-(C)
22-(C)	23-23	24-25	25-25	26-23	27-18	28-(H)
Fort Hall		31-10				
AUGUST 1838						
			1-15	2-15	3-12	4-30
5-(C)	6-35	7-25	8-12	9-26	10-20	11-35
12-(C)	13-40	14-25	15-25	– – – Fort Boise – –		
19-(B)	20-20	21-20	22-10	23-12	24-25	25-40
26-(C)	27-25	28-25	29-30	– – – Waiilatpu – – –		

The first figure indicates the day of the month, and
the second figure the mileage traveled that day.

Abbreviations: (L) = Fort Laramie   (H) = Fort Hall
(C) = in camp   (B) = Fort Boise

The party left Westport on April 23, and traveled
about 125 miles before May 1.

ministers were fresh from the sedentary life of students or from the relative quiet of a small parish.

As the mission party proceeded westward with the caravan, the men became more and more conscious of the fact that they were indeed working their passage to Oregon. Like the hired hands of the Fur Company's caravan, they too had to bear their share of the physical labor involved in packing and caring for their animals. The mere routine of camping out-of-doors and cooking over an open fire was often an exhausting experience for men and women alike. The missionaries frequently compared the hardness of their lot with that of others who were sent by the Board by ship to some overseas field. In the latter case the missionaries were passengers. Their fare was paid by the Board and they could take their ease. The diaries and letters of the members of the reinforcement of 1838 carry frequent references to this comparison of the overland journey with a sea voyage. The prairie was a vast dry sea with the rolling hills likened to frozen billows.

In a long letter to Greene written from Waiilatpu on October 15, 1838, Walker recounted their travel experiences and commented:

> It appears to me that if it is not proper or right for Missions who go abroad by sea to be compelled to work their passage & be exposed to all the hardships & sufferings incidental to a sailor on a voyage, neither is it right or proper that Missionaries should make the voyage across the Mountains & in such circumstances as will compel them to perform as much or more & the same kind of labor as the hired men of the company.
>
> The same may be said in regard to ladies. If it is not right & consistent with female delicacy for the wives of Missionaries who go by water to their various stations to act as cooks for their husbands & all who may be in their company, living on deck under miserable shelter, liable to be drenched at every passing shower & awake in the night & find that they were sleeping in water & often sitting on the deck in the open air without any thing to shelter them from the scorching rays of the sun in presence of the whole ships company — if it is not consistent with christian propriety & female delicacy for the wives of the Missionaries to do all this — then it is not right for them to cross the mountains where they will be compelled to do it.

Smith, also commenting on the travel experiences in a letter to Greene dated April 29, 1839, wrote: "I have not indeed worked my passage on board a vessel to a foreign port, but I can say in truth I worked my passage across the Rocky Mountains."

Whereas we have reason to marvel at the way in which the men, plucked out of the comfortable surroundings of their respective home or school communities, were able to adjust themselves to the hardships

Mrs. Cushing Eells . . .
A drawing copied from a photograph
and reproduced in Elwood Evans,
History of the Pacific Northwest.

Reverend Cushing Eells
From Myron Eells, *Father Eells*, 1894.

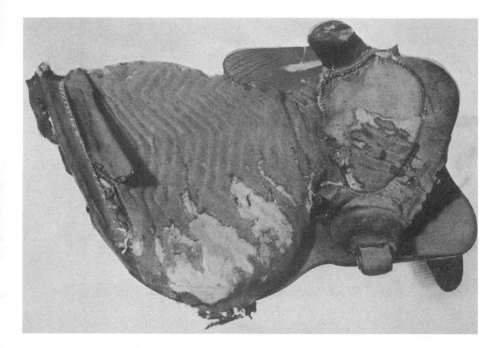

THE SIDE-SADDLE OF MARY WALKER
Two views of her saddle, the type which was used by the missionary wives for the nineteen-hundred-mile trip from Westport to Waiilatpu. Courtesy, Oregon Historical Society.

of overland travel, we have double reason to marvel at the stamina of these four women who accompanied their husbands. At least one of the women, Sarah Smith, was in delicate health before she started the long overland journey. Although the reinforcement took a wagon with them as far west as Fort Laramie, yet there are only a few scattered references to any of the women riding in it. For the most part each of the four women rode the entire distance of about nineteen hundred miles from Westport to Waiilatpu horseback, on the old-fashioned sidesaddle. There is no evidence that any one of the four was an experienced equestrienne before the party left the frontier. It might also be safe to assume that not one of the four women had had much if any experience in camping out-of-doors, cooking over an open fire, or sleeping on the ground.

Both Mary Walker and Myra Eells commented in their diaries on the novelty of their experiences when they first began their overland travels, but the novelty soon turned into drudging routine. And there was no turning back. Their trail led them through nearly two thousand miles of uncivilized country, across wide expanses of prairies which were sometimes swept by sudden and violent wind and rainstorms, over the Rockies where the wintry blasts from snow-capped peaks at times sent the thermometer below freezing even during the summer months, across swollen rivers, through areas where myriads of mosquitoes and other winged insects made life miserable for both man and beast, and then across the hot deserts of what is now southern Idaho.

The best way, yes the only way, to understand the magnitude of the undertaking and to appreciate the spirit of the participants and something of the privations endured is to read the documents which tell the story in detail. Since both Myra Eells and Mary Walker kept parallel diaries covering their journey from Westport to Waiilatpu and since the limits of this volume prohibit the publishing of both accounts *in toto*, the two diaries will be condensed and interwoven. Most of the passages in Myra's journal giving the daily mileage will be deleted since a summary of the distances covered is indicated in the above chart. Quotations will be made first from Myra's diary and then from Mary's. The name of each of the women will be given at the beginning of each quotation to indicate the source. It should be remembered that since Myra was writing for her family, her comments are more objective than were Mary's, who was writing just for herself. However, Mary does include much that is factual. The material in Mary's account which duplicates that given by Myra will be eliminated. All omissions in either diary will be indicated by the three-dot (. . .) ellipsis.[4]

---

[4] The manuscripts of *The First White Women Over the Rockies* together with the unabridged copies of the diaries of Mrs. Eells and Mrs. Walker will be deposited in the Eastern Washington State Historical Society, West 2316 First Ave., Spokane, Washington.

Before leaving Westport, the missionaries hired a man named Stevens to assist them in packing and caring for the animals. He remained with the party until they reached Waiilatpu. About a month later, another man, Paul Richardson, was hired to be their hunter. Thus the personnel of the party was increased to eleven.

The following section of the interwoven diaries begins with the entry for Monday, April 23, 1838, when the mission party left Westport, one day after the Fur Company's caravan had started.

Diaries of Myra Eells and Mary Walker
April to September 1838

WESTPORT TO THE RENDEZVOUS

Myra 23d [APRIL 1838] Started about noon. Dr. Chute accompanies us a day or two, see many things to interest us. Rode 5 hours, 12 miles; came into camp; pitched our tent, cooked and ate our supper in the open air and on the ground. . . Camp is any place where we stay for the night, or unpack our animals at noon. Saw four wild Indians, nearly naked.

Mary Left the States about noon. The baggage went ahead. Dr. Chute went as conductor to rest of us. We took a different way. Were missed. Mr. Gray went in pursuit. We found the camp but he rode till dark & then was obliged to camp. Returned to the camp early in the morning and found all safe. The prairie is spread out before us on every hand. . .

Myra 24th, TUESDAY. Mr. Gray comes to us about six o'clock, stayed about two miles from us but could not find us. Moved camp at seven, rode till noon, encamped two hours, then moved again and rode three hours; eight hours, 24 miles.[1] Encamped on one of the head branches of the Osage river. Met Mr. Meeker [2] and two Indians of the Ottawa Mission. . .

---

[1] The usual pattern of travel followed by the Fur Company's caravan was to make a morning march, observe a noon rest, and then make an afternoon march. Some time was given during the midday break to permit the animals to graze. There were two camps a day, at noon and at night. Sometimes the word camp was used as a synonym for march — as "a long camp" or "a short camp." Myra was more consistent in keeping daily mileage figures than was Mary. Occasionally the two did not agree.

[2] Jotham Meeker was a pioneer Baptist missionary printer who took his first press to the Shawanoe Baptist Mission, Indian Territory, in 1833. According to the *Baptist Missionary Magazine*, June, 1836, Meeker had up to that date printed some 6,000 pieces of literature in seven languages. For a time, Isaac McCoy, who entertained the Walkers at Westport, was associated with Meeker in the same mission.

Mary   Rested well on my ground bedstead [3] and should feel much better if Mr. W. would only treat me with more cordiality. It is so hard to please him I almost despair of ever being able. If I stir it is forwardness, if I am still, it is inactivity. I keep trying to please but sometimes I feel it is no use. I am almost certain more is expected of me than can be had of one woman. I feel that if I have strength to do anything it must come of God. . . May God help me to walk discretely, do right and please my husband. We came to camp about 5, having travelled about 23 miles. Very tired. Feel hardly able to sit up. Never had a poorer appetite. . .

Myra   25th.   After breakfast, Dr. Chute prayed with us and returned. Moved camp at seven, rode seven hours, encamped on a branch of the Kansas river, 20 miles. Saw no living creature except our own company, the prairie nearly covered with flowers of every hue. Crossed two creeks, banks steep on both sides, rode through some timber, rolling prairie, saw bluffs off at a distance. Think we must have worship night and morning, Mr. Rogers leads.

Mary   Cold but not rainy. Rode 21 miles without alighting. Had a long bawl. Husband spoke so cross I could scarcely bare it, but he seemed to pity me a little when he found how bad I felt. To-day has been very kind.

Myra   26th.   Moved camp at eight, road [sic] till noon, encamped on a small creek two hours, moved again till six, eight hours, 24 miles. . .   Thankful for a resting place, I am too tired to help get or eat supper. The weather extremely warm, see no living being.

Mary   Baked some biscuits. The first cooking I have done since I was married. Mr. Walker remarked that he thought I had done very well [for] one day. . .   Mr. W. impolitely selected the camp grounds. [4]

By Thursday night, April 26, the mission party was still half a day's march behind the caravan. Through inexperience with the thieving habits of the Indians, the men did not post a guard. That night their sleep was disturbed by the "howling of the wolves," undoubtedly signals that some Indians were giving to one another. [5]

---

[3] Mary began a letter to her family from Westport, April 23, 1838, which carried some later notations and was then sent back to be mailed. On the 24th she wrote: "We are now travelling on the dry sea. For days & weeks we shall see nothing but the big buffalow pasture. The buffalow however have deserted this end of the pasture. . .   We have two tents eight feet by twelve. Have a curtain to separate the families. All on the campground is still. Mr. and Mrs. Smith are sleeping loudly in the other part of the tent. Mr. Walker lies by my side telling me I have written enough." Original letter, Coll. Wn.

[4] The women took with them a tin reflector in which it was possible to do baking by a camp fire. Mary's reference to her husband "impolitely" selecting the camp grounds may be to the fact that the site afforded no privacy for the women, or possibly to her husband making a decision which Gray felt was his to make.

Myra   27th.   Husband, all but Mr. Gray, looking up the animals. Last night we were disturbed by the prowling wolves and we imagined Indians, to-day we have sufficient proof of it. Three of our best horses are not to be found, all go in search for them till nine o'clock. We then move camp. Mr. Eells goes back to look for them; have a thousand fears lest he will get lost in this great prairie. We ride . . . 6¼ hours, 20 miles. Mr. Eells overtakes us just before we get into camp, but can hear nothing from the horses. . . Husband so tired that the ground makes him a soft bed.

Mary   Some of our horses have strayed. Here we are waiting till the sun is high. Feel anxious. Some of the company feel disposed to murmur against Moses [i.e., Gray]   Mr. S. takes it hard if he has to be separated from his wife. I feel that dangers & perils await; that we ought to realize that every day may be our last.

Myra   28th.   Arose at four, proceed to business as fast as possible. Expect to overtake the company to-day. Move about six, overtake the company about nine o'clock, hope to travel a little more secure from the Indians.[6] The Company encamped and are making preparations to cross the Kansas river. Almost as soon as our tents were pitched, Captain Drips and Stuart [7] called on us, had a social talk, gave them some biscuit and cheese. They appeared pleasant, though they said we had better travel by ourselves, either before or behind camp, as they should have their animals guarded nights and it might not be convenient for our men to stand guard. Mr. Gray told them his men expected to stand their proportion of the guard. They seemed to think each company had better take care of their own horses. This gives us to understand they did not want us to travel with them. However, Mr. Gray did not mean to take the hint, as he knew it would not be safe for us to travel alone, and insisted on a due proportion of the guards being given to us. They leave us soon. Major Harris [8] comes, gives us a large piece of pork.

---

[5] Osborne Russell in his *Journal*, p. 56, gives a proverb used by the mountain men: "It is better to count ribs than tracks." Russell explains: "It is better to fasten a horse at night untill you can count his ribs with poverty than turn him loose to fatten and count his tracks after an Indian has stolen him." This truth the missionaries had to learn through costly experience.

[6] The missionaries averaged 20 miles a day for the first five days on the trail, which speaks well for the quickness with which they adjusted themselves to their new manner of life. They caught up with the caravan in the vicinity of what is now Manhattan, Kansas.

[7] The reference is to a Scottish nobleman, Sir (or Captain) William Drummond Stewart, who was traveling in the west for the love of adventure. He was with the caravan of 1836 when the Whitmans and the Spaldings went to Oregon.

[8] Moses Harris was also with the 1836 caravan. See vol. i of this set, part i of Mrs. Whitman's diary, fn. 36.

Indians on every side of us. Their clothing is principally skins and blankets. Their hair is cut short, except a narrow strip straight over the top of their heads. They are abundantly painted and ornamented. Their ears are filled with tin and pewter jewels, their ears having been bored all through, many of them are tied in with red ribbon. Their features are large. They would come around our tent to watch us like great dogs. Our dog grabbed one, who was nearly naked, Mr. Eells called him off, whipped him, and then tied him. After dinner Mr. Rogers goes back in search of the horses. Towards night three or four men came up to join the Company, say they have seen our horses with Indians on them. Dr. Chute comes up to us again. Feel that I have been preserved through dangers seen and unseen. Will God give me grace and wisdom and knowledge and strength equal to my day; make me useful in life, happy in death, and in eternity. Mr. Eells is so tired that he says a bed of stones would feel soft.

Mary Came up with the company about ten & the Captains called & were introduced. They sent us some corn & another gentleman sent us a piece of fresh pork. We expect to go in the morning. . . Would be glad not to have our flight on the sabbath. We cook up a little more than usual & I thought Mr. Smith acted hoggish. . .

Myra 29th. SABBATH. No Sabbath to us but in name. Husband obliged to keep guard during the night. After breakfast, every man is of necessity driven to his business in consequence of the companies crossing the river and we can not take our effects across only as they go with theirs.

Noon — Just crossed the Kansas river in a flatboat. Indians all along on the banks of the river. They came from the village on purpose to see us, and take what they could pilfer. . . A novel scene to see so many animals swim the river. . .

Even. — Seems a little like Sabbath. Our company all together once more. Dr. Chute with us. Thankful for a few moments rest from the distracting cares of the world. Mr. Eells leads in prayer and retired.

After joining the caravan, the missionaries were obliged to accept its routine. Often they arose before sunrise and sometimes rode twenty miles or more without stopping. The prairie showers, common at that time of the year, often drenched them making both traveling and camping unpleasant. In the following entry Myra gives one of the best descriptions of the Fur Company's caravan and of its method of travel to be found anywhere. She was describing a scene totally strange to her relatives and friends in the East.

Myra 30th. MONDAY. Many new arrangements to be made to travel with the Company. There are now about sixty men. It is necessary that five men be on guard during the night, which will give each man about two and a half hours to be on guard, as five are on during the day.[9] To make it easy, the night guard changes three times in the night, to be on guard every fourth night, and one day in every twelve days. There are ten or fifteen Indian women and children.[10] The Company have about 200 horses and mules; we have twenty-one horses and mules. They [have] 17 carts and waggons, we have one. We have 12 horned cattle. The waggons are all covered with black or dark cloth. They move first, one directly after the other, then the packed animals and cattle.

Sometimes we ladies ride behind the whole, sometimes, between the hindermost waggon and the mules; as circumstances may be. It is not safe for any to be far in the rear, because they are always exposed to be robbed of their horses and, if not killed by wild Indians, themselves left to wander on foot. The Company generally travel on a fast walk, seldom faster. When we are fairly on our way we have much the appearance of a large funeral procession in the States. Suppose the Company reaches half a mile — every man must know and do his own work.

Mr. Eells takes four animals, two to pack and each of us a horse to ride. These he is to catch morning, noon and night. At night they must be picketed, that is, fastened into the ground by a long cord. Mr. Gray takes three animals, one to pack, one for Mrs. Gray to ride, and one to go in the waggon, which he has charge of. Mr. Rogers takes three, two to pack and one for himself to ride. Mr. Walker takes three, one to pack and two for himself and wife to ride. Mr. Stevens takes four, three to pack and one for himself to ride.[11] Mr. Stevens is an old mountain-man[12] that we have hired to go with us. Our spare animals are all stolen.

At night the waggons are set so that they form a ring, within which all the horses and mules are brought in and picketed. At half past three they are let loose to feed outside of the ring until six o'clock usually, when they are to be harnessed and packed for traveling, which takes half or three-quarters of an hour. Before we start every man must put on his belt, powder flask, knife, etc., and then take his gun on his horse

---

9 Walker in his diary for May 8 wrote: "A regular guard is kept every night composed of five men. These are changed every three hours so that 15 men are on guard every night."

10 These would be the wives and half-breed children of some of the men connected with the caravan.

11 By an oversight, no mention was made of the number of animals for which Smith was responsible. It may be assumed that he had four which would have brought the total number to the twenty-one mentioned by Myra in her entry for this day.

12 This is the earliest reference the author has discovered to the use of the term mountain man. These were the men who were engaged in the Rocky Mountain fur trade.

before him.[13] Mr. Walker and Smith drive the cattle; Mr. Stevens, Rogers and Eells the mules and Mr. Gray the waggon. Move camp at eight, ride three hours on the river shore, trade with the Indians for dried green corn and some ropes. Buy one mule. A thunder shower. Move again two hours, 5 hours to-day 15 miles. Encamp on a small creek; cross one creek. Scenery delightful. The creeks are skirted with timber, the plains are covered with grass and flowers of every colour.

Myra MAY 1st, TUESDAY. A rainy night, wet this morning. Moved at eight. . . Meet Indians at every encampment, many of them entirely naked, especially the children. Met two blind Indians, one of them led by a little boy, the other by a middle-aged man; both of them old men. Dr. Chute comes us to us again. Has made inquiries of the Indians for our horses, but can not hear of them. Says we may take his horse and he will get one of the Indians or go down the river in a canoe.[14] He is now 136 miles from his home, as we have reckoened it. A thunder shower just as we come into camp.

Myra. 2d. WEDNESDAY. Dr. Chute bids us a final farewell. Think him a worthy man. Take his horse. A very rainy night, everything wet this morning. Move camp at half past seven. . . Encamped on a creek, crossed eleven, banks steep. . .[15] The scenery beautiful, roling prairies covered with green grass and flowers, the rivers skirted with timber. All in good health.

Myra 3d. THURSDAY. Moved at seven, rode three and one-half hours, 14 miles. A pleasant day. Finding we could get both wood and water ourselves, Mrs. Gray, Mrs. Walker and myself thought it a good time to wash. We dressed in our night dresses for washing, built a fire almost in the center of the creek on some stones, warmed some water, commenced washing in the kettles because we had nothing else to supply the place of wash-tubs. We would have got on well had the water been soft, but that being so hard, it took all our strength and a great portion of our soap, besides, our clothes would not look well, which spoiled our anticipated merriment, but we found that we could

---

[13] Writing from the Rendezvous on July 3, 1838, Rogers described his outfit: "My equipment is as follows: — a belt around the waist, with a butcher knife attached; powder, flask and bullet pouch over the shoulder; my rifle lying before me on the saddle, and a brace of pistols in my holster. These things except the pistols, every man and boy in the whole caravan carries; so that, in case of danger, all are ready for action at a moment's warning." Smith found the carrying of a rifle a sore trial to his conscience.

[14] Because of their desire to economize as much as possible, the missionaries had left the frontier with the minimum of animals. The loss of three of their best horses on the night of April 27 was most serious. Myra mentions the purchase of a mule on the 30th. Now Dr. Chute turns over his horse. Thus two of the three stolen animals were replaced.

[15] The banks of the prairie streams are often eight feet high or even more. These steep banks presented a real obstacle to wagons. Notice Myra's entry for the 4th when she mentions the use of ropes in getting the wagons across the streams.

heat water, wash, boil and rince our clothes in the same kettle. One of the Company brings us a little honey, have a little sport with the fire running in the dried grass in the prairie.

Mary   Rise before sunrise. Our company do nothing but jaw all the time. I never saw such a cross company before.

Myra   4th. FRIDAY.   Moved camp at seven, ride seven hours, 21 miles without getting off of our horses. Encamp on Burr creek, the bank of which was so steep we could not ride down; the carts and waggons were let down with ropes. Crossed three creeks, very windy, so that it was with difficulty we could sit upon our horses. . . Mr. Richardson kills a deer and brings us a piece. Sew on Mr. Roger's tent.

Mary   Better nature, a little. . . Mr. R. shot a deer. The first game we have had.

Myra   5th. SATURDAY.   Moved at half past seven . . . encamp on Blue creek, 15 miles. High roling prairie, deep ravines, the weather is so cold that we cannot keep comfortable with all our winter clothes on. The prairie is burning all around us. Mr. Richardson brings us a wild Turkey.

Mary   Rose before sunrise. Left the camp at eight. Very cold. Did not dismount till about two. . . Baked some bread & assisted Mrs. Gray in making a pot pie. Mr. Smith undertook to help Mr. W. correct me for dictating to Mr. Gray. I think the reproof quite unmerited. Feel so tried with Mr. W. I know not what to do. He seems to think more of Mrs. Smith than of me. Spends a great deal more time in her society than in mine. Do I deserve all this, or is not my dear W. to blame. I feel that I am cruelly neglected. I think I try to do all & the best I can.

Myra   6th. SABBATH.   My heart filled with mingled emotions. How can I, how can it be consistent for us to break one of God's positive commands to obey another? . . . 9 hours, 27 miles — encamp on rough ground where there is little water, and no wood,[16] very windy.

Mary   Last night a frost. Ice in the pail. Mr. W. rather sick. Travelled about 24 miles. Not a very pleasant way of keeping the Sabbath. Very cold, almost like winter. Had no idea that we were to experience so much wind & cold. Some of our company expressed regret that they have undertaken the journey.[17] I suspect more from aversion to the toil than real dread of sin. . .

Myra   7th. MONDAY.   Move camp at seven, ride five hours — noon — stop on nameless creek; then ride three and one-half hours — eight and a half hours, 26 miles. . .

---

[16] Walker in his diary for this day noted: "Our pack man took a mule & went off some distance & brought in a pack load so that we had enough [fuel] to cook our supper & breakfast."

[17] An evident reference to Smith. See Drury, *Diaries of Spalding and Smith* for this date. Smith wrote: ". . . it has been a day of hard labor, harder than usual. . . I fear we shall lose all our piety before we get across the mountains."

Mary 13 miles before dinner, 10 after. Cold in the morning, in the P.M. mild & comfortable. Mr. W. took an emetic & some calomel.[18] My own health good. Should feel quite happy if my dear husband were as well & in as good spirits as myself. Our company still have a good deal of unpleasantness among them.

Myra 8th. TUESDAY. Arise this morning only to seek a new home for the night. Moved at half-past seven . . . 5 hours, 16 miles. Encamp on Battle Creek.

Mary Husband sick.[19] In a big worry lest he does not feel as well satisfied with me as he ought.

Myra 9th. WEDNESDAY. All is hubbub and confusion; camp wants to move early, horses bad to catch, dishes not packed in season. Oh, how much patience one needs to sustain him in this life. . . Moved camp at half past seven, ride 7 hours, 21 miles, without food for ourselves or animals. Encamped on the west [side] of the Blue. The scenery is so grand, together with a pleasant sun and burning prairie,[20] that for a moment we almost forgot the land of our birth. Crossed Battle Creek. . .

Mary Travelled 21 miles. . . The first we have had no water the whole distance. Went it all at one pull. Rode with husband who is now only helping drive cows. About finished Mr. Rogers. A great want of devotion & some evidence of improper feeling toward each other.

Myra 10th. THURSDAY. Move at seven o'clock . . . 25 miles. Encamped on the Blue. . . Find the little calf so badly bitten by wolves, that Mr. W. and Smith think it best to kill it. Mr. Clark [21] gives us two ducks.

Mary Mr. W. still unwell. Laid till ten to strike tent. Rode only 10 miles in the A.M. . . Killed a calf. I dressed the head. The other family [i.e., the Grays and the Eells who shared the other tent] was displeased because the calf was killed. Refused to eat of it. I felt exceedingly tried to have things go on in this way. Resolved to talk with husband, think he had done wrong. Had been too much influenced by Br. S. & upheld him when he ought to have reproved.

---

[18] Calomel — mercurous chloride — was used as a purgative and was a popular remedy in those days for many complaints.

[19] The missionaries took a big risk in making so long a journey when they were dependent upon the caravan for their personal safety while traveling through dangerous Indian country. What if one member of the party had been so sick that he or she could not even ride in a wagon? Walker in his diary for this day wrote: "Brother Smith & myself drove the cattle accompanied by our ladies. The first time since I left home I have had the pleasure of riding all day with my wife."

[20] The Indians often started fires in the old grass in the early spring in order to promote the new growth. When fanned by a strong wind, these fires became spectacular, and sometimes dangerous to all living things before them.

[21] Eells, Reminiscences: "Two sons of Gen. Clark of St. Louis accompanied that expedition of the F. Co. . . The younger of those sons was a graduate of Yale. The use of alcoholic drink was to him ruinous." The reference is to Gen. Wm. Clark of the Lewis and Clark expedition of 1804-06. Coll. w.

Myra   11th. FRIDAY.   Move at seven . . . encamped on the Blue. Saw antelopes and sticks eaten by beaver.

Mary   Was gratified & pleased to find Mr. W. determined if possible to [effect] a reconciliation. I found it almost unnecessary to say what I had contemplated. Mr. S. & wife seem much less inclined to make concessions.[22] I think S. is stubborn & have about as lief things would go on & our family [i.e., the Smiths and the Walkers] devour the whole calf. . . It seems to me that he is more out of the way than Gray. He insisted in the first place that we should cook of the veal for dinner, but we did not. . . At tea he insisted again on my cooking veal but I told him until there was peace I would not cook or eat of it. Mr. W. thought as I did, so though he looked cross he said no more. After the horses were picketed, we went in Mr. Gray's sent & a treaty of peace was negotiated. It was agreed that the past should be forgotten, that they would commence anew. Several resolves were passed, but the peace so far as it related to Mr. Smith, I fear was a forced point. He could not in any decency have helped falling in with the proposition. But I believe the same wrong spirit remains. The other [tent] family agreed to share the calf with us.

Myra   12th. SATURDAY.   Rise early and prepare for a rainy day. . . Encamp on the Blue — 9 hours, 27 miles — got a thorough drenching. Met some eight or ten Pawnees, and many more are encamped on the other side of the river. We are in dangerous country. It rains so that notwithstanding we have a good fire, we cannot dry our clothes at all. Obliged to sleep in our blankets wet as when taken from our horses. Our bed and bedding consists of a buffalo robe, a piece of oilcloth, our blankets and saddles, our tents [are] our houses, our sheets our partitions between us and Mr. Gray's, when it rains they are spread over the tent.

Mary   Things go on more pleasantly than before. . . Feel in hope that it will rain tomorrow so the company may rest. . . We have a comfortable shelter from the rain.

Myra   13th. SABBATH.   Arise this morning, put on our clothes wet as when we took off, and prepare for a long ride. I am so strongly reminded of by-gone days that I cannot refrain from weeping. Moved camp at 7; ride 8 hours, 25 miles — without food for ourselves or animals. I do not get off my horse during the whole distance, cross from the Blue to the Platt river.[23] About nine o'clock the clouds disappeared and the sun shone bright and warm to dry us. Some of the Company kill three deer — gave us a piece. Encamp on the Platt.

---

[22] No members of the 1838 reinforcement aroused so much personal animosity as Gray, sensitive of his authority as the leader of the party, and Smith, who was hypercritical.

[23] The caravan had followed the Little Blue and on his day struck across some high prairie to the south bank of the Platte. After reaching the Platte, the caravan entered an almost treeless prairie country. Wood, except for a little driftwood found along the banks of the river, was practically nonexistent.

Mary   Reached the Platte about 3. . . . The last few miles seemed exceedingly long. I was as tired & faint as I could well be, having eaten breakfast at 6 & nothing untill near 5 p.m. . . . Think a great deal about home when we are obliged to travel all the Sabbath.

Myra   14th. MONDAY.   Last night the Pawnees came to our camp. Those we saw were better clad than any we had seen before. Their complexion lighter than the Kansas. They are painted; it is said that they are a war party going to war with the Sioux. In the night they sung a thief song; it is said they have three songs, the war song, the thief song, and the gambling song. Their noise to us appears like children at play. They make signs that they had two white ladies at their village, Mrs. Ellis and Dunbar, we supposed.[24] They appeared pleased with our manner of packing dishes. . .[25] 8 hours, 25 miles. Encamp on the head of Big Island on the Platt . . . suppose we are near the place where Dr. S[atterlee] missionary among the Pawnees, was killed about one year ago.[26] His bones and clothes were found not long after, but nobody knows how he was killed.

Mary   Very windy p.m.   12 miles in wagon.[27] Got rested a little. The river rose in the night a foot.

Myra   15th. TUESDAY.   A little rain during the night; moved camp at seven o'clock. . . Passed a number of Indian camps. A delightful view of the Platt. It is in some places a mile and a half wide.[28]

Mary   Fell in company with a gentleman from New Orleans who has traveled in Europe, Africa, &c., who has entertained us with descriptions of Switzerland, Italy, etc. Gave an account of Swiss dogs digging men out who are buried in snow.[29]

---

[24] The two Presbyterian missionaries, Rev. John Dunbar and Samuel Allis, who were sent out to the Pawnees by the American Board in 1834, were both engaged to be married at the time. Emeline Palmer accompanied the Whitmans and Spaldings to Liberty where she and Allis were married by Spalding on April 23, 1836. Dunbar went East in the fall of 1836 and was married to Esther Smith on Jan. 12, 1837. These were the women to whom the Indians were referring.

[25] Each of the missionaries had a tin dish, plate, knife, fork, and spoon.

[26] Dr. Satterlee and his bride went out to the frontier as missionaries to the Pawnees under the American Board with the Whitman-Spalding party in 1836. Mrs. Satterlee died on April 30, 1836. About a year later Dr. Satterlee was murdered on the prairie. Some thought he was the victim of a white man.

[27] This is one of the few references in the diaries to any of the women riding in the wagon. It should be remembered that Mary was going through the first months of her pregnancy and was not feeling well.

[28] A common characterization of the Platte was that it was a mile wide and a foot deep.

[29] This is a possible reference to Captain John A. Sutter who crossed the prairies with the caravan of 1838 and then accompanied the mission party to Fort Walla. Later Mary Walker makes several references to him by name. Sutter had spent the winter, 1834-35 in St. Louis and St. Charles. For three years he was engaged in the Sante Fe fur trade. Sutter had with him a party of six men and a Mexican servant.

Myra   16th. W<small>EDNES</small>.   A thunder storm, so that we stay in camp till eleven, when we move and ride five hours, 16 miles. Encamp on the Platt where we have no wood.[30] Mr. Gray sells his tinder box for a piece of dried buffalo meat — crossed Ash creek.

Mary   Rose early, kindled the fire, boiled my clothes, finished my washing before breakfast. . . Rode in the wagon. Mr. Smith short as pie crust. Mr. W. begins to see how things are.

Myra   17th. T<small>HURSDAY</small>.   Last night a tedious one, the rain pouring on us in torrents. Feel that we are safe only in the hands of Him who holdeth the winds and the storms. Very wet. All engaged in our domestic concerns. Obliged to improve all our time to the best advantage to meet our necessary wants. Moved camp at eleven . . . encamp in the open prairie — near the Platt, not a stick of wood in sight of us.

Mary   Last night had a pretty fair specimen of prairie shower. We were scarcely expecting rain & made no preparation. In the night it stormed tremendously. Our tent scarcely screened us at all. Our bed was utterly flooded & almost everything wet. It was windy but cleared away so we traveled about 15 miles & encamped where there was no wood . . . used prairie coal for cooking. Altho windy it was not very cold. Rode more comfortable than I have some other days. . . It was very pleasant & afforded us a good chance to get dry & prepare properly for another storm. For this, thankful.

Myra   18th. F<small>RIDAY</small>.   Moved camp at half past six . . . saw a large number of Indians [coming] up to us — encamp when they come up. Some of them had blankets or skins, some were entirely naked. Trade with them for a little dried buffalo meat and give them a knife. They always expect a present from white men, and will keep with them until they get it. . . Saw a number of buffalo skulls all lying towards the east. It is said they burn the first buffalo they kill as a sacrifice, and pray the Great Spirit buffalo may be plenty. One buffalo killed, several seen. Hire Mr. Richardson to hunt for us.[31]

---

[30] See entry in Mary's diary for the next day to "prairie coal," i.e., dried buffalo dung which made a good substitute for wood. See vol. I of this set, fn. 33, part I of Mrs. Whitman's diary. Myra Eells did not explain to her family how it was possible for them to cook their meals without wood.

[31] After traveling about four weeks over a distance of about 460 miles, the caravan drew near to the buffalo range. From there on buffalo meat was to be the main food. The missionaries were able to hire one of the men of the caravan, Paul Richardson, to be their hunter. He remained with the party until July 27, when he was sent back from Fort Hall with letters. Rogers in his account written from the Rendezvous commented on the large number of buffaloes the party saw after reaching the forks of the Platte. He wrote: "The meat is very sweet and easily cooked. Ten minutes boiling is enough, more will make it tough. When roasted, it is very juicy, and so highly flavored that no salt is needed. The meat is sometimes 'jerked' by being dried in the sun or over a slow fire. In this state it can be kept for three or four days in the most sultry weather."

Mary Saw Pawnees. . . Obtained buffalow. The scenery rather picturesque. Broken Mts. on one side, the river skirted with timber in through a verdant bottom land.

Myra 19th. SATURDAY. Move at half past six — ride 8 hours, 27 miles. Encamped in open prairie without wood or wat. The land wet. Husband and myself ride in the rear in the morning. As we passed along, we observed an Indian medicine lodge destroyed. The trail and the scattered wood indicated that it had been a great day with them. This led us to anticipate our future labour. Toward noon we came to a high bluff supposed to be 150 or 200 feet high. Mr. Gray & wife, Mrs. Walker and Mr. Eells went to the top.[32] They found heads and buffalo skulls left there by the Indians. The bluff is called a medicine mound.[33] Towards night we passed a buffalo which had been shot, lying near the road. A number of buffaloes seen to-day. Mr. Richardson brings five buffalo tongues.[34]

Mary. Passed the forks of the Platte. Ascended a bluff & had a view of the country. . . Supped on buffalow. . . Mr. R. our hunter killed five. Only brought in what he could of them on his horse. Pity to waste so much.

Myra 20th. SABBATH. The weather pleasant and the scenery calculated to lead the mind up to nature's God. Arise this morning at four, move at half past six . . . cross the south Fork of the Platt . . . forded the river in 20 minutes. The bottom full of quicksands.[35]

Mary Saw the hills covered with Buffalow. A large herd, perhaps 9 hundred. After noon saw a thousand perhaps. . . A pleasant day.

---

[32] These were the venturesome members of the mission party, always ready to examine some new wonder. Elkanah Walker, Myra Eells, and the Smiths were inclined to avoid such excursions.

[33] See reproduction of painting of circles of buffalo skulls by Miller in *The West of Alfred Jacob Miller*, 117. Miller writes of finding a number of these circles on the upper waters of the Platte. "They formed nearly complete circles of about 20 feet in diameter," he wrote, "with noses pointed each to the center." Undoubtedly the circles had some significance to the Indian medicine men.

[34] The tongues and cuts from the hump of the buffaloes were considered to be the choicest parts. The rest of the carcass was left as food for the coyotes or to rot.

[35] Of this Rogers wrote: "As soon as your foot is placed on the bottom, the water washes the sand from under and you are in danger of slipping and sinking." Eells, in his Reminiscences, gives the following account of the crossing of the South Fork of the Platte: "The wagon horse was strong and lazy. His name was Steamboat. Mr. & Mrs. Smith were in the wagon, following the carts. Steamboat and his load passed into the river and stopped. In vain the small whip was applied. Those acquainted with the water and bed of that river need not be told that to stop in the quick sand is hazardous, — to remain long stationary is to go down. I was in my place in the rear. The helplessness of the occupants of the wagon was apparent. I left my post, pressed to a convenient point and vigorously applied a severe scourge to so called Steamboat. Steam power was not thereby generated but locomotion was caused to that Steamboat and the craft in tow." The party crossed the river in the vicinity of what is now North Platte, Nebraska.

Myra   21st. MONDAY.   Nooned in a thicket of willows and tall grass. Mr. Smith made a fire and as soon as it began to kindle, the fire began to spread in the dried grass, which gave our husbands exercise enough for one noontime. This done, Mr. W's horse must be seen to and a stub taken out of his foot which he got in yesterday. Our dinner got & ate as soon as possible and prepared for another start. In two hours all riding again. . . Have seen danger on every side of us — the soil is sandy and the surface broken — deep ravines to go through, loose horses taking fright so as to put us in danger of our lives if they come near us. . . Capt. Stuart's mules frighten and his waggon upset, some of his goods in one place and some in another. Saw several herds of buffalo.

Mary   Mrs. Smith very much out with Dr. Gray,[36] in a fret all the time. Mr. W. seems to feel quite as I do toward them. Not any better. Hope we shall be enabled to treat them right, that they will see their error & reform. Fear I am not as plain with them as I ought to be. Rode in wagon with Mrs. Eells in afternoon. . . A company of Portuguese encamped on the opposite bank.[37]

Myra   22nd. TUESDAY.   Wait this morning to have Capt. Stuart's waggon repaired — moved at eight . . . 8 hours, 27 miles. Encamped on the river. . . Saw a great number of Buffalo.

Mary   No wood. Water freezes in the basin.

Myra   23rd. WEDNESDAY.   Moved camp at seven, ride nine hours without stopping — 25 miles. Did not see any water the whole distance. Crossed from the South to the North Fork of the Platt. The weather so cold that we could not keep comfortable.

Mary   Very cold, almost snows. . . Scenery peculiar. Cedar wood for fuel.

Myra   24th. THURSDAY.   Moved at six. . . Encamp on the Platt; saw few buffalo. Epsom Salts in large quantities. Soil sandy and surface broken, on our right hand the Platt — on our left, high bluffs — bank of the river low and not a stick of timber or a willow on it. Mrs. Gray sick.

Myra   25th. FRIDAY.   Mrs. Gray more comfortable. Move at six . . . 8¾ hours, 25 miles. . . Mr. Eells and myself hardly able to sit up, but obliged to eat, drink and work as though we were well.[38] Think it is trying.

---

[36] Gray was originally sent out with the Whitman-Spalding party in 1836 as a mechanic and was so listed in the Annual Reports of the Board for 1837 and 1838. After taking a few weeks at a medical college, Gray encouraged the members of the reinforcement to call him Dr. Gray. Dr. Whitman was irritated when this came to his attention and protested to the Board. See vol. I of this work, fn. 2 in section dealing with Mrs. Gray. After being listed once as a doctor in the Board's Annual Report, he was thereafter listed during the remaining years of his connection with the Mission as "Mechanic & Teacher."

[37] This company is unidentified.

[38] There was no stopping or turning because of illness in the party.

Mary   24th & 25th.   Nothing special only I was too busy & too much fatigued to write my journal. Mrs. Gray & Mrs. Eells sick.

Myra   26th. SATURDAY.   Mr. Eells could neither eat supper nor breakfast, but must do his duty in camp and ride, he knows not how far. Moved at half past six . . .   10 hours, 30 miles. Encamp nearly opposite Chimney [Rock] on the Platt.[39] Mr. Eells some better, eats a little gingerbread, and some water, which was given him at East Windsor.[40] Saturday night, but nothing but the name to remind us of the approaching Sabbath.

Mary   Passed what is called the fort, chimney & other bluffs, in appearance resembling castles, capitals of cities &c. . . Past 7 when we encamped. Feel real satisfied with the movements of my husband & cheerfully happy in anticipating our future labours. Mrs. S. tries my patience talking about Gray as she calls [him] all the time. I wish she could see how much like him only worse she acts.

Myra   27th. SABBATH.   Arise at half past three to work as hard as our strength will permit. Move at half past 6 . . .   9¾ hours, 30 miles. We left the Platt at noon and rode on a broad plain between the most splendid bluffs until we came to where they appeared to meet, where we encamped. The scenery grand. . .   The mountains on either side of us resemble a City covered with magnificent buildings. Husband and myself ride together; call to mind the many Sabbaths and sanctuary privileges we have enjoyed, but now they are not within our reach.[41] We are not disposed to complain or wish ourselves back, though to be deprived of the means of grace in reality and imagination are different things.

Mary   Scenery beautiful. The bluffs resemble temples, castles, forts, &c.[42] As if nature tired of waiting the advances of civilization had erected her own temples &c. Mr. Walker & Gray agree pretty well now

---

[39] Chimney Rock, sometimes referred to as Durls Chimney, and Scotts Bluff, in what is now western Nebraska, were two of the most famous landmarks along the Oregon Trail.

[40] In his Reminiscences, Eells wrote: "A special inconvenience was that when a supply of buffalo meat was obtainable, there was not much beside to use with it. The sudden change of diet was so great that weakness and slight sickness were thereby caused. I have a distinct recollection that late one P.M. I felt unable to sit in the saddle. I was in the rear. I dismounted, reclined upon mother earth, became rested and alone reached camp." It was at that time, perhaps, that his wife brought out a piece of gingerbread which had been given to him at East Windsor three months earlier. Mrs. Spalding, in her journey to Oregon in 1836, also suffered from the exclusive meat diet.

[41] The frequent references in the writings of the missionaries to traveling on Sunday is indicative of the deep distress of conscience suffered because of the necessity of breaking the Sabbath.

[42] An examination of a number of diaries of people who came over the Oregon Trail shows that the picturesque rock formations along the Platte River west of Ash Hollow made a tremendous impression upon them. Scott's Bluff, now in Scott's Bluff National Monument, rises 750 feet above the North Platte River.

THE POPO AGIE RENDEZVOUS SITE, NEAR RIVERTON, WYOMING

The picture shows the confluence of the Popo Agie, to the left, and the Wind River in the foreground. Simon Arthur, an Arapahoe Indian stands at left. The cottonwood grove in which the 1838 mission party camped is not shown, but is to the right between the two rivers. Photo by the author, 1960. See text page 95.

A PAGE FROM MARY WALKER'S DIARY

Showing entries for January 1839, and indicating that her writing is often most difficult to transcribe. See text pages 142-143.

& Mr. Smith & Walker apart. We have a strange company of Missionaries. Scarcely one who is not intolerable on some account.

Myra 28th. MONDAY. Moved at half past six . . . nooned on Horse creek; [43] then rode till half past five. . . Encamped a mile at least from the Platt, where Mr. Eells is obliged to get water for supper. Immediately after starting in the morning we passed down a steep declivity with just room enough for our horses to walk. The banks on either side are many feet above our heads. Obliged to look up to see anything but naked earth and then nothing but the azure sky. . . I know not with what better to compare the Mts. than a City with the streets just narrow enough to walk in. After passing through the Mts. we rode over roling prairie. In crossing Horse creek one of the [horses] mired in a quicksand so that Mr. Stevens and Mr. Eells [were] obliged to unpack him in the water; everything wet he had on, but a warm sun soon dried them again.

Mary Ride in comp [any] with our husbands, Mrs. Gray & I.

Myra 29th. TUESDAY. Moved camp a quarter past six . . . 8 hours, 24 miles. Encamp on the Platt. Husband faint and weak in consequence of not having such food as he can relish. I would gladly exchange appetites with him, because he is obliged to work so hard. It is true that nothing but the sustaining grace of God can carry us through. I trust we both have this grace. . . Dry wood in abundance on the bank of the river.

Mary Passed a Fort.[44] Encamped near it. Pleasant grounds. Not exactly wed to Grays. Talk about exchanging tents.[45]

Myra 30th. WEDNESDAY. Last night a number of Indian women came to see us. They were neatly dressed and ornamented with beads. Suppose they are wives of white men at the Fort and in the mountains. Moved camp at 6, rode 2 hours, crossed Larrimie's Fork and came to Fort William,[46] 5 miles. Sell Mr. Walker's horse to Capt. Fontinelle for 40 dollars.[47] Three Indian women, wives of Capts. Drips,

[43] One of the largest Indian councils ever held in the United States met at Horse Creek in September, 1851, when more than 10,000 Indians of the plains and foothill tribes met with government representatives to work out reservation boundaries.

[44] Possibly Fort Bernard, which was destroyed by fire in 1846. See Henderson, *Landmarks on the Oregon Trail*, p. 17.

[45] No indication is given as to what possible rearrangements might have been under consideration. It seems evident that by this time Elkanah would have preferred either of the other two couples in place of the Smiths.

[46] Fort William, better known as Fort Laramie, consisted of an eighteen-foot high palisade built around an enclosure of about 22,500 square feet with bastions in two diagonally opposite corners. Buildings, including some made of adobe, lined most of the inside walls. For fine exterior and interior views see reproductions of paintings by Alfred Jacob Miller in De Voto's *Across the Wide Missouri*, plates VIII & IX.

[47] As may be noted in Mary's entry for May 2, the missionaries received two horses from the Fur Company, perhaps in exchange for the wagon, and thus felt free to sell Elkanah's horse.

Fontinelle and Wood,[48] with their children call on us. The children are quite white and can read a little.

Mary Cross Laramey Fork. Just as we got our tents pitched it commenced raining. Cleared off in the afternoon. Mrs. Smith & Gray washed. I mended Mr. W's coat & marked blankets. In the evening received a visit from the wife of a fur trapper.

Myra 31st. THURSDAY. The ladies engaged in washing, mending, etc. Our husbands making repairs and arrangements for the remainder of the journey. Give the waggon [49] to Capts. D. & F. They, with Mr. Wood, take tea with us.

Mary Washed for myself & Mr. Rogers. Took me most of the forenoon. Almost blistered my arms. Not much fatigued, much less than if I had been riding. To dine with us had Mr. Clark, son of the Clark who accompanied Lewis. He & his brother are travelling in the company thro from St. Louis. In the afternoon arranged my trunks, &c.

Myra JUNE 1st. FRIDAY. Attend to writing. Indian women and children continually calling on us. The company give us a horse. Mr. Gray takes one he left here a year ago.

Mary Ripped & dyed my pongee dress. Made sundry repairs, &c. Recd. visits from squaws.

Myra 2d. SATURDAY. Leave here this morning, ride into the Fort. It is a large, hewed log building with an opening in the center. Partitions for various objects. It compares well with the walls of the Conn. State Prison. A Fort in this country is a place built to accommodate the Company as they go and come from the Mts. to trade with the Indians for firs.[50] Start at 7, ride 5½ hours — 12 miles. Encamp in the open prairie at a clear spring at the foot of the Black Hills. Left four of our cattle because their feet were so sore they could not travel. Hope to get them at some future day.[51] Mr. Walker and Rogers drive the cattle. Mr. [Gray] drives mules with Mr. S. and E. . .   Some of the Mts. appear to be above the clouds.

Mary Left Fort Williams or Larimier. Capt. Fontenelle & son, several squaws & children joined the Company. The fort is constructed of hewn timbers set in the ground. We rode into it. Inside were several big buildings, most of them without glass. The half breed children look

---

[48] Lucien Fontanelle was the leader of the 1835 caravan with which Whitman first traveled to Fort Laramie. A Mr. Woods, executive to Fontanelle, was in charge of the fort in 1838.

[49] Perhaps acting on Gray's advice, the missionaries decided not to try to take their light wagon any further west. The baggage which had been transported in it was thereafter packed on horses.

[50] Both Cushing and Myra Eells consistently spelt fur as f-i-r.

[51] So far as is known the missionaries were never able to reclaim the cattle left at the fort or to get any compensation for them.

as likely as any. Capt. Drips takes his Indian wife along. . . We are more than 7 hundred miles from the Miss[ouri], and more than 300 from Rendezvous.[52] Left four of our cattle at the Ft. Gave away the wagon and obtained two new horses.

Myra 3d. SABBATH. Moved at 6 . . . 9½ hours, 28 miles. Encamp on a little stream that runs into the Platt. Scenery delightful. Tops of the Mts. covered with snow. . . Mr. Eells troubled with a hard headache.

Mary A pleasant day. . . Have been so tired all day. Abundance of wormwood along the way.

Myra 4th, MONDAY. Moved a quarter before 6. . . Encamped on a creek that put into the Platt . . . saw juniper trees.

Mary Could scarcely forgive myself for not thinking that it was the day of the monthly concert.[53] Mrs. Smith & Eells being unwilling to give away milk, we divide & give away part of ours.[54] Think we shall enjoy what we have left as well as they.

Myra TUESDAY. Moved at six. . . Encamp on a dry spring. The face of the country broken. The Mts. covered with snow. Prickly Pear in abundance.

Mary A fine day. Frost last night. Rode over hills of a red appearance and passed over what we supposed to be gypsum. . . Was bled toward night.[55] Came near fainting. Sick some.

Myra WEDNESDAY. Moved at 6. . . Encamped on the Platt; soil, sandy; surface broken. Rode over one bluff, and through one ravine which seemed impossible for man or beast to go through. . . Rode up to one hunter and saw him take off the meat from a buffalo. Found wild hops and spearmint.

Mary 6 JUNE. Considerably out of health. Took a spoonful of wine, went without dinner at night. Felt better. . . Saw some minerals I wish very much to pick up.[56]

Myra 7th. THURSDAY. Last night, very windy and a little rain. Mr. W. & S. [tent] blew over. . . Encamp on the Platt. Soil sandy

---

[52] See section in vol. 1 of this work on the Rendezvous.

[53] A reference to a prayer meeting. Mary was remembering some stated "concert of prayer" held in her home community.

[54] No details are available as to what gave rise to the difference of opinion. Possibly both Mrs. Walker and Mrs. Gray were moved with compassion when they saw some Indian child in need of milk.

[55] Bloodletting was then considered a good method of treatment for many ills and diseases. The custom was followed as late as several years after the Civil War. According to modern medical opinion, such an extreme measure was most inadvisable for Mary at this time. She was then in the first months of her pregnancy. No wonder she nearly fainted.

[56] Mary did pick up samples of rocks and minerals along the way. At least one piece that she gathered, that from Independence Rock, is in the Oregon Historical Society's museum in Portland.

and covered with sedge,[57] surface broken. A hailstorm. . . Husband and myself find time and place for a short season of prayer.[58]

Mary In the evening gave Mrs. Smith a small piece of my mind about milk, mothers, &c.

Myra 8th. FRIDAY. Encamped on the Platt. Rode over bluffs and through ravines which it would seem impossible for us to do under other circumstances. . . It is said the Crow Indians are near us; Capt. Drips orders all the horses hobbled. A little rain. Our cloaks not uncomfortable.

Mary Think what I said to her [i.e., Mrs. Smith] had a good effect. Arrived at the crossing place.[59] Very tired. Everything almost excites my fears. It would be so bad to be sick in such circumstances. Find it difficult to keep up a cheerful flow of spirits. Think bleeding did me good tho it reduced my strength more than I expected.

Myra 9th. SATURDAY. Morning, rainy. The company making skin boats.[60] Mr. Clark calls on us . . . takes tea with us; wants to get some of our books.

Mary The workmen busy in preparing boats. . . Sewed most of the time on my dress. Mr. Smith in the tent all day with his wife. Kept up a constant whispering much to my annoyance. Mr. Walker busy here & there, hardly in the tent at all. I like my husband & like to have him with me but like to see a man attend to his business.[61]

---

[57] A reference to the sagebrush, a small shrub widely distributed on the alkali plains of western United States, especially common in desert areas.

[58] One of the trying aspects of the journey being made for the four newly-wedded couples was the lack of privacy. The brief time that Cushing and Myra were alone on this day was so unusual that Myra made special mention of it in her diary.

[59] The caravan had to cross the North Platte in order to follow the Sweetwater River to the Continental Divide. The crossing was made near what is now Casper, Wyoming.

[60] Eells, Reminiscences: "At the time we reached the North Platte, dissolving mountain snow had rendered the river not fordable. This was anticipated; therefore hunters had been instructed to bring skins newly taken from buffalo. Wicker work of willows in the form of deep boat was made. The skins, sewed together with sinew, were stretched flesh side out over the prepared frame. Then drying process followed by exposure to sun. Two such boats were prepared." However, Mary Walker in her diary for June 11, says that the boats were made by stretching buffalo hides over "the bottom of two wagons." Perhaps both types were used. The former kind was called a bull-boat. De Voto, *Across the Wide Missouri*, 116, describes one as being 18′ long and 5½′ wide. See plate XXII.

[61] This entry marks the end of the first of the series of sixteen notebooks containing Mary's diaries, owned by Huntington Library. She then began writing in a notebook in which her husband had made a few notations, while a student at Bangor Theological Seminary. See Montana *Frontier*, March, 1931, for an abbreviated form of Mary's diary, June 10-December 21, 1838, edited by Rufus A. Coleman. This was reissued as *Sources of Northwest History*, No. 15, by the State University of Montana.

Myra 10th. SABBATH. Although it is a rainy day, there is no rest for us. Husband on horse-guard. The Company taking their goods and carts across the river. Afternoon can hardly keep ourselves comfortable in our tents. Mr. Eells gets a thorough drenching. I think we know how to prize the comforts of a good house on a rainy day.

Mary To-day were designing to cross the Platte but the rain prevented. So we have for the first time an opportunity to lay by on the Sabbath. I am not sufficiently well to enjoy it as much as I would like, yet, I am glad of rest. I have reflected much on the goodness & mercy of God. I think he has given me a good husband & trust he will grant me favor in his eyes. He treats me kindly & I can but believe loves me. I however, experience some anxiety on this account. But I think I am rather gaining ground. That he feels more confidence in me & sees more plainly the defects of others. My attachment to him does not in the least abate. I feel as much anxiety as ever to please him. I regard my husband as a special blessing conferred by Heaven & I am determined if possible that my life shall evince my gratitude.

My health at present is rather feeble & I find it difficult to keep up a usual amount of cheerfulness. If I were to yield to inclination I should cry half the time without knowing what for. My circumstances are rather trying. So much danger attends me on every hand. A long journey yet before me, going I know not whither; without mother or sister to attend me, can I expect to survive it all? . . .[62]

Thus far I have been enabled to keep my temper on all occasions though my feelings have been tried exceedingly by some of the company. The uneasy, fretful disposition of Mrs. Smith, together with her persistent whispering are very unpleasant to me. Her husband is much of a hog at table as I have seen. He frequently treats me with what I deem rudeness. There is about them what looks a good deal like pure selfishness. Mr. Eells is very uninteresting and unsocial, and in his character the "I" eclipses the whole horizon. Dr. Gray is exceedingly fractious. It is rather difficult getting along with him. He however treats my husband & me rather politely, more so than for any other of the company. When Mrs. G. chances to hear her husband talked about, it is sure to be nothing good. But for me it is the reverse. My husband seems to gain friends, let him go where he will. I regret that he does not evince a greater engagedness in religion.

Myra 11th. MONDAY. A very rainy night; rains steady all this morning. Our husbands obliged to be out in the wet and cold. Say their hands are so cold they can hardly use them. The Capts. say we

---

[62] The missionaries had not yet reached the halfway point on their journey to Oregon. The more difficult part lay before them. Mary was also thinking of the child she was carrying, of her coming confinement, and perhaps of a possible miscarriage.

may have their boats to take our things over when theirs are over. About noon it slacks raining so that we and our baggage go over. Two Frenchmen rowing the boat. Mr. Gray, Mr. Eells and Mr. Rogers drive the horses and cattle over. Wade in the river up to their armpits but can not get across, and only succeed in getting the horses so far that they will swim over. Send the boat back to take them over. Night, all over safe. Encamped on the opposite bank. Snow falling continually a little distance from us.

Mary Rainy. The water comes into the tent. I was sick of diarreah. A little past noon we were summoned to cross the Platte, just at that time the rain ceased. We crossed safely in boats constructed of Buffalow hides & the bottom of two waggons. In the forenoon I cried to think how comfortable father's hogs were.[63] In the afternoon, felt we were dealt with in mercy. The snow capped Mts. appeared.[64]

Myra 12th. TUESDAY. Travel 7 hours — 12 miles. . . From the appearance we judged the snow was deep on the Mts. In sight of the Rocky Mts. Killed a rattlesnake, one deer, saw an antelope.

Mary Made only one camp. The Rocky Mts. covered with snow became in view.

Myra 13th. WEDNESDAY. Moved at six, rode 6½ hours. . . Continually crossing and recrossing high bluffs. Mrs. Gray and myself hold a short season of prayer for ourselves and husbands.

Mary Made a long camp in A.M. Short one P.M. Collected pebbles; drank sulphurous water. Sick a little.

Myra 14. THURSDAY. 9 hours, 28 miles. Encamped on the west side of [Independence] Rock,[65] at the foot of the Rocky Mts.[66] So cold that we need all our winter clothes. Saw a large number of buffalo.

---

[63] Eells, Reminiscences: "Mrs. Walker was a farmer's daughter — a country cultured lady. She was strong and cheery. Her common sense and her Christianity were practical. In her tent [while at the North Platte crossing] water was uncomfortably abundant. She considerately piled the bedding. Sitting upon her heels she thought and wept. Mrs. Smith entered the tent, and saw the tears. Seemingly surprised she said: 'Why, Mrs. Walker, what is the matter?' The reply was: 'I am thinking how comfortable my father's hogs are'." This became one of the most repeated incidents of their overland travels. Mary wished she were as dry and warm and comfortable as the pigs in her father's barn back in Maine.

[64] No doubt the rounded mountains of the Rattlesnake Range, rising to 6,000 or more feet.

[65] Independence Rock is one of the most famous landmarks along the Oregon Trail. It received its name from the report that Thomas Fitzpatrick, one of the earliest of the fur-traders, camped there on July 4, 1824. The turtle-shaped rock which rises abruptly out of the plain on the bank of the Sweetwater River, is about one-eighth of a mile long, 110 feet wide, and sixty to seventy feet high. So many passing travelers carved their names on its gray granite sides that it became the great Register of the Desert.

[66] Now the members of the caravan could see the jagged peaks of the Wind River range, rising to about 14,000 feet, a part of the Continental Divide.

Mary FRIDAY JUNE 15. Last night camped on the Sweet Water at the foot of Independence Rock, so called because the Fir Company once celebrated Independence here. This morning, there being no dew, went in company with Mr & Mrs Gray to the top of the rock. It is, I should judge more than 100 ft. high & a half mile in circumference, eliptical in form. The rock is a coarse granite, in which quartz predominates. It appears as if it had been scraped by something. . . We forded the Sweet Water & soon passed the place where the rock Mt. is cleft to its base & the Sweet Water passes.[67] The rock on either hand perpendicular, is perhaps 200 feet high. Rock Independence forms the entrance, some say to the Rocky Mts., others say not. . . The scenery has been beautiful & magnificent & with me the pleasure of beholding it has relieved in great measure the weariness of the way.

Dear God, the mountains speak aloud thy powers, and every purling rill proclaims thy praise. I wish Mr. W. would seem to feel as much interest in viewing the works of nature, as I do. I think the journey would be much less wearisome for him.

Myra 16th. SATURDAY. Moved camp at 6 . . . 9 hours, 20 miles. Many of the horses' backs sore, but none to change. Encamped on Sweetwater. Scenery awful [i.e., awesome].

Mary Nothing of particular interest. Near to the left, a magnificent wall of granite, far to the right another. The hunters shot 7 buffalo about 100 rods from the road.

Myra 17th. SABBATH. Moved at 7 . . . Encamped on Sweetwater. . . No Sabbath to us but in name.

Mary Very pleasant. More leisure than we have sometimes had. Met some of Capt. Walker's company.[68] Not so hard a day's work, picked a mess of gooseberries.[69]

Myra 18th. MONDAY. Moved at 7, rode 3½ hours, 10 miles, encamped on Sweetwater. . . Last night, two Indian girls [70] brought us some gooseberries of which we made sauce. To-day they came again. We gave them some needles and a few pieces of calico, upon which they sewed very prettily.

Mary Made only one camp. Not so much fatigued as sometimes. Weather quite warm & pleasant. Our tent close to the bank of the Sweet Water which is a remarkably pleasant stream; not turbid like most of those we have seen. Most of the country we have [been]

[67] Five miles west of Independence Rock the Sweetwater River breaks through a 400-foot ledge by way of a narrow canyon, with vertical sides, called Devil's Gate. Mary underestimated the height of the walls of the canyon.

[68] Joseph Reddeford Walker, who first went to the Rockies with Captain Bonneville in the spring of 1832. One of the most famous of the mountain men. Walker is reported to have discovered Yosemite Valley in California in 1833.

[69] Wild gooseberries and several kinds of wild currants are still to be found in these regions. See Myra's diary, July 13.

[70] Probably from the Crow Indian tribe.

travelling since leaving Ft. William has been sandy desert, bearing little but sedg & wormwood, flowers & greasewood. Most of the way plenty of fuel, though lately we have often had nothing but sedg. The minerals are interesting but I have to ride over most of them without picking them up. If I could only mount and dismount without help how glad I would be. Not at all discouraged by the way. Ride in company with Dr. & Mrs. Gray most of the time. Mr. W. gets along without quareling. A strange thing, for which I cannot be sufficiently thankful. If he had as much difficulty as most of the company I think I should be homesick enough.

Myra 19th. TUESDAY. Move camp at half past six, ride into camp at half past 4 o'clock. Travel 10 hours, ride 20 miles. Suppose we are not more than 10 miles from our last encampment. A hilly, barren desert. Crossed Sweetwater and left it in the morning.[71] Encamped on a small stream, but do not know any name for it. Mr. Eells and myself renewedly consecrate ourselves to the God of Missions.

Mary Made along over hills of sand. . . The country for miles appeared as if the foundation had given away & the land had sunk. . . I set off in company with Dr. G. who was so anxious to go ahead.[72] We went on not knowing where. Lost the company, was obliged to go back. . . Had a hard jaunt. But stood it quite [well.] Feel better able to drill about than a week or two since.

Myra 20th. MONDAY. Moved at a quarter before 6 and ride 5¼ hours — noon — move again at 3, ride 2½ hours — 7¾ hours, 12 miles. Cross the creek three times. . . Prickly [pears] in blossom, look like poppies. Colored like water lilies.

Mary Rode some time with husband which I had not done for some time before. I have rode with Dr. & Mrs. Gray and Mr. W. has driven the cattle. So I have been first on the spot and he last. Mrs. S. is a great hand to hurry, but her husband is a real poke and last ready about almost every thing. Encamped in a beautiful spot.

Myra 21st. THURSDAY. Move camp at 6 . . . encamp on the Popuasua [Popo Agie,] 12 miles. The water so high we can not cross the river, or we should be at the [rendezvous] which is on the oposite side. A shower.

Mary. Have reached the place near where they rendezvous. En-

---

[71] Rogers writing from the 1838 Rendezvous stated: ". . . followed a branch called Sweetwater to within 50 miles of the Windriver Mountains. We there left it and after proceding about 6 miles came to the Popo Agie, a stream which rises in the W.R. Mountains and runs in an easterly direction; this we followed for three days and arrived at this place on the 21st of June." In other words, instead of following the main trail through South Pass, the caravan made a detour along the east side of the Wind River Mountains to the site chosen for the Rendezvous of that year. According to the record kept by Myra Eells, the distance from the Sweetwater to the Rendezvous was about 40 miles.

[72] So characteristic of Gray — always pushing on ahead.

camped on the South W. side of the Popeasia. Have plenty of wood, water, grass, greens and thickets. Know not how long we may be detained here. Health good. The animals are in better order, most of them than when we started.

AT THE RENDEZVOUS OF 1838

The Rendezvous of 1838 was held where the Wind and Popo Agie (often pronounced Popushia) Rivers meet to form the Big Horn. The site is about nine miles southwest of the present Riverton, Wyoming. Rendezvous had been held at this place in 1829 and 1830. The site was not as favorably situated nor did it provide as large a pasturage for the animals as the location on Green River. One is prompted to ask why such a place was chosen. Cushing Eells in his Reminiscences stated: "The object was secrecy, and thereby to prevent the H[udson's] B[ay] Co. from interfering in their trade." Rogers, in his letter published in the December, 1838, issue of the Oregonian and Indian Advocate,[1] *commented on the intercompany rivalry as follows: "The American Fur Company must soon abandon the mountains. The trade is unprofitable, and the men are becoming dissatisfied; besides the Hudson's Bay Company will break down all opposition. Their resources are boundless, and they stop at no expense." By 1838 the Rocky Mountain fur trade was almost at an end. No more Rendezvous were held after 1840.*

The mission party crossed the Popo Agie on Saturday, June 23, and camped in a grove of cottonwoods within the forks of the two rivers.[2] Here they remained for nearly three weeks. The fact that the Rendezvous had been moved from the Green River to the Popo Agie gave them some concern for how would they be escorted to Walla Walla if no Hudson's Bay party appeared? Myron Eells in his Father Eells *explained the situation:*

> In passing east the year before, Mr. Gray had said to Mr. F. Ermatinger, of the Hudson's Bay Company, that he expected to bring a party out the next year; and as Mr. Gray had favored Mr. Ermatinger, the latter intended to meet the party at the old rendezvous.[3]

Finally on Sunday, July 8, Ermatinger[4] and his party arrived at the

---

[1] A complete file of this little known publication is in the Library of Congress.

[2] The author visited this site on July 15, 1960. There is still a cottonwood grove at the junction of the rivers, and gooseberries and currants may still be found. With but few exceptions the local residents have forgotten that this place was once important in the heydey of the fur trade.

[3] *Op. cit.*, p. 57.

[4] Francis Ermatinger, a Hudson's Bay man often in charge of the Company's pack trains, had escorted Gray to the Rendezvous of 1837. He was a jovial man.

Popo Agie Rendezvous to the tremendous relief of the missionaries. Even though it was Sunday when the Ermatinger party arrived, the missionaries were too excited to hold their religious services.

The presence of four women at the Rendezvous was as much of an event in 1838 as that of Mrs. Whitman and Mrs. Spalding in 1836. The boisterous welcome given by the mountain men to the mission party, in the form of a Rocky Mountain charivari somewhat frightened the women, especially Myra Eells. Some of the men painted their faces and, with a real scalp taken from a Blackfoot Indian, put on a scalp-dance, which the women considered offensive.

Here the missionaries met such famous mountain men as Robert Newell, Jim Bridger, and Joe Meek. With the Ermatinger party was the pioneer Methodist missionary to Oregon, the Reverend Jason Lee, on his way back to the States for reinforcements. Rogers reported that there were very few Indians at the 1838 Rendezvous. For the most part these were Shawnees and Delawares in the employ of the Fur Company. "There are a few lodges of the Snakes around the points of the mountains," he wrote, "but they will not come here."

Myra 22nd. [June, 1838.] Wash, mend & read a little. A shower at noon. Coffee, sugar and tea, two dolls. per pint; blankets from 15 to 16 dollars apiece; pipe, one doll., tobacco from 5 to 6 dollars per lb.; a shirt, 5 dollars.[5]

Mary Busy repairing. Concluding whether we had better cross Popeasia. Mr. & Mrs. S. went out and were gone several hours, so husband came & made me quite a pleasant visit.

Myra 23d. SATURDAY. The water so low it is thought we may ford the river. Mr. Gray and Eells go to find a fording place. Succeeded, though the water is high. All are busy getting the baggage across, which must be put upon the tallest horses. This done, the horses taken back, we mount them and follow our husbands in deep water, but in 20 minutes were all across safe, though some of us have wet feet, but this is nothing new in this country. Encamped in a grove of cottonwood trees near the Wind River.[6] Here we expect to spend a few days,

---

[5] In a letter to members of her family, Myra Eells wrote on July 9, 1838: "We have now traveled eleven hundred miles at the rate of three miles an hour and have not seen anything like a house but once and that made of logs . . . Goods in the mountains cost two or six times as much as in the States. Dr. Gray has just been out and bought a pint of tea for three dollars. . . Our salt is nearly gone and we cannot buy it at any price." Original letter, Whitman College.

Rogers in his letter published in the *Oregonian and Indians Advocate* wrote: "Rendezvous usually lasts 20 or 30 days, and the whole time is spent in drinking, gambling, horse racing, quarreling, fighting, etc. Alcohol is the only liquor brought here and is sold at $4.00 a pint. Some men will spend $1,000 in a day or two and very few have any part of their year's wages left when Rendezvous breaks up."

[6] Rogers wrote: "Our company encamped about 300 yards from the main camp; so we are a little out of their noise."

but know not how many. Hear nothing from Mr. Spaulding or Dr. Whitman or the Indians who were to meet us here.

Mary   About noon took a sudden start & crossed the river without the least difficulty. Mr. S. is going to construct a lodge, so we shall [have] our tent to ourselves. Our situation is delightful. In a little grove of cotton wood, consisting of some 20 trees, in the forks of the Popeasia & Wind Rivers. Husband looks more happy than I have seen him for a long time.

Myra.   24th. SABBATH.   To-day for the first time since we left Westport, we have a Sabbath of rest. Mr. Walker preached in the forenoon from 2d Peter 3:7. Mr. Eells preached in the afternoon from Ps. 66:13. Trust it has been a profitable day to us all. Hope some good may result from the sermons of this day. Some eight or ten men came from the company to attend our worship.

Mary   Mr. S. has gone to living by himself.[7] Query, does not the course he is pursuing cost him some misgivings? It will be pleasant not to hear so much fault finding. . .   Mr. Walker preached in the A.M. on judgment, sitting in the open air in the shade of our beautiful grove. He had 18 hearers. We enjoyed the meeting much. In the afternoon Mr. Eells preached. Had only our family. . .   Read "Saints Rest" between & after meetings. Husband seems to like to stay in the tent now. We all put on our Sunday dresses & acted as much like Sabbath at home as we could. I think I am rather happy.

Myra.   25th. MONDAY.   The gentlemen, except Mr. Eells, who is on horse guard, engaged in making a pen for the animals at night. Mr. [Joseph] Walker, an American trader in the mountains, comes to our camp with a large company, perhaps 200 or 300 hundred horses.

Mary   Spent most of the day talking & dividing things with Mrs. S.

Myra   26th. TUESDAY.   Our cattle could not be found last night; Mr. W. and S. go to look for them. Mr. Eells guards the horses. Mr. G. making a report to the A. Board. Mr. R[ogers] goes hunting buffalo. About one o'clock Mr. W., S. & S[tevens] return with the cattle — find them on the trail towards Walla Walla, at least 12 miles, walking on as regularly as though they were driven. Heat oppresive in the middle of the day.

Mary   The cattle strayed. . .[8] Think I enjoy myself, quite as happy as Mrs. S. for she has seemed to cry half of the time,[9] but I have

---

[7] The Smiths withdrew from the tent they had been sharing with the Walkers to a lodge which Asa had constructed. Thus these couples, for the first time since they left the Missouri frontier, had some privacy.

[8] The cattle were so accustomed to traveling every day that they started out on their own that morning. The mission party started with 13 head. They lost a calf along the way and left four head at Ft. Laramie.

[9] See Drury, *The Diaries of Spalding and Smith*, 17, for reference to the Nez Perces' memory of Mrs. Smith as "the weeping one."

not once since she left. Think I have [not] refrained as long before since we left Westport.

Myra 27th. WEDNESDAY. I repair my dress, which is about worn out. Mrs. Gray attends to baking. Mr. Rogers returns from buffalo hunting, kills two. I cut and help make a gown for Mrs. Craig.[10]

Mary Crag & Robertson came to get their dresses cut. Mrs. Gray baked mince pies; the day before yesterday she fried cakes. This morning Mr. W. got almost out of patience with G.

Myra 28th. THURSDAY. High winds. Mr. G. and wife, Mr. E. and myself take a ride up the river. More timber than we have seen since we left Fort William. . . Mr. Eells commences writing letters.[11]

Mary Mr. Walker traded for a pony & paid 80 dollars in goods for one that in the States would not be worth 20. Tent in a clutter all day.

Myra 29th. FRIDAY. Mrs. Drips, Walker and Robinson call on us. Wish me to cut a dress for Mrs. R.[12] I cut out a gown for Mr. Clark.

30th SATURDAY. The calico these garments are made of costs 2 dollars a yard, and is of ordinary quality.

Mary Baked pudding, sewed on a hunting dress, weather warm. Health good. Musquitoes plenty.

Myra JULY 1st. SABBATH. Worship in the open air under the cottonwood trees. Mr. Smith preaches in the morning, Mr. Walker in the afternoon, 50 or 60 men come from the other camp.[13] Feel that we have been fed with spiritual food to-day.

Mary Public exercises at half past ten. . . I judge as many as 40 persons from the camp, many of [whom] could not understand what was said but they enjoyed the singing. . . The day has been so warm, I feel languid enough.

Myra 2d. MONDAY. All in camp, hear nothing from any to escort us over the mountains. . .[14] Anxiously wait for the time when we shall get to our fields of labor.

3d. TUESDAY. Four Indian women called to see us last evening. Mrs. Gray and I make a rice pudding. An old Indian comes and seats himself at the door of our tent but [we] can not understand him at all.

---

[10] This was the Nez Perce wife of William Craig, who moved to the Lapwai Valley in November, 1839, and subsequently caused much trouble for Spalding.

[11] Several letters written by the men of the party to the American Board at this time are on file in Coll. A.

[12] Mrs. Eells' skill as a seamstress was put to good use. The women were the Indian wives of the mountain men. Robinson is unidentified.

[13] A religious service was indeed a novelty to the mountain men. Only a few attended the previous week but by now the word had spread and more turned out. Mary's estimate of the attendance is somewhat less than Myra's.

[14] By this time the missionaries were beginning to be concerned about how they would be escorted the remainder of their journey. No word had as yet arrived from Whitman or Spalding.

He then goes to Mr. Walker's tent and tries to talk, but can not be understood. Mr. Richardson and Stevens go hunting buffalo.[15]

Myra 4th. WEDNESDAY. No church bells, no beating of drums or roaring of cannons to remind us of our blood-bought liberty. How different one year ago. Then I attended a meeting for Sabbath school children. Here there is no Sabbath, even; no schools to learn the first rudiments of reading. Capts. Drips, Walker and Robbins take dinner with us. Major Harris comes to us again. Says that nine days out of eleven it rained and snowed constantly since he left us.[16] He said that the snow was 12 or 14 inches deep in the mountains. The men do business about camp and guard horses. Mr. Gray and Mr. Eells finish the report to the A. Board. Heat oppressive in the middle of the day.

Mary Rode out in the morning. . . Had baked pudding & greens for dinner. Washed a few things, made a few repairs. A fine day, hope friends at home have had some what of a good time. I *do* want to hear from [them] very much.[17] Could be quite content if I could hear, but not to see nor hear, it seems too bad.

Myra 5th. THURSDAY. Last night were troubled exceedingly by the noise of some drunken men. About one was awakened by the barking of dogs, soon we heard a rush of drunken men coming directly towards our tent. Mr. Eells got up immediately and went to the door of the tent in a moment. Four men came swearing and blaspheming, inquiring for Mr. Gray. Asked if Mr. Richardson was at home. Mr. Eells answered their inquiries and said little else. They said they wished to settle accounts with Mr. Gray, then they should be off.[18] They said they did [not] come to do us harm, had they attempted it, the dog would have torn them to pieces. They then began singing. Asked Mr. Eells to sing with them. He told them he did not know their tunes. They asked if they disturbed him by keeping him up. He made no reply. They said silence gave consent and went away . . . giving us no more trouble, only that we were constantly in fear lest they would come back again.

---

[15] Since buffalo did not wander far over the west side of the Continental Divide, it was most important for the missionaries to take with them a supply of dried meat.

[16] It is possible that Harris, perhaps on his own initiative, rode ahead of the caravan and visited the site of the Rendezvous on Green River before going to Popo Agie. If so that would explain the notice that Ermatinger found on the door of the log cabin at Green River, of which mention will later be made.

[17] Mary did not get her first mail from her home until Sept. 16, 1839, about eighteen months after she left.

[18] The coming of the drunken men at night was a disturbing experience for the whole mission party and especially for Gray, who discreetly kept out of sight in the tent. Gray had antagonized some of the mountain men at the Rendezvous the previous year. They felt that they had some old scores to settle.

All this while, Mr. G. and myself were making preparations for our escape, while Mr. Gray was loading Mr. E's gun, his own being lent.

Capt. Bridger's company comes in about 10 o'clock, with drums and firing — an apology for a scalp dance. After they had given Capt. Drip's company a shout, 15 or 20 mountain men and Indians came to our tent with drumming, firing and dancing. If I might make the comparison, I should say that they looked like the emissaries of the Devil worshipping their own master. They had the scalp of a Blackfoot Indian, which they carried for a color, all rejoicing in the fate of the Blackfoot in consequence of the small-pox.[19] The dog being frightened took the trail across the river and howled so that we knew him and called him back. When he came he went to each tent to see if we were all safe, then appeared quiet. Thermometer, 90 degrees.

Mary Last night disturbed by drunkards. Rose early and washed. A large company arrived under command of Capt. Bridger. Some of them came to salute us. One man carried the scalp of a Blackfoot. The musick consisted of ten horns, accompanied by the inarticulate sound of the voice. They halowed, danced, fired [guns] & acted as strangely as they could.[20]

Myra 6th. FRIDAY. Last night twelve white men came, dressed and painted Indian style, and gave us a dance. No pen can describe the horrible scene they presented. Could not imagine that white men, brought up in a civilized land, can appear to so much imitate the Devil. Thermometer, 100 degrees. Cut two dresses for children. About noon, the white men and Indians gave us another dance. All writing.

Mary Some of the squaws came to get dresses cut. We were again saluted by a company on foot. The same musick, scalp, etc. Their faces were painted. White men acted like Indians. It is said that many of the white men in the Mts. try to act as much like Indians as they can & would be glad if they really were so. Several squaws were here who united in the dance. They were warmly clad, [though] the weather was excessively hot. For several nights the noise in the camp has continued nearly all night. Some of the Capts. & I suppose many of the men are drunk nearly all the time.

Myra 7th. SATURDAY. Finish our letters, prepare for the Sabbath. . . Hear nothing from Mr. Spaulding.

Mary Baked some pies in the morning. Finished putting together my riding dress.

Myra 8th. SABBATH. Prepare for public services. An express comes from Dr. Whitman, Mr. E[rmatinger] and one Indian for a guide on the opposite side of the river to escort us over the mountains. Say that we have 4 fresh horses and provisions at Fort Hall, sent us by Mr.

---

[19] A reference to a scourge of smallpox which had visited the Blackfoot Indians.

[20] The mountain men in their own boisterous good-humored way were merely trying to welcome and entertain their women visitors. They probably had no idea that their demonstration was somewhat frightening to the women.

Spaulding and Dr. Whitman. . . Mr. Lee,[21] a Methodist missionary on the Columbia, Mr. Edwards and Mr. Ewen [22] come here with him and are going to the States, which gives us a safe conveyance for our letters. No public exercises to-day.[23]

Mary The day has been to us a day of rejoicing. A company of 14 from the Hudson Bay Co. arrived. Among them were Rev. Jason Lee, from the Methodist Mission, on his way to the States & several boys who are going to be educated.[24] They came to Green River, expecting to find the rendezvous there. But on reaching [that place] found no signs. The country full of buffalow. But in an old trading house, they found a line, "Come on to the Popeasia; plenty of whiskey & white women." [25] They accordingly came and on the fourth day found us.

Myra 9th. Monday. All writing. Messrs. Lee, Edwards and Ewen call on us. Mr. Edwards has been an associate in missionary labor with Mr. Lee, who is on his way to the States for a reinforcement to that Mission.[26] Mr. Ewen has been over the mountains for his health. Thermometer, ninety.

[21] Jason Lee and his companions, all men, made the overland journey to Oregon in 1834. They were the first Protestant missionaries to cross the Rockies. Lee returned to Oregon by sea aboard the "Lausanne," which sailed from New York on October 3, 1839, with a party of fifty-one missionaries.

[22] F. Y. Ewing, who is reported to have gone out to Oregon in 1837 for his health, was now on his way back to the States.

[23] Notice Myra's first entry for the day. The excitement resulting from the arrival of the Hudson's Bay Company made a religious service impossible.

[24] Lee took east with him two Chinook Indian boys whom he named Thomas Adams and William Brooks. Brooks died on May 29, 1839, and Adams returned to Oregon on the "Lausanne."

[25] Eells, *Father Eells,* gives the following explanation: "Some one who was somewhat friendly to the missionaries, either Dr. Robert Newell, an independent trapper, or a half-breed named Black Harris, who had learned of the rendezvous of the American Fur Company, had with charcoal written on the old storehouse door [perhaps at Fort Bonneville on the site of the Green River Rendezvous]: 'Come to Popoazua on Wind River and you will find plenty trade, whiskey, and white women.' The words 'white women' told them what was meant, and Mr. Ermatinger went immediately there, arriving only four days before the company was ready to start on their return to the States." pp. 57-8.

[26] An interview with Jason Lee appeared in the February 7, 1839, number of the Portland, Maine, *Christian Mirror,* which contained the following account of the Nez Perce delegation to St. Louis in 1831-32:
"A deputation of 6 persons, 3 of the Nez-Perce tribe, and 3 of the Flat-Head, had been sent to St. Louis to inquire for some one to teach them respecting the white man's God. Three of them died at St. Louis and two of them on their return home, and the only survivor could give but an imperfect account of their embassy from not having understood the interpreters through whom the deputation had communicated with Christian people at St. Louis."
In general the account agrees with other earlier reports. The statement about the Nez Perces not being able to communicate should settle once for all the oft repeated "Lament" which first appeared in an article by Spalding in the *Walla Walla Statesman,* February 16, 1866. As has been pointed out, the wording of the "Lament" evolved. See Drury, *Spalding,* pp. 72 ff.

10th. TUESDAY. Heat oppressive. Capt. Bridger and Mr. Newell dine with us. Two years ago [27] Dr. Whitman took an Indian spear [out] of Capt. Bridger's back that had been there three years.

WEDNESDAY. Make arrangements for the remainder of the journey. The gentlemen tell us we have not begun to see danger and hardship in travelling.[28]

Mary MONDAY 9, TUES 10, WED. 11. Wrote one big letter to all the folks and one small one to sisters.[29] Forgot to tell them how little Indian children ride & how the mothers do. How much the way is shortened by the company of plants & minerals; was sorry not to be able to write more.

Myra 12th. THURSDAY. About 20 men to go over the mountains [i.e., to Walla Walla.] Bid farewell to our new-formed acquaintances and move camp at half past nine; rode 7 hours, 22 miles; encamped on the Popiasua. Mr. Ermatinger eats in our tent; loses the letters Mr. Lee sent to his wife by him.

THE RENDEZVOUS TO WAIILATPU

Mary Enroute. Left rendezvous. Forded three streams, made a long camp. Like my pony very much. On reaching camp Mrs. Gray had lost her cloak & Mr. Ermatinger all his pack of letters. The cloak was found near camp. A man was sent after the letters; returned about noon the next [day.]

Myra 13th. FRIDAY. Wait in camp for Battes,[1] the guide, to go back after the letters. . . Moved camp at one — rode 16 miles; encamped on the Popiasua. . . Currants and gooseberries in our camp.

Mary Made a camp of 16 miles over hills of red rocks & earth. . . Poor King having his feet blistered, followed making great adieu. I think I have not felt so weak since I left the States.

Myra 14th. SATURDAY. Moved at 7 . . . 7½ hours, 27 miles. Encamped on a branch of the Sweetwater. Mr. Ermatinger says we are

---

[27] Myra was slightly confused as to dates. Dr. Whitman had removed the arrow head on the occasion of his first visit to the Rendezvous in 1835, three years previous.

[28] The warning given about the second half of their journey was correct. The mountains between South Pass and Soda Springs and those in what is now eastern Oregon were much more difficult to cross than anything the missionaries had previously experienced.

[29] The author has been unable to locate any letters written by Mary from the Rendezvous.

[1] A reference to Baptiste Dorion, son of Pierre Dorion who had been with Lewis and Clark, and an Indian woman of the Iowa tribe who was the heroine of the overland Astor party. Her remarkable story is told in Irving's *Astoria*.

on the back bone of America. Scenery, romantic; Mts. of red sand stone piled on Mts on every side of us, so steep that we can only go up and down them sideways. . .[2] Husband is fatigued and almost discouraged. Will God give us strength and grace equal to our day? Will He sustain and comfort him in every trying scene and carry him and me to our destined field of labour? May we be faithful and successful missionaries among the Indians.

Mary Rode ahead. Could scarcely keep [going.] I think they drive most too fast. Passed a patch of snow, eat some of it. A good deal of scolding because they drive so fast. Encamped for the last time on the waters of the Atlantic.

Myra 15th. SABBATH. It is said by our leader that we are in a dangerous country and we must travel; cannot feel that we ought to place ourselves where we break the Sabbath. Moved camp at 7 . . . 5 hours, 20 miles. Encamp on branch of the Colorado. . .[3] Soon after we moved in the afternoon, we saw a number of Indians coming towards us [with] all speed on horseback. When they came up they shook hands with several of the Gentlemen and said they wanted to trade. . . They went off to their lodges, got their skins & robes, and soon came to us to trade; Mr. E[rmatinger] bought some of both, and paid them with powder, knives, etc. They were greatly [pleased] with our things, especially our dishes and cattle. They appeared cheerful and happy. Mr. Stevens lost two blankets.

Mary Last night had quite a rain. Felt for the first time the leaping of [the fetus.] Followed close to the guide. On our right, snow capped mountains.[4] Saw a flock of antelopes. Last night a large band of buffalow passed so near we could hear them pant. Fell in with a company of Snakes [Indians.] Encamped to trade with them on Little Sandy [River.]

Myra 16th. MONDAY. Moved camp at 7, rode 2½ hours — noon —

---

[2] Riding over such terrain was a terrifying experience for Myra Eells. Eells in his Reminiscences wrote: "The ascents and descents were fearfully abrupt. It is believed that we passed the sides of mountains whose surface lay at an angle of 45 degrees with the horizon. In places, precipice above and beneath nearly perpendicular, and space only for loaded animals to move in single file. To Mrs. E. especially one Mt. appeared formidable. The trail led diagonally downward, thus there was a double declivity. She dismounted, scrambled down on feet, knees, and hands."

[3] On this day the mission party rode through South Pass, the gateway to Oregon. On July 4, two years earlier, Mrs. Whitman and Mrs. Spalding had passed the same way. The four women of the reinforcement of 1838 were the second party of white American women to cross the Rocky Mountains, but there is no evidence in any of the contemporary writings that any of them at the time attached any special significance to the event. July 15, 1838, was just another day of travel.

[4] These were the Wind River Mountains. South Pass skirts the southern end of the range.

then ride till quarter past 7 — 10¼ hours, 45 miles.[5] Morning rode over high mountains and through deep ravines, crossed two creeks, nooned on the last, then rode across a long plain, 35 miles, without coming to any water where we could encamp. Left one yearling calf and the dog on the plain.[6] All of us too much fatigued to write much. Our course s.w.; the soil sandy and covered with sedge.

Mary In the afternoon we rode 35 miles without stopping. Pretty well tired out, all of us. Stood it pretty well myself. But [when I] came to get off my horse, almost fainted. Laid as still as I could till after tea, then felt revived. Washed my dishes, made my bed & rested well. . . 45 miles to ride in one day is hard.

Myra 17th. TUESDAY. Sharp lightning and thunder with high wind and rain last night. Moved camp at eleven . . . ford Green river. . . Takes 2 hours to get all our effects across. . . Encamp on March creek. Crossed 11 streams of water. Find gooseberries so that we make a pie and some sauce.[7]

Mary Crossed Green river. It was quite as high as any we have passed. . . Travelled only a few miles. . . Feel much better than I expected to.

Myra 18th. WEDNESDAY. Moved camp at 7½ . . . 7¾ hours, 20 miles. Encamped on Marsh creek. In the afternoon we rode most of the time between two Mts. we judged to be from 300 to 500 feet high. We rode one and one-half hours on the side of the mountain, the angle of which we judged to be forty-five degrees, with a beautiful stream of water running below us, and no path but what we made ourselves; had our horses made one misstep, we must have been precipitated below to the depth of 100 or 150 feet into the water. We then went into the valley, crossing and recrossing the stream 13 times before reaching our encampment.

Mary Passed . . . along the steep side of a hill where had a horse stumbled, he & his rider must have been precipitated in the stream below. Encamped near the base of a snow capped Mt.[8]

---

[5] This was the longest day's ride of the journey, 45 miles on a side-saddle! Joe Meek, in Victor's *River of the West,* pp. 237 ff., related a dramatic story of the sufferings of the missionaries while crossing the desert which Eells in his Reminiscences branded as being "outrageously false." For further details of this grueling ride between the Sandy and Green Rivers, see Drury, *Diaries of Spalding and Smith,* p. 74.

[6] Mary in her letter of July 27, from Fort Hall, tells of the necessity of leaving the dog behind. All of the animals either had to keep up with the party or remain behind to perish.

[7] Mary in her letter of July 27 mentioned how welcome gooseberries were. "They are very refreshing," she wrote, "& we often find them or currants. They are both very sour, not like any I ever saw before."

[8] This may have been Wyoming Peak, 11,388 feet high.

Myra 19th. THURSDAY. Rode . . . 7½ hours, 24 miles, en-camped on Smith's fork.[9] Our course west through thick pine woods, over high mountains and through deep ravines. . . Mr. Walker loses his coat, Mrs. Walker loses the frill from her bonnet, all of us lose a piece of our veils. . . Snow all around us. One of the cases broken which contains our dishes. Crossed 28 creeks.

Mary Have passed most of the way through woods of pine & fir. Saw yellow violets & strawberries in blossom . . . I have been in camp an hour & husband is just coming. Very glad to see him alive, but sorry he has lost his coat.[10] Have suffered more from fear than anything else. Was so much excited in descending one hill that when I reached the foot I almost fainted. Have thot that God only could make us go in safety. Perhaps were my eyes opened I might behold angels standing by the way. . .

Myra 20th. FRIDAY. One of the company caught a beaver last night. . . Encamp in a pleasant valley after riding over the most frightful Mts., nooned on the salt springs — gathered salt to take on our journey.

After reaching Fort Hall, Mary Walker wrote a letter of nearly four thousand words which described her experiences of travel from the Rendezvous. This letter is now in the Walker Collection of Washington State University. In it she said: "A journal across the mountains is said to be incomplete without a bear story, and I have as pretty a one as need be to tell." She then related how the hunters had killed a brown and a black bear which had been discovered in a thicket alongside the trail. Both Myra and Mary, in their entries for July 20, give a description of the exciting incident which, for lack of space, is omitted.

Mary Encamped at noon on Thomas Fork.[11] Collected a supply of salt. The water of the stream is not salt. . . We made a long noon & our guide Batiste returned with Mr. W. to find a lost heifer. In the afternoon I rode the old pony supposing we had passed hills enough for one day. I rode on alone, but soon found there were hills left yet. We had some frightful places to pass. We passed along the steep sides of mountains where at every step the loose earth slid from beneath

---

[9] See entry in Mrs. Whitman's diary for July 25, 1836, in vol. I. The Whitman-Spalding party also camped on Smith's fork.

[10] From Mary's letter of July 27: "When he came I was glad indeed to see him safe & sound, with his clothes badly rent having lost his coat, his *wedding coat* . . . His watch too he gave such a tremendous jolting that it stopped & will probably have to be sent to England before it can be repaired." None of the women had watches. There is evidence that Eells carried one.

[11] A branch of the Bear River.

the horses feet & seemed to threaten to leave them without a footing. . .[12]

On reaching the foot of the mountains we passed a beautiful little grove & came at once to an open plain where the tall grass was in good state to mow. On entering the plain, my pony set off at an easy canter & I reached camp & unsaddled my horse before any of the company arrived. As there were abundance of rose, I picked rose leaves until my tent was pitched. Find my health very good. Husband came in with the lost heifer before tea, & glad was I to find we were all once more safe in camp. I have suffered considerable from anxiety lest both of us should not live to complete our journey's end. Find it difficult to be reconciled to the idea of separation by death. Find I [am] becoming every day more fondly attached to my husband. Indeed he seems every day to become increasingly kind & I am more & more confident of my ability to please him & make him happy. . . When the hunters came in they brought news that we [are] surrounded by [buffalo] cows. Decide to lay by & make meat.

Myra 21st. SATURDAY. Stayed in camp to prepare meat. From this place we expect to see no more buffalo, of course what [we] have must be caught and dried. The hunters off after buffalo; about noon some of them come in, say that Indians are near us and every horse must be caught; some of the Indians come up, appeared friendly. Every man is after his horse; Mr. Ermatinger [told them] to go for their skins, robes, etc., and he would trade with [them] which calmed our fears in a measure. Towards night they came in to trade.

Mary Hunters busy killing meat, others busy cutting & drying. About noon it was announced that a village of about ten lodges of Indians were approaching. The horses were brought to the pickets. . . Finding them peaceable, the horses were loosed. They were Banack. More savage than any we have seen [in] their appearance. Many of the boys were entirely naked. A knife was put in the hands of some of their squaws & they assisted in cutting meat. . .

Myra 22nd. SABBATH.[13] The Indians are about our tent before we are up and stay about us all day. Think they are the most filthy Indians we have seen — some of them have a buffalo [skin] around them, though many of them are as naked as when born. Mr. Walker read a sermon, and although they could not understand a word, they were still & paid good attention. They appeared amused with our singing.

---

[12] From Mary's letter of the 27th: "In the P.M. passed some more mountains at sight of which one might well exclaim *tremendous*. I shudder to think of them. In passing one I could scarcely believe it possible we could pass even after we were over it."

[13] After the missionaries left the Rendezvous, they were able to observe Sunday by remaining in camp each of the six Sundays that passed before they reached Waiilatpu, except the first. Being then in dangerous Indian country they felt it necessary to travel.

Mary Had a quiet Sabbath, tho the meat requires considerable attention. . . Quite a number of Indians collected around the door of the tent. . . Kept very still during the sermon & in prayer time remained with their eyes fixed on the ground. I was surprised to witness their devout appearance. . . I felt as if I would almost like to stay with & instruct them.

Myra 23rd. MONDAY. Moved camp at 8 . . . 23 miles. Encamped on a branch of Bear river. Scenery awful. Think the mountains would compare with the ocean in a storm, the mountain waves beating on the lonely vessel. We often say that this journey is like going to sea on dry land.

Mary At noon the horse flies were so thick that they could scarcely pack or saddle, P.M. reached the plain & left the Backbone of America. The flies seemed like a swarm of bees & plagued the horses exceedingly. Old Mountaineer men say they never saw the like.

Myra 24th. TUESDAY. Moved camp at half past 7 . . . 6½ hours, 25 miles. Encamped at Soda Springs, spoken of by Mr. Spaulding in the *Herald* — think that correct.[14]

Mary Nooned at cold spring, camped at the Soda. My horse fell & tumbled me over his head, did not hurt me.

Myra WEDNESDAY, JULY 25th. A rainy night. Wild geese singing all about us. Traveled twenty-five miles, and encamped on a branch of the Snake river. Soon after leaving camp in the morning we came to a soda spring, the orifice of which is six or eight inches in diameter. The water when boiling up, which is all the time, looks like artificial soda.

Mary In the morning baked soda biscuit & fried soda friters.[15]

[14] Extracts from Spalding's letter describing his travel experiences of 1836, including a description of Soda Springs, appeared in the October and December, 1837, issue of the *Missionary Herald*. The hot mineralized springs in the vicinity of what is now Soda Springs, Idaho, excited the attention of thousands who passed that way over the Oregon Trail.

The manuscript of Myra Eells' diary, now on deposit in the library of the Oregon Historical Society, does not contain the entries from the last part of July 24 to the first part of August 5. This portion of her diary is taken from the 1889 *T.O.P.A.*, pp. 82-85.

[15] Mary, in her letter from Fort Hall, wrote: "I made biscuit with it [i.e., the soda] as good & light as if I had used the nicest yeast & let the dough rise just enough. Used nothing but the water & a little salt & baked them as soon as mixed. Also fried fritters which were also nice." The Nez Perces had carried some provisions, including flour, from Spalding to the mission party. Thus Mary was able to do baking. Traveling with Ermatinger and the missionaries was the famous mountain man, Joe Meek, who years later told Mrs. Victor, author of *River of the West*, how he saw the missionary women baking bread in a "tin reflector before an open fire." His mouth began to water in hopeful anticipation, but he was not invited to partake. James, one of the Nez Perces from Lapwai, was asked by the missionaries to sing one of the hymns taught him by Spalding. This he did so creditably that one of the women rewarded him with a biscuit. Meek hurriedly

Both very fine. . . All about the springs [are] numerous little mounds with craters, evidently they were once springs but have filled up. We visited one which is about milk warm, the water spouts about two or three times in a minute, such as water gurles in a tunnel, or as it boils over a hot fire. The orifice whence it issues is on the brink of Bear River.

Myra THURSDAY, JULY 26th. Rode six and one-half hours, twenty-three miles; encamped on a branch of the Portsmouth [Portneuf]; two mules threw their packs, one into the river; crossed ten creeks.

Mary Yesterday we had a cold raw wind & I took cold in a tooth which ached so that I scarcely slept an hour all night.

Myra FRIDAY, JULY 27th. Move from the picket at half past four, ride five hours, eighteen miles. Arrive at Fort Hall; introduced to Mr. McKay,[16] one of the chief factors of the Hudson's Bay Fir Company; also to a number of Nez Perce Indians. They came here last night directly from Mr. Spaulding's, on an express to the Rev. Mr. Lee, with the painful news of the death of his wife and infant.[17] The same express will take letters for us to the States; nearly all improve the opportunity. Received kindly by all at the fort. Mrs. Walker almost sick. . .

Mary Left camp at half past four in the morning after a sleepless night with tooth ache.[18] Set out as usual with Dr. G. & wife, but Ermatinger & Batiste came on & they set off with them & left me behind. Capt. Sutor [Sutter] happened to be with me, and not having on his spurs was unable to keep up. So he & I were left alone without guide. I suffered my pony to do as he pleased; but having left the trail, & seeing no one ahead, he began to be alarmed & hastened over the sedge. I succeeded in checking him & turning his head the other way. Saw Mr. Richardson approaching, he came up & my pony kept up with him, so reached Ft. Hall after a ride of four hours. Pretty well exhausted with fatigue & toothache, & found breakfast ready which was acceptable.

Husband & rest of [party] arrived in about an hour after, so I think. After breakfast I laid down & tried to rest & compose myself but my nerves were so excited & tooth still aching. Tho I laid nearly all day, I

drew James aside and induced him to sing another hymn and to give him the biscuit should another be offered. "In this manner," declared Meek, "I obtained a taste of the coveted luxury, bread — of which, during nine years in the mountains, I had not eaten."

[16] Thomas McKay, who, with John L. McLeod, had escorted the Whitmans and the Spaldings to Fort Walla Walla, was in charge of Fort Hall in 1838.

[17] Mrs. Jason Lee had died in childbirth on June 26. It was at Fort Hall on July 27, 1834, just four years to the day previously, that Lee conducted the first Protestant service held in the Oregon country. See Brosnan, *Jason Lee*, 64.

[18] On April 3, while at Cincinnati, Mary had had some dental work done.

could not get even a nap, so unwell I concluded to have it extracted after which I felt better.[19]

Myra SATURDAY, JULY 28th. Attend to washing, mending, etc. No one willing to carry the express for less than five dollars.[20]

Mary Pretty much sick all day. Had to let my work all go. Wrote part of letter to our folks.[21]

Spalding had sent a party of six Nez Perces with five fresh animals and provisions to meet the reinforcement at Fort Hall. The hardest part of their overland journey still lay before them. The distance between Fort Hall and Waiilatpu was about five hundred miles, much of it through barren deserts. The missionaries were advised to leave their cows as there was little or no forage for them along the Snake River. In her letter to her parents, Mary lamented: "We shall now be deprived of our milk." By this time the four couples had been discussing their respective fields of labor. Mary wrote: "Mr. Walker is expecting to settle with Dr. Whitman. Dr. Gray among the Flatheads. Mr. Smith & Eells, I know not where, but unless some one should like Mr. S. better than at present, he will have to settle alone. He is as successful in gaining universal ill will as Mr. Walker good." The actual assignments were not made until the mission meeting at Waiilatpu on September 1.

Myra SUNDAY, JULY 29th. Mr. Gray lodges in the Fort. Mr. Eells and I have the tent to ourselves. We get and eat our breakfast before any in the camp are up. About 10 o'clock Mr. Ermatinger comes to invite us to breakfast; says he has just got up. After breakfast he comes again to invite us to have preaching in the Fort. Afternoon, Mr. Eells preaches in the dining room; some fifty or sixty hearers. Mr. Smith tries to talk with the Indians, who are constantly around his tent.

Mary Slept most of the day. Attended meeting . . . in the dining room.[22]

---

[19] From Mary's Fort Hall letter: "After riding fast four hours, arrived at Fort Hall where I found breakfast ready. . . Sat on a stool & ate at a table. After riding 16 or 18 miles before breakfast & going without sleep two nights, I found myself pretty well used up. After bearing it all day & finding no relief, I had it extracted, after which I got a good nights rest."

[20] The missionaries felt an obligation in forwarding the news about the death of Mrs. Lee. As will be noted in Myra's diary for July 30, they finally found it necessary to send Richardson, their hunter. He caught up with Lee at the Shawnee Mission near Westport on September 8.

[21] The original of this letter, of about 4,200 words, from which several quotations have been made, is in Coll. WN.

[22] Regarding the fort, Mary wrote: "The fort is built of doughbees which are clay made in form of brick two feet long, six inches deep. The wall is double & the room as cool as a cellar almost. We have our tents pitched out side the fort but have a room inside where we stay when we choose."

Myra MONDAY, JULY 30th. Mr. Richardson and Mr. Curtis go back with the express. Some of the company think it best for Mr. Gray to go on as soon as possible to Mr. Spaulding's and make arrangements for our arrival.[23]

Mary Quite well, washed [24] &c.

Myra TUESDAY, JULY 31st. Make arrangements for moving camp. The men of the Fort think it not best for Mr. Gray to leave the company at present. Hire two men, one for Mr. Spaulding, and one for the good of the mission, for one year. . .[25] Ermatinger gives ten pounds of sugar. At 2 o'clock bid farewell to our new formed acquaintances at the Fort; rode two and one-half hours, ten miles; encamp on the Portsmouth [Portneuf]. Mr. McKay and wife and two or three Indians go with us to our encampment, take tea with us and return.

Mary Left fort H. Mr. McCay [McKay] & Battiste &c accompanied us to our first encampment.[26]

Myra WEDNESDAY, AUGUST 1st. One of the mules gone back to the Fort, and Mr. Rogers goes back after it; had trouble in getting him; thinks some Indians drove him off, but could not catch him. Rode five and one-fourth hours. . . Grass as high as the horses backs.

Mary Encamped at falls in Snake river.[27]

Myra THURSDAY, AUGUST 2nd. Mosquitoes so troublesome that we can not go out of our tent without everything but our eyes covered; horses nearly black with them, and they cannot eat for them. Rode four and one-half hours, fifteen miles; encamped on Snake river. . . Passed through a lonely valley with a wall of rocks on either side of us, which we judged to be from one hundred to two hundred feet high.

FRIDAY, AUGUST 3rd. . . . Encamped on a branch of the Snake river. The face of the country is rough. . . We were met by a large party of Indians; one and another came up to our guides and

[23] The restless Gray wanted to push on ahead but was deterred for the time being. He and his wife did leave the others on August 13 and arrived at Waiilatpu on the 21st, a week or more in advance of the others.

[24] From Mary's letter: "July 30. . . I have got most well again. Am going to washing in the room at the fort which in form, size, & cleanliness resembles your hog sty."

[25] They were James Conner, who had a Nez Perce wife, and Richard Williams, both mountain men. See vol. I, page 214, note 10.

[26] The Ermatinger party with the missionaries remained on the south bank of the Snake River, across what is now southern Idaho. The Whitman-Spalding party crossed the river at what is now Glenn's Ferry and traveled on the north bank to Fort Boise. In Mary's letter from Fort Hall, we read: ". . . we expect in about twenty days to reach Dr. W's. . . there is one tribe we may pass who are very hostile. I shall rejoice to be once more where I can sleep without the loaded musket at our side."

[27] The American Falls, a famous landmark on the old Oregon Trail. The falls had a drop of 42 feet before the present dam was constructed in 1927.

shook hands, chatted awhile, then rode up to the hill, gave a war whoop. The women and children immediately ran into the ravines; the men came to meet us when they found we were friendly and the women and children came back. Most of them wished to shake hands with us; we suppose they were in all from seventy-five to one hundred. They were well covered with skins, their horses were fine; they had a large number besides what they were riding. The chief and five of his men turned and rode with us into camp; we gave them some dried bread and meat, some powder and balls with which they appeared exceedingly pleased. As they were about to leave, the chief sent his compliments and said he was destitute of a shirt. Mr. Eells gave him one that he had worn; he put it on and appeared satisfied. About 2 o'clock they went off.[28]

SATURDAY, AUGUST 4th. Rode seven hours, thirty miles, encamp on Snake river where there is plenty of grass for the animals on the Sabbath.

Mary THURS. 2 & FRI. 3, SAT. 4. No time to write journal. Encamped over the Sabbath on the big river among the tall grass.

Myra SUNDAY, AUGUST 5th. Observed a season in prayer, singing and special conversation. Afternoon, Mr. Smith reads a sermon.[29] Two men come from the Fort who will guide and interpret for us to Boise.[30]

Myra 6th. MONDAY. Moved camp at 7 . . . 8½ hours, 35 miles. Encamped on Rock creek and saw what we called a wild horse. At night an Indian called on us, enquired for the horse we saw at noon, said he had been lost a number of weeks; he gave us a dried salmon.

Mary 16 miles in the forenoon; nooned under the shade of a broad spreading cedar. P.M. 19 miles. . . Cold nights & rather cool, pleasant days. Had quite a pleasant rain Sat. night. Mr. S. preached in his old patched pantaloons. Sermon rather flat.

Myra TUESDAY, AUGUST 7th. Moved at 7 . . . 25 miles. Encamped on the Snake river; passed Rock creek . . . appears like a deep ravine walled in on both sides, the wall being from 20 to 30 feet high; and some of it very perpendicular. The Snake river, for some distance before we reach our encampment, is in a deep channel, said to be 400 or 500 feet to the water. Nearly opposite to us is a large spring coming out of a perpendicular bank.[31] The water has the appearance of salt at a distance.

---

28 No doubt these were the Snake or Shoshone Indians.

29 The manuscript of Myra Eells' diary in the Oregon Historical Society continues the text from this point to the last part of the entry for August 20.

30 Fort Boise was established by Thomas McKay in the summer of 1834 on the Boise River, about 10 miles above its mouth. In 1838 the fort was moved to a location on the east bank of the Snake near the mouth of the Boise River. This was the fort visited by the reinforcement of 1838.

31 The volcanic soil of this part of Idaho is such that often streams disappear only to gush forth as springs along the north bank of the Snake.

Mary   Made only one camp of about 25 miles. Opposite our camp, quite a stream of water gushes out of the rocky side of the hill. It is so white & gushing that at first I did not suspect it was water. Springs in this country are said to lose themselves in the sand & then gush out again in this manner. The roar of the water is heard for some distance. . .   Last night water in a covered dipper froze quite hard.

Myra   WED.   Moved camp at 7, rode 3½ hours, 12 miles. Encamped on the river and opposite a large spring which flows over the bank 150 or 200 feet high.

Mary   Br. D.T's birthday.³² Made only one camp, passed more streams gushing from among the rocks.

Myra   9th. THURSDAY.   Moved at 7, rode 7¾ hours, 26 miles. Encamped on the Snake river. Passed the Salmon Falls.³³ Several Indian lodges on the bank of the river. Some 50 or 60 Indians in them. Bought some salmon of them. Most of whom entirely naked, except a string or a bunch of willows tied around the middle. Mr. Gray [and wife] ride on ahead of camp, take a cross cut to where it is supposed the company will encamp; suppose they are about 12 miles before us, alone and with nothing to eat, and nothing but blankets and saddles for beds.

Myra   10th. FRIDAY.   Moved at eight — rode 3½ hours, overtake Mr. Gray and wife. Noon — then ride 2½ hours — 6 hours, 20 miles. Encamped on the Snake river.

Mary   Yesterday & today we are over what I call mountains, near the river, passed lodges of Indians. Procured salmon. . .   Mr. W. not very well for some days past.

Myra   11th. SAT.   Moved a quarter before 8 — 7½ hours, 35 miles. Encamped on the river. . .   Mr. Rogers' horse fails.

Mary   Passed hills of drifted sand. Plenty of Indians about; fear they will steal our horses. Passed over the hills into a level plain in the P.M.

Myra   12th. SABBATH.   To-day stay in camp. Indians about us most of the day. Two came with Mr. Rodgers' horse early this morning; said they stayed with him all night for fear some one would take him off. Gave them some meat, an awl and a fishhook. No public exercises on account of the heat.

Mary   SUN.   12. Rested. So warm had no meeting.

Myra   13th. MONDAY.   Rode 10 hours, 40 miles; encamped on Snake river.³⁴ Early in the morning, crossed two creeks, after which we came to no more water until our encampment.

Mary   Travelled 35 or 40 miles before stopping. We passed two

---

³² Mary frequently mentioned the birthdays of her brothers and sisters in her diary. Here she remembered her brother, Daniel Thompson, born Aug. 8, 1815.

³³ The falls were about 25 feet high. At certain seasons of the year, the salmon gathered there in large numbers, trying to hurl themselves over the rapids.

³⁴ The party covered 40 miles this day and again on August 25th. Fortunately, the weather was not as unbearably hot as it sometimes is in that area.

creeks, at one of which we should have stopped. It was almost three o'clock when we stopped, having rode eight & a half hours. The animals very hungry; [35] two gave out & were left by the way. Mr. & Mrs. Gray left & went ahead.

Myra 14th. TUESDAY. Move at 8 . . . 7¾ hours — 25 miles. Our horses feel the effects of yesterday; some of them do not get into camp for a long time, one does not get in at all. Crossed two warm springs; encamp on the river. A number of Indian lodges on the banks.

15th. WEDNESDAY. The wolves prowl about us and howl most hideously. This morning, a number of naked Indians came to sell us dried salmon and surface [service] berries [36] made into cakes and baked in the sun. Moved camp at half past 7 . . . 7½ hours, 25 miles. Encamp on the river opposite Fort Boise. Feasted with milk, butter,[37] turnips, and pumpkins and salmon. Mr. Gray and wife left here this morning, hope to reach Dr. Whitman's in one week. Met a large company of Indians, some of them follow us to the Fort. . . Stop here until Monday to recruit our animals.

16th. THURSDAY. Wash a little. The gentlemen walk about the Fort to see the country. Milk and plenty of vegetables to eat. Heat oppressive.

Mary Last night we encamped opposite Boisie. Had milk & butter for supper. . . Animals pretty well worn out. To-day had salmon, boiled pudding, turnip sauce for dinner. One cow at the fort gives 24 quarts of milk a day. Have pumpkins too.[38]

Myra 17th. FRIDAY. Some of the gentlemen at the Post send us a piece of sturgeon for breakfast; take a ride in the boat; Mr. Payton [39] and Capt. Sutter take tea with us.

18th. SAT. A restless night, the dogs bark, the wolves prowl, the horses take fright and break loose, some of the men about the Fort have a spree. The wind blew our tent over, the Indians about are watching for an opportunity to take whatever they could get — all

---

[35] In Mary's letter to her family written from Waiilatpu on Sept. 15, she said: ". . . nearly blistered my hand in trying to prevent my poor hungry horse from stopping to eat the dead dry grass by the way. . ." Original, Coll. WN.

[36] The service berry (also known as Shadbush) is a large juicy, full-flavored berry, common in the Pacific Northwest. The Indians dried the berries for winter use.

[37] Mary, in her letter of Sept. 15, wrote: "The cows were some that Mr. Spalding & Whitman left when they came over. They have grown so large they look like oxen. One cow gives we are told six gallons of milk per day."

[38] The milk and fresh vegetables were greatly appreciated by the members of the mission party who had subsisted so long on the monotonous and unattractive diet of dried buffalo meat. Smith also mentioned getting corn and melons at the Fort. See Drury, *Diaries of Spalding and Smith*, 83.

[39] Francis Payette was in charge of Fort Boise at the time. Captain Sutter remained with the mission party to Waiilatpu. This is the first time Myra Eells mentions him although Mary Walker has several references to him.

cause our sleep to be filled with anxiety and dreams. Prepare for the Sabbath and to leave on Monday.

Mary Baked etc. The fields are many of them yellow with sunflowers.

Myra 19th. SABBATH. The natural sun rises on the evil and the good here as in other places, but how few know anything of our Spiritual Sun, or of the requirements. Mr. Smith reads a sermon, a few come to listen, but suppose most of the people do not understand our language. Two Indians came from Fort Hall and will go with us to Dr. Whitman's. Mr. Payton sends another sturgeon.

Mary Rather quiet pleasant day. One service.

Myra 20th. MONDAY. Moved camp at 7 . . . 8½ hours, 30 miles. Encamped at the springs. . . Feel that I have great reason to be thankful that my health has been spared thus far.[40]

TUESDAY, AUGUST 21st. Awakened in the night by the cry of fire, which was set by some of the guard, and was running in the grass and near our tents. Moved at seven; rode four hours, noon, then rode eight hours, twenty miles; encamped on Burnt River. The grass and leaves begin to show that winter is approaching.

Mary Encamped on Burnt River. Found choke cherries, elder berries of the finest sort & Sumac, the first I have seen on the journey.[41]

Myra WEDNESDAY, AUGUST 22nd. Moved at seven; ride three hours, ten miles; encamp on Burnt river; one of the company sick, obliged to stop this afternoon; rode over long hills all the way, crossed three creeks; Indians come to us and want to sell berries.

Mary Made one camp over hills. Conner's squaw sick, had to stop.

Myra THURSDAY, AUGUST 23d. Prepare to move camp, find three of our good horses gone. After looking for and tracking them some distance over almost impossible hills, come to the conclusion that they were driven off by the Indians who are all gone this morning. All are sad enough. Rode four and one-half hours, twelve miles; encamp on Burnt River.

Mary This morning a number of animals missing. Suppose to be stolen. Con[ner's] squaw about to [give birth]. Can't move on account of the horses. Feel anxious to reach the end of this journey. Can't take much comfort riding. Concluded it was no use to try to recover the horses. We moved camp about ten. Climbed hills higher than any we have passed at all. They told us we were done with mountains long

---

[40] The manuscript of Myra's diary in the Oregon Historical Society ends at this point. The text following is taken from the 1889 *T.O.P.A.*

[41] Mary wrote on Sept. 15: "Found Sumack the first I have seen since I left N.E. A kind of Elder the berries of which are purple like grapes & good to eat. I should think some of the bunches have a pint of berries. We also found plenty of choke cherries. These resemble black cherries only they are a little chokey & somewhat larger."

ago, but if these are not hills I know not what they are. The woman [i.e., Conner's wife] safe in camp. Think it a hard case in such circumstances to ride some 12 miles up hill & down.

Myra FRIDAY, AUGUST 24th. Rode seven hours, twenty-five miles; encamped at "Lone Tree," so called because it can be seen miles distant and no other tree in sight. . .[42] meet an Indian three days from Dr. Whitman's, with an express, telling us of Mr. Gray and wife's arrival at his place, and wishing us to make all possible speed; Mr. S[palding] was there and would wait until we came.

Mary Encamped at the lone tree. This tree stands in the midst of a plain. On both sides are snow capped mountains.

Myra SATURDAY, AUGUST 25th. Rode ten hours, forty miles; encamped on a creek as we came into Grand Rounde valley; crossed ten creeks; Mrs. Conner sick and Mr. C., Mr. Smith and wife stop with her and do not get into camp.

Mary Just as we approached Grand Round, we descended a longer hill than I ever walked down before. Connor's wife was confined. She followed camp about 30 miles. At noon she collected fuel & prepared dinner. Gave birth to a daughter before sunset.

Myra SUNDAY, AUGUST 26th. Stay in camp to-day; a beautiful place. . . About ten o'clock Messrs. S. and C. and wife came into camp. Mrs. C. brings an infant daughter; suppose she rode twenty-five miles yesterday, fifteen to-day. In the afternoon, Mr. Eells read a sermon from Deut. 29:29. One Nez Perce present. Feel that we are near Dr. Whitman's, but not where we shall find our location.

Mary Another quiet Sabbath. The squaw came into camp about 10 with her child in her arms. Smart as could be. Grand Round is a Grand Round.

Myra MONDAY, AUGUST 27th. Rode twenty-five miles. . . In the morning, Mr. Rogers was thrown from his horse and hurt badly, but thought it not best to be bled. We move on; Mr. Rogers soon found that he would not be able to ride, being so faint; Mr. Eells overtakes us, got Mr. Smith to go back and bleed him; Mrs. S. and myself go back; the camp stops for Mr. R. to come up; Mr. S. bleeds him, but he can not ride; Mr. R. thinks he can ride and overtake the camp in three hours. It was then thought best that Mr. Rogers should stop. Mr. and Mrs. Smith and Mr. and Mrs. Conner stop with him until he is able to ride.

Mary As the company was catching up, Mr. Rogers horse threw him, hurt him considerably. He made out to ride as far as Big Creek where we left him. . . Crossed Grand Round & camped at a beautiful place for a settlement.

Myra TUESDAY, AUGUST 28th. Rode eight hours, twenty-five miles;

---

[42] See fn. 25, Part II, of Mrs. Whitman's diary in vol. I, for more information about this landmark.

encamped in the mountains at a beautiful spring. In the morning, the Indians came to ride a piece with us; pass an Indian village in a beautiful grove of pines, suppose there are fifteen or twenty lodges in it.[43]

Mary Travelled through woods of beautiful pine & fir. Down & over hills. Encamped at pleasant spot where we met Williams coming with fresh horses to hasten us on.

Myra WEDNESDAY, AUGUST 29th. Rode seven hours, thirty miles; arrived at Dr. Whitman's; met Mr. Spaulding and wife with Dr. W. and wife, anxiously awaiting our arrival. They all appear friendly and treat us with great hospitality. Dr. W's house is on the Walla Walla River, which flows into the Columbia river, and is about twenty-five miles east of Fort Walla Walla; it is built of adobe, (mud dried in the sun in the form of brick, only larger.) I can not describe its appearance as I can not compare it with anything I ever saw. There are doors and windows, but they are of the roughest kind; the boards being sawed by hand and put together by no carpenter, but by one who knew nothing about such work, as is evident from its appearance. There are a number of wheat, corn and potato fields about the house, besides a garden of melons and all kinds of vegetables common to a garden. There are no fences, there being no timber to make them of at this place. The furniture is very primitive. The bedsteads are boards nailed to the side of the house, sink fashion, then some blankets and husks make the bed; but it is good compared with traveling accommodations. Mr. Gray and wife have gone to Walla Walla.

Mary Left baggage behind, and hasten on. Rode my pony through the woods & then took Mr. W's & then cantered on. Arrived at Dr. Whitman about two P.M. Found Mr. & Mrs. Spalding there. Mr. Gray & wife gone to Walla Walla. We were feasted on melons, pumpkin pies & milk. Capt. Sutor was with us.[44] Just as we were sitting down to eat melons, the house became thronged with Indians & we were obliged to suspend eating & shake hands with some 30, 40, or 50 of them. Towards night we partook of a fine dinner of vegetables, salt salmon, bread, butter, cream, &c. Thus our long toilsome journey at length came to a close.

Myra THURSDAY, AUGUST 30th. Messrs. Smith, Conners, and Rogers arrive; Mr. Rogers is very tired. Mr. Gray and wife come back.[45] All have a feast of melons. After our repast is over, the Indians are called together to have a meeting in their own language. Mr. Spaulding addresses them through an interpreter.

[43] Smith in his diary identifies the Indians as being Cayuses.

[44] Before saying goodbye to the missionaries at Waiilatpu, Captain Sutter gave his French-English dictionary to the Walkers. Their youngest son, Samuel, presented this small volume to the author in 1938. He has turned it over to the museum at the Whitman National Monument, where it is now on display.

[45] For the first and only time all thirteen members of the Oregon Mission of the American Board were together.

Mary   Dr. Gray & wife returned. Mr. Pambre [46] came with things. Mr. & Mrs. Smith arrived & Rogers. So at last we all meet. Before breakfast & supper the Indians were collected. In the morning one prayer was offered in English & one in Indian language. It was truly affecting to witness what two years had accomplished among this people. The exercises in the P.M. were out of doors. Dr. W. & Mr. Spalding addressed first, then the other gentlemen addressed them & Mr. S. interpreted. Several of the chiefs replied. It was to us an interesting scene. The addresses of the chiefs were as sensible as those of the white men, & I think a little more so. One said, he was old & should die soon. Did not know whether he would go to the place above or below; perhaps he would go above. He had heard what the gentlemen of the Trading Company had been telling a long time. Had tried to persuade his people to listen. But they would not hear. But he hoped they would mind what was said to them.

A young Chief [47] spoke who said he liked what the Missionaries said to them but he was always concerned about trade, and pointed out Pambre as a bad man. An old chief seemed inclined to smooth over what the younger one had said. He said it was not his doings, binding Mr. Pambre, that he ordered the cords cut & he was alive still.[48] An old Flat Head Chief was present who said he was ignorant but he wished to be instructed & have his people [instructed.] [49]

I was glad to find so comfortable a house prepared for me & find it very gratifying to meet mothers who know how to sympathize with me.

Myra   FRIDAY, AUGUST 31st.   Settle with our hired help for services thus far on our journey. Have much talk about the prospects of the mission; hold a season of prayer for the guidance of all our future deliberations.

Mary   Morning a day of business. Some difficulty in settling with our men. Dr. G. was for having Mr. Stephens paid in goods. Rather than have trouble, our husbands paid their own specie. . .

Myra   SATURDAY, SEPTEMBER 1st.   After committing our cause to God, the missionary brethren proceed to do business.[50] Voted, that

[46] Pierre C. Pambrun was then in charge of Fort Walla Walla.

[47] Young Chief, also called Tawatowe or Tauitau, is mentioned several times in Drury, *Whitman*. At the time of the Whitman massacre, Young Chief was living in a house built for him by Pambrun on the Umatilla River.

[48] After Captain Bonneville's visit to Fort Walla Walla in the summer of 1834, the local chiefs became dissatisfied with the tariff received from the Hudson's Bay Company for their furs. Bonneville had been too generous with them. One day the chiefs seized Pambrun and, according to Allen, *Ten Years in Oregon*, p. 175: "beat him severely and retained him prisoner in rather unenviable circumstances till they gained to considerable extent their object."

[49] Identified by Walker in his diary as Old Chief. Since the Spokane Indians spoke the Flathead language, they were often called Flatheads.

[50] The women were not allowed to take part in the business meetings with the men.

there be but one new station; that Mr. Smith join Dr. Whitman's; that Mr. Gray [to] Mr. Spaulding, and Mr. Rogers be hired to teach at Mr. Spaulding's station for the present, and that Messrs. Walker and Eells form a new station in the Flathead counry. The reinforcement joins the Temperance Society.[51]

Mary It was decided that Mr. Smith remain with Dr. Whitman; that Mr. [no longer Dr.] Gray go with Mr. Spalding to assist in building a mill; that Mr. Walker & Mr. Eells go to explore. . . I find it hard to be reconciled yet trust it is for the best. . . It is very trying to me to think of having my husband gone. Inclination would make me wish to be where no one else scarcely could see me.

Myra SUNDAY, SEPTEMBER 2d. Have worship in English. The new members of the mission unite with the church already formed here, embracing seven members — in all, sixteen.[52] Celebrate the Lord's Supper. Have one service in the native language.

(the end of Myra Eells' diary)

Mary We all united with the little church, lately formed. . . Mr. Walker preached from the text, "Here [in] is my Father glorified" &c.[53] The communion was held. Mr. Spalding & Smith officiated. Mr. Spalding made an interesting & affecting address. Mr. Smith also made one. Mr. S. closed by explaining to the Indians what had been done. We had an interesting & I think a happy season, notwithstanding all the hardness that has existed among us. We feel that we [have] great cause for gratitude & much encouragement to go forward in the work.

ADVICE FOR WESTERN TRAVELERS

On October 4, 1838, a little more than a month after the arrival of the reinforcement at the Whitman station, Myra wrote a long letter to a sister in which she told of some of her experiences traveling and gave some advice as to what a well-groomed lady should wear on a horseback trip over the mountains. Her special interest in sewing is apparent. She wrote:

---

[51] The Spaldings and the Whitmans sponsored the organization of a Temperance Society before the reinforcement arrived. See Drury, *Diaries of Spalding and Smith*, 165.

[52] The First Presbyterian Church of Oregon was organized on August 18, 1838, with the Spaldings, the Whitmans, and the Hawaiian couple working for Whitman as the charter members. Charles Compo, the French Canadian, joined the church shortly after it was organized. All nine members of the reinforcement joined, thus bringing the total to 16. This was the first Protestant church to be formed on the Pacific Coast.

[53] This text, John 15:8, epitomized the Christian convictions of the little band of missionaries who voluntarily gave up the comforts of the East and accepted the hardships and dangers of life among the uncivilized Indians of Oregon. It was all for the glory of God.

We arrived here on the 29th of August almost six months after we left home. We had a long hard horseback journey, but suppose we are the better qualified to live in this country, as there is no other mode of conveyance here. Instead of finding everything necessary for livelihood, we are dependent on the mission family for everything at present. Everything of a cloth kind is brought from some foreign Post. There is nothing to make cloth of, and if there were, there was no means with which to manufacture it. Had I known that there was not a spinning wheel in this whole country, I should have been exceedingly anxious to have one sent with my things.

I can render some service to the Mission Family with my needle, but at present I cannot teach the Indians to sew or knit because they have no cloth to sew nor yarn to knit. . . The men of this country all wear striped cotton or calico shirts, sleep in Indian blankets and in buffalo skins. Of course they have no need of cotton cloth and have none. . .

Mrs. S.[palding] and W.[hitman] have obtained some earthenware dishes, but think it doubtful whether we can have any until we order them from England or the States. Perhaps you will wonder what we eat with. We have the dishes we used on the way which we have divided so that we shall each have a tin dish and a spoon, each a knife and fork and plate. I expect we can get tinware at Vancouver, I believe there is a tin-maker there. We must be content with what books we have until ours come. . .

For the horseback journey, they ought to have good strong colored clothes, a gentleman should have home-made blue cloth for his clothes, a strong stout box coat, thick boots and shoes, a cap and a broad brimmed felt hat. A lady should have a good green merino or pongee dress, and a loose calico dress to wear when she does not need her cloak. Her underclothes as well as the gentlemens should all be colored. They ought to have three changes to wear on the journey and at least four to wear in the States, and after they get here. They should have a Florence bonnet or a variegated straw. They should have a small dark bedquilt, a pr. of sheets, 4 prs of pillow cases and two pillows. Calico cases are best for the journey. A lady should have a pair of gentlemen's calf shoes, and be well-supplied with stockings and shoes.

She should take silks, ribbons, lining and trimming for bonnets, if she expects to have any after she gets here. She should also have two or three verage (sic) veils. When she journeys it is always in the sun. There are no trees here except a few in the Mts. and along the water courses. Mine lasted me here but it is all worn out now. If she ever expects a cap or caps she must take her laces and muslins with her. She ought to be well-supplied with pins, needles, scissors, pen knives, and silk and thread of all kinds and colours, have a large quantity of brown and coloured thread. . .

She should have an Indian rubber cover for her bonnet, and a cape made of the same. It is so windy that she cannot carry an umbrella, and besides they are likely to get broken. I believe mine is the only one that reached here.[1]

Even though there were times when the women could not use umbrellas to protect them from the hot sun or the rain, yet the very fact that Myra Eells succeeded in taking her umbrella through to Oregon seems to imply that on occasions she was able to use it.

MYRA EELLS — FORTY YEARS IN OREGON

An indication of the price Myra Eells paid in leaving her comfortable home in the East to become a missionary to the uncivilized Indians of Oregon is found in the letter she wrote from the Rendezvous on July 9, 1838. "It costs me tears," she wrote, "every time I write home, and every Sabbath when I think how neat and nice we used to go to church together. My tears are never suppressed; not that I wish to return or that I have once regretted that I have left you all, my dearest friends." [2]

Fortunately for timid Myra, she and her husband were not sent to occupy an isolated mission station by themselves, as was the case with the Spaldings. They and the Walkers were sent to Tshimakain where for over nine years they lived and worked together in close harmony. Two sons were born to Cushing and Myra at Tshimakain with Dr. Whitman present each time as the attending physician. Edwin was born on July 27, 1841, when his mother was thirty-seven years old, and Myron on October 7, 1843. Although there must have been times during the long years at Tshimakain when nostalgic memories of her home and friends in the East caused Myra to seek the privacy of her bedroom to weep, yet no written words of complaint or regret have been found in any of her letters. To the end of the mission period, she remained the loyal companion of her husband, the efficient homemaker, and the loving mother of her two sons.

The story of Myra Eells' life at Tshimakain will be indirectly unfolded in the diary of Mary Walker which follows. After leaving Tshimakain in the summer of 1848, the Eells family moved to the Willamette Valley where Cushing was active in educational and church work. For a time he was principal of the Tualitin Academy, which was chartered in 1854 as Pacific University. In 1860 the Eells family moved

[1] Original letter, Coll. WN.
[2] Atkinson and Eells, *Funeral Service of Mrs. M. F. Eells*, 8.

to the old Whitman mission site at Waiilatpu. Eells was then active in promoting Whitman Seminary, in Walla Walla, which later became Whitman College. Following the burning of their home at Waiilatpu on May 28, 1872, they moved to Skokomish where Cushing organized a Congregational Church, and where the two lived until Myra died on August 9, 1878. She was then seventy-three years old and had spent nearly forty years of her life in Oregon. Her son, Reverend Myron Eells, preached the funeral sermon.

In all probability either Cushing or Myra Eells had received some inheritance, for their gifts to educational and church institutions were large for that day and far beyond what Cushing could have saved during his ministry. When Cushing and Myra sold their land at Waiilatpu, they gave $1,000 to Whitman Seminary and another $1,000 to the American Education Society as a thank offering for the help Cushing had received from that society as a theological student.[3] Both before and after the death of his wife, Cushing Eells aided a number of newly-organized Congregational Churches in Washington and Oregon. The total amount of these gifts, including $10,000 given to Whitman College and contributions to sixteen different churches, was $24,654.65.[4] To this should be added a legacy of $5,000 to Whitman College.

[3] Eells, *Father Eells*, 196.
[4] *Ibid*, pp. 318 10.

Mary Walker's Diary
September 1838 - July 1848

The Crowded Whitman Home at Waiilatpu

The first concern of the enlarged Mission was that of making provision for the housing of all of its members. Winter was coming and there were but two cabins, the Spalding log cabin at Lapwai and the Whitman adobe cabin at Waiilatpu, to care for thirteen adults, two children, and several native or half-breed children that the Spaldings and the Whitmans had already taken into their homes. The men began their business sessions on Saturday, September 1, and continued them on the following Monday. Walker and Eells were authorized to open a new station among the Spokane Indians; Gray was to live with the Spaldings; and the Smiths were to remain with the Whitmans. Rogers was not assigned to any special station but probably lived at Waiilatpu when not with the natives. This meant that each of the three stations was to have two families. The Mission agreed that work on another house at Waiilatpu was to proceed with all possible speed and that Whitman was to go to Fort Vancouver for supplies. However, it took time to make adobe bricks and to build. It was not until December 4 that one room of the new house was completed. Into this the Smiths moved.

Walker and Eells left on September 8 to explore the Spokane country for a possible location. They selected a promising site about twenty-five miles northwest of Spokane Falls on the trail that led to Fort Colville, at a place called Tshimakain or "the place of the springs." They were able to erect the walls of two fourteen-foot square cabins before leaving for Waiilatpu, which they reached on Saturday, October 13. The season was then too far advanced to contemplate any move to Tshimakain that year. This meant that the Whitmans had to be hosts for three couples and a single man in limited accommodations originally built for their own needs. The arrival of the Walker baby on December 7 added to the problem. All of this explains the tensions that gradually developed at Waiilatpu during the winter of 1838-39. Nowhere else do we find such a clear picture of what was happening as in Mary's diary, and in some of her letters to her husband or to her family.

Lack of space necessitates some abbreviation of Mary's diary for her ten years' connection with the Oregon Mission. All of the important passages are retained.

MONDAY 3 [SEPT. 1838]   We formed a Maternal Association.   .   .[1]
[It] is to meet on the second & last Wednesday of each month. I am
appointed Vice Pres. We are to hold meetings at each station & report
to the Recording Secy. as often as practicable.

TUESDAY 4.   A social feast on Melons. Mr. Spalding & Gray & wives
left us.

WED. 5.   Husband, Eells and wife went to W. Walla. I regulated my
room and washed.

THURS. SEPT. 6.   Assisted Mrs. Whitman a little in washing; sewed
a little. Put up seeds &c.[2] Mr. W. & Rogers returned. Mr. E. & wife
took a wrong road & we know not what has become of them.

FRIDAY 7.   This morning rainy. Mr. E. & wife found their way back
without getting wet much. Worked some in the kitchen, finish making
Mr. W. lether pantaloons. Ironed.

SAT. 8.   .   .   .   Mr. E. commenced lessons in music, on the black-
board. Had an interesting group of 20 or 30 indians. They appeared
much interested. I feel anxious to be able to teach them myself. Think
there is every encouragement to labor for their good.

SUNDAY SEPT. 9.   Prayer meeting in the morning. Then instructions
to the natives, next sermon by Mr. Eells.   .   .   Two express from
Walla Walla.[3] Letters from the Methodist Mission. News of the [death]
of Mr. White's child.[4] Age 8 months old.

MONDAY SEPT. 10.   Rose early, worked as hard as I could untill Mr.
Walker got ready to start which was at three P.M. After crying a little,
picked up & found myself somewhat tired.[5] Oh! dear how I would like
to be at home about this time & see brothers, hear from all the good
folks. I wish I could have a letter from some of them.

TUESDAY SEPT. 11.   .   .   .   Had an express from Clear Water. Dr.
Whitman returned from W.W. Brought good news from our husbands.
Hope they will make a successful expedition.

WED.   Attended an Indian funeral for the first time. Our Maternal
Association was observed. Feel very much like doing very little. Don't
know when I shall do all my sewing, it tires me so.

---

[1] See section on "Columbia Maternal Association" in vol. I of this work.

[2] Thrifty Mary was making preparations for her garden to be planted the next
spring.

[3] The word "express" is here used to indicate a courier with letters.

[4] Dr. and Mrs. Elijah White were members of the reinforcement of the Methodist Mission in Oregon of 1837. He was the Mission doctor until 1840 when he
returned to the East. Their child, Jason Lee, was born July 10, 1837, and died
August 23, 1838.

[5] Walker and Eells left this day for their exploring tour of the Spokane country.
This was the first time that Elkanah and Mary had been separated since their
marriage. One of Elkanah's extant diary notebooks begins on this day with the
entry: "I was anxious to leave as time was wasting & we had much to do in order
to be prepared for winter if we located this season. Still it was hard to part with
my wife where her [condition] demanded more than ever my presence & attention."

THURSDAY 13.   Felt rather indisposed in the A.M. In the P.M. felt better, washed all the afternoon.

FRIDAY SEPT. 14.   Baked bread in the morning. Sewed for myself in the forenoon.   . .

SAT. 15.   Gathered seeds in the forenoon. Wrote in the afternoon. Mr. McCay came.

SUNDAY SEPT. 16.   Mr. Smith preached, finished writing my letters home to Mr. W's folks & one to mine.[6]

MONDAY, SEPT. 17.   Dr. Whitman set out for Vancouver. We rose early. I churned & wrote to Mrs. Perkins &c. In the P.M. began to work on husband's coat. The Dr. hurried & bustled about just as my husband does. Finally he got in such a fret that his wife began to cry which brought him to himself; he went on more calmly until he got ready to start.

TUES. 18.   . . .   Mr. Smith came to pantry & found nothing but milk & melons. Didn't like it. Mrs. W. [made] cut[ting] remarks on Mr. S. about milk, sugar, &c. At supper Mr. S. said he was very hungry, had had no dinner. In forenoon Mr. S. sent out to give a melon to some boys for pounding, Mrs. W. countermanded.[7]

WED. 19.   Mrs. Eells helped sew & we finished my Husb. coat. Then I washed and did up her silk dress. My health is good and I enjoy myself quite well, only I want to see my good husband so.   . .

THURS. 20.   Mr Rogers left for Mr. Spalding's. In the afternoon letter from Mr. S. informing that they were in trouble. Dick & Conner so alarmed they can neither eat nor sleep. He does not dare part with Compo.[8] I hope it will please God to turn the hearts of the savages & stay them from violence, & not suffer our hopes of success as missionaries to be blasted.

FRIDAY, SEPT. 21.   Sewed in the A.M. Washed in P.M. Hope when I get to our station I shall make a manage to do my washing in the

---

[6] Mary's long letter of September 15, 1838, contains not only a description of her travel experiences after July 31 but also her first impressions of Waiilatpu. The following are quotations: "At this very moment my window is full of faces gazing at me as boldly as you can imagine, & I cannot drive them away because I know not what to say. I get up every little while and draw my curtains till they go away. But as soon as I put it aside, along comes another gang of urchins. Big urchins too, some of them. They annoy me very much." "Dr. Whitman's house is built of doughlies or dry clay. Has three large rooms, two bedrooms. He is designing to build a better one & use this for a store house." "The Dr. is a good natured man, as tall as Mr. W. except the four inches." And "Mr. Spalding sees visions of the future, some bright & some dark & tells what he is going to do. Dr. W. shows what he has done." Original Coll. WN.

[7] Here is the first evidence in Mary's diary of growing tensions in the Whitman home.

[8] The reference to Dick was possibly to Richard, one of the two Indian boys taken East by Dr. Whitman in 1835. Nothing further is known of the difficulties which had developed with the natives at Lapwai. Although this incident was evidently temporary in character, it was a harbinger of more trouble to come.

morning. And a few other things I will try to have different from what I find here.

SAT. 22. Mrs. W., E. & myself went to visit the indians' lodges. Found some eating, some lying down, some dressing skins &c. and some were packing up to move. They, most of them, seemed busy, especially the women. If they only could have tolerable opportunities, I see not why they would not soon rise to a rank among civilized beings.

SUNDAY SEPT. 23. A.M. Morning worship & family prayer meeting. Worship with the Indians. Mrs. W. read from Mr. Spalding's book,[9] prayer in English, singing in Nez P. In the P.M. sermon by Mr. S. Text "Thy faith hath saved thee." Pretty good for him. Towards evening a marriage. Mrs. W. interpreted for Mr. S. I have read considerable today. But every little while I would find my mind on my husband, it seems a long time already since he left, & longer still before he will return. I can hardly refrain from tears every time I think of him. I know I am foolish but I can't help it. I ought to be more [thankful] than I feel that I have so good a husband & that I have enjoyed his society so much; & not be sad because he is gone a little.

MONDAY 24. Run here & there, accomplish but little. The weather so warm I can [find] little comfort.

TUES. SEPT. 25. Wrote verses a considerable part of the day. Had letters from Clear Water. Nothing said of danger & the like. Concert in the evening. All of us prayed.[10] I succeeded better I think than do sometimes.

WED. 26. Maternal Association. . .[11]

THURS. 27. Rain last night & this morning. Mended pair of gloves.

FRIDAY 28. Pleasant. Mr. S. is threshing wheat with his Indians.

SAT. SEPT. 29. . . . Got almost out of patience with Mrs. E's

---

9 Since the printing press had not yet arrived at Lapwai, Spalding's "book" was evidently in manuscript form.

10 See Mary's entry for October 2, about the propriety of praying "before folks." The Whitmans and the Spaldings believed that women should join in social prayer. The men of the reinforcement of 1838 did not. During the absence of her husband, Mary was induced to pray audibly before others, but she was troubled over what her husband might think. Narcissa, in a letter to her father dated October 10, 1840, wrote: "We have none in our mission of as high-toned piety as we could wish, especially among those who came in the last re-enforcement. They think it wrong for females to pray in the presence of men, and do not allow it even in our small circle here. This has been a great trial to me, and I have almost sunk under it." Again in her letter to her parents of October 6, 1841, she said: "In all the prayer meetings of this mission, the brethren only pray. I believe all the sisters would be willing to pray if their husbands would let them. . . My husband has no objection to my praying, but if my sisters do not, he thinks it quite as well for me not to."

11 The meetings of the Maternal Association were held with fair regularity every two weeks during the six months the Walkers and the Eells were at Waiilatpu. Most of the references to these meetings during these months in Mary's diary will hereafter be omitted.

habit of snuffing. I wish someone would tell her about it. We were hoping to hear from our husbands by this time. Mrs. E. manifests much solicitude about hers & I would at least like to hear from mine.

SUNDAY. 30.   Mrs. Whitman's babe is sick and [Sunday] exercises in consequence rather deranged. Was much interested in hearing an Indian go over the story of the prodigal son. His gestures were so expressive. No sermon in English. Mr. S. taught the Indians as well as he was able.

MON. OCT. 1 . . .   Had letters from Messrs. W. & Eells. . .[12] Fear my husband will suffer for want of his coat.

OCT. 2. TUES. . . .   Washed some & that is about all I have done today that counts. This evening weekly concert, made a prayer. I wish I knew whether my husband likes to have me pray before folks or not. When he comes home I will ask him. Fear when he comes home he will be disappointed to find me no more proficient in the language.[13] Hope I shall soon be able to give more attention to it.

WEDNESDAY OCT. 3 . . .   Ironed & made some blackberries pies [for] Mrs. E.W. & myself. Mrs. W. has said and done many things that do not suit Mrs. S. to-day.

THURS. OCT. 4 . . .   Helped hull some corn. Mrs. E. is in a great worry because she expects to be obliged to winter here & Mrs. Smith is worried for fear her husband will not get along so well [if] Mr. Walker & Eells are here. All goes well with me. Am glad I am not of the worrying sort. I know I do not seem to be doing much, but I do as much as I can & what is the use to be troubled & impatient. I have finished all my letters & wish husband could read them before I send them away.

FRIDAY, OCT. 5.   Sewed some, read some. . .   Female prayer meeting.

---

[12] Two letters from Elkanah to Mary written from Fort Colville and dated September 19 and 20, 1838, are in Coll. WN. In the first he wrote: "I would advise you to give all the attention you possibly can to learning the Nez Perce language. You will always find use for it and it will be of great assistance in learning other languages." And "Remember that you are not Mistress of the house & you have nothing you can call your own, that you are entirely dependent on others." In the second letter, he wrote: "I wish you to say to Dr. W. if he is not gone, to be sure & get me a watch at Vancouver if he can." See footnote 10, on page 105, where reference is made to the fact that Walker on July 19 had damaged his watch. Mary, in her letter to Elkanah of October 8, Coll. WN., reported that she had sent the broken watch to Vancouver to be forwarded to the Hawaiian Islands or to England for repair. See entry in Mary's diary for July 15, 1839, for reference to its return.

[13] Lawyer, a prominent chief of the Nez Perces, spent some time during the winter of 1839-40 at Waiilatpu teaching the language to Smith. See Drury, *The Diaries of Spalding and Smith*, 93. Since Lawyer knew the Spokane or Flathead tongue in addition to the Nez Perce language, it is possible that he also gave some instruction to the Walkers and Eells.

SAT. OCT. 6. Reading, sewing, commenced making my Dictionary. Mr. S. requested Compo to say something to the Indians. Mrs. E. [had] many remarks to make about setting babes to teach.[14] Mrs. S. wished Mrs. E. to assist her sew a dress of Mrs. W's. She [i.e., Mrs. Eells] declined because she pretended she did not like the fashion. She said too that Mrs. W. wrote all the time & her writing was of as much consequence as hers [i.e., Mrs. Whitman's] etc.[15] Just as [if] she did not feel under the least obligation & had as good a right to the house as Mrs. W.

SUNDAY OCT. 7. One service in Eng., two in P.M. Mrs. [Whitman] succeeded very well with the aid of Compo. Like Mr. S's discourses very [much.] Better than any I have heard him preach before. Have been searching my heart to-day to see how much sinfulness could be found there. Detect so much in others that I fear I do not see it quick in myself & husband, as I do elsewhere. Do not think I have so much of the small kind yet suspect the principal may be that [it is] implanted in my heart & secretly be working its mischief there. Oh! that in heart & life I were in some degree conformed to that of the Saviour.

MONDAY OCT. 8. Brother I.T's birthday.[16] Wrote to husband [17] & did some other things.

TUESDAY OCT. 9. Hear our husbands are at Mr. Spalding's. Weekly concert.

WED. 10. Have sorted out the more important words of one third of the Dictionary. In the evening plenty sing with the Indians a hymn prepared by Mr. Smith.

THURSDAY 11. Sent off more letters for the States. Washing, ironing, picking husks. Got quite tired. Worked about the house most of

[14] Charles Compo, a mountain man, joined the First Church of Oregon as a convert from Roman Catholicism on August 18, 1838.

[15] Four of Mrs. Whitman's letters written during September 18-29, 1838, are extant. See index of Whitman letters in Drury, *Whitman*, pp. 434 ff.

[16] Mary was faithful in remembering the birthdays of her nine brothers and sisters. Here she noted the anniversary of her brother Isaac Thompson, then 15 years old. Hereafter most of these references in Mary's diary will be omitted. Information about Mary's brothers and sisters may be found in Drury, *Elkanah and Mary Walker*.

[17] Mary's letter of October 8, 1838, to Elkanah, Coll. WN., has the following quotations: "Find it very unpleasant being with the Indians, the smell of them is so offensive. I am preparing me an English Nez Perce Dictionary, which I think will be very useful to you as well as myself. I shall try to associate more with the Indians & learn of them when my senses become less acute." "Think I am much more cheerful, happy & contented than Mrs. Eells. She is rather unreconciled to the idea of spending the winter here. She does not seem to like Mrs. Whitman very well." And "The weather will soon be so cold that I cannot stay in my little room away from the fire. I suppose Mrs. W. will let me take reffuge in her room as she will have a stove. But I think if you return in season you can prepare me a room so that I shall not be obliged to deprive Mrs. W. of her stove, as I would not like to do it."

the day, hulling corn, taking care of Alice [Whitman.] In the evening finished my Dictionary. Sat up till near eleven thinking it might rain before morning. Brought in the clothes.

Fri. 12.   Rained considerably last night. Mrs. W. & S. were much concerned about their clothes. Glad this morning to find them safe & dry.

Sat. Oct. 13.   Stewed pumpkin, baked pies. Mrs. Whitman quite out with Mr. Smith because he was unwilling to let her have Jack help her. Husband & Mr. Eells came about noon. Was glad once more to see my husband & he appears glad to see me & I suppose he really was for he has no faculty of making believe. Could not sleep all night for joy.

Sunday 14.   Worship out doors. Large assembly. Husband preached in the house in English.

Monday 15.   Were beginning to be anxious about Dr. W. But before breakfast he came. We were glad, glad, glad to see him. A day of rejoicing all day. Husband writing to the Secretaries.[18]

Wed. 17.   Dr. W., Mr. Walker & Eells went to W.W. Repaired a dress for Mrs. Whitman.

Thursday Oct. 18.   Husband returned from W.W. in the evening. When they came complained of the cold. Eat apples sent from Vancouver.

Friday 19.   Confusion all day. Dividing books &c, goods.[19]

Sat. 20.   Rain yesterday & to day. Fears that the winter is about to set in.

Sun. 21.   Mr. Eells preached. Text, Godliness is profitable, &c.

Monday Oct. 22.   Choring all day, hulling corn & make a little soap, wash & iron a little.

Saturday Oct. 27.   For several days past have been cutting out & fixing little things. Mrs. Eells has helped me sew. Today baked pies & hulled corn. Weather good. Dr. W's house going up. . .

[18] Walker's long letter of about 10,000 words to the Board is in Coll. A. In this he gave a report of their overland journey to Oregon, the Mission meeting of September 1-3, and the exploring tour of the Spokane country which he and Eells had just completed. He made mention of Chief Big Head who was eager for the missionaries to settle near his people. Big Head had a son who was sent to the mission school at Red River (near what is now Winnipeg, Manitoba) where he died. Walker wrote that the Chief said that he mourned ". . . not because he was dead but because he did not return to teach him about the way to heaven." Walker also gave the first description to the Board of Tshimakain where he and Eells had decided to settle. Since he had no opportunity to send the letter which he began on Oct. 15, Walker kept it over the winter and added a postscript in March describing their journey from Waiilatpu to Tshimakain.

[19] Occasionally missionary barrels arrived addressed to the Mission. These were often sent by churches or missionary societies in the East and contained clothing and other supplies. When such barrels arrived addressed to the Mission instead of to individuals, the contents were divided with scrupulous fairness. Mary may have been referring to such an incident.

SUN. OCT. 28. Mr. W. preached in Eng. Dr. W. instructed the Indians. There are many sources of happiness with me but I am ashamed & confounded when I reflect on the pride & self conceit of my heart; there is no coming to the bottom of it, go as deep as I will, pride still lurks under pride. Spend most of my time in my room now, though it is rather cold.

MONDAY OCT. 29. Washed & wrote a letter to Mother.[20]

TUES. 30. Cutting out small clothes & repairing old ones. Stay in my room most of the time, though it is rather cold.

WEDNES. THURS. FRI. Nov. 2. Busy about sundry affairs but up late nights & sleep well.

SAT. Nov. 3. Last night Mr. Pambrun sent us a quarter of beef. He was expecting some Catholic priests [21] to visit him & so he slew the old cream colored cow, which was 23 years old.[22] He also sent the tripe, so that I had the job of cleaning it. Mr. P. also invited the gentlemen to call over and make his guest a visit. They hardly knew what to do about accepting it, but finally concluded it was best. So Dr. W., Mr. W. & Eells have gone. Mr. S. declined saying that it looked too much like countenancing Romanism. Hope our husbands will manage discreetly.

[20] The original letter is in Coll. WN. Mary wrote in part: "Mr. Walker & Eells expect to spend the winter here. Are now assisting Dr. Whitman in building a new house." "I would like one of mothers feather beds right well. But as I have a husk bed & a dozen fleecy blankets, I think I shall not suffer for want of it. My bedstead which has neither sacking nor cord but is constructed of boards nailed up against the wall of the house unique fashion is snugly curtained with Sandwich Island cloth [tapa cloth] which is not cloth but paper." "We begin to have horse flesh served on the table. But I cannot overcome prejudice enough to taste it though it looks as tempting as any meat. Think I shall not learn to eat it while I can get plenty of something else." "Mr. W. is I am sure about the best son you have & merits well the rank of elder brother." And "Altho you have heard from me probably a great many times since I left you, yet you must remember I have not heard a word from home since I left Portland Maine & do not know who to suppose is living or dead. If grandmother is alive tell her, her old shears hang by the side of my window & remind me of her many times in a day."

[21] The first Roman Catholic missionaries to enter Old Oregon were Fathers Francois Norbet Blanchet and Modeste Demers who crossed Canada with the 1838 Hudson's Bay Express. According to Nichols, The Mantle of Elias, 72, the missionaries were called "Black Gowns" by the natives. The priests were welcomed at Fort Colville by Archibald McDonald. There they baptized nineteen, mostly half-breeds. From Colville, the priests went to Fort Walla Walla where they were warmly greeted by Pambrun, a Roman Catholic, about the middle of November. According to the baptismal record found in Nichols, op. cit., 260, the priests had three baptisms at Walla Walla on November 18, 1838. By the end of November, they were at Fort Vancouver.

[22] Eells in his Reminiscences under date of March 13, 1883, wrote: "In 1818 a pair of calves was taken by boat from Vancouver to Walla Walla (now Wallula). In 1838 the female of that pair was the mother of all living of the particular kind between the Cascade and Blue Mts. She was 20 years of age without a tooth in her head. . . She was slaughtered and distributed. A liberal portion was generously sent to the mission station of Dr. W."

SUNDAY Nov. 4.   A long day to me. A day seems a week as it were when my dear husband is absent. Worked too hard. Took cold or something so that I have not felt very well to-day, having felt too irresolute to read much, so have thought & prayed the more. This evening have been reading over my old journals & weeping over fond recollections.

I love my husband so much that almost the only thing that makes me feel unhappy is the fear that he does not love [me] as much. I find it hard to be reconciled to the thought of ever being separated from him. If he should be taken away, I should be so lonely & disconsolate. I could be more contented to die & leave him, could I know that he would obtain another better than myself. After experiencing so much of the goodness of God shall [I not place] myself, my Husband, my all in his hands? This I will endeavor to do. May God still be merciful to us. . .   May his blessing also rest on the little one which we fondly expect soon to welcome as ours.   . .

MONDAY Nov. 5.   Husband returned from W.W. as we were dressing in the morning. Did not see the Catholic priests. The boats having met with a disaster & 12 or 13 persons drowned. Very windy, unpleasant riding this morning. Mr. W. has laid in bed most of the day. Monthly concert in the evening. Mrs. Whitman did not pray. Perhaps did not like it because she was not urged to.

TUES. 6.   Slept little last night. Mostly in consequence of something husband said to me. Rather indisposed all day.

WED. & THURS. 7 & 8.   Making small affairs. Weather cold & freezing so they can not use the mud mortar, [i.e., to make adobes.]

FRIDAY Nov. 9.   So cold everything freezes. Door latches stick to the fingers only a few feet from the fire. Washed today & wrote to Mrs. Perkins.

SAT. 10.   Filled my bed [with corn husks.] Unpleasant weather.

SUN. 11.   Sacraments. Mr. Smith preached & officiated. Oh! I wish I had a little chamber where I could secrete myself & not see so many folks all the time.

MONDAY 12.   Staid in Mrs. Whitman's room & sewed all day. A little snow last night.

TUESDAY Nov. 13.   At work about house most of the day. Mrs. W. rather indisposed. Mr. Walker's favorite mule, Harry, kicked him.

WED. 14.   Dr. W. sick with toothache. His wife nurses him all day. Mr. Eells' mule threw him & lames him. Maria [Maki] is sick. Her husband, I found, sitting by her bed weeping. . .   The hills all around covered with snow.

FRIDAY 16.   Worked about house all day. Got very tired. Mrs. W. appears to feel cross at every body. Was so tired I thought I would not work so again. In the evening tried to sew a little. . .   Talked with Mrs. Whitman. She seems in a worry about [something.] Went out & blustered round & succeeded in melting over her tallow.

SAT. 17. Notwithstanding my resolution not to work so hard, I commenced in the morning & continued till night without ever stopping to warm my feet, which were rather cold. I should think the other ladies might consider me a little more. If I think I will do like the rest, let all go, there are so many suffering about me that I cannot compose myself to sit & not try to make those around me more comfortable. After breakfast Mrs. W. went to her room & there remained through the day without concerning at all how or what was done. I know not, I am sure, what she wishes or thinks. But I think her a strange housekeeper. It is hard to please when one cannot know what would please.

SUNDAY 18 Nov. Did not rest comfortably being too much fatigued & worried. In the morning tried to converse with my dear husband & get at least a little sympathy. But like Job's comforters, he only refered the cause of my trouble to my own imprudence. I think if he knew all & viewed things in their true light, he would deal more in pity & less in reproach. The other ladies are as much perplexed as myself. I feel very much the need of a comfortable retired room. My husband seems to think I expose myself more than is necessary, but what can I do? There is no place where I can be. Mr. Eells preached.

MONDAY 19 & TUES. 20. Not as well as I have been. Am obliged to let the work about house go. . .

WED. 21 . . . Fear I shall be sick before a room is ready for me. Mr. Walker & E. very much engaged making harness & whips.[23] Mr. W. has not bathed for some weeks. Maria not about yet. The weather not as cold as it has been for some time past. We eat now-a-days plenty of boiled wheat, potatoes, horse meat,[24] & salmon. No bread for a week past.

THURS. Nov. 22. Mrs. Whitman making soap. Somewhat raining.

FRIDAY 23. Mrs. Whitman washing. Cross time of it. Had to work about house more that I meant to because none else offered to do it.

SUNDAY Nov. 25. Rather indisposed yesterday & to day. Mr. Walker preached. . .

MONDAY 26. Quite better. Washed a little, sewed a little. Jack washed the floors. . .

TUESDAY 27. Washed with Mrs. S. A very pleasant day.

WED. Nov. 28. Casting candle wicks. My turn to lead the Maternal Association. . .

THURS. Nov. 29, 1838. Mrs. Whitman dipping candles. I iron sundry

[23] From a notebook in Coll. w. entitled "Mother Eells," p. 29, we read that the men made two sets of harnesses from rawhide and buffalo skins "sewing them with buckskin string, with the aid of an Indian awl."

[24] The Whitmans ate horse meat for five years, after their arrival in Oregon. In a letter to Greene dated October 22, 1841, Whitman reported that he had killed his first beef the preceding summer. Mary, at first hesitant about eating horseflesh, got over her squeamishness after the birth of her baby.

articles, on my feet most of the time. Husband at work on harness. Sits up with me till 12 o'clock much to the annoyance of br. Eells.

FRIDAY 30.   Dr. W. quite out of patience with Mr. Smith. Mrs. W. washing.[25] Think she has less help from the other ladies than she ought.

SAT. DEC. 1.   Rose as soon as I could see to dress by day light, having rested well. Mr. E. very careful to have me understand that he was much disturbed by my late hours. Have worked hard all day. Health good.

SUNDAY DEC. 2.   Mr. Smith preached. Have assisted Margaret [McKay] in doing the house work. Mrs. S. & E. not offering to do a chore. However, I have been able to do all that was necessary & suppose I have read more than either of them besides. Have been reading the Memoirs of Martha Read. Read two hours after returning to my room that poor Mr. E. may have a little chance to sleep. Hope his health will not be impaired by being broke of his rest so much.

MON. 3.   Monthly concert in the evening after which Dr., his wife & Mr. E. & wife, husband & self sit up till midnight talking about Mr. S. & G. Mrs. W. gets to feeling very bad, goes to bed crying.[26]

TUES. DEC. 4.   Mr. S. moves into the new house. Mr. W[alker] puts up a partition.[27] I work about the house some & make a cap. Mrs. W. in a sad mood all day, did not present herself at the breakfast table. Went out doors, down by the river to cry.

WED. DEC. 5.   Moved into my new room. Think to find it very com-

---

[25] Narcissa, in a letter to her mother, December 5, 1836, wrote: "You will scarcely think it possible that I should have such a convenience as a barrel to pound my clothes in for washing so soon; in this part of the world, & probably mine with Mrs. Pambrun are the only two this side of the Rocky Mountains. . . . she never knew the use of one untill I suggested it." Even with such an aid, washing clothes would have been a tedious chore with the necessity of heating water over an open fireplace. In a letter to her parents October 6, 1841, Narcissa commented on the Indians' reaction to the weekly wash: "It is difficult for them to feel but that we are rich and getting richer by the house we dwell in and the clothes we wear and hang out to dry after washing from week to week. . . ."

[26] The initial joy which the Whitmans experienced upon the arrival of the reinforcement had turned sour because of the little irritations and personality clashes which had arisen out of the crowded living conditions in the Whitman home. Mary, in her entry for the next day, mentions the fact that the Smiths had moved into the new house. Their absence made it possible for the three remaining couples to talk with some privacy about their common problems. By this time Narcissa was beginning to show signs of breaking under the nervous strain. She was so emotionally upset over the discussion which followed their evening prayer meeting, that she went to bed weeping. The next day she fled to a secluded spot along the river to weep some more. There was no other place to which she could go.

[27] Evidently Elkanah erected a more substantial partition to take the place of the tapa cloth which had been used to curtain off their bed. We do not have a floor plan of this first Whitman home.

fortable. A kind Providence always seems to provide for me all I need.

THURS. 6. Mr. Walker went to W.W.[28] I was busy all day regulating my room. Lay my bed spread. Had my room washed. After which I went out several times & brought in fuel and built fire to dry it. Put up my curtains in the evening & after nine o'clock made two table clothes. Retired about 12.

FRIDAY DEC. 7. Awoke about five o'clock A.M. As soon as I moved was surprised by a discharge which I supposed indicated approaching confinement. Felt unwilling it should happen in the absence of my husband. I waited a few moments. Soon pains began to come on & I sent Mrs. Smith who lodged with me to call Mrs. Whitman. She came & called her husband. They made what preparations they deemed necessary, left me to attend worship & breakfast. After which or almost nine I became quite sick enough — began to feel discouraged. Felt as if I almost wished I had never been married. But there was no retreating, meet it I must. About eleven I began to be quite discouraged. I had hoped to be delivered ere then. . . But just as I supposed the worst was at hand, my ears were saluted with the cry of my child. A son was the salutation. Soon I forgot my misery in the joy of possessing a proper child. I truely felt to say with Eve, I have gotten a man from the Lord.[29] With Hannah for this child I prayed.[30] Thanks to a kind Providence for so great & unmerited a blessing. The remainder of the day I [was] comfortable. Husband returned in the evening with a thankful heart, I trust, & plenty of kisses for me & my boy. Mrs. Smith stayed with me thru the night, her husband being gone from home. . .

SATURDAY DEC. 8. Quite comfortable. Mrs. W. dresses the babe.

SUNDAY 9. Took medicine. Mr. Eells preached. Mr. Walker remained with me.

MONDAY 10. Up for the first time. Mrs. Smith took my washing.

TUESDAY 11. Nipples very sore. Worry with my babe. Get all tired out.

WEDNESDAY 12. Mrs. Eells takes care of me. Very nervous. Milk so caked in my breasts, have apprehensions of 2 broken breasts. Have it steamed & drawed alternately till it seems better, then cover it with sticking plaster. Husband sleeps but I get very little.

THURS. DEC. 13. Little Cyrus,[31] for so we call our son, having slept

---

[28] No reason is given for Elkanah's trip to Walla Walla just at this time. Although he was able to return the next day, he was not present at the birth of his son.

[29] See Genesis 4:1.

[30] Mary's thorough knowledge of the Bible crops out in many such casual reference in her diary as this. Here she refers to Hannah's joy upon giving birth to Samuel. 1 Samuel: 2.

[31] Contrary to statements sometimes made (including one by the author in his *Whitman,* 210), Cyrus was not the first male child born of white American parents

all day was troubled some all night, so that his father got very little rest. Mrs. Eells is my nurse by day & Mr. Walker by night. Margaret draws my breasts for me else I know not how I should do.

FRIDAY, 14 DEC.   Nipple still very sore. Think I have rather a tedious time of it. Very little strength on account of suffering so much with my breasts. Hope they are beginning to heal a little. Have just brought my journal up to the present time which was a week behind.

SATURDAY DEC. 15.   Rather smarter today than yesterday. Eat some broth, beef[32] & potatoes. Nipples sore as ever. Babe nurse all I have & has to [go] a begging. . .

SUNDAY DEC. 16.   Gaining in health & strength. Breasts some better. Mr. Walker preaches. Stays in my room most of the time. Converses with [me] a good deal. Enjoy his society very much. Think he never seemed kinder. Have commenced reading today for the first time since my confinement.

MONDAY DEC. 17.   Felt quite out of sorts this morning because they did not bring me plenty to eat. Was very faint for want of food. At breakfast took hold of horse meat with a pretty good relish. Through the day have been well supplied. Tonight felt had been ungrateful to murmur. My breast still a cause of much suffering. Sat up & tended my babe about half the day. Took a nap. This evening made a cap for my babe, the first time I have sewed any. Fear I have worked too hard today.

TUESDAY 18.   Very sick all day. Steam pads over my breasts all day. Have taken cold. Experience soreness in all my breasts, relieved by sweating. Take morphine and calomel.[33] Go to bed, sleep some.

WED. 19.   Margaret continues to draw my breasts. . .[34]

on the Pacific Coast. In 1833 Mr. and Mrs. Thomas O. Larkin became the parents of Thomas Jr. at Monterey, California. The father was then the American Counsul at that place. Cyrus has the distinction of having been the first white male child to be born in the Pacific Northwest who lived to maturity. He died at Albany, Oregon, May 5, 1921. See footnote 4, page 126, for reference to the birth and death of Jason Lee White.

32 Possibly some beef from the meat sent by Pambrun to the Whitmans several weeks previous. The meat would have kept for this period if frozen or possibly if dried.

33 Calomel, or mercurous chloride, was somewhat of an universal panacea in those days. As an effective cathartic, it not only emptied the stomach but was supposed to stimulate the liver.

34 Mary began a letter to her parents on March 25, 1839, (the original of which is in Coll. WN.) in which she gave considerable detail regarding her difficulties in nursing her child. She wrote: "My babe weighed at first about nine pounds & when he was twelve weeks old, sixteen. I think him without exception the strongest & most healthy infant I ever saw." She refers to the use of a breast pump and added: "I soon found that a forced projection unlike a natural would not bear to be used. In a few days they [i.e. the breasts] became exceedingly sore & swollen so that it was with great difficulty I nursed." The full text of this letter is in Drury, Walker, pp. 255 ff.

THURS. 20. One breast quite comfortable. The [other] sore as ever.

FRI. 21. Eat and drink all I can & keep nursing my babe in order to make milk. Mrs. Whitman plenty jaw at me.[35] Right breast very painful.

SAT. 22. Slept pretty well last night. Quite comfortable, all except sore npls. Wish much to write a good deal in my journal but suppose it is not prudent at present. Have abundant cause for gratitude notwithstanding I suffer much pain & anguish.

SUNDAY 23. My very kind husband spent the whole day with me. What would I do were it not for my husband?

MON. DEC. 24. Was restless & uncomfortable the first part of the night. This morning quite discouraged. Fear I shall not be able after all to nurse with more than one breast.

TUES. 25.[36] More comfortable, partly because my boy is unable any longer to draw my breast which is nearly dry. The other about as it has been for some time. As painful as I can bear without ado.[37]

WEDNES. DEC. 26. Letters from Mr. Spaldings. More peacable than some former ones. Dr. Whitman half resolves to go to Clear Water partly on little Eliza's account who he is apprehensive has the dropsy in her head.[38]

THURS. 27. Am up & stiring about my room again to day. Hope I

---

[35] In the same letter Mary wrote: "I was very anxious about my babe & extremely reluctant to relinquish the idea of nursing him but I had experienced so much torture that I was at last glad when no alternative was left me. Mrs. Whitman at first assisted me but the babe found it so much easier to draw from her breast than mine that he refused to do it & she thinking at all events to oblige me to nurse him weaned her own child and even refused to let me have a bottle to feed him with cow milk but I made out to find one & so fed him." Mrs. Whitman's child, Alice Clarissa, was born March 14, 1837, and was, therefore, nearly two years old.

[36] Christmas day but the missionaries, true to their Puritan tradition, made no note of it.

[37] Again in her letter to her parents, we read: "I was quite unable to hold him [i.e. the child] to the breast myself but my husband had to hold me & the babe too. The pain I experienced was so intense that my hands would be clinched & a paroxism produced much like a fit. I think I can say with truth that I never knew what pain was untill then. But for this trouble I think I would have been about the house in a week or so but this confined me to the bed, my clothes wet with sweat. I would get up a little & then take cold & be down again. My room was very open & I had to have my bosom so much exposed that I could not avoid taking cold & to prevent a broaken breast would be obliged to have recourse to steaming. But at the end of six weeks the troublesome things partly rotted off & the rest drew back & all my suffering amounted to nothing but a fruitless attempt."

[38] Spalding's diary gives no indication of any such trouble. During the winter of 1838-39 hundreds of Indians were helping Spalding dig a mill race. He paid them in part with potatoes. In the evenings he conducted religious services. It was at this time that Timothy and Old Joseph were converted. Whitman arrived at Lapwai on January 4 and remained until the 10th and took part in the revival meeting.

shall not take cold again. My left breast still quite sore, feel much concern least I lose also that.

FRIDAY DEC. 28. Looked for the first time since my confinement beyond the confines of my little apartment. Husband & Dr. W. are gone to the mountains. . .

SAT. DEC. 29. Try very hard to invent artificial nipples. Do not succeed. Feel very much unreconciled to the idea of being unable to nurse my babe.

SUN. DEC. 30. Took supper with the family. Find my health in a good measure restored. Babe in good health, no appearance of sore mouth. Nurse him mostly with a bottle. Feel more reconciled than I did yesterday. Tho the dispensations of Providence often appear dark, yet they are in the [end] for the best. How do I know but the want of means to nurse my babe may be the greatest of blessings? . . .

MONDAY, DEC. 31. Have obtained a maires tit [teat]. Hope to succeed in using it. If so I shall rejoice.[39]

I have now reached the close of another year. It has been a year of mercies. A year ago to night I sat with my sisters by the fireside of my father & watched to see the old year [go out.] Now I find myself on the other side of the continent. A wife & mother. Surely this is a changing world. With no one has God delt in more mercy than to me. O! may I be quickened to a sense of my duty to God & men, to myself, my husband, & my child. Affection drops a tear at thought of the friends & home I have left, but it is not a tear of regret. I rejoice to find myself where I am with a prospect of entering long on the labours I have so long sought. Farewell departing year. I number thee among my happiest. Thanks to God for all his goodness.

1839 — MOVE TO THE SPOKANE COUNTRY

The atmosphere became so strained at Waiilatpu during the winter of 1838-39 that Mrs. Whitman eagerly grasped the opportunity to accompany her husband on a camping trip, just to get away. They left on January 22 and did not return until February 9. Ten days later the Whitmans left for Lapwai and Mrs. Whitman did not return to her home until after the Walkers and the Eells had left for Tshimakain. If it should be thought strange that missionaries, who have given their lives to the high calling of preaching the Christian gospel, should disagree, we should remember the abnormal conditions under which these people were living. The very fact that they were willing to go

---

[39] Evidently Mary did not have an artificial nipple made out of rubber such as are so common today. From this entry it appears that a mare suckling a colt was killed and a teat skinned with the hope that such could be used. There is no evidence to show that such an experiment was successful.

out to the wilderness of Oregon as missionaries to the uncivilized Indians shows that they had strong opinions. Otherwise they would not have volunteered. Personality differences are common on the foreign mission field of this generation, when people are forced to associate with others whom under other circumstances they would never select for their close friends — in some restricted compound surrounded by people of another language and culture. The unhappiness which developed at Waiilatpu during the winter of 1838-39 was unfortunate but understandable.

The year 1839 was a momentous year for Elkanah and Mary. Now for the first time they could begin their evangelistic labors for the "benighted heathen," for whom they had sacrificed so much and had traveled so far. Cornelius (Chief Big Head) with four men and four women from his band arrived at Waiilatpu on February 26 with thirty-five horses to escort the missionary families to the Spokane country. On March 5, which was the first wedding anniversary of both the Walkers and the Eells, the caravan got under way. A fresh milch cow was driven along in order to provide milk for the three-months old baby. A number of factors and events slowed their progress. There was first the necessity of stopping frequently to build a fire, warm milk, and feed the child. A snow storm forced them to remain in camp one day. Another day was spent in camp when Elkanah was so injured by a kick from a horse that he could not ride. Of course they did not travel on Sunday. It took them over two weeks to make the journey of one hundred forty-to-fifty miles.

TUE. JAN. 1, 1839 . . . Dr. W. left for Clear W.

WED. & THURS. 2 & 3. Rather indisposed. Mrs. Compo nurses my babe.[1]

FRIDAY 4. Husband went to Walla W yesterday, returned tonight. Had a stormy unpleasant ride. Have very little hopes of being able to nurse much. Some times am tempted to murmur. But then when I reflect how many other blessings I enjoy & especially what a "worthy portion" I possess in my Elkanah,[2] I feel that I do not do well to complain of any affliction consequent on my union with him. My mind often turns with strong emotion to the home of my childhood & youth. But I would not return. I some times feel discouraged & fear I shall never do anything to benefit the heathen & might as well have stayed

---

[1] From Mary's letter of March 25, 1839: "But fortunately an Indian woman the wife of the hired man had a babe three weeks younger than mine & milk enough for her child & half enough for mine so with her aid I got along nicely." The Indian woman continued to nurse the child until March 5 when the Walkers left for Tshimakain.

[2] One of the rare times that Mary refers to her husband by his first name.

at home. Self must be taken care of & that requires more than all my time & strength.[3] Is it always to be so?

SUN. JAN. 6.   Mr. Walker preached. I am still afflicted with care. How long is [it] to be so? Am glad my babe can be supplied with milk tho it comes from a black breast.

MON. 7.   The day observed in part as a day of fasting & prayer.[4] Not the most pleasant feelings existing in the family. Think we should so fast in this manner to cause our voice to be heard on high. Mr. Pambrun here on a visit. Mr. Walker not very sociable because he was not as cordially received at W.W. as he anticipated.

TUES. 8.   Mr. Walker went to the mountains. Soon after he left I was taken sick again. Much pain in my limbs & breasts. Babe can no longer draw the left or best breast.

WED. 9 . . . through the day sick, again in the evening had Margaret draw my breast.

THURS. 10.   In much pain through the former part of the night but about midnight got more easy & rested pretty well. Mr. Walker was very tired & sleepy but took care of the babe. This morning feel better.

FRI. 11.   Mrs. Whitman said nothing about Female prayer meeting. Keeps aloof from my room. Looks rather volumes.

SAT. 12.   Mr. W. hunts horses.[5] Finds his mules. Mrs. E. spends most of her time with me now, helps me sew & take care of babe. Am very weak myself.

SUN. 13 JAN.   Mr. W. preaches. Mr. Smith unwell. Came from W.W. yesterday. Went with Lawyer. . .[6]

MON. JAN. 14.   Able to go to the kitchen to eat again & work considerable.

---

[3] Here Mary touches on a problem that gave her increasing concern with the passing of the years. Since the American Board supplied funds for only the barest necessities, so much of the time and the strength of the missionaries had to be expended on self-support that little was left for missionary work for the natives.

[4] By this time the custom of observing the first Monday of the new year as a day of fasting and prayer was well established in the Protestant churches of the United States. Without exception, she made note of this day each year during the time she lived at Tshimakain.

[5] Because of the lack of fences, the animals were allowed to roam for forage. As will be noted, both Walker and Eells were obliged to spend an inordinate amount of time looking for their animals after they settled at Tshimakain. Gradually they were able to erect rail fences to enclose limited areas.

[6] The first discovered use of this name of the famous Nez Perce Indian who later, 1848-71, was the Head Chief of his tribe. See further identification in Appendix II. Also see article by Drury, "I, The Lawyer" in New York Westerners, May 1960. Smith in a letter to Greene on August 27, 1839, wrote: "He exhibits more mind than I have witnessed in any other Indian. He is the one who has been much in the mountains with the American Fur Co., & on account of his knowledge of different languages & his talent at public speaking he was called by them Lawyer, by which name he is now generally known."

Tue. Jan. 15. Dr. Whitman returned from Clear Water. Mr. & Mrs. Eells took tea with Mrs. Smith. In the evening discussion concerning women speaking.

Thur. 17. Wrote a note to Mrs. Spalding & Gray.

Fri. 18. Went out of doors for the first time for six weeks.

Sat. 19. Babe very worrisome. Mrs. Eells has made my cape, but it has been as much as I could do to take care of my boy. Dr. W. and Mr. Smith in trouble. We do not agree about celebrating the Lords Supper without wine.[7] Mrs. W. busy preparing to go to the Tukanan.[8]

Sun. 20. Mr. Eells preached extempore. Mr. W. took care of the babe. Dr. W. very sad.

Mon. 21. Mrs. W. washed in the morning. Query. Did she ever do such a thing before.

Tue. 22. Dr. & his wife left. Mr. & Mrs. Eells, Margaret & myself accompanied them about three miles, it being the first time I have rode out or been on horse back since I arrived at Wieletpoo. Mrs. W. has dealt so largely in powder & balls of late that perhaps her absence will not detract much from our happiness.

Thurs. 24. Washed & ironed my Pongee dress as a commencement to washing again. Rogers & Coner arrived from Mr. Spaldings.

Fri. 25. A fine day. Mr. W., S. & wife, Mr. Rogers & myself rode out, had a fine ride. This is a beautiful country. Still a kind of gloom seems to prevade it as if nature were asleep or rather the face of the ground. The whole country might be supposed to be enjoying a long sabbath.[9]

---

[7] Two minor matters divided the small mission band at Waiilatpu. The men of the reinforcement of 1838 objected to women taking part in prayer meetings, even within the mission family, and preferred the use of wine instead of grape juice for the communion. Of this Narcissa wrote on May 17, 1839, in a letter to her sister Jane: "We need help very much, and those who will pray, too. In this we have been disappointed in our helpers last come, particularly the two Revs. who have gone to the Flatheads. They think it not good to have too many meetings, too many prayers, and that it is wrong and unseemly for a woman to pray where there are men, and plead the necessity for wine, tobacco, etc.; and now how do you think I have living with such folks right in my kitchen for the whole winter? If you can imagine my feelings you will do more than I can to describe." Elkanah is the only one of the mission group who used tobacco. He chewed it. See also footnote 10, page 128.

[8] The tensions arising out of the crowded conditions in her home were becoming greater than Mrs. Whitman could stand. So when her husband proposed that she and their little girl accompany him on a camping trip to the Tucannon where he could spend some time in language study with a band of Nez Perces, Narcissa quickly agreed. They left on January 22 and returned on February 9. See Drury, *Whitman*, 211 ff. The departure of the Whitmans greatly relieved the strain at Waiilatpu. Notice Mary's entry for the 25th when she broke forth in poetry.

[9] Mary plays with the idea that once a race of men had inhabited that land who had incurred the wrath of God and then had vanished. With prophetic insight she looked forward to the day, closer than she then could conceive, when that same valley would be dotted with the farms and towns of the white man.

A feeling of sadness with beauty is mixed
As the eye ore the country is cast
Say why is the soil of its timber bereft
And still no inhabitant there?
Say once as in Pallestine dwelt a race
Of men who obeyed not their God
And when in his wrath have vanished away
That the land may in quiet
Its sabbaths enjoy
And be washed by the rain of heaven?

Will these hills & these vallies for ever remain
As if in a quiet repose?
Shall such beauty & grandeur
Be witnessed for aye by the eye of the savage alone?

Not long can it be so.
This silence   .   .   .   (?) now around
Is beginning to break
And the sod that for ages has laid unturned
Is broke by the Red mans spade

Not long ere hamlets & towns shall be seen
Up springing on either hand
And the song of the husband-man
Cheerfully chime with the glee of the school boys at play
Not long ere the church bell
So distance a far
Its sound shall extend ore the land.

TUES. JAN. 29. I dipped 24 doz. candles. Mr. Ermatinger arrived. . .

WED. 30. Mr. E left for W.W. having sold Mr. Walker his watch. My own babe's health good. Washed my floor.

FRI. FEB. 1 . . . Babe quiet. Grows fast, is very healthy. Mrs. Compo nurses him about three times a day. . .

SUN. FEB. 3. Everything seems to move on pleasantly. How easy it would be to have every thing to one mind if people only knew how. I have been thinking to day that if I did not know I should sooner suppose myself in the house of a Southern plantation than a Christian missionary. I witness much that seems wrong to me. Mr. Smith preached. A cold day.

SAT. FEB. 9. Dr. and Mrs. W. returned. Adieu to peace & order. Mrs. W. on first reaching us seemed in good humor & I hoped she had made her a better heart. But at supper table & even before she began to show out.

SUN. 10. Nobody knows what to depend upon now, everything goes just as it has formerly. I am half-resolved to call for an explanation. Last night we recd. a large package of letters. One from Mr. Perkins giving an account of the Revival at Willamette. It seems as if while it was yet seed time they had to begin to reap. . .

MON. FEB. 11. Nearly completed my wash before breakfast. Husband & Mr. Smith left for Mr. Spalding.[10]

TUE. 12. Mrs. W. who had kept her room since Saturday appearing in the greatest agitation requested prayers & asked forgiveness. Her appearance did not satisfy us of her penitence.[11]

SAT. 16. Have felt very badly for some days as Mrs. W. did not

[10] Walker and Smith went to Lapwai to assist Spalding in getting some mill-stones. Upon their arrival on February 13, they talked with Spalding, Gray, and Rogers, and found so many problems demanding consideration that all felt a special meeting of the Mission should be called. Word was sent to Whitman and Eells to go to Lapwai. The meeting opened on February 22 and continued until the 26th. Smith was adamant in his insistence to open a new station. He no longer wanted to live at Waiilatpu. Walker and Eells, contemplating the opening of their new station about 175 miles north of Lapwai, felt that the Mission doctor should be more centrally located and therefore were in favor of the Whitmans moving to Lapwai. Gray also wanted a station of his own. Some important decisions were made at this meeting which were later reversed. See Drury, *Diaries of Spalding and Smith*, pp. 94 ff.

[11] Two letters from Mary to Elkanah, dated February 12 and 17, and one from Elkanah to Mary, February 14, are in Coll. WN. Here in the intimacy of the personal correspondence between wife and husband, further light is thrown upon the personality clashes and petty differences which existed in the Whitman home. On the 12th Mary wrote: "Mrs. W. presented her self at table this morning which if I am not silly to mention it is spread without a cloth. I was so provoked at this fresh mark of disrespect, as I deem it, that I was half tempted not to eat. It was true she had no brown cloth ironed but she has plenty white ones. If she does not begin to put away her bad heart soon I am resolved to call her to account & if I have wronged her know what my offence is." In this letter Mary refers to Timothy, one of Spalding's first converts. She wrote: "I was much affected this morning to hear Timothy pray. He burst into tears & almost wept aloud. I have never witnessed any thing of the kind before in an Indian."

In Mary's letter of February 17 she tells of how, at the close of the evening prayer meeting, Mrs. Whitman in great agitation "confessed to those present that she had abused them & intreated their forgiveness." Mary was not present at the time so Narcissa went to Mary's room. Mary wrote: "I desired her to be seated & expressed a wish to converse with her. I did not hesitate to admit the accusations she brought against herself to be true. . . How the conversation proceeded I hardly recollect, but she desired us to tell her if we had ought against her, & I for one was not reluctant to do it. I told her plainly that her treatment of us had been such as to render our residence in the family very unpleasant. . . I told her that her treatment of me in accusing me of not loving my babe, not nursing it when I might if my heart had only been big enough or I had had a mind to, & in refusing to let Margaret draw my breasts, & trying to force me to do what was impossible for me to do . . . was cruel & without reason . . . she was disposed to justify her conduct in every particular. She said we did not know her heart. That we thought her out of humor when it was anxiety for the salvation of sinners caused her to appear as she did. . . This rather stumbled us & we almost felt that she designed to make a cloak of Religion. Can it be, we thought,

come out to eat with us. Had half concluded not to eat my breakfast at her table this morning unless she was present. But much to my relief on going out I found her at the table. She has pretended to be sick the week past but she now wishes to accompany her husband to Clear Water. To night she appears a little more pleasant, prayed at evening worship. I find it exceedingly unpleasant to have the woman of the house conduct as Mrs. W. does. She says we do not know her heart. I fear she does not know it herself. I would like to know how so much unpleasant temper can consort with such high pretentions to piety. If she is a good woman, I hope grace will so abound in her as to render her a little more pleasant.

Had a letter from Mr. Walker tonight. My health is very good, my babe quiet but disturbs me considerably by night so that I seldom have more than six hours sleep, as I cannot prevail with myself to abandon my old habit of sitting up late.

There are now a great number of Indian lodges at Wielatpoo. I like Mr. & Mrs. Eells better than I used to do, think we shall live quite happily. I begin to feel anxious to be at Spokan. When I get there I think I shall not be a slothful servant.

Sun. Feb. 17.   No preaching in English, the services in Indian. Considerable excitement among the Indians. They are very anxious to devise some way to get to heaven without repenting & renouncing their sins. Mrs. Whitman has appeared to be much in prayer to day. I fear we are too severe in judging her & that we are not after all as pious as she. Perhaps our beseting sins are as heinous in the sight of God as hers. She appeared rather pleasant this evening.

Mond. Feb. 18.   Wrote to husband & Mrs. Gray. Wrote with so much freedom to her I fear I shall be sorry.[12] Baked plenty of gingerbread for Mrs. W. Got supper.

Tuesday Feb. 19.   Wrote to Mrs. Spalding. Mrs. W. with her family

---

that anxiety for sinners can cause one to appear so petulant, morose & crabbed? We almost felt worse than before."

According to Mary, Mrs. Whitman retired to her room that Tuesday evening and did not join the family group again until Saturday morning. "She was said to be sick," wrote Mary, "& I have no question she was. However, letters arrived from Mr. Spalding's. We heard no more of her sickness. She determined at once to accompany her husband. There were many reasons that would justify such a step. Her difficulty with Mrs. Gray was of itself a sufficient reason." See Drury, *Diaries of Spalding and Smith,* p. 255, for a discussion of this particular difficulty. Mrs. Gray was pregnant at the time of her arrival at Waiilatpu in September, 1839, and accused Mrs. Whitman of making known what was supposed to have been kept a secret — at least for a time.

[12] Mary's letter to Mrs. Gray is not known to be extant. However, Mrs. Gray's reply of February 23 is in Coll. c. In this letter Mrs. Gray told how Mrs. Whitman by persistent questioning had learned of Mrs. Gray's pregnancy soon after the arrival of the reinforcement of 1838. Mrs. Gray felt that Mrs. Whitman had then told others. See Drury, *Diaries of Spalding and Smith,* 255, where Spalding claimed that Gray himself had done the talking. "A very little matter indeed," wrote Spalding, "to cause such a difficulty."

left for Mr. Spalding's. She seemed in pretty good humor for her.

WED. 20. Mrs. McCay [McKay] made us a call. Was sorry Margaret was gone. . . Wrote a hasty letter to Mrs. Perkins.

THURS. & FRI. 21 & 22. Mrs. Eells making hoods. Indians come in & tend my babe. Carried him to an Indian lodge for the first time.

SUN. FEB. 24. Last night up with my babe but once. At the usual hour the bell rang for Indian worship. Mrs. S. & myself attended. The room was full. At first there was some hesitancy about who should lead. Telockak [Tiloukaikt?] put it upon Hull Hull [Lawyer?] who officiated & he himself made an address. At the close H.H. pronounced the benediction with due solemnity.[13] The Indians today have been more noisy & mischievous than I ever knew them. They say the Dr. says they will go to hell any way & they are not going to restrain their children to try to be good any more. I am sorry to find them so ill disposed.

MONDAY 25. So much pleasant weather, it seems wasteful.

TUES. FEB. 26, 1839. The valley is full of horses & people coming & going. There is almost the stir of a city. Cornelius has arrived to conduct us to his country. Soon adieu to Wielatpoo. My health as good I think as when I was married.

WED. FEB. 27 . . . Visited Indian lodges. Cornelius' daughter called to see us. Frogs are singing.

THURS. FEB. 28. Husband returned from C[lear] W[ater], have had a bad time enough at their meeting.

FRI. MARCH 1. Mr. Walker & myself went to W.W. Sat. returned, had a pleasant visit & rather a cold ride.

SUN. 3. Mr. W. preached. Mr. Smith administered the Sacrament. Had rather a pleasant time.

MON. 4. Busy packing up. This evening it snows. Hope we shall be able to leave here tomorrow.

After living at the Whitman home at Waiilatpu for a little more than six months, the Walkers and the Eells left for their new mission station at Tshimakain on March 5th. They camped the first night on Mill Creek, a branch of Walla Walla River near what is now the campus of Whitman College in Walla Walla. The next day they moved north to the Touchet River near what is now Prescott. On the 7th they reached the Tucannon River at what is now Starbuck. The next day they rode about five miles to what came to be called Lyons Ferry on the Snake River just below the mouth of the Palouse River which enters from the north. On Saturday, March 9th, the party crossed the Snake River. The people and the baggage were conveyed across in

---

[13] All of the men of the Mission were at Lapwai. However, according to their custom, the natives gathered for Sunday worship. Tiloukaikt was the chief who took the leading part in the Whitman massacre of November 29, 1847.

canoes with the assistance of some local Indians. The animals swam. The trail led up the west side of the Palouse to Cow Creek and then along that stream to its source in Sprague Lake. Eells in his Reminiscences dated June 12, 1882, wrote: "On March 14, 1839 . . . [we] camped at a spring a short distance west of Sprague." From there the trail led in a northly direction past the west side of Medical Lake to a ford on the Spokane River at the mouth of Tshimakain Creek. They crossed the Spokane on Tuesday, March 19th, and the next day arrived at Tshimakain.

TUE. MARCH 5. About sunrise Dr. W. reached home [14] & about noon we left W. Dr. W. accompanied us to our first encampment about 5 miles. We talked with him all that time would allow & he left us feeling much better than when he came home.

It commenced raining just as we encamped but we had time to pitch our tent before it rained fast. It continued to rain all night. We were so well housed that the rain did not hurt us much. Little Cyrus very quiet.

WED. 6. Travelled 15 miles. The rain ceased so that we could move camp or prepare to at nine. Had some trouble to get the calf along.[15] We stopped, struck fire & warmed milk twice.[16] The weather very moderate & pleasant. Surely a kind Providence seems to smile on us. Do not find myself so fatigued as I used to do last summer.

THURS. 7. A pleasant day. Travelled 20 mls. perhaps. Came to a pleasant encampment. Constructed a small lodge at the mouth of the tent in which we build our fire. All goes pleasantly.

FRI. MARCH 8. Thought in the morning we should have rain. But it only threatened. Reach the Palluce. Had word that Dr. W. & Mr. Spalding would meet us in the morning.

SAT. 9. Dr W. & wife & Mr. Spalding with [his wife and] the babies came to meet us at our crossing place, had not a remarkably pleasant

---

[14] Knowing that the Walkers and the Eells were planning to leave on the 5th, Whitman hastened back after making arrangements for the Spaldings, his wife, and Alice Clarissa to follow. After accompanying the Walkers and the Eells to their first encampment, Whitman pushed on and joined the party coming from Lapwai. It was arranged for all to meet at the Snake River crossing.

[15] Walker had gotten a cow and calf from Spalding. It is possible that Walker and Eells also had some other cattle from either Lapwai or Waiilatpu. We know that they had several head after reaching Tshimakain although they may have gotten some of these at Fort Colville.

[16] In the closing sections of Eells' unpublished Reminiscences (Coll. w.), he has a diary of the days spent on the trail. He refers to the fact that the cow was milked each morning, and added: "When the little one indicated the calls of hunger, I would ride forward, kindle a fire, warm the milk and have it in readiness as the train arrived. In those days we did not enjoy the luxury of matches now used abundantly. Flint steel, homemade sulphur match, and pitch pine were used."

interview with them.[17] Parted without a social prayer. Had a pleasant time crossing the river. Made a short camp over imposing mountains of basalt & encamped between them on the Palloose.[18]

SUN. 10. Quite rainy last night, but we were very comfortably sheltered to day. Pleasant but windy.

MON. 11. 20 miles, pleasant riding.

TUES. 12. 20 miles, a cold stormy day. Not very comfortable taking care of babe. Had to stop but once, get along quite well.[19]

WEDNES. 13. A snow storm, had to lay by. Made out to keep pretty comfortable tho we were rather crowded. Had to step one over the other. The geese were very plenty & annoyed us by their squaking but we got none to eat. The Indian women dug camas.[20]

---

[17] This was the last time that Mary and Myra were to see Narcissa for over a year. Narcissa accompanied her husband to Tshimakain three times — May 1840; July 1841; and May 1847. Mary made three trips to Waiilatpu before the massacre — May 1842; April 1844; and May 1845. With the passing of time, the strained relationships between the two women passed. Mary's diary shows that a number of letters passed between them.

[18] Eells in his Reminiscences wrote: "The crossing of the Snake river was always anticipated with dread. At the time indicated, it was accomplished with satisfaction. From the river we passed up on the west side of the Palouse to an island distant from the [Snake] river some eight miles. . . The next day we continued to pass up the west side of the Palouse about four miles to the Little Falls. The scenery was grand, almost frightful. . . In places the bluff was a hundred or hundreds of feet above us and nearly perpendicular. . . At the distance of twelve miles from its junction with Snake river, there is a beautiful fall of some 11 or 12 feet. At that point the trail and creek part. Mostly over high rolling prairie the trail passes."

[19] In Mary's letter to her parents on March 25, she wrote: "Tuesday, March 20, a cold stormy day. Rode 20 mls. On unwraping my poor babe found his feet so cold that they were swollen like a puff. We pitched tent & secured ourselfes as we were able against the weather. During the night or next day several inches of snow fell so that we could not move camp." In this letter she stated that sixteen animals were needed to carry their baggage. Allowing 250 pounds per animal, this means that the two families had about two tons of baggage.

[20] The camas had an edible root, resembling an onion, which was a main item of food for the natives of that area. The new crop of camas came into season in May. Father De Smet in his Oregon Missions and Travels, pp. 117-18, wrote regarding the camas: "It is abundant, and, I may say, the queen root of this clime. It is a small, white, vapid onion, when removed from the earth, but black and sweet when prepared for food. The women arm themselves with long, crooked sticks, to go in search of the camash. After having procured a certain quantity of these roots, by dint of long and painful labor, they make an excavation in the earth from twelve to fifteen inches deep, and of proportional diameter, to contain the roots. They cover the bottom with closely-cemented pavement, which they made red hot by means of a fire. After having carefully withdrawn all the coals, they cover the stones with grass or wet hay; then place a layer of camash, another of wet hay, a third of bark overlaid with mould, whereon is kept a glowing fire for fifty, sixty, and sometimes seventy hours. . . It is excellent, especially when boiled with meat; if kept dry, it can be preserved a long time." The baked root turned black in the baking. After being pounded, the camas could be baked into

THURS. 14.   Very cold this morning, dreaded to start. Travelled 15 mls & encamped in a quiet place. Crossed some ponds. Came in sight of pine timber. Picked and cooked a duck larger than a goose.

FRI. 15.   Our breakfast was ready, the morning fair & we were all in fine spirits except little C. who had a sore mouth. The horses were driven in & husband went out to catch them. Soon Mr. E. came leading Mr. W. who was faint. Mrs. E's horse had kicked him. The horses were loosed & we were to lay by. Never did I realize how frail we are. I felt so glad my husband was not killed that I hardly felt that a wound was anything.

SAT. 16.   Mr. W. able to travel. Went ahead at a fine rate. Encamped in the pine timber where Cornelius' wife was baking bread, strange bread. They brought us some tongues & camas. Babe very worisome, mouth quite sore.

SUN. 17.   Last night babe rested well, slept six or seven hours. Is a little better I hope, tho he demands my whole attention.

MON. 18.   Made a short camp. Babe slept through the whole.

TUES. 19.   Reached Spokan river about noon, crossed & encamped on the bank. The water beautiful, the soil sandy covered with stones, granite.

The next day the party reached the mission site which the men had selected the previous fall and where a beginning had been made on the two log cabins, fourteen feet square, and twenty feet apart. Without roofs or floors, they were nothing more than "log pens." Myra Eells described the location as being "a pleasant one, at the foot of a small wooded hill, near a good spring of water, with the open prairie in front." The valley of Tshimakain Creek is several miles wide at this place. A farm house now occupies the original mission site and the water from the spring has been piped into the home.

Since the missionaries were running short of food, one of the natives, whom they named Solomon, was sent to Fort Colville seventy miles to the north to get a fresh supply. Solomon returned on the twenty-sixth with a cordial invitation from Archibald McDonald, chief trader at the fort, for the women to stay at the fort while the men were completing the building of the cabins. Walker escorted the women to Colville, while Eells remained at the site. The women did not return to Tshimakain until May 4.

WED. 20.   Reached the log cabins. Think the location pleasant. Mr. Eells occupies the tent. Mr. Walker his house, find it quite comfortable.

THURS. 21.   Have stowed away our baggage so that we have quite

loaves like bread. No doubt this is what Mary noticed as mentioned in her diary for the 16th.

a clear spot in the middle. The Indians have covered our house with grass & boughs & chinked it so that we are very comfortable. Little C. is getting better. Weather quite warm.

FRI. MARCH 22. We washed, find the water hard. Worked rather hard & took some cold.

SAT. 23. Not as well as common. Husband building a baggage house & writing.

SUN. 24. Not well. Babe worisome. Mouth not quite well. Mr. W. took the raising of Lazarus for his subject.[21] This P.M. went to Indian worship. 26 persons present, appeared very attentive.

TUES. MARCH 26. Solomon returned from C[olville] with abundant supplies & an invitation from Mr. McDonald to make a visit. We baked the last flour we had in the house for dinner & cooked the last meat. I felt very little courage to think of journeying again so soon. But set about getting ready.

WED. 27. We left home about noon,[22] made a short camp.

THURS. 28. Camped at the Fool's place.[23] Find the road to C. very good & the scenery magnificent. Think it surpasses anything I have yet seen. We have a view of mountains without climbing.

FRI. MARCH 29. Sent back the cow.[24] Made very fast all day, stopped two or three hours. Think we have travelled more than 35 miles. Reach C. about sunset.[25] Mrs. Eells very tired. Not very tired myself nor my babe.

---

[21] Evidently a reference to a worship service held for the two couples as Mary writes of an Indian worship service in the afternoon. There is evidence to show that the natives were holding some form of a religious service long before the missionaries arrived.

[22] Mary's first reference to Tshimakain as "home." In her letter to her parents which was begun on March 25, she wrote: "After the lapse of more than a year, I now find myself at what I contentedly call *home*. It is some 60, or 80 miles, from our nearest neighbor. I have been here but a few days & the only description I can give of the place is that our cabin which is sixteen feet squair, without door, window, chimney, or roof, except a few boughs & grass, stands at the western end of a plain on the verge of a pine wood. The plain is 6 or 8 mls. long, elipticle or somewhat crescent form."

[23] The names given to the natives by the white men, perhaps sometimes by the missionaries themselves, reveal a certain sense of humor. Among the names mentioned by Mary in her diary, some of which are listed in Appendix II, are the following: Mufflehead, Old Queen, Simpleton, Old Jezebal, and Wild Boy. Of course the natives most probably had no idea of the real significance of the names given to them.

[24] In Mary's letter to her parents, we read: "We made the journey in three days. Two days we made short camps taking along a cow on which our little son is unfortunately dependent for sustenance. The third day . . . we sent back the cow taking a supply of milk for the day."

[25] Mary described Fort Colville as follows: "The site . . . is pleasing & romantic. It is on a fertile plain on the Columbia encircled by mountains." Elkanah in his letter to Mary of September 1838 (Coll. WN.) wrote: "It was truly pleasing after being nearly half a year without seeing anything that will bear to be com-

SAT. 30. Not very pleasant. Glad we are here . . . writing home.

SUN. 31. No worship except by ourselves. Like Mr. McD's family.[26] But dislike the wine on the table.

MON. APR. 1. My birthday. 28 years old. Finish writing to my Father's family. . .[27]

TUES. 2. Wash & iron. Find that I have so many conveniences here that I fear I shall not like to go away & leave them.

WED. 3. Mr. W. returned. . . Make out bill for Vancouver.[28]

THURS. APR. 4. Mr. Black . . . left. Little C. I think is not thriving so fast as he has been formerly.

FRI. 5. Very pleasant weather. All goes well. Mr. M. pursuing my geology.[29] Mrs. Eells wants to see her husband so.

SUN. 7. A very quiet Sunday. The men at least in some of the houses teach their children to read.

MOND. 8 TUES. 9. Washed & ironed &c.

WED. 10. Had our maternal meeting. Mrs. M. & her children attended, quite an interesting meeting. Mr. M. making his garden. Very windy, has to watch hard against fire.

---

pared with good farming, to see fenced fields, houses and barns grouped together, with large and numerous stacks and grain, with cattle and swine feeding on the plain in large numbers. . . Mr. M[cDonald] estimates his wheat this year at 1500 bushels and his potatoes at 7000. Corn is in small quantity. . ." McDonald built the first sawmill on the Pacific Coast north of California at Colville. The Fort stood in the middle of a prairie, about one and a half miles wide and about three miles long. It was an island of fertility surrounded by rocks. The site is now covered with water backed up by the Coulee Dam.

[26] McDonald was first married to Princess Sunday (or Princess Raven), a daughter of Chief Concomly who lived near Fort George (Astoria). They were the parents of Ranald (who spelt his last name MacDonald), who deliberately became a castaway on the shores of the northern island of Japan in June 1848. See Lewis and Murakami, *Ranald MacDonald,* and Drury's article "Early American Contacts with the Japanese" in *Pacific Northwest Quarterly,* Oct. 1945. His first wife died. In 1825 McDonald married Jane Klyne (1810-1879) to which union thirteen children were born. Mary, in her letter to her parents, wrote: "Mr. McDonald is a Scotch Presbyterian, very kind & hospitable, has a pleasant wife who is nearly white & speaks good English. Their children appear as well I think as any I ever saw in N.E. Their mother attends to their instruction having been herself educated by her husband." See Mary's entry for April 10. Mrs. McDonald joined the Columbia Maternal Association and seven of her children were listed in its record book.

[27] See footnote 34 of previous section.

[28] The original bill of Walker and Eells for supplies purchased from the Hudson's Bay Company is in the archives of the American Board. They ordered a great variety of items needed in their homes and for trade with the natives. Included are such items as blankets, scalping knives, ink powder, handkerchieves, nails, brass kettles, tools, hoes, cotton cloth, fish hooks, and some food supplies as flour, spices, raisins, etc. The cost was about double that in London.

[29] Mary's deep interest in science is evidenced in the fact that she carried a book on geology on her long journey across the continent.

THURS. 11. Mr. & Mrs. McD., Mrs. Eells & myself went to the Indian village, a mile distant. They have a lodge for worship.[30] In the middle is an isle which is swept clean. On either side the ground is covered with grass, at the far end is a piece of cloth — spread for a pulpit. The little chief leads the service. He is now sick but getting better. . . The disease appears like chicken pox or measles. Had a pack of letters from our husbands & friends. . .[31]

SAT. 13. Wrote to Mrs. Spalding, Gray, Smith & Whitman.

SUN. 14 & MONDAY 15. Wrote to Husband. . .[32] Plenty of rain yesterday & to day.

WED. 17. Had a letter from husband,[33] very good & affectionate.

[30] In Eells' letter to the Board on Feb. 25, 1840, he described an Indian lodge: "While the weather continued warm, the place for worship was under some pine trees; but as it became cold, a house was prepared entirely by the people, expressly for worship. It resembles somewhat in form, the roof of a house in New England, making the angle at the top much smaller than that of modern houses. The frame is made of poles four or five inches in diameter, and covered with rush mats. Most of the Indian houses are made in the same way." The lodges made for group assembly could be as long as was needed. Even before the missionaries arrived, the natives had secured some idea of Christian worship and were observing some of its forms as keeping Sunday, repeating the Lord's Prayer, and perhaps singing some songs taught to them by the white men. After the missionaries became better acquainted with such observances, they felt that a great deal of paganism was mixed in with a few simple Christian ideas and forms.

[31] Coll. WN. contains two letters from Elkanah to Mary written during April 1839 — the 9th and the 15th — and two from Mary to Elkanah — the 14th and the 17th. In his first letter, Elkanah wrote: "We are in rather hot water here now about the dogs. Eleven have already been killed & more must be soon or the plain will not hold us." DeSmet, *New Indian Sketches*, p. 115, wrote: "The Indian dogs are as bad as their masters are good. Their masters abhor theft, but these dogs make it their business, and subsist entirely by pilfering. The dogs are found to the number of six or seven in each family. . . For the most part they work at night, and become very cunning and expert: hunger sharpens their rapacious instincts." The missionaries were obliged to declare a war of extinction on the dogs and, strange to say, the natives did not seem to object.

[32] Included in Mary's letter is the following: "We find our situation here very pleasant. Still we shall welcome an invitation to return to our husbands & our homes. It is not difficult for a female to abandon a palace for a cottage if by so doing she can enjoy the society of a beloved companion."

[33] Elkanah in his letter of the 15th wrote: "I am tired of keeping an old bachelor's hall. Things do not go to suit me when I come in from work tired almost to death. I want some [one] to get me a good supper & let me take my ease & when I am very tired in the morning, I want some one to get up & get breakfast & let me lay in bed & take my rest. More than all I want my wife where I can have her company & to cheer me up when the blue devils chain me down." He reported that the plain had been cleared of dogs. "We were determined," he wrote, "to have no more worship with the Indians unless they would kill these dogs. . . We told them they might make their own hearts about killing the dogs & we would make our hearts about staying with them. If they had not killed the dogs we were determined to move off."

Answered it this evening. Ironed before breakfast. Am making a dress. . . Still the rain continues.

THURS. 18. Little Cyrus laid all night for the first time without feeding. He begins to sit alone.

FRI. 19. Have spent most of the day in reading Goldsmiths Nat. His. This evening took a lesson in Indian.

SUNDAY APR. 21. Have been reading to day the Memoirs of Mrs. L. Huntington. In reading of parting with her husband I have reallized how I should feel if called to part with [mine.] I fear I could not be reconciled to such & I dread to think of it. O may it please God to spare his life & that of our dear little son. How frail a thing is an infant. I treamble in view of afflications because I know I need chastisement. Why I have hitherto received so many mercies I do not know. One thing I know, it is not because I have deserved. I have been so ungrateful I have reason to fear they will all be taken from me.

I have desired to become a missionary & why? Perhaps only to avoid duties at home. If I felt a sincere interest in the salvation of the heathen, should I not be more engaged in acquiring the language that I might be able to instruct them? But instead of engaging with interest in its acquisition, I am more ready to engage in almost anything else, & as I do not like others to excell so I feel a wicked satisfaction in seeing them as little interested as myself. O Lord may I not be left to cherish such feelings. But from this time forth may my attention be directed to the language & may I be willing to forego other studies when they interfere with this. May I reallize now the awful responsibility that rests upon me. I have great reason to fear that the object of pursuit with me is not to glorify God but to please myself & my husband. I have at time, yea, frequently the most distressing fears that there is no such thing as experimental religion or if there is that I am a stranger to it. Why is it that I feel so much inclined to shun the [prayer] closet? Is it not because I have not pressing need to be there. O me, the mournful truth is I am not willing to humble my heart before God. I have no adequate sense of his goodness & holiness. I do not have the Savior & I fear he [is] indeed a root out of dry ground to me without form or comeliness.

O may I not be left to embrace a delusion and finally perish. . . O may we two be quickened to renewed zeal day by day & may we be a blessing to each other & to the poor heathen among whom we have come to labor. I have never with more satisfaction anticipated meeting my dear husband. O what a comfort & blessing it is to have so dear a companion.

MON. APR. 22. Mrs. E. & myself went to the mill with Mr. McD., had a pleasant ride, but all that amounts to nothing so long as I have made no proficiency in the language.

Tues. 23. I feel vexed. This is the third morning I have omited the sweeping when I first got up just to see if Mrs. E. would not take her turn. Sunday morning when I commenced sweeping she remarked she would have done it but supposed I had already. But the floor was so dirty had she looked at it she could not have thought so. Yesterday morning I went to washing thinking she could not decently avoid sweeping. But some how she managed to get to the tubs & I would not be so impolite as to crowd her away, so while she was washing her clothes I just swept the room. This morning I wished to make haste & iron while babe slept so left an opportunity for her to sweep again. But I left it go till ten o'clock when she took her knitting & walked off after cracking & scattering about nut shells. So I have swept the room with a vengence. I have washed the room every week while we have been here & she not once & I think she shirks more than is decent. Evening, have got plenty words to day.

Wedns. Ap. 24 . . . Little Cyrus gives me very little trouble, is asleep or off with the girl [34] most of his time. I observed him take & hold a thing in his hand for the first time.

Thurs. Apr. 25. Mr. and Mrs. McD. & family, Mrs. E. & myself walked to the shoots [Kettle Falls] Two & a half miles. The river passes through a ledge of rocks where it evidently had to break through. . . The river & rock present one of the grandest spectacles I have ever seen.

Sun. 28 . . . Have little time to read on the Sabbath as I have to tend my babe more myself than on other days. Hope to spend next Sabbath with my husband. O! it will be good to be with my husband again. . .

Tues. April 30. Washed before breakfast & ironed before nine. Husband arrived about eleven.[35]

Wed. May 1. Went to the Shoots with our husbands (Mrs. E. & myself.)

Thurs. 2. Left Colvile for home. Mr. McD. accompanied us some miles. But did not wait for Mr. W. But went ahead with Mr. Eells. Wonder why he did that.

Sat. 4. Reached home about noon, very much fatigued. Commence house keeping.

THE WALKER HOME AT TSHIMAKAIN

The drawing of the mission site at Tshimakain made by the German botanist Charles A. Geyer, in 1844, shows six buildings. (See page 185 of this volume.) These were the Walker and Eells houses, each a story-

[34] In Mary's letter of April 17 to Elkanah, she wrote: "Lazette a half-breed girl takes care of him most of the time when he is awake which is only a small part of the day. I have been learning her to knit & she stays in my room most of the time."
[35] Mary neglected to mention that Eells also came.

*and-a-half high with gabled roofs, two barns, and the two original
cabins with slanting flat roofs. Originally the cabins erected in 1838-39
were only fourteen feet square, but each was extended by the addition
of another room in the fall of 1839. The larger houses were not started
until the spring of 1841. Because of the lack of help, it took about two
years to complete them.*

*When Mary Walker and Myra Eells were ushered into their first
cabins in May, 1839, they found them to be without windows, doors,
or floors. Heavy cotton cloth or finely dressed deer skins filled the
window spaces. Mary does not refer to window glass until January,
1845. The whipsawing of logs into boards was a slow and laborious
process. The first lumber thus secured was used to make doors, shelves,
and some necessary articles of furniture. Mary did not enjoy the luxury
of a board floor for at least five months. Eells, in his Reminiscences,
tells us that his first table was made by driving four stakes in the
ground and fastening over the top three three-foot boards which had
been packed up from Waiilatpu. No doubt the Walkers had a similar
table. They had nothing but stools to sit upon, until the spring of 1841.*

*The spaces between the logs were chinked with mud. Indian rush
mats,[1] or possibly tapa cloth from the Hawaiian Islands, were used to
line the interior walls. Beds were made by nailing bunks against the
wall, "sink-fashion," as at the Whitman home. On October 19, 1839,
Mary mentions the fact that she had secured enough feathers from
wild fowl to stuff a mattress. All of the cooking was done over an open
fire in the fireplace, as neither the Walkers nor the Eells had the
luxury of a cooking stove during their entire nine years' residence at
Tshimakain. However, Mary does refer to the acquisition of a heating
stove in May, 1844. In August of that year she writes about painting
the woodwork of her house and the furniture. Their dishes were the
tinware used on their overland journey, supplemented by items secured
from the Hudson's Bay Company.*

*At first the roofs were nothing more than grass and sod laid over
poles. After heavy rains these roofs often leaked large globules of
mud, to the dismay and discomfiture of the inhabitants. There is
reason to believe that the missionaries soon discovered the ease with
which cedar could be split into what are called shakes. These made
excellent shingles. Elkanah, in his diary, referred to the board roof of
his new house.*

Busy days followed the return of the women to Tshimakain. The

---

[1] According to J. A. Teit, *The Salishan Tribes of the Western Plateaus,* p. 47:
"All the best mats were of rushes . . . and tule . . . woven with In-
dian-hemp twine. Long mats of rushes and young tule were used in the lodges as
floor covers and for couches and seats. . . Some coarser mats woven in the
same style were made of bark stripped from dead trees, generally willow." Although
Teit was writing of the Coeur d'Alene Indians, no doubt the Spokanes had the
same type of mats.

rudely constructed cabins had to be made liveable. Gardens and fields had to be plowed and planted. Eells, in his old age, remembered how he and Walker secured a plowshare, before leaving Waiilatpu, which they fitted with native wood to make a plow after their arrival at Tshimakain. Then with three teams of mules using homemade harness, the two men broke the virgin sod and made a beginning in agriculture. Of course always weighing upon their minds and troubling their consciences was the realization that they had to master the language before they could effectively preach the gospel to the natives. Although the natives were friendly and even eager for the missionaries to live in their midst, yet they were strangers to one another. The white people knew little or nothing about the red men's customs, superstitions, and traditions. Mary's diary, with its detailed descriptions of her experiences in the untamed wilderness, gives a vivid picture of the self-sacrificing toil to which the four gave themselves so freely.

TUES. 7.   Went down to the creek to wash.

WED. 8.   Cyrus not well, afflicted with an eruption which I suspect is chicken pox, suppose he took it of the Indians at Colvile.

THURS. MAY 9.   Have hard work to get along & take care of my babe.   .   .

FRI. 10.   SAT. 11.   SUN. 12.   MON. 13.   TUES. 14.   WED. 15.[2]   Dipped candles.

THURS. 16.   Washed. Have had to work very hard since I returned home. Rise before sunrise most of the time. Find my health very good which is a blessing for which I ought to be thankful. Regret I am able to devote so little attention to the language. Live very comfortably in my little house without floor, door, or windows.

FRI. 17.   Received letters from numerous friends, bringing intelligence   .   .   .   that Mr. Bingham's church [3] has made our mission a present of about 400 dollars & that our goods from V[ancouver] are at Walla Walla.

SAT. MAY 18.   Mr. Walker writing letters. A Frenchman called, the first traveller we have entertained. Rainey. We have thus far had frosty nights often.[4] Corn planted not up yet, also potatoes.

---

[2] Mary had no calendar hanging on the wall. Undoubtedly she listed the days of the week with the corresponding number of the month as a convenient method by which she could keep track of the passing days when she was too busy to make her usual daily entry. Hereafter all such listing of dates will be omitted.

[3] Hiram Bingham, founder of the Sandwich Islands Mission, was pastor of a large Hawaiian church in Honolulu. It is most interesting to note that the Hawaiian Christians were taking an interest in what was to them foreign missions at so early a time in their history.

[4] In this particular locality, frost was possible every month of the year. In his letter of Feb. 25, 1840, to the American Board, Eells wrote: "The nights during

SUN. 19. It rained hard all night. I slept little expecting any moment when the roof would commence leaking as this is the first rain since it was [put] on. But it did not leak at all. . .

TUES. 21. Did my washing & ironing & finished before eleven A.M. . .

SAT. 25. No worship in the morn with the Indians on account of a dog have broken into the house in the night. They talk rather bad but finally said they had killed the dog so all goes on right again.

SUN. 26. Attended worship. Mr. Eells led.

MON. 27. Washed & ironed before dinner. In the P.M. helped plant garden seeds.[5]

TUES. 28. Mr. Eells & Walker went to the Camas Plane about ten or 15 miles distant.[6] After they returned had a heavy thunder shower & some hail. But it did not injure our windows. I take very little care of Cyrus now except to dress & feed him. He cries to go from me to them[7] but when tired & hungry is glad to come back. He begins to want play things in his hands. Sits alone pretty well. Eats mostly milk porridge. . . He is very playful, sleeps but little by day. . .

WED. 29, MAY. Went out & worked in the garden two hours before other folks were up. In the P.M. Husband cut out a window & built over in part his chimney.[8]

SUN. JUNE 2. We were designing to have the sacrament but Mr. McDonald arrived & not exactly liking to commune with him nor without him, we thought best to differ it.[9] Mr. McD. found us very comfortably situated, as much of every thing good to eat & drink as we could wish.

---

the summer were generally cold. Sometimes there were fifty degrees difference between the temperature of the day and night. . . The extremes of heat and cold have been ninety-eight and five below zero." Later he found that the extreme temperatures were greater than here indicated.

[5] A careful check of Mary's diary shows that she had the following growing at one time or another in her garden: beans, cabbage, corn, cucumbers, melons, onions, peas, potatoes, radishes, "salad" (possibly lettuce or rhubarb), squash, tomatoes, and turnips. Mary grew and saved her own seed.

[6] The favorite camas prairie of the Spokane Indians who lived in the vicinity of Tshimakain was called Seakwakin. Mary makes many references to it in her diary.

[7] Soon after her arrival at Tshimakain, Mary secured the help of an Indian girl. See entry for Nov. 12, 1839, where Mary wrote: "Kwantepetser, my Indian girl."

[8] Mary's diary is sprinkled with many references to the difficulties they had with the adobe chimney. Sometimes the grass or straw used in the manufacture of the adobies would catch fire. When this happened the fireplace would have to be torn down and the burning part removed.

[9] Although Mr. McDonald came out of a Scotch Presbyterian home, the missionaries hesitated to invite him to the Lord's Supper and did not wish to embarrass him by holding the service without inviting him to join them. Notice Mary's entry for August 17 of this year, when she noted that McDonald had become a Catholic.

Mon. 3. Saw the plain from several places where there are springs but do not know as any up there are better than this. Mrs. Eells sick. Their house leaks as it is rainy. . .

Tues. June 4. Mr. McD. left in the morning.

Wed. 5. The first salmon. . .[10]

Sat. 8. Churned & baked, washed & ironed. Got very tired. . .

Mon. 10. Left home about ten a.m.[11] Pleasant weather. Mrs. Eells accompanied us to the River. On reaching camp found we had lost a kettle.

Tues. 11 & Wed. 12. Pleasant riding, travelled rapidly.

Thurs. 13. In the morning crossed a high mountain from which we had a very extensive view of the country.[12]

14. Reached Clear Water about noon. Our friends seemed glad to see us. Mr. Spalding & Gray both out of health. Mr. Gray & wife just returned from a visit to Mr. Smiths. Mr. & Mrs. Hall here from the Islands.[13]

Sat. 15. Went to the old house.[14]

Sun. 16. The sacrament was administered by Mr. Spalding. The occasion rather interesting. I have been thinking much of the circumstances in which the child of a missionary is placed, have had many anxious thoughts in regard to my own. What is to become of him? His parents one or both may soon be taken away & then who will care for my child? I hope I can with some degree of faith & confidence commit him to the care of his maker. . . If I have done right in

[10] Eells in a letter to the Board dated Feb. 25, 1840, wrote: "In June salmon begin going up the river. . . At first a barrier was constructed near some falls, ten miles from this place. . . At that place salmon were taken only during high water, and then not in great quantities, as the barrier extended only a part of the way across the river. . . As the water fell another barrier was built farther down, and extended across the entire river; and when completed men, women, and children made a general move to the place. If I judged correctly I saw there at one time near one thousand persons, and the number rapidly increasing. From four to eight hundred salmon were taken in a day, weighing variously from ten to forty pounds apiece." The salmon run stopped about August 1. Dried salmon was one of the main items of food for the natives. The missionaries frequently had salmon on their tables during season and there are some references to the use of dried fish.

[11] The Walker family started this morning for Lapwai, some 125 miles distant.

[12] The reference is to the Thatuna Hills a few miles north of the present Moscow, Idaho. The author lived for ten years at Moscow and remembers the magnificent view that is unfolded before a spectator who stands at the top of one of these hills on a clear day. It is possible then to see the Blue Mountains of eastern Oregon at least 150 miles distant.

[13] E. O. Hall was the printer of the Sandwich Islands Mission of the American Board. He took the mission press to Oregon, arriving at Lapwai on May 13, 1839. Mrs. Hall was an invalid who could not ride horseback but had to be conveyed up the river in a canoe.

[14] Mary visited the first cabin which Spalding built in the fall of 1836, located about two miles up Lapwai Creek from its mouth.

becoming a missionary, surely he will do what is best with my child. O may the blessing of the Father, Son & Holy Ghost rest on my own. May . . . his earthly portion be such as his Father in heaven sees best for him.

MON. JUNE 17. Washed with Mrs. Spalding & [Mrs.] Gray.

TUES. 19. Husband set out with Mr. Spalding to go to Mr. Smiths. Mr. S. was unable to ride. They returned. Mr. Rogers went with Mr. Walker. I have been ironing as Mrs. S. & G. are neither of them well. The weather is very hot, the thermometer at 96 almost every day.

THURS. 20. Mr. W. & R. arrived about one P.M. having made the distance from here to Mr. S[mith's] in eight hours.[15] Mrs. [Spalding] likes Mrs. Whitman as well as any of us.

SAT. 22. Yesterday & today made my husband a spencer.[16] Heard that Dr. W. is sick. Mr. Hall recd, some 40 or more of letters from the Islands.

MOND. 24. Left C.W. about 9 A.M. At our nights encampment an express overtook us informing [us] that Alice Clarissa W. is drowned & inviting us to return & attend the funeral. But we had travelled about 40 miles in an opposite direction & did not deem it expedient to return.

TUES. 25. Husband very much out of tune all day, scarce spoke pleasant. Out of patience because in accordance with my wish, he took along some chickens all of which except one died. Rode about 60 miles.[17] On the yellow pony in the P.M. Very much fatigued.

WED. 26. At half past two in the morning husband call[ed] on me to be up & preparing to start. Little son was sleeping soundly. I, tired, sleepy & half sick, entreated for a little more rest as we would have plenty of time without starting so early. But I met with [nothing] but an impatient, unfeeling moroseness, enough to melt the heart of the most insensible. The morning was pleasant & my horse went finely. I might have been so happy but the sadness of my heart spoiled it all. Oh can it be that I am the wife of a man that does not love me? In the afternoon my dear husband, for dear he still is, seemed more pleasant. We reached home about 4 P.M., having had a pleasant & prosperous journey.

THURS. 27 JUNE. Thought husband had got to feeling pleasantly again, but find I am sadly mistaken. He reproached [me] again this morning most severely on account of some ingentillities of which I had indeed been guilty. He almost said had he not supposed me more

---

[15] Kamiah, where the Smiths lived, was about sixty miles distant. To cover this distance in eight hours meant hard riding for the men.

[16] A short coat or jacket.

[17] So far as is known, this established a record for a day's travel by any of the women of the Mission. Sixty miles in one day on a side-saddle! The longest distance covered in any one day on the transcontinental journey of 1838 was forty-five miles.

accomplished, I had not been his wife. I am almost in dispair & without hope of his ever being pleased or satisfied with [me.] I do not know what course to persue. I can never with all my care make myself what he would like me to be. I never intended to be the wife of a man that did not love & respect me from his heart & not from a stern sense of duty & this I fear, yes I have much reason to fear is all that secures me that share of kindness that I receive. I know for the most part I am kindly treated. But I am but too often treated as tho my convenience & wishes were not to be regarded. The thought often occurs, I am glad my friends do not witness & can never know it. This morning as I sat sobing with my little son in my arms he looked as if he was worrying & I was endeavouring to quiet him, but when he saw me he seemed amazed, sat & looked at me in almost breathless silence till he fell asleep without moving a limb. He had never seen me weeping before & he seemed to say as plainly as looks could utter, Mother what ails you? Has your son been naughty or grieved you? . . . I never witnessed any thing [more] interesting in a child.

I am tempted to exclaim, Woe is me that I am a wife. Better have lived & died a miserable old maid & with none to share & thereby agrivate my misfortune. But it is too late. O may he who in his providence has suffered me to become a wife bless me in that relation & enable me to discharge every duty with Christian discretion & propriety. Yes, God helping me, I will endeavour tho faint & disheartened still to merit the love & esteem of my unfortunate but much loved husband. Perhaps tho I may be an affliction I am given to him in mercy to avert a worse. But reflections like these are but a poor solace to a grieved and disappointed wife. Disappointed, not because he is not as good as I anticipated, but because I have not gained that place in his heart that I fondly expected & which I think a wife ought to possess.[18]

O! the sad, sad emotions that seem almost more than I can endure. And how can I avoid them? I can only weep in silence for there is no sympathy for grief like mine. How can my heart be cheerful when oppressed with such sadness. O Leah, poor hated Leah, thou art my sister.[19]

THURS. EVENING. Tonight told husband how bad I was feeling. He only laughed at me. Said I was mistaken in suspecting he did not love me, for he certainly did. He confessed he had spoken wrong, said he was sorry I had felt so bad. That he had not intended to make me sad. So I think I will try to feel better.

SAT. 29. Mr. Eells & wife went to pass the sabbath at a camas

[18] The section beginning "Thurs. 27 June" to this point was later marked over with large "Xs." Evidently, after her husband had reassured her of his continued love, Mary regretted writing the lament.
[19] The unloved first wife of Jacob. See Genesis, ch. 29, 30.

ground ten or 15 miles distant. A company of Ponderra Indians arrived. I shook hands with about 70 at one time. My hand was quite numb from repeated & hard shakes. It is very interesting to see such a company coming for the purpose of receiving instruction. When I witness a scene like this I do not regret that I have left my home & come to this wilderness. But I feel impatient to be able to impart instruction.

SUN. JUNE 30, 1839.   A very pleasant Sabbath, more than a hundred Indians present. Appear very attentive. Every thing goes on well & my domestic enjoyment was never greater. O for a grateful heart to God for all his mercies.

TUES. JULY 2.   Wrote a note to Mrs. McD.   Mr. W. left for Colvile before sunrise.

WED. 3.   My Indian awoke me before sunrise. I set him to work in the garden till milking time. Very warm weather, the thermometer above 90°. Was much disturbed last night by mice & wolves. Cyrus is very healthy & good natured, fear we do not reallize as we ought how great a blessing it is to have so healthy a child. Last night was the first time . . . I have spent in a house alone.[20] It seems more lonely to have husband gone.

THURS. JULY 4.   Suppose much that is good or much that is bad is going [on] at home. Would like much to know how all my brothers & sisters are employed. My friends, what has become of them, are they yet alive.[21]

FRIDAY, JULY 5th.   Husband arrived about noon. Having dined the 4th at Colville.

SUN. JULY 7.   Cyrus Hamlin was baptized by Mr. Eells. Mr. Walker administered the sacrament for the first time. It was also the first time it [i.e. the Lord's Supper] was ever celebrated among our people, but through some misunderstanding, probably, very few attended. The occasion was to me solemn & interesting.

[Mary's Prayer.] O may the blessing of the Father, Son & Holy Ghost rest on our son. May his infant heart be cleansed that he may as soon as he knows his maker love and serve [him.] O may my heart be spared the anguish of seeing him running in the broad road to destruction. O may he be indeed a son of consolation & a pillar in the church of Christ.

May we feel that he is in the Lord & train him up for him. May the blessing of the God of so many of his ancestors, as were they thy true followers, rest & abide with him whether his days be few or many. Whether his parents have to see him attain a mature age or leave him

---

[20] The reader should remember that the Eells' cabin was but twenty feet from the Walker's.

[21] The Fourth of July in those days was the great holiday of the year, having much more importance in the mind of a New Englander than either Thanksgiving or Christmas.

an orphan. Into thy hands, as to a faithful Father, O God, I commit [him.] He is thine & thou hast a sovereign right to dispose of him as thou shalt [deem] best. Be merciful O Lord to my child & bless him. As he grows in stature may he grow in favor with God & man. May he be saved from the vices of the heathen about & be an example worthy of imitation to them. Thanks [be] to God for all his mercy to him thus far in blessing him with health & preserving life from its most incipient state uncommonly exposed to danger.

Mon. July 8. Heard that Cornelius was sick. Mr. E. went to see him. Mrs. E. quite unwell. . .

Tues. 9. Mrs. E. worse. Cyrus got choked with something he picked up, was more alarmed about him than ever before.

Thurs. 11 July. Mrs. E. very sick. Our little skill in medicine entirely baffled. Almost despair of her life.

Fri. 12. Almost contrary to our expectations, Mrs. E. survived through the night but to appearances no better till about 9 o'clock perhaps, when I ventured to apply cold water to the lower part of the bowels. This produced an immediate effect, occasioned a throbbing & stopped in some degree the flowing; she was also relieved from the nausea tho the faintness continued & she is still very sick & I think by no means out of danger. Mr. W. is also sick under the operation of calomel. Able only to sit up & take a cup of tea & go out to the door. O may it please God to deal with us in mercy & not in judgment & if it can be for the best, restore to life & health & usefulness.

Little Cyrus is good as a little child [can be] and he is off with the Indians from morning till night except when he requires washing, feeding & dressing.

Sat. 13. Mr. McLean arrived before 8 o'clock A.M. from Colvile, having travelled all night. Mrs. E still better. Mr. W. quite sick, sits up very little. Make out to get along better than I expected.

Sunday 14. Mrs. E. still appears to be doing well. I gave her an injection which operated favorably. Have very little immediate apprehension of her immediate safety. Mr. Walker able to go out & talk to the Indians a little. Weather very warm. The thermometer at 98.

Mon. About noon a Catholic Priest called. Brought letters & Mr. Walker's watch, invited him to dine but he declined & went on his way. We were not sorry to see him off.[22]

Tues. 16. Sent off Solomon for Dr. W. Quite discouraged about

---

[22] In all probability this was Father Modeste Demers who spent a month in the vicinity of Colville during the summer of 1839. Mary shared the antipathy to the Roman Catholics common to her associates. The watch returned was the one which had been sent to the Hawaiian Islands in the fall of 1838 to be repaired. In the meantime Walker had purchased a watch from Eells. See Mary's entry for Jan. 30, 1839. The repair bill amounted to £2.

Mrs. E. Mr. Walker yesterday some better but not able to work much.

WED. JULY 17.   Mrs. E. appears to be doing well.

THURS. 18.   Mrs. E. still better, got from her bed onto the floor without assistance.

FRI. 19.   Mrs. E. up & dressed.

SAT. 20.   Washed & ironed, baked . . . besides much other work. Cyrus quite unwell. Mr. W. still able to sit up but little. My own health very firm.

SUN. JULY 21, 1839.   Mr. Walker was very anxious yesterday to go to the River where the Indians are fishing but concluded it was not prudent. Think it is well he did not attempt it as he is scarcely able to sit up. Isabell Payett's mother [23] has come & wishes to take her away. I shall be glad to have her go. She is only an addition to my cares without having any assistance, (comparatively.) 9 o'clock in the evening Dr. Whitman arrived.[24]

TUES. 23.   We are enjoying a pleasant visit from Dr. W. I feel to rejoice exceedingly that there is so fair a prospect of more pleasant feelings among the members of this mission.[25] O may it be permanent. Mrs. Eells is recovering as fast as could be expected.

This is the end of the fifth notebook of Mary's diary. The next notebook begins with a letter to her husband. It appears that Mary had discovered that Elkanah had been reading her diary including the long entry for June 27, in which she poured out her heart because of her husband's criticisms and moroseness. As a dutiful and obedient wife, Mary was somewhat hesitant about speaking her thoughts to her husband. She felt greater freedom in writing.

[23] This is the only reference to Isabel Payette in Mary's diary. Evidently she was the half-breed daughter of Francis Payette, who was the Hudson's Bay official in charge of Fort Hall, at the time the reinforcement of 1838 passed that way. Probably the Walkers were asked to take the girl into their home when they were at Fort Colville. There are many instances of the mountain men and Hudson's Bay men being eager for their children to be trained and educated by the missionaries.

[24] Eells, despairing of the life of his wife, had sent an urgent message to Dr. Whitman begging him to come to Tshimakain. This was the first of eight visits that Whitman made to Tshimakain, six of which were professional calls and two on mission business. Of the professional calls, five were for confinement cases. Since the round-trip from Waiilatpu was about 300 miles, this meant that Whitman covered about 2,400 miles on horseback on these trips. When we remember that he made many such trips to Lapwai, Kamiah, and to Fort Walla Walla and Fort Vancouver, we realize that much of this time was spent travelling. There was also his trip East in 1842-43, which took a full year.

[25] There is much evidence to indicate that the death of Alice Clarissa on June 23, 1839, had a mellowing influence upon the whole Mission. Whitman was able to tell the Walkers of a reconciliation which had taken place between him, his wife, and the Spaldings.

164

FRIDAY JULY 26, 1839

To REV. E. WALKER

MY DEAR HUSBAND I find it in vain to expect my Journal will escape your eyes & indeed why should I wish to have it [so] ? Certainly my mind knows no sweeter solace than the privilege of unbosoming itself to you. It frequently happens that when I think of much I wish to say to you, you are either so much fatigued, so drowsy or so busy that I find no convenient opportunity till what I would have said is forgotten. I have therefore determined to address my journal to you. I shall at all times address you with the unrestrained freedom of a fond & confiding wife. When therefore you have leisure & inclination to know my heart, you may here find it ready for converse.

WED. JULY 24, 1839.[26] My Dear Husband in company with Dr. Whitman, who was returning from a visit to Mrs. E., left for Walla Walla. Your health is so poor that I feel rather anxious about you. When you first mentioned going I thought nothing of it, not reflecting how long a time it would require. After you left I felt exceedingly lonely. Hardly know how to dispose of myself. Observed the Maternal Meeting alone & enjoyed much. Felt more interest in attending evening worship alone than I often do. Mrs. E. is apparently recovering. Mr. E. wishes me to bake him some bread and let him live at home. . .

THURS. 25 . . . Let Mr. E. milk the black cow instead of the brown, hoping to succeed better with her than he as she troubles much about giving down her milk.[27] Mr. E. & the Indians burning ashes for soap.

FRI. JULY 26. Attend Mr. Eells worship. He is particular to mention you but never alludes to son or I in his prayers. I have felt for many days a boading [i.e. foreboding] of trouble. Have wept many times to think how soon & easily my husband may be taken & I left a widow. It seems to me I could not be consoled. If son were taken away it would seem so light a stroke compared with this, I should hardly feel it. If I were left a widow, I think I should not return home. I would devote myself to the language, to making book & teaching & to the education of son till he was old enough to send home. But why do I devise schemes like these? My dear husband, I trust, is yet alive. May it please God to spare his life many years. I was indulging in very sad feelings when opening the Hymn Book I read the 170 hymn. Two lines in particular afforded me much comfort:

Thy watchful eyes, which cannot sleep
In every place, thy children keep.

[26] Sometimes Mary failed to make daily entries and then would write in retrospect. This seems to be the case on July 26. After writing the letter to her husband in her diary for that day, she went back and made the entries for the two previous days.

[27] Among her many other duties, Mary for most of the time, did the milking for the Walker family.

I know that God is able to keep you & restore you in health. But the time of your absence seems long & I wish to see you very much. I hope to be able to devote some time to the language. Yesterday I filed all our old letters.[28] Today I have washed & so I am all the time busy about something. But is this kind of labor all a missionary has to do?

SAT. JULY 27. Mr. E. still busy making ashes. But says he has given up the idea of raising any turnips. That he tried repeatedly to get you to help him plough the yard, but could not get you about it. Do not know whether he is displeased about it or not. Was almost tempted to whip son today but feared it was not best. I wished I knew when it would be best to commence; I think I will endeavor never to do it hastily but with deliberation & prayer. As to his learning the language, I think we can determine better about it some time hence than now. . .

Have attended to the language more today than usual. Hope to begin to progress a little soon. Mrs. E. comes tottering to my house every day, looking more like a ghost than any thing else. Fear it will be long before she is well again if she recovers at all.

SUNDAY 28 JULY. I have enjoyed a very quiet sabbath day. Have not attended Mr. Eells worship, son makes so much disturbance thought it not best. Only about a dozen Indians here today. Have had more time for reading & meditation than usual. Have composed a letter in answer to Mrs. Whitney [29] which I design to copy if it suits you.[30] The time till your return begins to look shorter. Would like to know how it seems to you to be at Dr. Whitman's again.

MON. 29. Have spent most of the day attending to the language. My boy [31] is a good one to get words from. Fear he may not be as correct as some one older would be. He discovers an eager desire to

---

[28] Thanks to Mary's methodical nature, these letters were saved. The author secured this collection of old family letters from Sam Walker, the youngest son of Elkanah and Mary.

[29] The schoolteacher, Samuel Whitney and his wife, Mercy, were members of the pioneer company of missionaries who went out to the Hawaiian Islands on the "Thaddeus" during the winter of 1819-20. They were the parents of the first white child born on the Islands. On February 11, 1839, Mercy Whitney wrote to Mary Walker, saying in part: "Though personally unknown, permit me to address you by the endearing appellation of sister for such I trust we are. . . What a long and tedious journey you must have had from the United States, across the Rocky Mountains. . ." The two women carried on a correspondence throughout the nine years the Walkers lived at Tshimakain. Several of Mrs. Whitney's letters, including this which Mary answered on July 28, are in Coll. WN.

[30] The use of the pronoun "you" reminds us that Mary was expecting her husband to read her diary, so she would be directing some of her comments to him. After her entry for Sept. 21, Mary rarely made such references.

[31] Myron Eells in his *Father Eells*, p. 155, refers to the fact that the Walkers took into their home or their employ in 1839 a sixteen-year old Indian lad by the name of William Threemountains who was "cheerful and faithful and learned well." William was baptized by Spalding in 1873 and became a leader in the Deep Creek Presbyterian Church. See Drury, *A Tepee in His Front Yard*.

learn to read & write. Is not quite retiring enough, otherwise like him, shall hate to send away one so anxious to learn. I wish I could keep & instruct him. I have been thinking to day that nothing would tempt me to leave the missionary field to return to spend my days at home. I know of no place no situation in the world where I would prefer to be rather than here. I trust if my life & health are spared I shall yet be able to [do] much for these benighted people, & if I do not live to labor myself, my dying entreaty to my brothers & sisters should be come to the heathen. I have been thinking to day how much I wish I had one of those brothers of mine here to study the language with us Would it not be pleasant? I think I will write to them & see if I cannot stir them up to become missionaries.

TUES. JULY 30. To day is Sister Phebe's birthday, 20 years old. I was 20 years ago attending school . . . I recollect a great many little incidents that occured about that time. I have washed & ironed [32] & spent most of the day studying the language.

WED. JULY 31. Had boiled corn [33] & green pumpkin for dinner today. Mrs. E. does not mend as fast as I hoped she would. Her appetite very poor. Have had a group of Indians around me all day, have been trying to teach them the figures. There are so many interesting young people & children among them, I wish I could do more for them. It grieves me to see them idling away so much time that might be employed in acquiring knowledge, if there were only books & some one to teach them.

AUG. 1. Well my dear husband, I think I can sympathize with you a little to night for I have been sitting right here all day with half a dozen women at my feet talking & listening to them & writing words as fast as I could get them till I can hardly recollect where I am. Mr. Eells is busy writing letters home, hardly looks at an Indian, fear he will not get much knowledge of the language in that manner, [34] tho I suppose it is necessary one should let friends at home know he is alive. Poor little son, I hardly know what becomes of him. But he is a busy quiet happy looking child as I ever saw. After playing in the dirt all day & being handled first by one dirty Indian & then by another, he enjoys a fine frolick in a pan being washed. I then dress him clean, give him his supper & soon he is fast asleep for the night. I dont know but I neglect him more than I ought to but I console myself with the idea that if I do not spend all my time almost worshiping him, he will be less likely to die.

[32] Heating a flatiron over an open fire in the fireplace must have been doubly unpleasant on hot days during the summer months.

[33] Mary, in her entry for Sept. 11, 1839, refers to drying the corn, and again on Nov. 19, to eating "hulled corn." Some corn was carried to the mill at Fort Colville and ground into corn meal, for Mary also refers to "corn cakes."

[34] Both Mary and Elkanah were critical of Eells' failure to study the native language as they thought he should. Although Eells had the better education, it was Walker who became the better linguist.

A GROUP OF SPOKANE INDIANS WHO LIVED NEAR TSHIMAKAIN

Left to right: Father Abraham, Old Solomon, Zachariah, and Mary Magdalene. Solomon is mentioned many times in Mary Walker's diary, and is the one who brought the news of the Whitman massacre to the two families living at Tshimakain. Picture date is unknown, probably between 1880 and 1890. From Myron Eells, *Father Eells.* 1894.

MARY WALKER

ELKANAH WALKER

When the Walkers returned to their homes in Maine in 1871, they had their photographs taken by Bowers, Lynn, Massachusetts, on September 27, 1871. Courtesy, Oregon Historical Society, owner of the originals.

I have had two women sewing on a shirt to day, they have nearly completed it & do much better than I expected they would.

FRI. AUG. 2. Have spent to day much as yesterday. Hope to see you tomorrow, but fear you are sick or have been. I shall be glad to see you return in safety as an anxious wife need be.

SAT. AUG. 3. This morning I churned & did up all my chores, hoping this afternoon to see my husband and Mr. Eells went to the river to meet you When I was milking, the people said you were near & I supposed it was so but it proved to be only Mr. E. I should be very anxious about you but I think you have had scarcely time as yet. I listened till I was half amazed to day to an old woman who attempted to make me understand their method of computing time. I got ten divisions of the day, the changes of the moon & its name. I gave them a description of the elephant & showed them the picture which interested them very much. Just as I was finishing, some new Indians came. An old woman whispered to me to put away my book & not show them because they were bad Indians. Probably she wished to have the distinction of telling them herself, thinking thereby to acquire distinction. I am not quite done looking for you. I think by this time you would like to see home & little son in particular.

SUN. AUG. 4. My dear husband. I have just been having a chat with the people. They seem much gratified with my spending so much time in conversing with them & now & then I impart a little instruction. I find I understand them better every day. I have been thinking a good deal to day about Cyrus. Fear I indulge him too much. But really I can find no occasion against him that seems to demand chastisement. I do not wish to discourage him in his wish to gain knowledge of every thing & when he is hungry or in pain I wish him to make it known & the poor boy can do it only by crying. I do not think it is best to provoke a child in order to bring out the latent depravity that you may correct it early. I think it best to avoid a contest till a child has sufficient knowledge of words to know at least what is said to him. I know I lack wisdom & I will endeavor to ask of him who giveth liberally and upbraideth not.

MON. AUG. 5. Noon. I have just been exercising some boys in adding numbers. I never could make white children understand half as quick. They added the digits to 10 & get it right the second time. . .

P.M. My anxiously awaited husband returned in better health than [when] he went away.[35] The goods he went after had not been left at W.W. so he had nothing [to] pack. I was very glad to see him arrive safe as I had feared he would be sick. He also brought the intelligence that the receipts of the A.B.C.F.M. were sufficient to pay its debts & send out those who were waiting to go. This was indeed cheering intelligence. . .

---

[35] When Whitman started back to Waiilatpu on July 24, Walker went with him to get supplies. He was away for nearly two weeks.

WED. 7. Ironed & picked up a few words. Mrs. Eells not so well. Applied a blister this morning. I feel very irresolute about doing anything. Do not know whether my mind or body is out of tune. Perhaps it is both.

AUG. 8 . . . Mrs. Eells had a severe ague fit to day. We succeeded in sweating her but she is still very low. Fear she will not recover soon if ever. Her blisters will not draw.

FRI. AUG. 9. I made soap. Mrs. Eells no better. Very low. Have to neglect her more than I like to.

SAT. 10. Mrs. E. has several blisters that draw well. Her former difficulty has returned but not with violence. Know not what to think of it. She needs much more attention than I can bestow. Fear her husband is less attentive than he ought to be. I am lately much troubled with salt rheum in my hands.[36] Hope I shall be able to do something to help them.

SUN. 11. Attended Indian worship. Very few people here.[37]

MON. 12. Mrs. E. had a sick night last night, seems to be failing fast. Can not speak loud. Conversed considerably to day. Lamented her luke-warmness. Mentioned one or two instances in which I had injured her feelings. Wished to know if I had any thing treasured up against her, I would tell her so &c. Told me to keep half a dozen of her tea spoons if her things came round the [Horn.][38] Named some things to be given to Mrs. Smith & others. Said she wished Mrs. S[mith] to have as much as any one. She seems to think she shall not live long. I think perhaps she may live till fall if no longer.

TUES. AUG. 13. Mrs. E. seems a little better, but is very low. She is left alone more than I like to have her. I cannot stay with her much & her husband is off much of the time. I have had a large wash to day for me & then I had husband to fix off & son was not as well as usual.

[36] Possibly some irritation of the skin, resulting from working with lye in the making of soap.

[37] Eells, in a letter to the Board dated Feb. 25, 1840, explained how the Indians were obliged to move from fishing sites to camas plains to hunting grounds in their never ceasing search for food. He wrote: "When they ceased to take salmon, about the first of August, they returned to the camas ground, where they remained till October, and then began to make preparations for taking the poor salmon as they went down the river. During this month they were very much scattered, though not very remote from each other. In November they went to their wintering places. From March to November our congregations varied from thirty to one hundred; not more than half of whom usually remained with us during the week. They often came ten, fifteen, and sometimes thirty miles on Saturday, and returned again on Monday. Since November near two hundred have remained with us almost constantly. In addition to those just mentioned, there have been frequent visitors here from neighbouring bands, coming in various numbers, from three or four to sixty at a time. They usually spend one or two weeks here, and then return."

[38] The boxes of personal belongings which the Walkers and the Eells shipped from Boston in the spring of 1838 did not arrive at Tshimakain until February, 1840.

So I have only made out to get through the day. Charles was here this afternoon. I talked with him some or tried too but could not understand much about matters. I sent for S. & she came.[39] I had to go to attend on Mrs. E. so she took Cyrus & remained during worship. . . Charles wished to take the gun and shoot a bird but I told him I thought you would not like it.

You know I dislike to have you gone so much, yet I am determined to be as contented in your absence as I can & give myself as little anxiety [as possible.] I know I cannot protect you or make you well & he who guards you at home is equally able to do it abroad. To him I will ever try to commend you & yours.

WED. 14. Mrs. E. rested but little last night. Seems not so well this morning. P.M., almost thought she was dying.

THURS. AUG. 15. Mr. E. finds that he made a mistake in giving morphine instead of giving one of the doses [of another medicine] Dr. W. left out. He gave that which was not left out. A great wonder he did not kill her. But perhaps it will do good in the end. She is still very sick. Has slept some for several nights. Vomits nearly everything she takes . . . seems to feel fretful. Have hardly found time to day to eat.

FRI. AUG. 16. Little son has been rather a naughty boy all day. Towards night I gave him a camas root but [he] let it fall so often I gave him a bit of bread instead. He took it & threw it on the floor with a spite. I gave it to him again & he threw it again. Pretty soon he saw an Indian at the door & cried to go out. I did not let him go & he acted vexed, straightened himself & screamed. I concluded a child who knew enough to act so naughty would understand what correction meant & accordingly I summoned resolution to give him a slap which he could not mistake for a pat. I expected he would set up a loud scream & be grieved about it. But instead of this he immediately took his milk which he had just refused & snuggled up to me as if he would go to sleep. He appeared to understand what he was corrected for & seemed to cling to me with more than ordinary affection, & was very quiet & happy till the girl let him fall & bump his head. I hope he will be a good boy so I shall not have to correct him often.

Mrs. E. seems to be doing well if consumption does not take her or has not already commenced its ravages. I think she may get about again & perhaps enjoy a measure of health.

SAT. AUG. 17, 1839. Toothache, half sick. Son cross. Got another slap. Husband returned from Colvile. Had a prosperous journey. Got his goods. Mrs. McDonald has a pair of boys three weeks old.[40] Is

---

[39] Mary found it necessary to have a girl help her from the beginning of her residence at Tshimakain. Just who this "S" was we are not sure. Beginning in 1842, Mary frequently refers to two girls, Shoshenamalt and Sillapal.

[40] The twins, Donald and James, were born July 23. They died of scarlet fever at Edmonton, Alberta, on May 13, 1845.

smart at work [again] at the wash tub. The Catholic priests very active.[41] Hope they will not be suffered to mislead these poor heathen. The pious Mr. McD. is a Catholic now. Had a letter, or Mr. W. did, of Mr. Rogers who is now in the buffalo country.

SUN. AUG. 18.   Not much going on.

MONDAY 19.   Frost last night, killed the vines and injured the corn. Not as well as usual myself. Hardly know whether Mrs. E. gains any or not. Cyrus cross as a child need be, suppose of course he is not well. We have two Indian children who seem happy & contented.[42] Husband is reaping the wheat to day.[43] Very tired tonight. He asked me to pray. Was glad I declined for he made a better prayer than usual .

TUE. AUG. 20.   [Prayer] concert in the evening.

WED. 21.   Washed. Toothache a little. But on the whole pretty well. The saw commenced sawing to day.[44]

FRIDAY AUG. 23.   Baked. Tooth ache still. Weather rather warmer than it has been lately. Son pretty good. Gets a little whipping almost every day, but do not have to whip him much. He minds well. Mrs. E. sits up to have her bed made.

SUN. 25.   Staid at home all day, read in the Mis[sionary] Her[ald] & Mothers Mag[azine.] [45] Mrs. E. went out of doors. Cornelius & quite a number of the people here. Sometimes feel almost discouraged, fear we shall never benefit the Indians at all. Wonder why I am so reluctant

---

[41] Nichols, *The Mantle of Elias*, pp. 110, 271, states that Father Demers baptized seventeen at Fort Colville during the summer of 1839 including a son of Peter S. Ogden and "Julie of the Spokane Nation." A fundamental difference regarding when and to whom the sacrament of baptism should be administered separated the Roman Catholics and the Protestant missionaries at Tshimakain. The former believed that the souls of infants were lost if they were not baptized. This was not a teaching of Calvinism. The Roman Catholics would baptize adults after a brief period of indoctrination. The Protestants insisted not only on a longer period of instruction but also upon a personal experience of salvation. The activities of the priests among the Spokanes was a most disturbing factor to the missionaries at Tshimakain.

[42] As did the Spaldings at Lapwai, so the Walkers tried the experiment of receiving into their home a few native children. However, since both families soon gave up this practice, we may assume that the experiment was not a success. All of the missionary families were more willing to receive half-breed children.

[43] We should remember that all of the work of harvesting and threshing was by hand. This was tedious, hard work.

[44] Walker in his diary has many references to hiring natives saw logs into boards. The Indians did not know the value of money. All payments to them for services rendered was in trading goods which the missionaries had purchased from the Hudson's Bay Company.

[45] True to their conscientious scruples regarding the observance of the Sabbath, Mary and Elkanah did no more work on that day than was absolutely necessary. This gave Mary her only time during the week to read. The magazines noted in this entry were probably one or two years old and probably had been borrowed from the Whitmans or the Spaldings.

to lead in prayer, perhaps it is because I pray so little in secret & why do I do this? I like to unite in the prayers of others & why I am no more prayerful I cannot tell. I fear I have not a right spirit; that I do not love God & seek to glorify him but am actuated by a feeling of selfishness in regard to myself & of sympathy for others. That I am grieved not because they have sinned against a holy God but because their sins render them miserable.

MON. AUG. 26.   Have been thinking how very unprepared I am for life or death. O could I live as seeking him who is invisible.   .   .

WED. 28.   Wrote to Mrs. Gray & Whitman.[46] Husband left for Mr. Spaldings about noon. Mrs. E. seems to be mending fast, walked as far as the garden. Had our Maternal meeting for the first time at our place.

THURS. 29.   Washed. Got very tired. The fire which last night threatened very hard went out pretty much.[47] Mr. Walker returned not being able to find his way on account of the smoke, and fearing also we should be burnt out. Think it as well he should return.

SAT. 31 AUG.   Mrs. Eells came to eat with us, seems to be gaining quite fast. Has a good appetite.

SUN. SEPT. 1.   My dear husband. I feel quite discouraged. I have been reviewing my life, particularly since I indulged a hope that I had experienced a change of heart. It is now almost nine years, and what progress have I made?[48] In what respect am I the better for having lived? I cannot see as in anything. I am just as prone as ever to indulge in vain & wicked thoughts, to forget God, and the high vocation with which I am called. I am still the same stupid indifferent creature. If called this day to deliver up my account, I fear I should do it with shame & confusion of face. What good can such a vile creature expect to do among the heathen? I should despair of doing any thing were it not for the prayers of Christians & for the glory of God himself to save souls. My dear husband, is there any thing you can do to make me better? If you know just what I am, I fear you could not love & respect me. How much you need a prayerful, devotedly pious wife to assist & to strengthen you. If I am so unfaithful in the discharge of my duty to myself & my maker, how can I be faithful as a wife or a mother? These are not idle reflections but awful truths which serve to depress me

---

[46] Mary was evidently replying to a letter written to her by Mary Gray dated July 19, 1839, the original of which is in the Coe Collection, Yale Univ. This collection contains seventeen letters from Mrs. Gray to Mary; three from Mrs. A. B. Smith; two from Andrew Rodgers; and twelve from Mrs. Whitman. In addition are letters to Walker and/or Eells. For further information about this collection, see Drury, *Diaries of Spalding and Smith*, 187.

[47] Forest fires have always been common in that region. Some of these were started by lightning and some occasionally by the natives.

[48] Mary dated her conversion from the time of the Methodist revival at the Maine Wesleyan Seminary in the fall of 1830.

with a sense of guilt & shame without effecting that repentence which need not be repented of. Often when the fire of devotion seems extinguished on the altar of my heart, I am able to catch a spark from your altar. If my ungrateful heart is grateful for anything it is that God has given me a husband of whom I am indeed unworthy. But now shall I turn my eyes from these reflections as from a glass & forget what manner of person I am. Is there no way by which I can attain a more devout & prayerful frame of mind. . .[49]

TUES 3. Kwantepetser[50] left. Miss her very much. Cyrus hinders me so much. He is not so full of glee as formerly, appears more sober & is frequently inclined to repose quietly in my arms.

WED. 4. Had green peas for dinner, the first we have had. Have been thinking how much I resemble the unproffitable servant who accused his master of being an austere man. I am inclined to feel that I am under no obligation to God for his unnumbered mercies because it cost him nothing. But can I not realize that the sufferings & death of the Saviour cost him something?

SAT. 7. A man arrived today from Walla Walla who brought the intelligence that Mr. Lee is on his way. So that I expect soon we may receive letters from home.[51] Kwantepetser returned tonight. Mrs. E. is still about, has a great appetite, fear every day when she will make herself sick.

SUN. 8. Attended worship today. The Chief appears not so friendly as formerly.

May we have grace & wisdom to conduct [ourselves] so as to benefit the people. And may we never forget that except the Lord build the city, they labor in vain that build it. I trust that even among these poor heathen God will raise up a seed to serve him. May every fresh exhibition of the depravity of their hearts serve to awaken our sympathy & to kindle afresh our zeal.

MON. SEPT. 9. Harvesting corn & pumpkins to day. The people seem not to feel pleasantly about something. The Chief is not willing

---

[49] Mary frequently wrote in this self-searching vein in her earlier diaries. On April 1, 1835, on her twenty-fourth birthday, she wrote in poetry:

So speed my years nor care I how
  You speed. Vain years how little can
Ye tell of duty done to God or man
    . . . And I have
Striven too to mend my heart
Hard heart which tho I strive
And much of labour do bestow on
It yet barren is and yield scarce
    Any gracious fruit.

[50] The first mention by name of the native girl who was Mary's most faithful helper for about two years.

[51] Mary was misinformed about Jason Lee being on his way. The Methodist reinforcement did not leave New York until October 9, 1839.

to renounce his medicine men.[52] To night quite a penitent confession. I hope it will please God to enlighten him & lead him to sincere repentance.

TUES. 10, 1839. Very much tempted to be offended at Mr. E. Wish he knew a little better what belonged to politeness or even kindness. Told my grievances to husband. He seemed to think he meant no harm. So I suppose it is better not to seem to mind it.

WED. 11, 1839. Husked the corn, the Indians [helped.] Twenty boys spread it on the house top. Mrs. E. & myself cut some half dozen pumpkins each day. Fine weather to dry them. Little son . . . can say boy, pa, &c. . . He has not worn squairs [i.e., diapers] for some weeks, seldom soils his bed. Creeps from one house to the other. Eats in addition to his quart bottle of porridge a little solid food & drinks plenty of water. I feel very anxious to know if we are to have any letters from home. It is time we were writing [53] but I cannot think of doing it until I hear from home.

THURS. 12 SEPT. Plenty of Indians cutting pumpkins to dry.

FRI. 13. Had our Friday prayer meeting. Never heard Mr. E. make so good a prayer. . .

SAT. SEPT. 14, 1839. Waited till P.M. Hoping to receive letters from home before writing, but none came so I set about writing. Commenced a letter home.

SUN. 15. Attended worship quite a number present. In the evening write in my letter again.

MON. 16. About noon heard that some white man was coming. The Indians said it was an English man. An inquiry being made if they were certain it was not a Frenchman, they said they were sure it was not because he stoped over the sabbath. Pretty soon Mr. Gray and wife arrived. They brought us letters from home from across the Mts. & by way of the Islands.[54] The intelligence they contained was much of it cheering tho they mentioned the death of many a friend or relation. The excitement felt was perhaps greater than on the day I left home. . .[55]

---

[52] The conflict between Christianity and the primitive religious beliefs of the natives came to a focus in the medicine man. The diaries of both Elkanah and Mary contain many references to this problem.

[53] The westward bound express of the Hudson's Bay Company usually passed Fort Colville early in the fall. Letters could be sent by this express to Fort Vancouver from whence they would be forwarded by sea to the United States.

[54] Gray carried letters that were brought to Oregon by sea and possibly some that might have been carried overland by the Mungers and Griffins, independent missionaries, who made the transcontinental journey in 1839.

[55] These were the first letters from her home that Mary had received since her departure about eighteen months previous. Some extracts from letters written by her sister Charlotte may be found in McKee, *Mary Richardson Walker*, pp. 182, 221.

WED. 18 SEPT. 1839. This morning arose before day & finished writing my letter to J. C. [a brother] & father. Mr. & Mrs. Gray left after dinner.

FRI. 20. Mr. Walker left for Spokan.

SAT. 21. Left son in bed awake & alone & went to milking. When I returned found him lying just as I left him but still awake. He has taken a fancy to a little girl not much larger than himself who has amused him by creeping from our house to the other many times to day. Poor little son, I wish he could have better playmates.

Have been thinking of my brothers & sisters to night. Have thought how pleasant it would be to meet again in this world, but I have thought how much more I would rejoice to know we were all prepared to meet in another. Find it very difficult, my dear husband, to do just as I suppose you would wish me to when my own judgment & inclination would induce me to act otherwise. I mean in regard to my treatment of the natives.

SUN. 22. Husband gone, a very quiet day. Have given the 29th Report of the A.B.C.F.M. a very cursory reading.[56] Feel some disheartened from the circumstances that so little has been done for Indians. I fear a final extermination awaits them. Why is it thus?

MONDAY, 23. Spent some part of the day in writing to Mr. Caldwell.

TUES. SEPT. 24, 1839. Husband returned from Ponderas, having had a prosperous journey & witnessed much interest in the people.

WED. 25. Washed, baked pies. . .

THURS. 26. Build the chimney over again, that is repair it. Feel vexed with the Indians. Charles has been coaxing away our girl. Should be glad if he might not succeed.

SUN. 29. Cornelius, tho here, absented himself from worship. He is evidently very much offended.

MON. SEPT. 30, 1839. Mr. Eells is building his chimney. I am getting some lazy, shall feel glad when Mrs. E. gets to keeping house again. The Chief has been here to day. Is very mad apparently. Son is getting to be a naughty boy, cries to go out doors almost all the time. Strikes when anything does not suit him. As soon as he is put on the bed, he begins to frolic, & I often have to whip him to make him lie still & go to sleep. He is full of mischief as a child can be.

WED. OCT. 2. A new floor & bed stead. Son was naughty when I washed him. Had to slap him much harder than ever before, but he minded pretty well at last.

SAT. 5, 1839. The Indians who came in to night say they heard we

---

[56] The 29th annual report of the Board appeared in the Nov. 1838 issue of the *Missionary Herald*. Less than a page of this report was devoted to the work of the Board among American Indians. Eells once wrote of how he carefully laid aside the accumulation of a weekly paper which was sent to him and then read in chronological sequence only one copy a week.

were going to leave them & their hearts were very small. Feel encouraged a little.

MON. 7. Mr. W. draw the timbers for a room.[57]

TUES. 8 & WED. 9. Yesterday & today Mr. E. helped Mr. W. & the room is up & covered. Washed today. Find it pleasant to have a floor to wash again. Little C.H. [Cyrus Hamlin] can not quite walk yet. He sits on a stool while I am getting breakfast. I can keep him quiet in this way. He knows when I say no.

FRI. OCT. 11, 1839. Mr. Walker recd. letters from his father & sisters by the H.B. Express. Also one from Mr. McD. who expresses hopes that the U.S. & Eng. will not engage in a war.[58] May it please God to not suffer such a thing to be.

MON. 14. Our best cow ate poison & died.[59] We feel it a great loss but are thankful it is no worse.

WED. 16. Sat up most of the night to finish letters. One of three sheets to Prof. Caldwell of Carlisle, Penn. & one of one sheet to Mrs. Whitney. . . Mr. Walker left for C. Mrs. Eells commenced keeping house last Sat. But I have given her about half the victuals I cooked as yet. Hope she will be able to get along for her sake & mine too for I find it rather hard to do her work & mine too. Tho she sews a good deal for me. Cyrus has one tooth.

THURS. 17 OCT. 1839. A very cold night. Our girl slept out of doors with another. I intended she should sleep in the house but [I] did not like to harbor the other. But I was worried about them all night but they seemed bright this morning. . .

SAT. 19. Mr. E. has Indians helping dig potatoes. Filled my feather bed. So we are in possession of one of the comforts of civilization again.

SUN. OCT. 20 . . . Little Cyrus commenced walking to day. . .

TUE. 22. Dipped 16 doz candles, hope they are good ones. Expected my husband but he does not arrive. Left son asleep in bed. Went to milking. Heard him cry, ran in, found him near the door. Not much hurt I think.

WED. OCT. 23. Husband returned from C. having enjoyed a pleasant visit tho he did not meet the express as expected.

THURS. 24. Mr. and Mrs. E., Mr. Walker, Cyrus & his bearer [i.e. his mother] took a ride down to the sand bank.

SAT. 26. Recd. letters from Clear W. & Wielatpoo. Mr. Gray in

---

[57] Walker was building an extension to the original cabin.

[58] During the winter of 1838-39, a dispute arose between Maine and New Brunswick over the boundary in the Aroostook region. Both sides called out the militia. However a truce was arranged in March, 1839, before any blood was shed.

[59] Smith also lost a cow in the first part of February, 1840, because it ate a poisonous plant. Smith called it "wild parsnip." Drury, *Diaries of Spalding and Smith,* 125.

trouble about establishing a new station.[60] Pity his wife but do not know what ought to be done.

TUE. 29. Moved my bed into my new room. It is more comfortable than we have had before. It is lined with mats & mats for a floor.

FRI. Nov. 1. The first snow we have had this fall.

SAT. 2. Very rainy this morning. Mr. E. returned from Colvile, reached home a little before noon. . . Brought some kittens so I hope we shall soon be less troubled with mice.

SUN. Nov. 3 . . . Had the communion. We have innumerable blessings to our benefits. I wish I could realize more the importance of living for eternity.

WED. 6. Recd. letters from Mr. Gray who is in a big trouble. Mrs. E. dipped candles.

THURS. . . . Husband is helping Mr. E. put up a house.[61] I am anxious to sew but my hands are so bad I am scarcely able to. One of our cows gives a good mess of milk, so son fares well as to milk yet.

SAT. Nov. 9, 1839. Rather warm rainy weather. . .

MONDAY 11 . . . One of the horses got bit by wolves. Weather not very cold most of the time. A little rainy, damp or foggy.

TUE. 12. Kwantepetser, my Indian girl, washed without much of my assistance. . . Husband watched horses.[62]

WED. 13. Find the pork we had from C. the other day so tainted fear we can never eat it.

THURS. 14. A rainy night. Husband out watching horses.

SAT. 17. Have been think[ing] much today on the prospect of doing good among these or any other Indians. Feel disheartened because they all seemed doomed to melt away like the snow on the approach of summer & all we can do seems only calculated to hasten their doom. Yet perhaps they should not yet be given over in despair. I do reproach myself for my indolence & want of zeal in acquiring the language & trying to do something for them. I am often much perplexed in applying the rule of doing to others as I would they should do to me in my treatment of them. Wish I could realize more that we can do nothing without the blessing of God & the influence of the Spirit.

Little Cyrus now very well. I have left off feeding him porridge &

---

[60] The Mission meeting held in Sept. 1839, gave Gray the right to explore for a new station. When Gray returned to Lapwai on Oct. 18 with the news that he had selected a site at Shimnap, about a day's travel on the Columbia River above Walla Walla, Spalding informed him that the Mission had granted him only the right to explore and not to move. This vacillating policy caused much unhappiness.

[61] Eells was building an extension to his cabin even as Walker had done.

[62] As has been mentioned, until the missionaries were able to erect rail fences, they were obliged to let their animals run loose to forage. Both Walker and Eells had to spend much time hunting for their horses and cattle and driving them back home.

he sits at the table. His food is milk boiled for drink & he eats a little of anything but much bread & hulled corn.

WED. 20.   The cows were not found till late — had a bad time milking. Got somewhat vexed & out of patience.

THURS. Nov. 21.   Had trouble catching my calf. Mr. E. came to my assistance. Gave it a most severe threshing & lamed himself. Think as ever that mild treatment is best, to be sure the calf acted provokingly but what good could whipping do it?

SUN. 24.   Attended Indian worship in the new lodge. Have been reading the memoirs of S. Pierce.[63] Husband is off this evening guarding horses. Being alone I have indulged in many reflections. It affords me much satisfaction to see my husband persue the arduous labors before him with so much diligence & perseverance & apparent satisfaction. I think I am truly thankful it is thus. I feel much solicitude about our little son. I feel to leave him in care of a merciful Providence. I feel much satisfaction in the idea that I have him not at my disposal & that God will spare his life or take him away as he shall see best. What a mercy we all enjoy good health. But with all my blessings how small my return. How inactive I am. I do nothing, feel nothing as I ought. I cannot think of heaven as a place to which I am destined. I see so much in my heart that is unholy.

MON. Nov. 25, 1839.   An eventful day to the Flat Heads. An alphabet was formed [64] & the first lesson given in learning to read. They seem much interested. Poor creatures. I hope they are destined to see better days.   . .

THURS. 28.   A sad lonely evening on account of the reproaches of my dear husband. If I deserve them I am sorry, if not, am no less so. I do not know what the most dutiful wife could do for the most deserving husband that I have left undone. I never forget that he is a frail treasure of which I may soon be deprived. I endeavor to discharge my duties faithfully as in the sight of God & when I find my best endeavors fail to receive that confidence & affection I so much prize, it is as tho a milldew had blasted all my hopes. Must my happiness be thus snared always? What can I do that I have not done?

FRI. Nov. 29.   All day the dejected countenance [65] of my husband caused me to feel no less so. But he seemed more cheerful in the evening. Drilled his Indians till one was fast asleep at his feet.

SAT. 30.   We have a long thaw. The snow is gone. More or less rain

---

[63] A review of the titles of the books that Mary listed in her diary shows that she majored on the lives of missionaries and famous ministers.

[64] The missionaries had for their guidance in this great task of reducing a language to writing an essay by John Pickering on "A Uniform Orthography for the Indian languages of North America," published in the *Memoirs of the American Academy of Arts and Sciences*, Cambridge, 1820.

[65] Elkanah was often subject to moody spells when, as he once stated, "the blue devils chain me down."

for many days past. Clothes put out on Mon. did not dry till to day. The weather now clear but very mild.

SUN. 1 DEC. A remarkably pleasant day. Have read till I am tired. If I had a news paper or something just from press, think I would sit up & read till late. How I wish I could hear from home at this interesting season of the year.

MON. DEC. 2. Concert. TUES 3. Prayer Meeting.

WED. DEC. 4. The weather is still warm & rainy. Husband quite indisposed. I think I never before felt so unreconciled to the idea of our little son being [with] nothing but Indians & . . . [that he is denied] the blessings of civilized life. Yet how much happier his lot than that of any Indian child. If ever I look back it is when I think of him. For his sake I could wish we[were] back. But it was my duty to come hither. I trust my child will be provided for. But it is a subject in which my faith almost fails me.[66]

FRI. 6. Cold, pleasant weather. Husband still somewhat indisposed.

SAT. 7. Son is one year old today. Has three teeth. Walks most of the time, but continues to creep yet. He is into all manner of mischief. I hope we are not unmindful of the goodness of God in sparing his life & blessing him with health. May it not be in vain that his life is spared but may he live to be a blessing to his generation & those that come after. Our hope is in God who sheweth mercy to thousands of them that love him. May the prayers of our progenitors who sleep in Jesus, the prayers of those who still suplicate his mercy, be answered in behalf of our dear child. In anticipating the life of a missionary, nothing seemed so trying as the thought of becoming a mother & seeing my children exposed to the influences of heathen or shut from the privileges of civilization & Christianity. And now I fear I may more than realize my darkest anticipations. But I can but hope that he who has so mercifully provided for me will not forsake mine.

SUN. DEC. 8. Husband more unwell. May his life & health be very precious in thy sight, O Lord.

MON. 9. Begin to feel much alarmed about my husband. Through the day he seemed rather stupid but to night he appeared to be delirious. I am filled with apprehensions & concern. The Lord deal mercifully with us.

TUES. 10. Husband seems in his right mind again. It affords me some relief. But still he is sick. We gave him asafetida last night & applied a blister to his arm. He was very restless till past 12 last night when he seemed [to] get easy & slept pretty well till morning. He walked to Mr. Eells to day. . .

WED. 11. In the morning husband seemed no better. Took a potion

[66] Here Mary touches on a problem which has been of deep concern to all Christian missionaries who have children while stationed among peoples of other religions and of different cultures.

of calomel which operated well after which he began to vomit. He then took an emetic which had a thorough operation. His head seems relieved & I trust he is in a fair way to recovery. I am glad & I think I may add thankful.

FRI. 13 DEC. I proposed when I commenced this journal to let you know my heart. But I think I do not always do it. My heart to night is that when my husband scolds me it makes me feel very unhappy & I wish when he does so again he would stop to consider whether his poor, frail wife deserves it.

SAT. 14. Received letters from below [i.e. Waiilatpu.] [67] Mr. Gray has returned to Clear Water or proposes to. Mrs. Spalding has a son. Mrs. Hall a daughter. Mrs. Gray is in great trouble. But do not know who is to blame.

SUN. 15. Wrote in the morning to Mrs. Perkins & a note to Mrs. Hall.

MON. 16. Wrote to Mrs. Whitman.

WED. 18. Husband left for Colvile. Rainy most of the day. . .

SAT. 21. Still rainy. Have hard work to keep the people out & harder still to keep Cyrus & his girl in.

SUN. 22. A long sabbath. Have been reading Andrew Fuller's Memoirs.[68] Reports say Mr. McLean is at Colvile. Fear husband will be tempted to engage in conversation not proper for sabbath day. It makes me feel sad to sit down & read to myself all day & think how many about me have nothing profitable to occupy their minds. I hope I shall some day know enough of this language to be able to instruct them. But I feel discouraged when I attempt to impart anything to them.

TUES. 24. Have heard that husband did not leave Colvile yesterday. Am some tired of living alone.

WED. 25 . . . Husband returned altho he did not leave C. till yesterday. Mr. McLean reached C. on Sunday. Mr. McDonald loaded him [i.e., Elkanah] with good things, pork, beef, buffalo tongues,[69] cheese, &c. So we are likely to live very comfortably.

THURS. 26. Still raining & snow alternately.

---

[67] Mrs. Whitman's letter to Mrs. Walker, dated Dec. 3, 1839, now in Coll. c., Yale Univ., contains the following: "The afflictive Providence of God in removing our darling babe from our sight taught us to *forgive as we would be forgiven.* . . As I have once asked your forgiveness for injuring your feelings, so I now do again."

[68] Among the items received by the author from Sam Walker, the youngest son of Elkanah and Mary Walker, in the summer of 1939 for deposit in Coll. WN. were a number of volumes from the "Columbia Mission Library." Included as No. 207 was "The Complete Works of the Rev. Andrew Fuller." Fuller was a famous English divine who lived 1754-1815.

[69] Dried or pickled buffalo tongues were considered a great delicacy. These had been carried to Fort Colvile from the buffalo country by McLean.

FRI. 27. Succeed very tolerably in making mince pies without apples. To day the weather warm & pleasant, to night cold & freezing & clear. Hus. still rather indisposed, considerably so when he left Colvile but think his journey was beneficial tho he had a hard jaunt home. . .

SUN. DEC. 29. Husband able to talk to the people once, at least he did tho perhaps not well able. Feel lonely to night. Wish husband would converse about something. Fear we are not that society for one another which man & wife ought to be. Wish I could find what it is prevents our being [so.]

TUES. Thanks to God for all the goodness & mercy which have crowned the departed year.

1840 — HOUSEKEEPING IN THE WILDERNESS

By 1840 life in the Walker home at Tshimakain had settled down to a routine. Much of Elkanah's and Mary's time and energy had to be given to the necessary duties of providing for their material wants. Elkanah had to cultivate the garden and the fields. Hours were spent in hunting for his animals which had wandered away in search of forage. In his letter to Greene dated September 12, 1839, Elkanah reported: "In addition to my other labors I have travelled in regular journies about two thousand miles." Of course this was on horseback. In 1840 he was to travel even more. Not counting his short trips to Indian camps in the vicinity of Tshimakain, Elkanah made seven long trips for supplies or on mission business, including three to Fort Colville, two to Lapwai, and two to Walla Walla or Waiilatpu. Counting the days of departure and return, these trips consumed a total of fifty-four days.

Mary's diary reveals the extent and the monotony of the never-ending tasks which devolved upon her. To begin with she had to do her cooking, baking, washing, and ironing under the most primitive conditions. In addition she had to dip candles, make soap, milk the cows, work in the garden, churn butter, dry or pickle fruit and meat, and sew. Their rudely constructed cabin brought its problems. The door did not always keep out the cold wintry wind. Once a portion of the wall collapsed bringing down with it a part of the roof. And in rainy weather the dirt covered roof leaked. Fortunately through all of the vicissitudes and labors of the year, Mary's health remained excellent.

The year was highlighted by three important events. In February the boxes of personal belongings, which had been sent nearly two years previous by sea around South America, arrived. On May 24 a daughter was born. And in September Elkanah and Mary with their two children made a two weeks' trip to Fort Colville. For Elkanah this was in addition to his other trips previously mentioned. For Mary this excursion was the second time she had been away from Tshimakain since her arrival about eighteen months earlier.

Added to all such duties was the continuing necessity to study the language and to impart such religious knowledge as was possible to the natives. Both Elkanah and Mary bemoaned the fact that they could give but little time to the object of their going to Tshimakain. On September 18, 1840, Walker wrote to Greene saying in part: "It is impossible for me to do much at studying the language when I am worn out with labor." However, the missionaries began a school for the natives in the fall of 1839, which continued through the following winter. Eells in a letter to Greene, dated February 25, 1840, wrote: "At first it was composed of little more than thirty members, but has been gradually increasing so that it now numbers more than eighty." The Indians constructed a lodge to be used for the school and as a meeting place for their worship services.

Although the presence of the white people in their midst continued to be a novelty to the Indians, yet both of the white families increasingly felt the need for privacy. Mary mentions the difficulties she sometimes had to keep the natives out of her home and of the annoyance caused by the Indian children who loitered outside her door. Limitations of space demand that some of the entries for the year be deleted. However, the new and the unusual together with Mary's observations and soliloquies will be retained.

WED. JAN. 1, 1840.   Mr. & Mrs. E. dined with us.[1] We had roast beef, baked pork & plum pudding, mince pies, fried cakes, bread, butter, cheese & hulled corn for dinner. Commenced writing letters home.

FRI. 3.   For a week past our roof has leaked very much, so that the house is now very damp.

SUN. 5.   I wish I had any feeling or activity about me. I am as one asleep. When shall I awake to a just sense of my own situation & that of the perishing about me. It seems as if I were a disciple of Christ I should be more like him. Have much more I might do if I had a heart to do it. . .

TUES. 7.   About 60 Indians came to day from the barrier. Our house still continues to leak. . .

FRI. 10.   Last night a powerful rain. Our roof still continues to leak some To night an express from W.W. Dr. W. sent us some sugar & molasses.[2] Also a dozen apples apiece. The first we have had at Tshimakain.

TUES. 14 . . .   last night clear & freezing. Husband still con-

---

[1] According to Mary's diary, the one holiday each year which was the most regularly observed by the missionaries was New Year's Day. A special feast was held on that day in either the Walker or the Eells home.

[2] Undoubtedly the sugar and molasses were a part of the gift from the Honolulu Mission, mentioned by Mary in her entry for May 17, 1839.

tinues quite unwell. . . I forbear to write my gloomy thoughts & say prepare me Lord for whatever awaits me in mercy or affliction. [End of sixth notebook of Mary's diary.]

WED. JAN. 15, 1840. Visited to day the Indian lodges for the first time. . .

FRI. 17. Cool pleasant weather for several days past, still writing letters. Husband some better I think.

SAT. 18. Mr. Angus McDonald arrived on his way to W.W. Mr. W. concluded to accompany him.

MON. 20. Mr. Walker left this morning about nine We had to do more to prepare for his starting on Sunday that we ought perhaps. I feel not very anxious about him. Trust he will have a prosperous journey. But the time till his return seems rather long in anticipation. I sent letters by him to Mrs. Smith, Gray, & Griffin, also to my three sisters by [way of] S.I.

21. TUES. Took as I suppose some so called cream of tartar but it operated so powerfully as an emetic that I think it is tartar emetic. . .

WED. JAN. 22 . . . Had quite a fuss getting Simpleton out of the house this morning. But succeeded with the help of Mr. E. He was however so mad or ashamed that he did not attend worship. Have fixed up a mat in the kitchen so that it suits me pretty well. . .[3]

FRI. 24. Have worked as hard as I dared to, fixing the kitchen & putting up mats. . . The children kept crowding at the door all day till I got out of patience. I had them go away but they did not mind so I took a stick & shook it amongst them, but could not hit any but they fled & were out of the way the rest of the day. . .

SUN. JAN. 26. More stormy to day than any day before this winter. My husband has reached Waiilatpu. Think if it is as wintry there as here he will feel anxious about home. The day has seemed long tho I have been much interested in reading Baxter's Memoirs.[4]

MON. 27. Colder. Several of the children & big girls crowded into the house & stayed till I drove them off. Finished working on the house. The poor cattle are very cold & hungry but the ground is only partly covered with snow.[5] The cow gives scarce a pint of milk. Poor son will have to go without soon. . . Fear husband has taken a wintry time for his journey.

TUES. 28 JAN. The Indians stayed out well & did not trouble me at all.

---

[3] Both the Walkers and the Eells lined the walls of their homes with Indian mats.

[4] Among the items given to the author by Sam Walker (fn. 68 in preceding section) was vol. 155 from the "Columbia Mission Library," entitled *Select Practical Writings of Richard Baxter*. This is now in the library of the Eastern Washington State Historical Society, Spokane. Another volume given to the author by Sam Walker was Bunyan's *Pilgrim Progress*, No. 44, now in Coll. w.

[5] As yet the missionaries had no barns, so their animals had to stay out all winter. When the snow was deep, they had to paw through it to get forage.

TSHIMAKAIN MISSION DRAWN BY GERMAN BOTANIST, K. A. GEYER, IN 1843
The Eells family occupied the house in the central foreground, and the Walkers the
house to the left. The original drawing is at Washington State University, Pullman.

TSHIMAKAIN MONUMENT
This granite memorial was dedicated
on October 29, 1908. Descendants of
the two families took part in the
ceremonies. The above picture, taken
in 1940, appeared in the *Spokesman-
Review* for July 31, 1960.

THE TSHIMAKAIN MISSION SITE AS IT APPEARED IN JULY 1960

The farmhouse stands near the site occupied by the Eells cabin. The spring still flows through the building to the rear of the house. Back of the small center building is the well. Immediately to the left of the house is a large lilac bush or tree which must date from the mission period. Further to the left are two crab apple trees, also very old.

The view from the hill back of the house looks across Walker's Prairie in a northwest direction. A small stream flows at the edge of the trees. The view east across the prairie to the present buildings is from the bank of Tshimakain Creek. Photos by the author.

WED. 29. A rainbow about three o'clock P.M. such as I never saw before. The weather clear & cold. The bow was nearly overhead & instead of bending as usual towards the horison, it described about one third of a circle about the zenith. . .

THURS. 30. The people have kept out. Have succeeded in doing quite a large wash tho cold as ever.

SAT. FEB. 1. Felt quite out of patience this morning on account of the miserable old door. The cats & the Indians, first one & then the other, would knock out a piece & the wind came in without the least ceremony so that I could not be comfortable in the room long enough to get my breakfast. I was tempted to fret but concluded I would go & work to see if I could not fix it up. So I nailed it together as well as I could . . . so that it is quite comfortable. . .

SUN. 2. Weather more moderate. Finished reading Baxter's life.

MON. FEB. 3. As much or more snow than we have had. . . Should like to know how husband is. Feel some anxious about him. Half hope he is still at W. engaged in preparing a small book. I wish I could do something. It seems to me I am not a very good missionary.

WED. 5. More snow. Wish I knew where husband is & how he fares. Son talks about him a great deal & seems to want to see him. We were nearly out of wood but to day Mr. E. has drawn us some. Shall be very glad to have husband at home again. Tired [of] keeping watch against [the] Indians. But they were never in the house less.

THURS. 6. Plenty of rain last night. Very lonely to day, feel anxious about my husband. . . Have felt very bad in thinking of our little son. Fear when it comes warm weather he will be out with the Indians all the time. Feel that the responsibility resting on a parent is more than I know how to sustain & shrink at the prospect of renewing the relation. . .

SUN. 9. More snow to night, fear husband will have as much of travelling in the winter as he will want. Have been writing letters most of the day as I could not bring my mind into a reading mood.

TUES. 11 FEB. Still more snow. The Indians think that Snake River is frozen so that husband cannot get home. I wish I could hear from him. Think . . . he must be obliged to travel very slow. . . Shall be glad [if] we had more wood.

FRI. 14. More snow & rain. About despair of seeing husband very soon. Very anxious about him. Spend most of the day trying to compose verses in Flathead. In the evening our prayer meeting. After which Mrs. E. & I were talking that probably Mr. Walker was at W. still when we were surprised by his arrival. I was never sensible of greater joy. He is in good health for him & has had a prosperous journey. Did not find snow of any consequence till three days before reaching home.

SAT. 15. Unpacked & looked at my things, find very little injured. A pleasant day for drying & airing them. . .

WED. 19. Washed. Still we have snow but not very cold weather. Glad Husband is not travelling.

SAT. 22 FEB. A bad cold & inflamed eyes. . .

TUES. 25. Showers & sunshine. Thermometer at 50°. Snow goes fast. Husband watched horses last night. The Simpleton having deserted. My eye still prevents me from reading or sewing much.

SAT. 29. My eye has got better. Son complains some on account of milk, tho he gets a half gill a day. The snow is going fast. . .

SUN. MARCH 1. Reading life of Brainard.[6]

MON. 2. This morning a part of the wall of our house fell. Husband was in bed in the room when it began to fall. He escaped without being hurt much. Sons little chair was broken to pieces, after he has been sitting in it in the very spot where it fell. Scarcely the least thing besides was injured. The chimney fell with the wall & roof. Just as they fell it was beginning to rain . . . but it soon ceased & it was determined the roof must be removed . . & having cleared out the books & some other things & covered the bed with skins, they set about removing the roof. After working a little while, they left to attend a funeral, were detained some time. Just as they returned, there was a shower of rain sufficient to have wet the room pretty thoroughly . . . they were unable to remove the roof till the shower was over. They succeeded in getting the roof on again & the room in so comfortable a fix we can sleep in it to night. We have much to remind us that here we have no abiding place & that soon our earthly tabernacle will be dissolved. Thus we have great cause of gratitude that no more calamity has befallen us. . .

WED. 4. Husband repaired the fallen chimney so we [are] getting quite comfortable again.

THURS. 5. A year ago to day we left Waiilatpu & two years ago [from] Baldwin [Maine.] Surely thus far goodness & mercy have followed us.

SAT. 7. Putting up mats & fixing our house which is now as good as before it fell.

SUN. 8. Went this morning to the lodges. . . This P.M. communion, Mr. Walker administered. . . This evening I feel sad that my husband cannot be content to spend one hour with me. It must appear to other people that he is better contented anywhere than at home.

TUES. 10 MARCH. Pleasant weather. Indians moving off. The plain

---

[6] Probably a reference to Jonathan Edward's, *Memoirs of David Brainerd.*

is flooded. Trying to make soap & preparing letters to be sent to the States. Son plays out of doors most of the time. To day is entirely without milk for the first time. He seems to be quite as well as when he had milk but requires much care in feeding. . .

THURS. 12. With the help of our Indian children, make a big wash. The wind commences blowing violently.

FRI. 13. More wind that we have ever had at this place. Blows down a tree near the house. It fell partly on the store house.[7]

SAT. 14. Last night the wind abated. . . A pleasant day. Dried the clothes washed on Thurs.

MON. 16. Mr. Walker has gone with the horses to the big river. Mr. E. says the grass there is six inches high. Last night we had several inches of snow. . .

WED. 18 MARCH. Last night the thermometer was nearly as low as it has been this winter, that is four below zero. Husband came home with the horses having had a cold time. . .

SAT. 21. Make out our bill for Vancouver . . . finishing letters to send by Mr. E. who designs to start on Monday for W.W.

MON. 23. Mr. E. left for W.W. The weather mild & pleasant. Cut Cyrus' hair for the first time.

FRI. 27. Mr. Walker commenced ploughing to day. . . Snow mostly gone. Cyrus happy as can be, plays out of doors most of the time. When he is thirsty he comes in, find a cloth & puts it under his chin to signify he is ready to drink. When sleepy he hides his head in my lap & breathes hard to let me know he wishes to go to sleep. . .

SUN. 29. Feel discouraged in view of the little good I seem to be doing or have ever done or am ever likely to do in view of my stupidity. . . A very pleasant sabbath, have been reading Brainard's Life. I wonder that God in his Providence should ever suffer one so little fit for a Missionary to be sent out. O that the blessed influences of the Holy Spirit would so operate on my heart as to prepare me for greater usefulness.

TUES. 31. Washed with snow water probably for the last time this spring. The ground in many places begins to look green.

WEDNES. APRIL 1. My birthday, 29 years old. So teach us to number our days that we may apply our hearts unto wisdom. . .

SAT. APRIL 4. Husband ploughing. The plain looks green. . .

MON. 6. A fine gentle rain. Find myself of late in not so good health as I have often been. Cyrus is trying to spell & count. . .

WEDNES. 8. Mr. Eells returned from W.W. having had a prosperous journey. We have indeed a very few things compared with him. But

---

[7] One of the first buildings erected at Tshimakain was a small storehouse with a locked door.

it looks wasteful to see so many nice things almost without use in this country.[8] We are now about to have milk again. . .

MON. 13. Mr. Walker & Mrs. Eells left for Colville about 9 o'clock

SAT. 18 APR. Mr. Walker returned from Colvile. Weather pleasant but a cold raw wind. Mrs. E. stood her journey well & has received a letter informing her of her father's death which occurred Dec. 1838. Have been reflecting on the prospect of death. Find that children are a stronger tie than any other to bind me to earth. I feel that it would be trying indeed to think of dying & leaving them. . .

SUN. 19. Attended Indian worship not having done so for a long time. Feel discouraged in view of the little we are doing to benefit the Indians. Fear I am criminal in not doing more. It seems a pity they have nothing more to sing. I am certainly stupid to give myself any rest till [I] have sufficient command of the language to enable me to translate hymns.

FRI. 24. Mr. W. & E. have planted a part of their potatoes. Cornelius has returned apparently in a pretty good state of feeling. I ought to pay more attention to writing but get so tired I am not able.

SAT. APR. 25. Our Indian boy [William Threemountains ?] came later than usual in the morning. Mr. W. said nothing to him. I inquired the reason and it not being very satisfactory, I told him perhaps as he had not been awake long perhaps he was not hungry. He said he had already eaten at the lodges. I told him if the people fed him, perhaps it was good for him to help them instead of us. He remained about the door a few moments, look not just pleasant & then went to the lodges.

SUN. 26. Attended Indian worship. [In] P.M. Mr. McDonald the younger called on his way to W.W.

TUES. 28. To day all the Indians left except our girl. She appears to feel rather lonely. Thus we have no help now. Know not how we are to get along but trust some way will be provided. Am concerned to see my husband so constantly worn down with care & toil.

WED. APR. 29. For two nights past the cold has been quite severe, so as to freeze in our sleeping room quite hard.

FRI. MAY 1. Mr. E. [and Mrs. E.] set out for Colvile. Husband left

---

[8] Included in the boxes which Mrs. Eells had packed were silver spoons, fine linens, etc., which reflected the home of some means and culture out of which she had come. Eells, in his Reminiscences, tells of having shipped a small writing desk and a big bass viol with his other goods. While on the trip back to his home from Walla Walla with his household goods, one of his Indian assistants used the box with the desk and the viol as a hitching post. The animal, becoming alarmed, dragged the box over some rocks, completely demolishing its contents. As long as Eells lived at Tshimakain, he was never able to replace his beloved musical instrument. The only other member of the Mission who is known to have played an instrument was Gray, who played a flute.

alone. . . Mr. W. out till nine in the evening hunting horses so that I began to feel concerned lest some accident had befall[en] him.

SAT. MAY 2. Here I am far away in this remote wilderness alone with little son & happen what may, I know not where another human being can be found. Our girl left the house an hour or two since & for ought I know may have eloped. Husband has gone, I know not whither in search of his horses. Perhaps will miss his way or something else will befal him.[9] Things look dark, but I trust all will turn out well in the end.

Scarcely had I closed [my diary] when the girl returned & soon husband but without finding the horses. It was about noon & he sent off the girl to hunt. She found the track & followed it to the S. River, found the horses, rode one home driving the rest & arrived about sunset. Two Indians arrived expecting to find the people here.

SUN. MAY 3. A very quiet Sabbath. No Indians about except one of those who came yesterday. Have felt some concern lest I should be laid by [i.e. confined] before Mrs. E. returns.

MON. 4. Observed the M. concert in our solittude. . . Busy making soap.

TUES. 5. Dipped candles.

WED. 6. Washed &c. Mr. and Mrs. E. do not arrive.

THURS. MAY 7. Mr. & Mrs. E. returned from C. Arrived about noon. Brought Sarah Goudy & a boy home to live with them.

FRIDAY 8. Achieved with the aid of our girl the long dread job of cleaning out the store house. Mr. W. & E. give a horse a tremendous whiping. Felt ashamed of my own conduct on the occasion. Expected a reprimand from my husband which I happened to escape.

MON. 11. Made another dipping of candles, partly for Mrs. E.

TUES. 12. Washed. Was much fatigued.

WED. 13. Prepared & salted our buffalo tongues of which we have about two dozen. Mr. W. & E. planting corn. A few Indians returned. Among whom is the boy evidently not as well off as when he went away.

FRIDAY 15 MAY. Sowed our garden. About 5 P.M. Dr. & Mrs. Whitman arrived. We were not looking for them so soon.

SUN. 17. The Dr. & wife being here, observed the communion. No Indians & no Indian worship.

MON. 18. Dr. W. & wife left for Colvile. Mr. W. accompanied them as far as the Fool's place.

TUES. 19. Mr. E. left for Walla Walla. His wife much afflicted with headache.

---

[9] Mary's frequent reference to her concern about the welfare of her husband reveals a deep inner sense of anxiety. Far removed from her relatives, she was haunted with the thought of what would happen to her and her child if something happened to her husband.

SAT. 23. Very busy trying hard to get a little the start of my work. Have accomplished most that I expected to. Especially a job of baking. . . Much work is suffering to be done. Mr. W. able to do but little. Dr. W. & wife arrived from C. about 5 o'clock this evening.

MAY 24, 1840, SUNDAY. Rested well last night. Awoke about 4 o'clock A.M. Rather restless. Arose at 5. Helped about milking. But by the time I had done that found it necessary to call my husband & soon the Dr. Had scarcely time to dress & comb my hair before I was too sick to do it. Before eight was delivered of a fine daughter with far less suffering than on the birth of our son. The morning was pleasant. In the P.M. fine thunder shower. Babe very quiet. Think it weighs not more than eight pounds.

MON. MAY 25. Rested pretty well last night. Husband slept near; the babe required to be taken up by once. Succeed pretty well in nursing it. . .

TUES. 26. Dr. W. left. I took medicine. Babe quiet. All getting on well. Am greatly rejoiced that I succeed so well in nursing. Mrs. Whitman seemed to feel better than when she came.

WED. 27 MAY. Mr. W. washing. All continues about so.

THURS. 28. Last night slept but little. My milk having wasted so that I had not enough to satisfy the babe & nothing prepared to feed it. The nipples too are getting bad so that she can hardly draw them. So having spent much of the day in fruitless attempts in which I could not avoid exposure, took cold. Was much exhausted by fatigue & want of sleep. Also experienced a great degree of nervous excitement.

FRI. 29. The former part of the night sick & restless. Took assefedita, applied hot rocks to my breast which seem to afford much relief. After midnight got several naps. This morning felt much better & continue to do so through the day. Feed the babe for the most part, mostly with breast milk. . . I sweat profusely most of the time so that it is almost impossible to avoid taking cold. Do not begin to eat anything yet but gruel, bread, water & milk.

SAT. MAY 30. Very rainy. Roof leaks. Mr. E. returns from W.W.

SUN. MAY 31. Up and dressed for the first time. Feel pretty well tho I was very tired last night in consequence of a long worry with the babe. Suspect I have stirred quite as much as I ought to day.

JUNE 1. MON. Plenty of Indian help to day. Mr. W. puts on the mud roof again over our room The garden fence is built & the people are trying to get away our girl. Went out of doors this morning.

TUES. JUNE 2. Very anxious this morning about my babe, having [given] it some paregoric [10] last night which caused it to sleep almost

[10] Paregoric was used to assuage pain. It was a camphorated tincture of opium. We are amazed that Mary should have given such a medicine to a week-old infant. See Mary's entries for Aug. 15, 1839, and Jan. 21, 1840, where mistakes were made in the use of medicines.

without waking all night & till past noon when she awoke & continued awake for several hours. Went to dinner in Mrs. E's [house.]

WED. 3.   Feel pretty well to day. Have taken a walk in the garden, picked sallad & radishes. The air very clear & dry, enjoy it much.

THURS. 4.   Mrs. E. is nearly sick. I have made my bed & taken care of my children & it takes nearly all my time. The little one wakeful to day.

SAT. 6.   Rode out in the morning. Was less fatigued than I expected to be. In the afternoon baked & commenced eating at home Think I have gained strength surprisingly fast for several days past.

SUNDAY JUNE 7.   Feel much rejoiced . . . to find my health so far restored & my little ones doing so well. I feel encouraged to hope that I shall finally succeed in nursing. My babe is very quiet. . . She does not require to be fed or taken up in the night. (Have been reading Mrs. Trollopes Domestic Manual of the Americans the past two weeks, find her disgustingly interesting.) We have given the babe the name of Abigail Boutwell. . .

TUES. 9.   Yesterday morning Mr. W. left for C. I arose at three in the morning, assisted in fixing him off. Milked, baked bread & did a part of my washing. Towards night found my babe was beginning to have a sore mouth. She was very worrisome so that I could not retire to rest till eleven o'clock in the evening, tho so tired & sleepy I almost let my babe fall from my arms. The latter part of the night rested well. Cyrus slept quietly. Towards night he began in a mournful tone to say papa. Since I have been sick, he has expected no care from me but has clung to his father. He seems to admire his sister & kisses her altho he has scarcely been prevailed on to kiss any one else. Being at loss how to [show] his kind feelings, the other day he put his fingers in her hair & then in his mouth in imitation, no doubt, of an Indian looking [for lice in] another's head. He probably sees them doing thus & supposes them discharging to each other an act of kindness. I worked so hard yesterday I feared I should be sick to day. . . Altho I rose so early I could not find a moment's time to lie down the whole day.

THURS. 11.   Mr. W. returned from C. well supplied with pork & flour. . .

FRI. 12.   This morning by an express from Colvile learned that Mr. Lee's reinforcement has arrived & that plenty of letters are on the way for us. . .[11]

SUN. 14.   Son quite sick. Little daughter wakeful & tearful. . . Have scarcely read any to day.

TUES. 16.   An express arrived with our letters. They contain less bad intelligence than I expected. . . The news that Mr. G.[12] is

---

[11] The "Lausanne" with the Methodist reinforcement of fifty-one, including women and children, dropped anchor at Fort Vancouver on June 1, 1840.

[12] Undoubtedly a reference to her former suitor, Joshua Goodwin.

living in a good house does not make me less contented in my own miserable hut. Surely it is better to dwell in the corner of a house with one than in a big one with another. Sat up till 1 o'clock at night to read & then could not read nearly all.

WED. JUNE 17. Cyrus is some better but very cross. Babe wakeful. So much excited myself I can do little tho I have much that needs to be done immediately. The Indians trouble me in trying to get away my girl again. Sometimes almost wish her gone.

THURS. 18. The girl [Kwantepetser ?] went to worship in the morning. Did not return as usual. Soon her father came to inquire why she was crying. We told him we did not know, but if she wished to go away & not return, she might go. Towards night she returned, took her things & went away. On some accounts, I felt very sad to see [her] go, on others very glad. I trust the affare is directed by an all wise Providence & all is for the best. It will be much more pleasant for me to get along alone if I can. But I fear it will be nearly impossible for me to do it.

FRI. 19 JUNE. Thus far miss the trouble of the girl as much as the help. Felt this morning as if I could sing as heartily as any Methodist

> There's better days a coming
> For I feel it in my soul.

SAT. 20. Find more & more every day in the character of the Indians to try & perplex me.

JUNE 21. The Old Chief [13] came to the house this morning, seemed quite pleasant. . .

WED. 24. Yesterday washed alone & cleaned my room better than it has been for a long time & thought we looked quite comfortable. But this morning the roof over the kitchen was found to be falling in & had to be removed. A dirty bad job enough.

THURS. 25. Got the house cleaned a little again.

SAT. 27. Cooked provisions for husband's journey.[14]

SUN. 28. The children & other things take all my time. Read not a word the whole day. . .

---

[13] After this date, Mary preferred the title Old Chief to the name Cornelius. Lt. Charles Wilkes, USN, who visited Tshimakain in June, 1841, gave the following description of Cornelius: ". . . is about sixty years of age, tall and slender, with a dignified carriage; has a thin, wrinkled face, and a far-retreating forehead. He has an expression of intelligence and self-possession, which impresses a visitor very favorably. He is represented as being very pious; and, as far as outward appearances and loud praying go, is certainly entitled to be considered." *Narrative of . . . Exploring Expedition*, IV: p. 438.

[14] Walker and Eells both attended the annual meeting of the Mission which began its sessions at Lapwai on July 4. At this meeting, Walker was chosen Moderator. Both Walker and Eells exercised a moderating effect in the growing tensions which were so apparent at the other stations.

Mon. 29 June. Mr. W. & E. left for Clear Water about half past five this morning. Have taken all their horses [15] & left the cows in charge of the chief. The Indians have behaved well.

Tues. 30. All goes well. Have made out to take care of my babes, milk & wash.

Thurs. 2. Very warm. No Indians about except the Chief & his family who all conduct [themselves] with the utmost propriety. . .

Sat. 4. Tended my babe most of the day. Picked greens & washed them with her in my arms. Mrs. McDonald arrived with her family about five o'clock P.M.

July 5. Mrs. E. dressed the children & took care of the babe. I milked & got breakfast for the company. We seem to get along better than I feared. . .

Mon. 6. Have put up some curtains to our bed. Took a walk. We are on very neighborly terms with Cornelius. He sent us to night a big fish. Mrs. McDonald & children call our large bowls saucers. . .

Tues. 7 July. My little babe very quiet. Have milked three cows, got breakfast, dinner & supper for the company & worked a little in the garden.

Fri. 10. Washed, ironed, baked, & what is worse than all, milked. The cows & calves so unmanageable, it takes so long I get all out of patience. Shall be glad to [have] husband home again

Sat. 11. Mr. W. & E. returned. Arrived about five P.M. . .

Sun. 12. Mrs. McDonald & her family all attended worship. . . The thermometer above 100.

Tues. 14. Mrs. McDonald, her family & ours all except Mrs. E. went down to the Barrier. Saw Indians spearing fish. Met Mr. McD's men returning from V[ancouver,] also the Catholic priest who took tea with us.[16]

Wed. 15. Mrs. McD. with her family left us a little after sunrise.

Sun. 19. Attended the Indian worship, a large number present. The school is now in operation & pretty well attended. The aspect of our mission is rather encouraging. Mr. W. is quite unwell much of the

[15] Being unwilling to leave their horses and mules unattended during their absence of nearly two weeks, Walker and Eells felt it necessary to drive the whole band (exact number unknown) with them to Lapwai.

[16] Father Modeste Demers was back at Fort Colville during the summer of 1840. Walker in his letter to Greene, of Sept. 12, 1839, reporting on the activities of Father Demers at Colville during the preceding summer, wrote: "He said among other things [i.e. to the natives,] that they must not come to us." And, ". . . he told them that he should soon baptize them & that when they died they would go to heaven." The Protestant missionaries were not willing to baptize until the candidates had a conversion experience. In the light of this background, we know there was a strained feeling between the Roman Catholic and the Protestant missionaries even though Father Demers accepted the Walkers' invitation to take tea with them.

time. We need help very much. My hands are very bad now & make me feel rather discouraged some times. Cyrus grows fast in stature & mind. Abigail is very quiet & patient, very unlike her brother. I feed her in part with cow's milk.

MON. JULY 20. Mr. Walker left for W.W. I spent the day cording my bed & sitting our little room at rights.

TUES. 21. Washed & got a boy to help me mend the chimney.

WED. 22. Put up mats; traded berries,[17] &c.

THURS. 23. Busy as ever, scarcely time to eat. Trade berries, &c.

FRI. 24. A fine shower today. Ironed, boiled brine &c. . .

SAT. 25. Finished putting up mats & picked over feathers which nearly completed a lot of little jobs on hand. My hands are too bad to allow me to sew. I trust Providence has some good design in thus afflicting me, yet I am anxious to have once more the free use of my hands. Last night a frost killed the vines a little.

SUN. 26 JULY . . . Attended worship. Few present except the children. Feel very anxious to be doing something more. Perhaps I could teach if I should undertake [it.]

MON. 27. Made a first attempt at teaching. Think I succeeded pretty well as the children seem pleased & are telling over their new ideas, & just now when I asked who would bring my washing water, several answered. I went out to the lodge, took both my children & they were very quiet. I gave them a lesson in geography on an egg shell which I had painted for a globe.

TUES. 28. Have got alone with milking, washing, teaching & taking care of my children very well. . .

THURS. 30. Detected a girl to day in thieving.

SAT. AUG. 1. Got along better than I expected I could in teaching. . I have now every day the satisfaction to think I have imparted a lit.tle information & learned generally several new words every day. Felt vexed with the Indians about the door because they ventured to enter the house while I was milking against orders.[18]

SUN. AUG. 2, 1840. Attended Indian worship. Should think I could have talked better than Mr. E. did. Was going to teach as on other days except would give a religious instruction, but Mr. E. said I had better not. . .

MON. 3. A.M. washed & ironed. P.M. husband returned from W.W.

---

[17] Mary made many references to various kinds of berries which ripened during the summer months including huckleberries, strawberries, "sepet or whurtleberries," "mountain berries," and the service berry. She mentioned making syrup out of "thorn berries" and making gooseberry preserves. Some berries were dried.

[18] The missionaries had to be constantly alert against petty thieving. Considering the fact that the white people were living among Indians who had an entirely different concept of property rights than those they held, we are amazed at the relatively little trouble the missionaries experienced on this score.

SUN. 9. Last week I went four time to teach the Indians. But it is all I can do to get along, do my work & take care of my children. How I can answer a single letter I do not know.

SUN. AUG. 16, 1840. The past week the weather has been very warm & as there have been but few children, I have not been to teach. . .

SUN. 23. Have felt the past week several times as if I could no longer endure certain things that I find in my husband. I find it difficult to gain relief on a subject like this. For I cannot speak of him — nor to him — & if I write I fear he will read. I suspect there is wrong on my part as well as his but I know no way to remedy it. What grieves me most is that the only being on earth with whom I can have much opportunity for intercourse manifests uniformly an unwillingness to engage me in social reading or conversation. I remember it was not always so & that actions & words promised it should never be. But thus it is & every day I feel it more & more & can see no way to remedy it. I would fain render myself more deserving by improving my [mind] but this I can not do as I am so pressed with care & labor that I can hardly find time to read even my bible & thus it is that makes me feel much more sensibly the need of social intercourse.

SUN. 30. The past week we have had frost enough to nearly kill the vines. On Friday Mr. W. went to Spokane to spend the Sabbath [with the Indians.] . . . My hands do not get well, yet, tho not as bad as they have been some times. The children are very well. Cyrus weighs more than 30 lbs & Abigail 12.

MON. SEPT. 7. Monthly concert this evening. Mr. Eells & W. are trying to make a book. . .

SUN. 13. We had Eng. worship out doors between our houses. Mr. Walker preached, the only sermon he has written since he has been in this country & administered the sacrament. Our little daughter was baptized by the name of Abigail Boutwell. May we be enabled so to discharge our duties to our children that a convenant keeping God may own & bless them.

Tonight Cyrus asked for his skiam [i.e., milk], his father told him to say please. But he would not & still he goes without it rather than to humble himself enough to say please. He has gone to sleep with a smile of exultation depicted on his countenance. I hope if he is ever called to suffer at the stake he will be as unrelenting.

TUES. 16 [15]. Washed, ironed &c. Got ready to start in morning.[19]

WED. 17 [16]. Left home half past eight in morning, overtook the express, received letters. . . Encamped at the Fool's. A fine moon shine. The children rested well, did not seem much tired.

---

[19] Elkanah and Mary and their children left this day for a short visit to Fort Colville. They returned to Tshimakain on September 26.

THURS. 17 SEPT.   Left camp half past 7. Arrived at C. at sunset.

FRI. 18.   Wrote a letter to my mother.

SAT.   The express left this morning.[20]

THURS. OCT. 1, 1840.   Last night the first severe frost. Killed all the potatoes & froze all the melons & our squashes.

SAT. 3.   We came from Colvile a week since. Had a pleasant time, rather cold coming home. . .

SAT. OCT. 10.   Mr. Eells returned from Colville, brought some pigs.

MON. 12.   Have written to Mr. Caldwell. . . A. begins to sit alone, is afraid of Indians.

TUES. 13.   Washed & ironed. Get along very well with my work. . .

MON. 19.   Mr. W. left for Colvile.

SUN. 25.   Yesterday Mr. Walker returned from C. was so fortunate as to meet the express but so unfortunate as to receive no letters. My three last letters were in season, tho I fear they would not be so. So I have succeeded in finishing my letters to the U.S.A. The people are now collecting in considerable number. Hope we shall be able to do something to benefit them.

MON. 26.   Mr. Walker gathered his garden sauce.[21] I churned. . .

WED. 28 . . .   About noon husband concluded the roof must be taken off over our bed room again & went right about it. Just at night an express arrived from Mr. Spalding. Mr. Smith has trouble with the Indians &c.[22] Dr. Whitman & others concludes best to give up the Mission, that is he proposes to sell it to the Methodists.[23] We are astonished & somewhat indignant to think they should think of such a thing.

THURS. 29 OCT.   We all wrote that we were not inclined to sell the Mission.

SAT. 31.   Trying to clear & regulate my house again. . .

TUES. Nov. 17.   Mr. Walker left for Mr. Spalding's yesterday morning. Towards night we received letters from the S.I., one from Portland, Maine. . . For several weeks I have been very busy, as my neglected journal will testify. Last week, Mrs. E. had, with a little help from me, [made] a duffle coat for Mr. Walker. The children are pretty well. Cyrus begins to repeat verses after me very well. I have felt lately to pray earnestly that he might not be taken from us without

---

[20] Possibly a reference to some special express leaving Fort Colville for Fort Vancouver. In her entry for Oct. 25, Mary seems to refer to the arrival of the trans-Canadian express which sometimes brought letters from the United States.

[21] An old use of the word sauce refers to all table vegetables as roots and greens.

[22] See Drury, *Diaries of Spalding and Smith*, 199, for an account of the crisis at Kamiah when the Indians threatened the lives of the Rev. and Mrs. Asa B. Smith.

[23] Smith in his letter to the Board, on Oct. 21, 1840, had suggested selling out to the Methodists. See also reference to this proposal in Drury, *Whitman*, 242. Actually Whitman was not in favor of giving up the Mission. In a letter to Greene dated Oct. 15, 1840, he stated: "No: Do not withdraw it."

experiencing a change of heart & giving evidence of the same. A. sits alone. . .

SUN. 22 Nov. I have spent some time the past week in fixing our bed room & now live in [it] most of the time. I find it almost as much as I can do to take care of the children, milk, tend my fire, &c from 6 o'clock in the morning till 7 at night. When I find so much that needs to be done, I can spare very little time to sleep. For several weeks I scarcely retired earlier than eleven & frequently sit up till 12 or one. I sometimes feel almost out of patience & discouraged not to say tired. Sarah G.[24] stays in our house most of the day. She helps me some & tires me more. . .

Cyrus arose this morning & after drinking went to see Mr. Eells. Then amused himself with books awhile, trying frequently to repeat — "I must not work" &c. but [his] pious mood was soon over & he began to tease for the hammer which I thought best not to give him, so he cried. Before noon he chased the pigs into the horse pen & there fell into a dirty puddle & came crying back in a sad plight. . . Mr. E. went to afternoon worship. Sarah & Cyrus both cried to go. To divert them I gave them the Encyclopedia [25] to look at the pictures. While they were looking, something troubled the hens & Sarah ran to see what it was. Cyrus ran too but not without first placing the big [book] on the table. He discovers every day a disposition to put things in their proper place.

Nov. WED. 25. This afternoon visited the lodges. Found several sick. . .

THURS. 26. Had a girl to day making C. some shoes.[26] Am up again till 12 [midnight] ironing, cooking &c.

FRI. 27. Rains to night. Have had a fire in the kitchen to day & baked, &c.

SAT. Nov. 28. Mr. Walker arrived from Mr. Spalding, of course without a book.[27] The printing press was not ready. To night gave little A. a smart slap & she minded but whether she understood that I hurt her designedly or not, I am not sure.

---

[24] Sarah Goudy, a half-breed girl from Fort Colville, was then living in the Eells home. At this time she was probably not more than five or six years old.

[25] Among the books received from Samuel Walker by the author in the summer of 1938 was an illustrated Encyclopedia, possibly the same volume as here mentioned by Mary. Now in Coll. WN. Note the remark of Cyrus: "I must not work." Since this was a Sunday, it is possible that Mary refrained from giving the hammer to Cyrus, for the use of it implied working on that day.

[26] All of the Walker children wore moccasins as did the Indians. Mary's diary contains frequent references to cutting out and sewing on them.

[27] See Mary's reference to a book in her entry for Sept. 7. The printing press from Hawaii had arrived at Lapwai in the spring of 1839. Walker took some copy for a Spokane primer to Lapwai but found that the press was not ready for use. The Spokane primer was not printed until 1842.

Mon. 7. Cyrus' birthday. Mr. Eells' folks took supper with us on the occasion. . .

Sat. 12. Rode to the river. The weather very mild. Children enjoyed it much.

Sun. 13. Attended worship at the new lodge.[28]

Mon. 14. Washed to day. Mr. E. left for Ponderie.[29]

Sat. 19. Mr. E. returned yesterday. Saw Gary.[30] Had rather an interesting visit.

Dec. 25. Have had as yet very little cold weather. The Indian school house seems prosperous. The girl who lived with us last year, on account of misconduct, is not allowed by the people to attend school or worship.

Mon. 28. Last week made my woolen dress and read some.

1841 — DISSENSION WITHIN THE MISSION

After 1840 we have a double look into the activities of the Walkers at Tshimakain because Elkanah resumed the keeping of his diary. Comments from his journal will be added as footnotes when such are pertinent to the entries Mary made. Among the main events of the year

[28] Mary occasionally dignified the lodge erected by the Indians for their worship services and for a school by calling it a chapel.

[29] Judging from many entries in Elkanah's and Mary's diaries, the two men took turns making trips to the Pend Oreille Indians (sometimes spelt Ponderay) living by the lake of that name.

[30] This is the first mention of Spokane Garry in Mary's diary. It was he who was so largely responsible for the Nez Perce "delegation" of 1831 which went to St. Louis for the white man's religion. See Drury, *Spalding*, pp. 76 ff., and his *Diaries of Spalding and Smith*, 107. Contrary to expectations Garry refused to cooperate much with the missionaries. Jessett, in his *Spokan Garry*, gives the following explanation: "Of the Calvinistic revivalism of Walker and Eells, with its demand for an emotional experience of conversion, he had no experience, and it probably repelled him." p. 76. Jessett develops the theory that Garry preferred Anglican ritual and doctrine and concludes, p. 91, that "The tribe preferred to stay with the simple Christianity taught them by Garry, and which they still practiced." Wilkes, who saw Garry in June, 1841, stated that upon his return from the Red River Mission school Garry's influence "was great in the tribe; but now, owing to his propensity for gambling, he has lost all influence." *Narrative*, iv: p. 460. Sir George Simpson of the Hudson's Bay Company, who was mainly responsible for the sending of Spokane Garry to the Red River school in 1825, visited the Spokane country in August 1841. Simpson in his *Journey Around the World*, p. 91, wrote that for a time after his return to his people, Spokane Garry was active in trying to teach his people but that "he had gradually abandoned the attempt, assigning as his reason, or his pretext, that the others 'jawed him so about it'." Simpson claimed that Garry then "relapsed into his original barbarism, taking to himself as many wives as he could get; and then, becoming a gambler, he lost both all that he had of his own and all that he could beg or borrow from others. He was evidently ashamed of his proceedings, for he would not come out of the tent to shake hands with an old friend."

*was the burning of the interior of the Eells' home on January 11 when
the thermometer registered 8½° below zero. The days that immediately
followed, when the house was being repaired, were even colder. In
March W. H. Gray arrived to help in the construction of new and
larger houses for both the Walkers and the Eells. He was supposed to
stay for five months but left after three weeks. The Walker house,
which measured 22 x 32 feet, was not completed until August, 1843.*

*Edwin, the elder of two sons born to Cushing and Myra Eells, ar-
rived on July 27. In June a party under the command of Lieutenant
Robert E. Johnson from the Wilkes Exploring Expedition, which was
then in the Pacific Northwest, visited Tshimakain. Other members of
this expedition came in September. Also in September, Henry and
Eliza Spalding arrived for a visit.*

*This was a troubled year because of dissension within the Mission.
The annual meeting was held at Waiilatpu in June, which both Walker
and Eells attended. Here the difficulties came to a climax before a
reconciliation was temporarily at least achieved. Both the Walkers and
the Eells were sick at heart over the developments. At Tshimakain the
two men carried on their evangelistic and educational labors to the
best of their ability and within the limits of available time. Mary
found herself so engrossed with the duties of her home that she had
little time for anything else.*

FRI. JAN. 1, 1841.   We are permitted to enter on the commencement
of another year under circumstances of great mercy. In regard to
habitation, food & raiment, we are comfortable & all in tolerable
health except Mrs. E. who tho now distressingly ill, will, we trust, soon
recover. Cyrus . . . is inclined to spend nearly all his time in the
house, occupies himself with tools & in trying to build houses. . .
He is fond of singing. Any thing almost serves him as a tuning fork.
Abigail is very healthy, fat & good natured. I get along with my work
very well tho I do not know whether I shall be able [to do] all that
will be necessary for Mrs. E. Mr. E. took [New Year's] supper with
us. I have made my dress that Mother sent me & like it well. In regard
to the Indians, all seems going well. The Chief behaves like a gentleman, is furnishing himself with implements of husbandry.

SAT. JAN. 2.   Have made an Indian a shirt. Attended on Mrs. E. a
little &c. . .

SUN. JAN. 3.   Did not attend worship.[1] Mrs. E. still seems better.

---

[1] E.W. (hereafter this abbreviation will be used to indicate a quotation from
Elkanah Walker's diary.) "Worship with the Indians at or near sunrise." This
seemed to have been a favorite time for the natives for their worship services.
The Missionary Herald, Dec. 1841, p. 435, gives the following quotation from a
letter of Eells dated March 8, 1840: "It has been a general impression among the
best informed Indians, that thieves, gamblers, Sabbath breakers, and such like will

Appears rather patient & resigned. Feel concerned for her but hope she will be carried safely through all that probably awaits her.

Mon. 4. The annual fast was observed in part. . .[2] This evening I have been baking but my mind has been very much in contemplation. I have been wishing I were more pious, regretting my coldness & stupidity with little resolution to do better. My husband & children seem to engross my heart & I fear they will be taken from me. I was thinking of the rose bush in Mother's garden when I was a child. I was so impatient to have the roses bloom that I used to pick the buds open, or try to, so that when the flower opened it was but a mangled flower. I have thought that parents often, and perhaps we are of that number, feel the same impatience in watching the opening of the infant's mind. It is certainly better to leave nature uninvaded. I wish not to see a forced maturity in children.

Tues. Jan. 5. Washed for Mrs. E. & myself. Had her Indian girl to help me a little. Garry came to our place for the first time. I had no opportunity to converse or scarcely to speak with him, altho anxious to do so. Hope he will yet become a blessing to his people.

Wednes. 6. Several inches of snow last night. Mr. Walker has gone to the river to stay a few days. Mrs. E. still seems mending. I have spent the evening filing & perusing old letters.[3]

Thurs. 7. Washing floors & baking for Mrs. E. & myself. . . Snowed all day. Mr. W. has a fine time to improve his health.[4] This evening busy with old letters.

Fri. 8. Husband returned to day. Ironed. Mrs. E. washed her floor this evening, think she is getting smart fast.

10. Jan. . . . Atten. worship. It is interesting to see so many people in so commodious a place of worship. The weather very cold to night. Mr. McLean informs us the priests are busy. I hope they will not be suffered to do much mischief.

Mon. 11. Rose early. Found I had taken cold in my breast. Set to work to doctor it. Worked till time for breakfast. Was dipping some

go to the place of misery when they die. But that such as are not guilty of open vices and attend to a form of worship will go above. We have labored to correct this and kindred errors, and unless we greatly mistake, our labor has not been in vain. The language of the chief is, 'I formerly thought my heart was good, but I now see it is not'." The essential message of the missionaries was not contained in a series of Puritanical do's and don'ts, but rather in the necessity of the individual having a living faith in Jesus Christ. They stressed the necessity of conversion after which a high morality would naturally follow.

[2] E.W. "The day set apart by the church universally for fasting & prayer for the spread & triumph of the gospel throughout the whole world."

[3] Many of these old letters which Mary so carefully filed, and which were used by the author in the writing of this work, are now in Coll. Wn.

[4] Elkanah with an Indian companion had left on a hunting trip. Only rarely do we find references to any of the missionaries making trips for recreational purposes. Elkanah noted in his diary: "Killed nothing."

toast when I heard an alarm call. Mr. E's house was on fire.[5] We exerted ourselves all we could to save it. Much lost & much saved. I worked as long as I could, almost froze my fingers. Found I was sick or something, gave up & went to bed. Sweat & steamed my breast, worked till I hope I got in a safe state. Feel much better. Mrs. E. has got through the day much better than I should have supposed she could. We all feel grieved for the loss. . . I hope this providence will be sanctified to us & to the Indians; some seem to feel that it is on their account. May we feel as we should.[6]

TUES. JAN. 12.   We have [passed] another day very comfortably. Mr. E's house is partially repaired. He has more saved than we at first supposed. We all feel that we have great reason for gratitude.

WED. 13.   Busy most of the day cooking. Mrs. E. making a tick & surveying the ruins of her house.

THURS. 14.   The coldest weather we have experienced in Tshimakain. Quite windy. If we should have to fight fire today it would be worse than it was the other morning. Think we have great reason to be thankful that both houses were not burnt. Am glad we had no difficulties to settle in order to live in peace all in one house.

FRI. JAN. 15.   Cold, cold. All we can do to keep comfortable.

SAT. 16.   So cold most of the family left the table to finish breakfast. The potatoes freeze in the cellar, have to build fire in it. Found the house was taking fire in consequence of the chimney being heated. Had to repair it, a cold treat for so cold a day. Our house is so open & so crowded & the weather so cold we can hardly make out to cook our food. Have not been able to wash this week. Mrs. E. is tolerably well but feels most discouraged sometimes. Mr. E. insists that he has always done right.[7] Perhaps he has & perhaps not. I am sorry to see him so severely punished even if he does deserve it. Shoshenamalt [8] came today with her leg badly frozen. She froze it yesterday getting wood. I dare say there were several young men sitting idle at the fire she built.

SUN. JAN. 17.   Just at sunset we were surprised by the arrival of Mr. McLean & another gentlemen with four men to assist Mr. E. The weather is still cold so I fear they will not be able to do much. We

[5] Evidently the mats which lined the walls of the Eells home had become ignited from the fire in the fireplace. E.W. "This has been one of the most sorrowful & sadest days ever seen in Tshimakain." The fire and the subsequent days of rebuilding came in an extremely cold period. Spalding noted in his diary for January 16 that the thermometer at Lapwai dipped to 26° below zero.

[6] Mary, like Job's comforters, assumed that the calamity came as a visitation of divine judgment for sin. Note her entry for the 16th, where Eells rejected such an assumption.

[7] E.W. "I fear Mr. Eells does not feel right about his loss — is disposed to justify himself too much."

[8] First mention of the Indian girl who, after Nov. 1842, was Mary's most faithful assistant for over five years.

hardly know how to manage for want of room. Mr. McDonald expresses much sympathy & we can hardly express our gratitude for his kindness.

Mon. 18. The weather much more mild. The men are at work trying to repair the burnt house. We are crowded but get along rather pleasantly. All I try to do is to cook. . .

Wed. 20 Jan. Mr. McLean & McPherson left this morning. Mr. Walker has gone to the river to guard horses.[9]

Thurs. 21. Washing & scrubbed a little. Mr. W. returned. . .

Fri. 22. Have gone thru the old course of affairs once more. Have felt a little racked at Mr. E's remarks about my husband & myself. Wish he had more pity or politness. . .

Sat. 23. Mr. E's house is ready to live in again as soon as the men are gone.

Sun. 24. Mr. E. continues his course of polite observations which keeps me in anything but a pleasant mood. I hope the poor man will soon be able to live more remote from an object of so much disgust and aversion. I find it difficult to imitate the example of him who when he was reviled, reviled not again.

Mon. 25. Mrs. E. is trying to clean a little. The men left to day. They observed a more quiet sabbath yesterday than they are accustomed to perhaps. I find our little hut has had a severe drubbing & requires to be thoroughly cleaned.

Tues. 26. Cleaned Mrs. E's earthen ware. Cooked for both families. Got offended as usual once or twice with Mr. E. Cyrus told a lie. He broke an ink bottle while I was out of the room & when I came told me his sister had done it. He was sitting by the fire when I left & when I returned was in the same spot. He was evidently frightened when he found he had broken the bottle & so resumed his seat in order to deceive me. I was disposed to punish him but his father let him go, but I fear he did wrong for it seems to me when a child can contrive so wilful a lie he knows what it means to be punished for it.

Wed. Jan. 27. Solomon returned bringing letters from Dr. W & Walla Walla. The Dr. is sick. The weather has been more severe than for five years before.

Thurs. 28. Had a boy to help me wash with whose help I made out to get a good share of washing done. I began before breakfast & have finished now about midnight, but I have had perhaps twenty rests. Little A. is not well & needs care. Mr. E's family still eats with us. So there is always enough to keep me busy.

Fri. Jan. 29 . . . Ironed & put up our bed curtains. Mr. W. not very well.

---

[9] There were meadows along the bank in the Spokane River canyon which, because of the lower elevation, had less snow and more grass than could be found on the highlands.

SAT. 30.   Getting the worse for wear. Mrs. E. sick so she just keeps about.

SUN. 31.   Mrs. E's family eat at their own house. She takes care of A. I go to worship. The weather fine. It is always affecting to me to attend the Indian worship & see so many poor almost naked people. One with the skin [of] one animal & another of another. May God grant them so to hear as to be saved.

MON. FEB. 1.   Mr. Walker left for Colvile about noon.[10] I ironed some, baked some &c. Mrs. E. washing altho hardly able to keep about. . .

TUE. FEB. 2.   Have found time to day to sew a little. Made a stew for Mrs. E. & us a supper. Some snow falling.

WED. 3.   Quite snowy. Think Mr. W. has not a very pleasant time. . .

THURS. 4   . . .   Mended a window & stockings & took care of the babies. A. has climbed up by things to day for the first time. She is in the fire or some mischief & requires constant watching. . .

FRI. 5.   Sick all day. Do nothing but tend my babies. Wish husband at home.

SAT. 6.   Husband has not returned, feel anxious about him   . . . washed up my children, milked, mended the chimney, &c.

SUN. 7.   A cold windy day. Should be glad to know my husband was in a comfortable place.[11] Have been reading the report of the A.B.C.F.M. . .

MON. FEBRUARY 8.   The weather still cold. Had the Indian bring plenty of wood to the door as I almost got out yesterday. Have an Indian girl make Cyrus a pair of shoes. . .   Reread a number of old letters.

TUES. 9.   Felt very anxious about my husband this morning lest some evil had befallen him. How soon I may be left to bathe my orphans in the tears of widow-hood. The girl who was so badly frozen came to make me a call, tarried several hours.

WED. 10.   Just at dark Mr. W. reached home. Brought a cow. All well. I am glad, I trust thankful. . .

FRI. 12.   Mr. Walker went to the River. He & Mr. W. returned with the horses. In the evening Mr. E. fell & cut his knee. Hope the wound will not prove bad.[12]

---

[10] Elkanah was out of chewing tobacco and felt it necessary to make the 140 mile round-trip to Colville in stormy weather to replenish his supply. At the Fort he got lonesome and wrote in his diary on the 5th: "There is no place so sweet as home. No man has a wife more deserving of the warmest affection than I have."

[11] Elkanah took advantage of his visit to Fort Colville to hold services there for the natives. He noted in his diary: "Walked about two miles to attend worship with the Indians. Had quite a congregation."

[12] E.W. "He felt doubtless some vexed with a cow & went to chastising her when he fell down & cut his knee quite bad & fainted."

SAT. 13. Cleaning & settling in order our little hut. Hope the day may come when we shall have a better house tho I could be content to live as we now do all my life long. Surely there are enjoyments sweeter than good houses & such like things can afford. . . The assurance I receive of the love & esteem of my dear husband is to me a source of gratitude & consolation. May we both grow more & more deserving of mutual regard.

SUN. FEB. 14. Mr. Walker has all the labor with the people today, Mr. E. being lame. He succeeded much to his joy in obtaining several important words.

MON. 15. Have done a fortnights washing besides my other chores. I wish I could do something besides house work to write about.[13]

TUES. FEB. 16. Went to the lodges to day. Took the children with me. Found very few sick, tho many seem rather destitute of food.[14] One said he was laying still because he had nothing to eat. Their homes appear very comfortable & I thought we could live in them. . .

WED. 17. Ironed & did plenty besides. Mr. W. quite unwell. Talks of setting out for W.W. on Monday.

THURS. FEB. 18. Our folks have built pens for pigs to day. . .

FRI. 19. Received the sad intelligence of the murder of Mr. Black at Thompson's river. Wrote to Mrs. Whitman & Mrs. Gray.

SAT. 20 . . . Solomon went with the express. . .

SUN. 21. Much pleased to find husband is trying to abandon the use of tobacco. Hope it will improve his health.

MON. FEB. 22. Rose early & washed. Mr. W. concluding to set out for W.W. Prepared his food &c. His health seems a little improved.

TUES. 23. Mr. W. left in good season this morning. After he was gone I employed an old man & woman to get some dry wood. He cut & she brought it. They got a good supply of excellent pitch wood. I sent word to the girl who lived with us last winter to come & help me wash. . . Mr. E. . . . has sent word to her not to come . .[15] I do not know what is right. I have compared the case with the example of our Savior in the case of the woman taken in adultery & of the woman of Samaria. . . I cannot determine exactly how we should treat the present case. Or whether Paul . . . would have us as far as practicable avoid all intercourse with persons of bad character.

[13] Mary's repeated references to her household duties as cooking, baking, washing, ironing, sewing, cleaning, milking, gardening, and tending the children strikes a monotonous refrain. Yet the very accumulation of these words builds up an emphasis and paints a picture of her daily life.

[14] Walker, in his diary for the 15th, referred to an Indian who came to them begging for food. He wrote: "Gave none, think it best not to for if we should give one we should have the whole camp upon us."

[15] Eells objected to the employment of the girl who had been caught in some act of immorality.

WED. FEB. 24.   Mr. E. expected that I would resent his interference by doing the washing alone, but he missed it that time, for I assured him with all good nature that I was not disposed to do any such thing but that I should like to have him provide a girl to suit himself. He by accident got two sisters instead of one & Mrs. E. being a little smart employed one & I the other. So we have accomplished a good day's work. We washed all the burnt ticks.   . .

FRI. 26.   Cleaned my room & then fixed the mats. Children both cross.   . .   Snow going fast. Hope if ever any one reads this they will remember I write when half asleep.

FEB. 27.   A. quiet. Have tacked her frocks so she can run if she pleases. Baked bread & fried cakes for Mrs. E. & baked tarts for myself. Cyrus who never wants a name for any thing calls them berries cakes.   . .   I would like to know where husband is &c. Feel some what guilty & ashamed because I have worked so late to night.[16]

SUN. 28.   Attended worship, also Mrs. E. The Indian carried A. When Mr. E. was about half through, recollected that I did not notice on leaving how the fire was. Felt alarmed & the time was long till I was out where I could see that the house was safe. How vain is all our caution except all we have is kept by God. This evening have been reading letters between myself & husband. Think some of them I could write better were it to be done again. Think I realize in my connection with Mr. Walker all I anticipated.

MON. MARCH 1.   Had a girl to assist in washing for Mrs. E. & myself. She partly washed & I finished this evening.   . .

THURS. 4.   Solomon returned. Had a note from husband. He finds [it] mudy traveling. Thinks if he gets back by a week from Saturday he will do well. Yesterday was the anniversary of our marriage, but I did not think of it. I can not realize that it has been three years & we have not written to Mr. Emerson yet.[17]

FRI. 5.   Employed a man to get wood & a girl to sew to day. Ironed before breakfast. It has been a long day & I have accomplished something.

SAT. 6.   Worked fast & hard all day, had a girl helping. Thought I had finished repairing the burnt bed tick but found to my surprise when most done, a long seam was done wrong. Shall have to take it out. The old man who was to get the cow did not &c.

SUN. MARCH 7.   A long day to read.   . .   A. is gaining on C. fast. To night took a shoe & tried to put it on her foot. She manifests a more selfish disposition than C. Cries for every thing she sees him have.   . . I am beginning to long for the time when I shall see my husband again. Hope he is a good piece towards home.

---

[16] Mary had a guilty feeling because her work extended so late into the night that it encroached on the Sabbath.

[17] Mary was confused as to her wedding date. The anniversary came on the 5th. Mr. Emerson was the minister who officiated at the marriage.

Mon. 8. Finished mending the tick. In the evening washed, enjoyed it well. Such beautiful moon shine & children asleep.

Tues. 9 March. Teeth ache a little all day. . . The people are leaving to dig popo.[18]

Wed. 10. Nearly all the people gone. . . Gary called at Mr. E's. Have done many little chores among which mended a small looking glass.

Thurs. 11. Fried two big pans of cakes. Baked two ovens full of bread & plenty of tarts. Hope husband will smell them & come where they are. Made a little soap & cleaned a little, &c.

Fri. 12. Exchanged a burnt basin for a soap basket with the Chief's wife. . . Have had the tooth ache for several days — better to day.

Sat. March 13. Mr. E. went to the river to meet Mr. Walker & returned without him, but soon after he returned & Mr. Gray came with him. Mr. Gray is to assist in building a house.

Sun. 14. Have been reading the Christian Mirror,[19] sent from Portland. Sometimes almost imagined myself at home. Mr. Walker is talking of going with Mr. McLean to the Flathead proper to be gone several months.[20] I hardly know how to be reconciled to the thought. But if it seems for the best, I will submit.

Mon. 15. Mr. Gray has made a plan of a house. I have looked over our things from Portland. Find most of the things good & acceptable, altho worn.[21]

Tues. March 16. Washed. Had a boy to assist me. Kept A. shut up in the bed room alone. Prayer meeting this evening after which a long & interesting coversation.[22]

Wed. 17. Mr. G[ray] is getting on with his work. . . A. is still threatened with croup. . .

Fri. 19. Ironed, starched clothes & mended chimney once more, tho I had designed not to do it. Got very tired. Yesterday got into trouble with some lice.[23]

---

[18] Sometimes spelt poh poh, a root which was dug during March and April.

[19] This was the paper which carried the correspondence of Dr. J. A. Chute. See page 59, footnote 13.

[20] Walker's sense of obligation to preach the gospel to the Flathead Indians at some distance from Tshimakain, possibly in the Bitter Root Valley of what is now western Montana, led him to consider seriously the advisability of leaving his family for several months for this purpose.

[21] Possibly a reference to a missionary barrel of used clothing sent out to Oregon by some church group in Portland, Maine.

[22] The Walkers and the Eells, being far removed from Waiilatpu and Lapwai where most of the dissension within the Mission centered, seemed to have been completely ignorant of what had been transpiring. Gray undoubtedly told the Walkers and the Eells of the letters of criticism about Spalding which had been sent to the Board by himself, Smith, and Rogers. This information was most disturbing to the two families at Tshimakain.

[23] Walker in his diary tells of camping with some Indians while on the trip to Walla Walla. After telling how "a poor looking Indian" had spent the night with

SAT. 20 . . . Mr. Walker has a letter from Mr. McDonald. He seems not to favor much his going with Mr. McLean to the Flatheads. I hope he will give it up & think he will. We have a good large settee & find it very comfortable after sitting for two years on stools. . .[24]

TUES. 23. Washed. Had a girl to help me. Had seven Indians in our employ. Fed them at noon. . .

WED. 24. Mrs. E. was bled this morning.[25] The cow not found yesterday nor to day. . . Mr. W. now drawing the house timber.

THURS. 25. How I am to write a letter, I do not know. All I can do is to cook, wash, iron, tend the children &c.

SAT. 27. The house is up as high as my head. The gentleman have passed towards the Flat Head country & I am glad my husband is not with them.

SUN. 28. Reading the Christian Mirror two years old. How much I would like some new ones.

MON. 29. Trying to write.

TUES. Writing. Mrs. E. gives no encouragement of our going to gen[eral] meeting unless it is here. Mr. W. is working very hard instead of resting, fear he will be sick, indeed he is already.

WEDNES. 31. Have succeeded in writing two letters, one home & one to Mr. Emerson & wife.

THURS. APRIL 1. 30 years old to day. Mr. Eells & Sarah set out for Colvile. . . Mrs. E. to supper.

FRI. APR. 2. With Indian help washed & ironed. Had quite a chat with Mrs. E. in regard to Mr. G.

SAT. 3. Mrs. E. heart sick about my talk to her yesterday or in consequence of getting too much excited thinking about it, she could not sleep. Sorry I said any thing considering her state of health, but I did not think of its having so much effect. Feel very much in doubt how we ought to do. Meet with a great deal in Mr. E. to vex & try me. . .

SUN. 4. Mrs. E. came in & staid with A. who was asleep while I went to worship. This evening she is sick in consequence of taking Cream of Tartar as she supposed. I have felt much distress with the state of our mission.

MON. APRIL 5. So much troubled, thinking how things have been in this mission, and are likely to be & have been & ought to be, & now so little hope of their going right, that it is with difficulty I can attend

him and his helpers, he wrote: "He was up very early and took his leave. But we soon had evidence that he had left much behind for the Indians with me found that they were swarming with lice & I have felt all day as though I was covered with them." No doubt Elkanah carried some home with him.

[24] The presence of Gray, the cabinetmaker, at Tshimakain made it possible for the Walkers to have made such common items of furniture as a settee and a few weeks later a rocking chair. See Mary's entry for April 6.

[25] No doubt the bleeding was done by Gray, who prided himself on having had a brief course in medicine in the Fairfield Medical College during the winter of 1837-38.

to my domestic duties. O that the Lord would show us the right way & incline our hearts to walk therein.

TUES. 6. About half sick. . . This evening for the first time enjoyed the comfort of a rocking chair in our own house & it really seemed very comfortable.[26]

THURS. 8. Mr. E. returned from Colvile. Met the express. . . Brought home Mr. McLean's daughter [Elizabeth].[27] Took dinner with us. After dinner went in [&] had a talk with Mr. E. which relieved my mind very much & I hope all will go right again.

FRI. APR. 9. Mr. Gray left for home. . . In what state of feeling Mr. G. left I do not know.

SAT. 10. Have so much to do & see no way that I can ever expect to have less that I some times feel almost discouraged. . .

SUN. 11. My mind ill at rest in regard to things lately occuring. Would give much to know how & want to do & whether it is I more than others who err. I know that I am a wicked wretch & fear my associates are no better.

MON. 12. Brother S.S. [Samuel] 20 years old. . . I wish I could get a peek at him & see how he looks. It makes me feel badly to think my brothers & sisters are growing old so fast. . .

TUES. 13. Was much troubled last night & on waking this morning. Felt afraid I was more to blame than any body else in the Mission & that altho I might have kept up a better appearance, yet perhaps my motives about every thing had been wrong & in the sight of God I was more sinful than any one. I went about my business but still my mind dwelt on the subject. . . Mr. W. went to hunt the cows & Mr. E. came in to finish our talk. I told him some things he had said to me & in what light I considered them. Talked more about Mr. Gray & as a kind of wind up of the whole, told Mr. E. what it was I disliked in him, that was egotism. He did not attempt to deny the charge. I feel in a great measure relieved & hope to be able to turn my attention to other things. Abigail commenced walking to day.

WED. APR. 14. Cut out two Indian shirts & made one with little assistance. In the evening, picked & dressed two ducks. . .

FRI. 16. Really made a shirt. Elizabeth's mother came thinking to take her away, said the people told her she was hungry. She offered the child food but she declined eating so after a little while she went off apparently quite well satisfied.

SUN. 18 . . . Attend the afternoon worship. The Indians came

[26] E.W. "We now have one chair, the first that we ever had. It is a rocking chair & it is really good to get into it."

[27] Elkanah was doubtful over the wisdom of taking Elizabeth, for he wrote that day in his diary: "I was sorry to see her but will try & do the best with her that we can."

from the river to attend worship. Mr. W. thinks to go tomorrow with the people to popo. Hardly feel reconciled to his absence.

Mon. April 19. Mr. Walker left to accompany the Indians to popo. I hope he will spend his time profitably & pleasantly. . . Little A. walked from our house to Mr. E's alone. She discovers much more naughty temper than her brother ever has done. Elizabeth is not a pleasant tempered child & I fear will injure the temper of our children unless she can be reformed. I saw Cyrus to day trying to treat her in return as she had him. He appeared very unlike himself.

Tues. 20. Milked before the children were up. . . Washed all my clothes while A. was sleeping. Mended some. Mrs E. looks tired enough. Think she works harder than ever before. . .

Thurs. Apr. 22. Milked & strained tallow for candles. Cleaned out the store house. Mr. Walker returned not being able to prosecute his proposed journey. The after express from W.W. arrived bringing us letters. Mr. Rogers is dangerously sick. Mrs. Spalding has been sick but is better. Mrs. Munger is thinking to cross the Rocky Mts. with an infant at the breast & a deranged husband.[28] It seems to me like preseumption.

Fri. April 23. Have been talking all day about all going to general meeting. Cast wicks & dipped 19 dozen candles.

Sat. 24. Before breakfast packed away candles, &c. In the course of the day prepared the tallow & wicks for Mrs. E's candles. Baked first time in the baker. . .

Sun. 25. Indians all gone except those with us. Had worship in English. . .

Mon. 26. Dipped 26 dozen candles. . .

Tues. 27. Mr. E. left for pohpoh. I wash in the afternoon. Mr. Walker received a most affectionate letter from Mr. Spalding. . .[29]

Thurs. 29. Churned some butter for the first [time] this season.

Fri. 30. Feel quite rested, having spent most of the day sewing. The Indians are burning more ashes for soap.

Sat. May 1 . . . In the p.m. the chimney took fire & continued burning till in the night when we got up & had to throw down a part of it in order to extinguish the fire. Had we neglected to do this our house would in all probability been burnt before morning. . .

---

[28] Osborne Russell in his *Journal of a Trapper*, p. 90, tells of travelling with the Mungers from Fort Hall to the Green River Rendezvous, which was reached on July 5. There they learned that there was to be no Rendezvous that year. The Rocky Mountain fur trade was practically over. Since the Mungers could find no escort to the States, they were obliged to return to Oregon. They went to the Willamette Valley where Mr. Munger committed suicide the following December.

[29] Probably by this time Spalding had learned that Walker and Eells were the only ones in the Mission who had not sent critical letters of him to the Board.

SUN. 2. A beautiful day. In consequence of sleeping little last night, feel not so well. Mr. Walker very unwell & low spirited.[30] Think he must go some where. . . It makes me feel very bad to think of his leaving the field of labor. It is much easier for me to think of encountering hardships than being laid aside from labor. I feel that I can not long continue to labor as I now [do.] That as yet we have accomplished very little missionary labor. I [think] almost none. I feel troubled about many things, among others fear our associates feel unpleasantly towards us.[31]

MON. MAY 3. Husband sick & dejected & out of tobacco. What would I not give if he would forever relinquish its use. Cut out two spencers for my husband. . .

WED. 5. Washed & baked & made a new hearth in the bed room. Mr. W. sowed cabbage seed & made some saddle bags & whipped E[lizabeth.] [32]

THURS. MAY 6. Mr. E. returned from pohpoh, brought something we think may make soap.[33]

FRI. 7. Tried divers experiments in making soap, now seem to succeed. But the soda is very good to boil clothes in & I think will save soap. . . Set up a leach [34] for soap.

SAT. 8. Made two kettles of soap.

SUN. 9. Communion to day. . . Have said too much to my husband about leaving off tobacco, he is getting out of patience. Feel much concern on this subject, being more & [more] satisfied that his ill health proceeds from the use of tobacco. Resolved to pray more on the subject if peradventure the Lord will open his eyes.

MON. 10. At home the cattle are just wintered out. O what long winters in the [East.] Mr. W. left for C. Besides fixing him off, have salted tongue, boiled brine. drawed off lye, &c., besides having to bring 8 pails of soft water.

TUES. 11. Commenced working in the garden before breakfast,

---

[30] E.W. "Have felt miserably all day, hardly know what to do. . . O how I long for the presence of some good cheerful friends with whom I can converse & be as I once was. My associate is no company to me & is no help about the language & unless I can in some way be relieved I fear I shall be bereft of my reason." The reference is to Eells, regarding whom Walker became more and more critical in the pages of his diary.

[31] The high idealism which had sent Elkanah and Mary into the mission field was being severely tested. Were the meager results worth the sacrifice? Should they leave the field? Mary was also concerned by what appeared to be a temporary lack of cordiality with the Eells.

[32] E.W. "Gave Elizabeth quite a severe whipping but made her mind & do as she was told & think she feels better for it."

[33] No doubt Eells had discovered some soda deposits in the vicinity of what is now called Medical Lake. Caustic soda was needed in the making of soap.

[34] Mary was referring to a process of passing water through wood ashes in order to get lye to be used in the making of soap.

worked till perhaps three P M, except now & then stopping to eat & feed the children. Sowed four beds, planted squashes, melons, &c. Got up another leach.

WEDNES. 12.　Made some more soap, commenced cleaning &c., churned & baked some bread. The mosquitoes trouble A. so that she's quite worrisome.[35]

THURS. 13.　Mr. Walker returned from C. . . Concludes to set out again for B[ay] in the morning.

FRI. 14.　Arose before sunrise & fixed away my husband once more. Spent most of the day mending. Used an awl in sewing for the first time. Some indications lead me to think we may not be long without milk next winter as there is a prospect of two early calves. Showers with thunder this evening.

SAT. 15 MAY.　Washed a little, sewed a little &c. Have seen more bad conduct in Cyrus of late than ever before, especially to day. Think his associates are an injury to him, know not what course to pursue. Feel much concerned & distressed on his account. I dread the idea of his becoming a great wicked boy. . . Have been very lonely to day & wished to see my husband very much.

SUN. 16　. . . A long lonely day. Mr. E. had English worship in his house, read a sermon. Have been reading Stuart's account of his visit to the S.I. with much interest.[36] Tho I think he might have told shorter stories with less of egotism.

MON. 17.　Wrote a letter to the Sew. Cir. Portland. Found another cow to milk this morning. Mr. W. returned from the Bay Mt. in the most pleasant state of mind on account of some [thing] which had occured to his mind that I said some time since. . .

FRI. 21.　Mr. E. just making his garden.[37] One of the hens came off with eleven chickens, all the eggs she sat on

SAT. 22.　Took a long ride up the plain. . .[38] Mr. E. carried C. A. rode most of the way in my lap. . .

SUN. MAY 23.　All quiet. The Indians [gone] except one Mr. E. has under censure. Had Eng. worship. A warm pleasant day. We have

---

[35] Walker, in his diary for the 15th, also mentioned the mosquitoes. While on his itinerating trip to the Bay he wrote: "Had another hard time last night on account of musketooes." No reference has been found in any of the contemporary documents to mosquito netting.

[36] Charles S. Stewart, a former chaplain in the U.S. Navy and later a missionary in the Sandwich Islands, wrote a two volume work, *A Visit to the South Seas*, which appeared in 1833.

[37] E.W. "Commenced repairing the fence around our garden." By this time the men had been able to erect rail fences to protect their gardens. Later they built such fences to protect their fields and to keep their livestock within bounds.

[38] E.W. "We all took a ride . . . quite a distance. It was too long for comfort. . . Mrs. W. had some unpleasant feelings towards me thinking I did not show as much disposition to accommodate her as I ought. I regret that I did not comply with her wishes."

spent time enough looking at a fine brood of 32 chickens hatched by three hens. . .

WED. 26.   Mr. W. left for Colvile about sunrise.[39] I have washed for Mrs. E. & myself. . .

SAT. MAY 29, 1841 . . . In the afternoon the Indian who accompanied Mr. W. returned. Mr. W. arrived just in season for the boats. We received a budget of letters from below. The intelligence they contain is of a most disheartening character. I am sorry, sorry, sorry that things are as they are.

SUN. 30.   Rose very early this morn; it has seemed a long day. And I have felt sick about the distracted state of this Mission. Have written notes to Mrs. Whitman & Gray.

MON. 31.   Churned & planted more hills of cucumber seeds.

TUES. 1.   Washed & picked up the things to be sent to Mr. Walker . . . The Old Chief returned to take charge of things while Mr. W. & E. are absent.

WED. JUNE 2.   Wrote a letter to Mr. Walker. Mr. E. left for W[aiilatpu] alone. . .

FRI. 4.   Have milked six cows morning & night. . . Covered the plants in the garden to night for fear of frost. Mrs. E. quite sick.

SAT. JUNE 5.   Was not disappointed in looking for frost. Everything in the garden froze stiff to the ground. The squash & melon vines escaped except a few I did not cover. About eleven o'clock Mr. McD. surprised us by a call. He brought me three letters from my dear husband for which I am very thankful.[40] Poor Mr. Pambrun is dead. . . After he [McDonald] was gone, we all went out to see the Indians take their food from the oven. Found it very good eating. It was the little onion they call sa. . .

MONDAY 7 . . . Baked some more cakes, bread &c., churned.

TUES. JUNE 8.   Washed & ironed. Mrs. E. not well at all. Sometimes helps with her cows, sometimes does not.

[39] According to Elkanah's diary, he rode the full distance of seventy miles to Ft. Colville in one day. Walker was on his way to the annual meeting of the Mission scheduled for Waiilatpu. He was a passenger in a boat from Colville to Walla Walla. Eells went by land.

[40] Coll. WN. contains the following letters from Elkanah to Mary: May 27, 1841; two for May 31; and a letter from Mary to Elkanah, June 9. Elkanah wrote: "I am far from feeling easy when you are left alone." He reported that both Rogers and Smith were leaving the Mission. In spite of the dark days which the Mission faced, Walker declared: "I never was so determined to hold on as at the present moment." Regarding Dr. Whitman: "The Dr is not in very good spirits but is not discouraged." And of Smith, Walker wrote: "It is very plain that he has worked all manner of ways to get off without appealing to the Mission for advice or consent." Mary in her letter told of how she had covered the vines and plants in the garden with bark that had peeled off the logs used in the rail fences. Regarding Smith's determination to leave the Mission, Mary commented: "If he can do no good by staying, the sooner he is off the better. . . I think he makes a big fool of Mr. Gray."

Wed. 9.[41] Have written a letter to my husband. Mr. McLean & family pass the night here. . .

THURS. 10.   Mr. McLean left in the morn.

FRI. 11.[42] I have hoad all the vines & transplated some cabbage plants & weeded & thinned out the beds & the Chief has set one man to work on the potatoes. I planted a few pumpkin seeds & cucumber. This afternoon made me a milking bonnet. . .

SAT. JUNE 12 . . . Big Head's dog killed a chicken. Commenced buying strawberries.

SUN. 13.   Quite a number of Indians about . . I want very much to see my husband. It seems long to think of waiting another week . . .

MON. JUNE 14 . . . Worked a while in the garden. . . Just as I was finishing my evening chores & washing my children . . . we were surprised by the report, gentlemen have arrived. We could not imagine who they were till informed one was a gentle[man] of the Company & was conducting Mr. Johnson of the U.S.A. Navy [43] to Colvile from Okenargan. They left their company at the mouth of the Spokan R. at three o'clock P.M. & arrived here a little past sunset having eaten nothing since breakfast. We prepared them as good a supper as we could & they did ample justice to our eatables. It was midnight before we finished . . . or before I was to retire. . .

TUES. JUNE 15.   We took breakfast about 9 o'clock. It continued to rain all the forenoon but ceased about noon. Mr. Johnson was trying all the forenoon to trade some horses of the chief. I had to do most of the talking . . . we succeeded in obtaining three of the chief's best horses. For which he took a written order on Mr. McDonald for nine blankets, one capote, & one shirt. We were a long time parleying with the Chief but seemed to come to nothing when I assumed an air of earnestness & told the Chief the man was in haste to be gone & wished to bring his horses quick & say what he would take &c. After the gentlemen were gone, the Chief complimented me very highly for my eloquence. Said I talked as powerfully as Mr. Walker, or E. would have done & that the gentlemen would not have got the horses but for me.

It was half past four P.M. before they took leave, taking a drink of

[41] Mary starred this date in her diary as an aid in computing time. Her third child, a son, was born the following March 16.

[42] Elkanah wrote this day in his diary regarding the heated words being spoken at the Mission meeting: "It came on so sharp that I was compelled to leave. It is enough to make me sick to see what the state of things [are] in this Mission."

[43] In 1838 the U.S. Government sent an exploring expedition into the Pacific under command of Lt. Charles Wilkes. The squadron of four ships arrived at the mouth of the Columbia in April, 1841. Several exploring parties were then sent into the interior. One of these parties visited Tshimakain. Mary was thrilled with this experience.

milk in the stirrup & leaving apparently well pleased with the entertainment they received, tho regretting as we also did that our husbands were absent. Mr. J. was much charmed with the appearance of Abigail. . . Mr. J. took a specimen of soda & several minerals that I happened to have. He said our latitude was 48°40′. He had the misfortune to break the thing containing his quicksilver for taking observations of the sun & begged a bottle of molasses to use instead. . .

WED. JUNE 16. The gentlemen had only been gone a short time when it commenced raining again. . . I was much concerned for the gentlemen as they had only a blanket each. We might have lent them an oil cloth if we had only thought of [it]. . . Wish my good husband would come home.

FRI. 18 . . . notes & compliments from Mr. Johnson saying he will be at our place Sat. eve. Very rainy. My husband reached home in the evening leaving Mr. E. behind.

SAT. 19 JUNE. Mrs. E. & myself cooked & prepared to receive company. Made a frock for Cyrus as the poor child had none fit to be seen. Our company did not arrive & we were not much sorry as we were apprehensive they might wish to leave on Sunday.

SUN. 20. A pleasant day, we all attended worship in the Chief's lodge. In the afternoon just as I was going to milking, Mr. Johnson arrived. After remaining in the house a few minutes, I hastened to the cow yard thinking to have time to milk before the rest of the company should arrive. But I hardly had commenced when they began to arrive & all passed me while I was milking.[44] We concluded to make our kitchen the eating room & Mr. E's study the sleeping room. Sat up very late. . .

MONDAY JUNE 21. The gentlemen could not get ready to leave in the morning, remaining to dinner. We had a plum pudding. In the afternoon two of the gentlemen left. Mr. W. & myself with the children accompanied them a few miles. Two of them being botanists, I had a pleasant time as I found they knew much more than I on the subject, gained several items of intelligence. . . In the evening baked some bread & cake for Mr. J. to take with him.

TUES. 22.[45] Mr. Johnson & Stearns left in the forenoon. . . Mr. Walker & E. accompanied them over the Mt. It felt very lonely when they departed. We had a pleasant visit from them & Dr. P[ickering] remarked that the most pleasant sight he had seen in Oregon was a lady milking her cows. It is a rare treat indeed to meet literary men in such a wilderness. They have gone to Mr. Spalding & from thence to Dr. W's. . .

[44] E.W. "They made rather a dirty appearance for officers of the A. Navy."

[45] E.W. "I have some fears that their visit will not be attended with any benefit to the heathen & there are stories reported rather against the moral character of some of their party."

Fri. 25. Getting ready to go with my husband to spend the Sabbath with the Indians.

Sat. 26. In the afternoon we came to this place Seakwakin.

Sun. 27. We enjoy a quiet sabbath. . . I am so lifeless I have not improved the day as well as I could wish. We were disturbed last night by the dogs coming into the tent. Abigail cried in the night & after' attempting in vain to quiet her, found an insect bitting her head.

Mon. 28. Made a long sleep this morning till the people called us to worship because they wanted to be off to their work. We reached home in safety about noon. Glad once more to be in a house. . .

Thurs. July 1. Commenced teaching Cyrus to read. . . Mr. Johnson is much pleased with the improvement of the Indians. Mrs. S[palding] is teaching them to spin & knit.

Mon. 5. Too lazy to write in my journal or too busy. . .

Tues. 6. Washed. Mr. Walker very busy irrigating his garden.

Wednes. 7. Churned & ironed. The flies so thick the animals can take no comfort. . .[46]

Wed. 21. Ironed: just as [we] were ready to dine, heard Dr. W. & wife were at the river. Took the children & went to meet them. Received letters from the States but none from home.[47]

Sun. 25. We all attended worship with the Indians, also had English worship. The Dr. & wife took supper with us tho they seemed disposed to stay in Mr. E. house most of the time. Fear it is because [they] do not feel quite right towards us.

Mon. 26. The Dr. & wife eat at our house all day, Mr. E. & wife at noon. Mrs. Whitman & Mrs. Eells do quite a large wash. Mrs. E. very much fatigued.

Tues. Was designing as soon as Mr. Walker should leave for Colvile to go to washing but Mrs. E. was taken ill in the night. Mr. W. at first was going to tary at home but we concluded it might be a false alarm . . . he however went on. . . I have baked & been pretty busy all day. Hope she will yet get along pretty well.

Evening. Mrs. E. was delivered of a son about half past nine as we judged. She had rather a tedious time but not more so than we expected. . .

Wed. 28. Could sleep none last night. Rose some time before the sun. Went in to see Mrs. E. She rested some, babe quiet & I can see nothing why she is not as comfortable as I was the first time. Tho it does seem to me if a little of the care & kindness which she receives had been bestowed on me, I should at least get on much easier. Have washed a large wash to day. Dr. & [Mrs.] W. think to stay two weeks.

---

[46] For want of space, more and more entries of Mary's diary will hereafter be omitted. These deal largely with routine duties.

[47] E.W. for the 22nd: "Was bled this morning & in the afternoon rode to the river in company with the Dr. & dealt out medicines to quite a number."

THURS. 29. Had our Maternal meeting to day. . . All our children present. Have reason to be thankful that I feel so well able to do all the work I have to.[48]

SAT. 31. Mrs. E. continues smart. . . The fire on the mountain south of us threatened us very hard, but our husbands with the help of several Indians succeeded in preventing it from coming too near. . .

MON. [AUG.] 2. Mrs. E. took cold in consequence [became] alarmingly ill. Dr. W. administers ipecac oil & bleeds. She gets some relief. I bake & churn, &c, &c. Get so tired, sleep but little.

TUES. 3 AUG. Mrs. E. is bled again but seems some better. . .

WED. 4. Finish washing. Trade some berries of Gary's wife. Have a tooth filled & two teeth & three fangs of another extracted. . .[49]

FRI. 6. Mr. Walker seems rather discouraged. Thinks he shall not be able to keep the saw running & that nothing will be done to our house this fall.[50]

SAT. 7. Husband 36 years old.

SUN. 8 . . . We had the communion to day & Mrs. E's child was baptized by the name of Edwin. I am blessed with a good measure of health & work very hard. . .

WED. 11. Ironed & baked & cooked potatoes, squash, peas, &c.

THURS. 12. Churned before milking. Mrs. Whitman washed. Mrs. E. gets on slowly. Has done trying to nurse. Is threatened with a broken breast.

FRI. 13. Husband & the Dr. gone to the Barrier. . .[51] In the evening a long talk with Mrs. W.

SAT. 14. Had cabbage for dinner. Mrs. E. came to eat at our table for the first time. Baked eleven bakers full of eatables. Worked till perhaps near midnight. Ready for sabbath. . .

MON. 16. Dr. W. & wife left about noon. . .[52]

THURS. 19. Feel lifeless as need be to day. The weather oppressive. Had boiled corn for dinner. In the evening an express arrived bringing letters from the U.S. One from home. Some of my dear friends are dead but most are living. I am not pleased with the course my brothers are persuing in regard to certain young ladies.

[48] Walker, who had gone to Colville for supplies, returned on the 30th.

[49] Whitman was not only the Mission doctor, he served as the dentist as well.

[50] Walker had hired some Indians to man the whipsaw. In his entry for Aug. 4, Elkanah referred to a cart. This is the first reference to a wheeled vehicle at Tshimakain.

[51] Walker and Whitman made an excursion to the Spokane River to see some stones which some one had reported to be marble. Elkanah wrote on the 14th: "The Dr. has been as full of Geology as if he had eaten half dozen of great volumes on this subject."

[52] E.W. "Was rather displeased with the Dr. this morning. . . They left us today to return home & I must say I did not regret to see them depart."

FRI. 20. Sat up late to read letters.[53] Felt sick all day but got through a large ironing.

SAT. 21 AUG. Baked squash pies & bread & got dinner but had hard work to force myself to do anything. . .

SUN. 22.[54] Mrs. E's folks commenced eating at home. I have read considerable to day but feel miserably sick except when lying down. Am afflicted with nausea & faintness. . .

TUES. 24. Some better, make out to get my floors & Mrs. E's washed up. . .

FRI. 27. More unwell. After dinner rode out. After returning from the ride was quite sick. Took castor oil & calomel.

SAT. AUG. 28 . . . Mr. W. received a letter from Colvile informing that . . . the Pres. of the U.S. was dead.[55]

MON. AUG. 29. Felt pretty well when I arose this morning, went & milked, returned tired & sick & have been rather so most of the day. . .

TUES. 31. Have felt pretty well today. Made me a new corn broom [56] & washed my floors. . .

THURS. [SEPT. 2] Washed & afterwards went into the garden & picked melons &c. . .

MON. 6. A severe frost last night, everything frozen except covered. . .

TUES. 7. Washed. Were agreeably surprised by the arrival of Mr. & Mrs. Spalding with their family.[57]

THURS. 9. Mr. Spalding left for C. & Mr. E. for Okenorgen. Ground froze last night. . .

SUN. 12. Thought to retire early last night & be prepared to enjoy reading to day but about bed time a dog came & killed a hen & to catch the poor little chickens, I sat up till very late. I only found 6 leaving the rest to perish with cold. To day another hen has adopted

[53] Among the letters received was one from the Islands which brought the information that the two couples, Mr. and Mrs. W. H. Rice and Rev. and Mrs. J. D. Paris, who were originally assigned to the Oregon Mission, had arrived in Honolulu on May 21, 1841, and because of the unhappy conditions reported in the Oregon Mission had been advised to remain in the Islands. There are many descendants of the Rice and Paris couples still in the Hawaiian Islands today.

[54] E.W. "Mr. E. prayed in Indian, the first time I ever heard him." It took Eells over two years to obtain even this modest command of the language.

[55] President William Henry Harrison had died April 4, 1841. The news reached Oregon in less than six months, a record for those days.

[56] In a letter dated July 7, 1842, to Maria Pambrun, Narcissa Whitman wrote: "Our broomcorn did not do well last year." *Oregon Native Son,* May, 1899, p. 29. The broomcorn was a canelike grass of which brooms were made. Perhaps Mary got her broomcorn from the Whitmans.

[57] E.W. "The most important event that took place to day was the unexpected arrival of Mr. Spalding & family. We have had an interesting time & I hope a profitable one. They appear disposed to make friends and be at peace."

them altho her own are a month older. There are quite a number of Indians now here & attended worship.[58]

WED. 15. Mr. Spalding & family returned. . .

SAT. 18. Mr. S's eat at our table.

SUN. 19. 50 or 60 Indians present. We all attend worship. In the afternoon Mr. W. preached & Mr. Spalding administered the Lords Supper. We enjoyed for the first time the opportunity of communing with a native. The one present is called Timothy [59] & seems truely pious.

MON. 20. Mr. Spalding & family left. We went with them to the river.

TUES. 21. Washed. Just as I was finishing a gentleman by the name of Sinclair called. He is conducting a company of emigrants from Canada. They expect to settle at the Cowlitz. There are a hundred & twenty five, 80 of whom are children. The women are mostly half-bloods. Several births have occured on the way, & since leaving the buffalo country they have been obliged to kill 8 oxen. An ox only lasts them a day or two. Thus we see Oregon is fast filling up. . .[60]

SAT. 25. Baked pies & cleaned up & put away one thing or another. Concluded while we were eating supper we should get no other house than this this winter.[61] But just as we were rising from the table, two men arrived. We at first supposed Mr. G. had come but it proved to be Mr. Hale of the Exploring party & with him a man who is engaged to finish our house. . .[62]

---

[58] The regularity with which the missionaries conducted Indian worship and the faithfulness with which the natives attended such services are impressive. During their nine years' residence at Tshimakain, the missionaries did not have the satisfaction of having a single native show sufficient understanding of the Christian faith to be baptized and received as a communicant member into the Mission church. However, even if they could not count results in terms of baptisms and conversions, they did have the satisfaction of knowing that Sunday after Sunday through the years, they were able to give Christian instruction. Years later, in the 1870s, Spalding took part in a great revival which swept through this part of the Spokane tribe when hundreds were baptized. See Drury, *A Tepee in His Front Yard*.

[59] A reproduction of a painting of Timothy, made from an old photograph by Rowena Lung Alcorn, is to be found in Drury, *Spalding*, p. 214. Timothy was the most faithful of all of Spalding's converts.

[60] In 1865 Spalding mistakenly placed the arrival of the Red River migration in 1842, and made it one of the reasons why Whitman rode East that fall. See Drury, *Spalding*, p. 285.

[61] Elkanah had labor trouble with the natives. On the 20th he wrote in his diary: "Paid off the sawyers today and they are most dissatisfied. I must be more cautious about employing them & I think it will be a long time before they are again asked to saw or do anything else."

[62] Gray sent a mountain man by the name of Overton to help Walker build his house. E.W. for the 27th wrote: "Commenced putting the roof on the house." See Drury, *Walker*, pp. 161, 165, for copies of the inscriptions made by Johnson and Hale in Mary's Autograph Album.

WED. 29. Ironed & boiled dinner. Mr. H. eat with us. We have commenced eating the little keg of butter I had laid down. . .

MON. [OCT.] 4. I cut pumpkins to dry. . .[63]

THURS. 7. Got an Indian woman to help & cut about 20 pumpkins for Mrs. E. Killed our pig.

MON. 11. We are all busy preparing for Mr. E. & Overton to leave. Mr. Walker has most of his potatoes dug. . .

TUES. OCT. 12. Mr. E. & O. left. . Washed, had Kwantepetser to help me. In the evening ironed. The Chief's wife came with the soda & the Chief came & had a long talk in the evening.

WED. 13. The cows were not found last night not till near night to day.

THURS. . . . The Indians are most of them moving off to winter elsewhere. . .

SUN. 17. The weather is rather mild & fair. . . I have been reading to day in the Missionary Her[ald]. Think I would like to go & visit the missionaries at the Islands. I think perhaps we have no more reason on the whole to be discouraged than there. . .

THURS. 21. Mrs. E. & myself cut out a cap, pantaloons & vest for Mr. Walker.

FRI. Baked pumpkin & mince pies. . .

MON. 25. We took down the old mats in the kitchen & put up new ones.

TUES. 26. Mr. Walker fixed some shelves & made a much more convenient place to keep our dishes than we have had before. Our kitchen is now in much better fix than ever before. . .

FRI. 29 . . . Mr. E. reached home. Brought a cow for himself & one for us. He also brought much sad intelligence from W[aiilatpu.]

---

[63] E.W. "The Old Chief came in to day with the most of his family to dig his potatoes & some other Indians came with him & attempted to encamp near our house. Mr. Eells requested them to go further off which did not please them." This shows that some of the natives were making a beginning in cultivation and also that the missionaries objected to the Indians camping near their houses. In April, 1842, the famous Roman Catholic missionary, Pierre Jean DeSmet, camped near the Tshimakain mission. In his *Letters and Sketches,* 367, he wrote: "Here, on a gay and smiling little plain, two ministers have settled themselves, with their wives, who had consented to share their husbands' soi-distant labors. During the four years they have spent here, they have baptized several of their own children. They cultivate a small farm, large enough, however, for their own maintenance and the support of their animals and fowls. It appears that they are fearful that, should they cultivate more, they might have too frequent visits from the savages. They even try to prevent their encampment in their immediate neighborhood, and therefore they see and converse but seldom with the heathens, whom they have come so far to seek." Walker's diary shows that he had daily worship with the Indians when they were in the vicinity. The missionaries found it necessary to discourage the Indians from camping near their houses for the sake of privacy and for the protection of their gardens and fields.

The Indians have acted out some of their wickedness.[64] We have reason to believe it.

Nov. 1. Washed with the aid of Mungo. . .[65] Mr. E. killed his pig, much fatter than ours. . .

TUES. Nov. 2. Mr. W. left for Colvile. Had Mungo clear out the store house & hen house & cleared up in the bed room a little.

WED. 3. Churned & ironed. No cows to be found. . .

THURS. 4. Rainy. Mr. E. & Mungo hunt the cows and find them

SAT. 6. Mr. Walker returned from Colvile. . . I find it a great help to me to have Mungo, think I can now get some of my sewing done.

SUN. 7 . . . We attend worship out doors. Yet a considerable of a number present. Most of the Indians have left to winter where food can be obtained as they are likely to come short. . .

THURS. 18. Finished writing to Mr. Caldwell. I wrote at first a letter of 16 pages but have copied it on to 8 very closely written. I will not spend so much time writing another letter. . .

SAT. 20. Baked nine times in the old tin baker. . .

WED. Nov. 24, 1841. Mr. Walker moved the book shelves & made a trundle bed. . .

FRI. 26. Mr. W. & E. butchered an ox, the first beef we have killed. In the evening cleaned the tripe with the help of Mungo.

MON. 29. We had our chimney fixed, better the crane too. In the evening washed.

WED. DEC. 1. Rainy. Emptied a barrel so we have two.[66]

THURS. 2. Boiled brine, scalded pickles, roast beef.[67]

SUN. 5. E[lizabeth], the little girl who lives with us, is a great trial to me. She does not seem amiable & I can not love her. I feel that it is

[64] E.W. "Busy the fore part of the day upon the roof of my house. Mr. Eells came & brought much news from below. They have had hard times with the Indians at W. & the Dr. came very near losing his life." See Drury, *Whitman,* 259, for an account of how Tiloukaikt (who led in the massacre of Nov. 1849) demanded pay from Whitman for the mission site at Waiilatpu and in a belligerent mood struck Whitman twice.

[65] Mungo Mevway, a half-Hawaiian and half-native lad about seventeen years old, was sent by Whitman to spend the winter of 1841-42 with the Walkers. Since he could speak English, he proved to be a valued assistant.

[66] Barrels were highly prized by the missionaries. The women used them for the washing of their clothes or for the salting of fish and meat. E.W. for this day noted: "An Indian came in from the Buffalo country & left the priest on the Sabbath & the priest travelled on that day." The strictness with which the Protestant missionaries observed Sunday set them apart from the Roman Catholics.

[67] E.W. "Finished cutting & salting our meat & Mungo went & got a mule & we drew wood the rest of the day. . . Spent a part of the day at the lodge of my Teacher." Hereafter Walker's diary has many references to this Indian whom he called Teacher who was helping him translate the Gospel of Matthew into the Flathead tongue.

wicked to cherish such feelings towards any one as I do towards her. I should not be willing to have my children entrusted to the care of those who feel towards them as I feel towards her. . .

TUES. 7. Cyrus' birth day. Mr. E's family took supper with us. Rainy. Mr. Walker off till after dark hunting a cow, found her with a young calf. . .

SUN. 19. Attended Indian worship. Feel concerned in view of my slothfulness as a Christian. . .

SAT. 25. Made, cut & made two pair drawers for A. & a dress & one pair for Elizabeth. My health good except I can not sit long without my sides aching so I mix in my house work to rest me & sew a great part of the time. Sit up late nights. . . There is plenty of snow & the weather for a week past has been so cold we have not used our beef because it was frozen too hard to cut any.[68]

TUES. 28. I cut up my old plaid dress & make A. a new apron.

WED. 29. Cut out shoes & employ two girls in sewing them.

FRI. 31. Thanks to God for the many mercies that have crowned the closing year.

1842 — A YEAR OF TRANSITION

The eleven-year history of the Oregon Mission of the American Board was divided into two parts by the events of 1842. The first period of six years was characterized by discord within the Mission, which climaxed in the fateful order of the Board of February 25, 1842. This called for the closing of the stations at Lapwai and Waiilatpu; the dismissal of Smith, Gray, and Spalding; and the removal of the Whitmans and Rogers to Tshimakain. However, by the time this directive reached the field the situation had greatly changed. Smith and Rogers had withdrawn from the Mission and Gray was on the point of leaving. Whitman and Spalding had reconciled their differences. The work Spalding was carrying on at Lapwai was the most promising in the whole Mission, while Whitman could point out the strategic importance of Waiilatpu as an outpost on the Oregon Trail. The first period came to a dramatic climax when Whitman mounted his horse, on October 3, to go East to intercede with the Board for Spalding and for the two southern stations.

The second period is characterized by a steadily growing hostility without the Mission which came to a tragic end in the massacre of November 29-30, 1847. Beginning with the first trickle of immigration in the fall of 1842, the Indians began to view the incoming white people with increasing suspicion and alarm. The old order was changing. The white men threatened to take their hunting grounds, to settle upon

---

[68] Although this was Christmas day, Mary fails to make any reference to it.

their camas prairies, and to destroy their age-old manner of life. The year 1842 was the year of transition.

As far as the Walkers were concerned, the year was marked by four major events. A baby boy arrived on March 16, who was christened Marcus Whitman. The two families at Tshimakain, with their children, made the long trip to Waiilatpu in May to attend the annual Mission meeting. They were away from their homes for about six weeks. Thirdly, the dreaded letter arrived in September which showed the Board as being far more drastic in its judgments than the missionaries had expected. And finally Walker visited Lapwai in November of that year, with the text of a primer in the Flathead language. This was the only item printed on the Mission press for the benefit of the Spokanes.

Mary's life as revealed in her diary was crowded with the ordinary and routine duties of keeping house and caring for her growing family. Much of the diary covering these activities will be omitted as enough has already been given to indicate the pattern. Since the reasons for Whitman's decision to go East have been the subject of so much controversy and since the contemporary writings of the Walkers and the Eells throw considerable light upon the subject, these references will be given in full. There is no indication in the letters and diaries of any of the members of the Mission for these days that there was any political motive prompting Whitman to make the trip. Rather, they all stress the fact that he rode on mission business. This conclusion does not preclude the fact that Whitman while in the East interceded with government officials in behalf of Oregon.

SAT. JAN. 1, 1842.[1]   We are all in health & took supper with Mr. E's folks. . .

WEDNES. 5.[2]   Washed. The Indians killed five deer.[3]

THURS. 6.   Quite a fall of snow last night. Have had the Teacher's two daughters this three days past, paid them to night a knife each for four days work nearly.

SAT. 8.   Baked mince pies. Mungo mended the hearth. Our Indian teacher killed a deer. We have cooked the last of our fresh beef.

---

[1] E.W.   "Rose about the same time as usual & wished my wife a happy New Year. . .   We took tea in Mr. Eells', had a very good supper."

[2] E.W. in regard to the annual observance of the fast day: "O how I long for one of the days I have spent in happy New England."

[3] The Indians were short of food so the killing of deer meant much to them. They sometimes passed through periods of great want during the winter months. Walker, in his entry for the 6th, commented on how he and Eells had gathered all of their animals together "for the first time for some time" to protect them from the wolves and also to guard them against the possibility of the Indians killing a horse for food. "If they get deer meat enough," he wrote, "they will not I think trouble our horses."

SUN. JAN. 9.[4]   Snows.   .   .   Elizabeth is a smart active child, but to me very disagreeable. I find she is not trustworthy but disposed to take advantage of my absence to do mischief, lying, stealing, and deceiving.   .   .   Cyrus is a very pleasing child. I have little cause to reproach his Maker for making him what he is. I hope he will give me wisdom to train him as I ought. Abigail is a smart child.   .   .

MON. JAN. 10   .   .   .   Mungo kills a deer.

TUES. 11.   One year since Mr. E's house was burnt. Washed, had a girl to help me. A rainy day, so easy getting water, wished to improve it. Took down my bed curtains & washed them.   .   .[5]

SAT. 15.   Take care of venison. Cook the last of our squashes, put up bed curtains.   .   .

SUN. 16.   Gary here, but declined rehearsing.   .   .[6]

SAT. 22 JAN.   Garry returned from Colvile with the Indian who carries the express from C. on snow shoes.   .   .

SUN. 23.   We all attended worship, Mr. E. talked. Gary assisted some at evening worship, gave them a plain talk. I think if we could have him about us he would assist us much.   .   .[7]

FRI. 28.   Last night half a foot of snow fell. The two girls have helped me five days this week & I have paid them each six loads of amunition,[8] two basins [of] potatoes & given some dinner. Think they will have enough to pay them for their labor. They have sewed this week mostly on pantaloons & aprons.   .   .[9]

TUES. FEB. 1.   One girl helping Mr. Walker make saddle bags.   .   .

[4] E.W. "We have one advantage here, a stormy day does not keep the people from worship. They attend as well on a stormy day as any other."

[5] E.W. "Concluded to draw the logs.   .   .   Have had four mules harnessed together for the first time for a long time." It was much easier to draw the logs to the building site over snow than over dry earth.

[6] The reference is to interpreting. There was no member of the Spokane tribe as able to assist in the work of translating as Spokane Carry with his knowledge of English. E.W. "When the time of worship came, he refused to rehearse & left me to my own resources. I felt quite at a loss at first, & hardly knew how to get on alone. But commenced & made quite a speech, spoke with more energy than common & I think gave them more instruction than common."

[7] According to Walker, Garry on this day interpreted once for Eells. At the close of the service conducted by Walker that day, he called upon Garry to say something. Walker wrote: "He was long in commencing & began very low saying he was ashamed & how could he help it.   .   .   I did feel considerable when listening to Garry to hear him pour the truth on to them & when he was illustrating the awful condition of the finally lost, that all will be in vain without a blessing from God."

[8] After this date, both Elkanah and Mary refer to using "loads of ammunition" in making payments to the natives. The reference is undoubtedly to some accepted measure used in handing out powder. *In Adventures of Zeans Leonard, Fur Trader*, p. 9, we read: "For twenty or thirty loads of powder you can generally get eight to twelve dollars worth of fur." That was in 1834. Figuring twenty-five loads at $10.00, this means that a load was worth .40¢.

[9] E.W. for the 31st: "Commenced my sawing & made very good progress."

WED. 2. Washed in the evening, cut out trousers for Mungo. A horse belonging to the Co. died.

THURS. 3. The Indians are carrying off the carcas of the horse. . . It still continues to snow very frequently.

FRI. FEB. 4, 1842 . . . Solomon arrived with letters, travelled the last two or three days on snow shoes. We are informed of the death of Mr. Munger. He locked himself in his shop, drove two nails through his hand, & then burnt it to a cinder & nearly roasted himself. His hand was amputated, but he survived only a few days. . .

SUN. 6. FEB. Have felt unhappy in view of my stupidity in regard to our eternal welfare & that of my children & others. Have felt much interested in reading what is doing in other parts of the world particularly in Siam. . .

WED. 9. The Cour de Lain Chief came to invite Mr. E. to go to & teach his people. Garry came with him. They say half of this people are in favor of the priests & the other Mr. W. & E.[10]

FEB. 10, 1842. Mr. E. left this morning to go as he was desired. Rather a stormy day.

SAT. 12. Had to exert myself very much to keep my Indian girls employed. . .[11]

TUES. 15. Mr. E. returned from his excursion.

THURS. 17. Dipped candles in the evening. Have 15-20 dozen very white & nice made of beef tallow.

FRI. 18 . . . Mr. W. has an Indian sawing with Mungo so I have quite a large family to feed at noon.

SUN. 20. Attended worship, found the walk rather long. Think I will not return again this winter. . .

TUES. 22. Glad Shoshenamalt to help me wash. Her sister went to help bring home a deer her father killed.

WED. 23. Cut out eight pairs of shoes. . .

FRI. 25. Have sewed some but have not felt as well as usual. Have three dresses nearly finished but fear I shall not be able to complete them before I am sick . . . [child birth]

---

[10] Father DeSmet spent the winter of 1841-42 among the Flatheads. He spent some time with the Coeur d'Alene Indians in the spring of 1842 and founded a mission for them. In a letter to Chamberlain in Honolulu, Walker on Sept. 6, 1842, wrote: "I had some conversation with De Smet in the language. He remarked that as our belief was the same in regard to the Trinity, he thought we had better adopt one common phraseology. He gave me some of his phrases & my knowledge of the language would not allow me to adopt them. . . I am yet to be convinced that we ought to borrow words from him. We were first in the field & we shall hold our right to make our own words."

[11] E.W. "Have hunted horses all day but could not find two of mine & have engaged an Indian to go for them in the morning. I hesitated some but fearing they might kill themselves by eating rushes, I thought it my duty to send for them." When the snow lay too deep for the animals to paw through it for grass, they sometimes ate the rushes along the streams. On the 13th Elkanah wrote of having Garry's help in translating the Lord's Prayer.

TUES. MARCH 1. Had Kwantepetser to help me wash. . . Feel very tired. The snow is going off fast. Trust Dr. W. is on his way. . .

SAT. 5. The anniversary of our wedding. In the P.M. Mr. Walker rode out to see if he could meet the Dr. Soon met him. We feel much relieved to have him here as we have feared he would not arrive in season. . . I succeed in doing a good job of baking; baked hard bread, mince pies, & pound cake. Hope the Dr. will not be detained long. . .

TUES. 8. Washed, has Soshenamalt to help me. Health very good. . . The Old Chief returned yesterday. Quite a blustering snow storm, hope it will prove the last for this year. We have two calves, found yesterday so we may hope for a good supply of milk. . .

THURS. 10. Had but one of the girls who helped me iron & mend. Baked again nine loaves & three corn cakes, as the children call [them.]

SAT. 12. Health still good, but so many to feed it takes more of my time than I can well spare as I still have much sewing that I am anxious to do.

SUN. 13. Pleasant weather. The Dr. took breakfast with Mr. Eells' folks. His time is spent mostly in revising a translation of the first ten chapters of Matt. which keeps him busy & contented. . .[12]

WED. 16. Rose about 5 o'clock, had an early breakfast, got my house work done up about 9. Baked six more loaves of bread. Made a kettle of mush & have now a sewet pudding & some beef boiling. My girl has ironed & I have made out to put my clothes away & set my house in order. May the mercy of the Merciful be with me through the expected scene. Nine o'clock P.M. was delivered of a son.

THURS. 17. Rested pretty well last night. The rain disturbed me some. My little boy laid still all night. We call his name Marcus Whitman. Had Kwantepetser help me wash &c. . .

SAT. MARCH 19 . . . The babe laid all night, only I nursed him several times. Have now about as much milk as he requires & succeed well at present with the artificial nipple. . .

SUN. 20. Dressed myself & got up about eight in the morning. Sat up till afternoon. After worship Mr. E. came in to see me & his family with ours eat dinner in our house. In the afternoon read most of the time in Josephus.[13] Went out in the kitchen several times in the course of the day. . .

MON. MARCH 21. Dr. W. left this morning. . .

WED. 23. Rose about seven. Got my breakfast, cleared up my room, dressed my babe for the first time. Made a kettle of mush &c, delt out

---

[12] During the winter of 1841-42, Spalding had translated the first ten chapters of the Gospel according to Matthew into the Nez Perce tongue. Evidently Whitman had been asked to check the work.

[13] Josephus, *Antiquities of the Jews,* an important reference work for the history of the Jewish people to the end of the first century of the Christian era is dry, heavy reading.

dinners to the family . . . made some pea porridge & washed the children. . .

FRI. MARCH 25, 1842. A very windy day, took some cold in one breast but with a warm stone succeeded in removing it. This is an Indian medicine & the best I can find. . .

SUN. 27 . . . Took a short walk out of doors for the first time since the 16th.

MON. 28. Arose at six, dressed my babe. . . While we were at breakfast, Mr. McPherson arrived, prepared a breakfast for him. Swept, washed dishes, made a plum pudding & baked two bakers full of biscuit. . . Had milk for supper. Mrs. E. boiled the dinner & dined with us.

TUES. MARCH 29. Was able to get breakfast in good season. . . Find myself every day a little stronger. O that I could thus find my spiritual strength increase. . .

FRI. APR. 1. My birthday. 31 years old. Passed an almost sleepless night on account of Mungo who was missing & a girl too.[14] Garry came in the night.

SAT. APR. 2. Mungo tells a fair story not however very creditable to the girl. He is disposed to take her as a wife. It is rather humiliating to see human nature acted out with so little disguise. . .[15]

THURS. 7 .. . . Mungo has gone to Mr. E's house to live tho he is to do our milking. He has concluded a bargain for a wife but is going to wait a while & see the Dr. & know his mind. . .[16]

SAT. APRIL 9. My babe has still a sore mouth. Nurse him mostly without the artificial nipple, tho not without considerable pain. Mrs. E. has given me considerable many things that she has lately received from home. . .

FRI. 15. Ironed . . . boiled beef brine. We have more than a barrel of beef left yet. . .[17]

---

[14] E.W. for Mar. 31. "We were quite annoyed last night by the conduct of Mungo. learning that he was off with one of the teacher's daughters. But on inquiry this morning found that he had no bad design in it but was making a bargain with her for a wife." Also for April 2: "Had some more talk with Mungo & found that the proposition was made to him by the girl."

[15] E.W. "Gave Garry some wheat & potatoes for seed. . . He wanted to trade a small piece of deer tallow for a shirt. I lent him two hoes. He wanted six. He may cause us much trouble but we must learn (sic) him that we can not give him all he wants."

[16] E.W. "Told Mungo this morning that he better not take her now as there was no place to keep [her] & asked him if he had any thing to keep house & told him furthermore that he ought to get the chief's consent as that was the way they did here. Had some talk with her parents & found them quite anxious on the point."

[17] E.W. for Monday, the 25th. "Did not feel very Mondayish to day." I.e., not lethargic. Elkanah frequently referred to a "Mondayish" feeling in his diary, no doubt referring to the feeling many ministers have on that day after a busy Sunday.

THURS. APRIL 21. The express arrived. Brought letters from the States & the Islands. My friends all alive.

FRI. APRIL 29. Kwantepetser came. . . Mr. W. & E. have engaged Solomon to remain in our absence. . .

MON. [MAY] 2. Busy all, preparing to start. . .[18]

THURS. 5. Rose early & was about ready to start at nine. Mr. E's folks were not ready till eleven, when we mounted. Charles & Mungo had gone ahead with the cow & to get the boats which were on the other side. We nailed & locked the houses as snug as we could, turned the calves loose to take care of the cows & left the hens to manage themselves, charging Solomon to feed [the] chickens, should there be any.

Scarcely had we mounted than one horse took a fancy to scatter his pack about the plain. This put others in a restless mood. I dismounted & Mr. Walker took my horse & rode a while to tire him & in a short time we started again. Rode to the river. I carried the babe. Mr. W. [had] Abigail & Kwantepetser, Cyrus. . . It was about four o'clock when we encamped on the south side of the river. There were two boats & they crossed several times with each. The horses swam. . .

FRI. MAY 6. A fine morning & we designed to start early but Mrs. E. finds that several things are missing that were thrown from the pack yesterday. Concluded to return & seek them. It is now about 8 A.M. & Mr. E. has returned having found his lost things. To night encamped about 5 on a low wet spot where mosquitoes were plenty.

SAT. MAY 7. Moved about 8. At our nooning place saw Indians passing near us. Were informed that a village was near our trail. We went to it. Garry was among them . . . we went to his lodge & found him. . . Mr. E. & Walker told him they would return & hold worship with them. I carried my babe in the forenoon & Mr. W. in the afternoon. We encamped about 5.

SUN. MAY 8. We are encamped on the side of a hill.[19] The sun shines & the wind blows so that we can hardly keep our tents from blowing down. . . The children are so full of business we have our hands full to take care of them. Babe claims most of my time. . .

MON. MAY 9 . . . We are encamped near a small pond not far from where we once stopped in a snow storm. . .[20]

---

[18] The 300-mile round-trip to Waiilatpu was quite an undertaking for the two families with six small children, including the two half-breed girls Elizabeth and Sarah. A cow would have to be driven along to provide milk for the babies. During their absence, they left their houses, much of their livestock, their poultry, their fields and gardens in the care of the natives.

[19] To the missionaries, traveling on Sunday except in cases of great emergency, was wicked. For conscience sake, they preferred the difficulties and inconveniences of remaining in camp with little children to the easier alternative of continued traveling.

[20] E.W. "Rested badly last night. Laid cold & hard & late."

WEDNES. 11. Went to the falls on the Palouse. The water falls in a sheet down a precipice so steep that the water is reduced to a mere spray. Crossed the Snake river which is now very high & encamped on it. . .

THURS. 12. We arrived at & crossed the Tusha.

FRI. In the afternoon reached the station where we met a cordial reception. . . Mr. Eells makes his home at Dr. W's. We with Mr. Gray. Mr. Spalding writes that he does not expect to attend the meeting. I feel sorry. . .

SUN. 15. Mr. Walker preached twice.[21] Mr. Eells being sick. During recess we had a Sunday School. In the afternoon Mr. & Mrs. G., Dr. Whitman & Mrs., Mr. Walker & myself presented the children for baptism. . .[22] We had good singing & it seemed affecting to witness anything so much like civilization.

MON. 16. The meeting commenced. The ladies were invited to attend the sessions. . .[23]

WED. 18. Atten[ded] the meeting part of the day. . .

THURS. 19. Several boxes [of] belongings are divided by lot.

FRI. 20 . . . Mr. Rogers left for Clearwater. . .[24]

SUNDAY 22 OF MAY. Have spent so much of my precious time dressing this morning, will try to avoid doing so again. P.M. The sacrament was administered by Mr. Walker. . .

THURS. 26. Mr. Rogers & Spalding arrived about ten A.M.[25]

FRI. The meeting goes on again. . .[26]

---

[21] E.W. "It has been a very interesting day to me. It seemed so much like home. I should like to spend every Sabbath in the same manner as I have this so far as religious duties are concerned." After being isolated for over three years at Tshimakain, the very fact of having worship with two other families was stirring.

[22] The Whitmans had taken a forlorn little boy between three and four years old into their home the preceding March. They called him David Malin. He, Mary Sophia Gray, and Marcus Whitman Walker were the three baptized this day but no record of these baptisms was made in the official minute book of the First Church of Oregon. Since Spalding was not present and since he had custody of the book, it is probable that the omission was just an oversight.

[23] Although invited to attend, the women could not take part in the discussions nor vote. Elkanah in an entry in his diary for June 8, 1841, mentioned the fact that Mrs. Whitman and Mrs. Spalding were present at the Mission meeting held in Lapwai and added: ". . . they called upon me to take the lead of the meeting. I was rather perplexed to know how to get along without calling on the women to pray but managed in such a manner as not to." Elkanah took literally Paul's injunction for the women to keep silence in the churches. I Cor. 14:34.

[24] Spalding's absence was an embarrassment, so the other men by unanimous vote passed a resolution calling for his immediate presence.

[25] E.W. "About noon Mr. Spalding came with Mr. Rogers & it produced quite a sensation in many minds. Had no sitting this afternoon."

[26] E.W. "Had a session this morning. . . Mr. Eells in the chair & commenced considering the difficulties in the Mission. Each one made out statements of what was considered the difficulties, which occupied most of the forenoon. In the afternoon specifications commenced."

MON. MAY 30. We all attend the sessions & hear much to make our ears tingle. . .[27]

TUES. 31. Washed a little &c.[28]

WED. JUNE 1. Meet in the afternoon & adjourned. The question under consideration, how shall the differences be reconciled.[29]

THURS. JUNE 2. Felt distressed this morning on account of the state of the mission. Felt to say, help Lord for vain is the help of man. Talked with husband who was nearly sick for abstinence [i.e., from eating] & anxiety & perplexity. Mr. E. came in & talked with Mr. Walker. They talked with Mr. G. & I believe with Dr. W. W[alker] talked with Mr. Spalding after which he began to take courage. After much private consultation, the meeting commenced. . . There was much talking but little determining.[30]

FRI. 3. Soon after the opening of the session, Dr. W. began to call Mr. Spalding to account. Mr. Rogers thought Dr. W. wrong. Much talk followed, & the Dr. was allowed to proceed. The appearance is such as to excite much concern on the part of some if not all & to lead us to fear that there will be no sound settlement after all. If any restraint is laid on the Dr. or if he suspects he is not to have his own way entirely, he immediately threatens to leave the mission.[31]

SAT. JUNE 4. In the morning, Mr. McKinley, Mr. Ogden & Mr. Frazer arrived from W.W. They brought the sad intelligence that five men were lately drowned in the Col. R. . . There was some hesitating what course to persue & much fear in regard to the course the Dr. was likely to persue. But he & Mr. Spalding after some private conversation announce their wishes to have all assemble in haste. Whereupon Mr. S. commenced to making a confession as humble as could be wished. Dr. W. seemed not quite right, but after being called to account for his threats the day before [said] he could not recollect them but said he did not mean so exactly. . . Mr. E. question[ed] the Dr. closely & he said he saw nothing why he & Mr. Spalding could not come to a settlement. The minds of all were relieved.

---

[27] E.W. for Sunday, the 29th: "Preached my big sermon today."

[28] E.W. "Had a hard session to day & there was so much bad feeling manifested that I said that I thought it was an abomination for us to meet to pray. We had no meeting this evening."

[29] E.W. "Made an end of specifications. . . Mr. Eells & myself took a long ride in the rain & felt that all hope was gone."

[30] E.W. "Much talk was had to day on the awful consequences that would follow if a reconciliation should not take place. I felt much & said considerable & I hope it was not in vain & I think that there was a better state of feeling than there had been at any time during the Mission & I was quite confident that a settlement would be made."

[31] E.W. "Had a hard time & my feelings have been any but calm. I have been moved in view of some threats the Dr. made that if he was not allowed to pursue his own course he would leave the Mission. The Dr. asked to be allowed to go on in his own way without being checked."

SUN. JUNE 5. Mr. Walker preached. . .[32]

TUES. 7. Mr. Rogers left. . .[33]

WED. 8. Mr. Spalding left, the difficulty settled. Mr. Walker wrote to Mr. Green. . .[34]

FRI. 10. Preparing to go home.[35]

SAT. 11. Left W. about noon. Dr. W. & Mrs. [Whitman], Mr. Gray & family, Mr. & Mrs. McKinley came out a short distance. . .[36]

MON. JUNE 13. Rode to Snake river & crossed & came up a little way & encamped on the Palluse. . .

WED. 15. The weather for most of the time very warm. Got most too tired riding & carrying my babe. We find plenty of berries, red, yellow & black currents. . .

THURS. 16. Made one camp to Ki-ha-kilin. Mrs. E. was sick in the morning but grew worse & we laid by on her account. She had had a diarrhea for several days which stopped suddenly. She ate some berries which was probably the occasion. We gave her rhubarb. We tried injections which afforded practical relief. Next we gave calomel followed by salts, obtained a thorough operation. She seemed feverish, tongue coated somewhat.

FRI. 17 JUNE. Mrs. E. is better this morning tho weak from taking so much medicine. . . It would be very bad to be sick long in such a situation as we must be in here. Evening — made only a short camp. . .

SAT. 18. Took an early start, stopped twice to rest & eat, reached the [Spokane] river in season to have crossed & gone home had there

---

[32] E.W. "Had rather a sleepless night notwithstanding I took two pills to make me sleep. . . Preached again to day & preached my Missionary sermon. . . I liked my sermon well, think it quite good. Wish I had more time to write sermons."

[33] Rogers never received an appointment from the American Board but was always a voluntary assistant without voting privileges in the Mission. He left the Mission in 1841 and for a time in the fall of 1841 was employed by members of the Wilkes Expedition. No explanation has been found as to how he happened to be present at this May-June 1842 meeting of the Mission. Perhaps he was in the vicinity and was invited to take part in the discussions as a witness.

[34] The report of the meeting sent to Greene contained the following which later proved of great importance to Spalding: "It was the unanimous opinion at the close of the investigation that, should the Prudential Committee have taken any action on any communication yet unanswered, that the Mission ought to wait until this communication can be answered." When that action was voted, the Board's drastic order to close the southern two stations and to dismiss several including Spalding was already on its way to Oregon.

[35] After arriving back at Tshimakain, Walker wrote in his diary on June 24: "Have been thinking about the affairs of the Mission & did take the credit of Mr. E. & myself saving the Mission." Undoubtedly this is correct.

[36] It was customary for the hosts to ride with their departing guests for a few miles on their homeward way. Evidently the McKinleys were at Waiilatpu awaiting Mrs. McKinley's confinement. It came the next day.

been a boat. But not being one . . . went to the upper crossing place. It was near dark when we reached it. We missed the way. I had to climb & descend mountains & pass a ravine or defile, the most grand perhaps we ever saw, hugh precipices, &c, crags of granite overhanging on either hand. I carried my babe over the whole not without apprehensions. . .

SUN. JUNE 19. Weather warm. Long day lounging in the tent . .[37]

MON. 20. Crossed the river early & reached home about nine. Found all safe except that the hens had only five chickens. One calf had been killed. They [had] eaten a bag of fine flour that we did not intend they should. The frost did all the mischief it could. There was a swamp like growth of weeds in the garden. Found all our meat keeping well.

TUES. JUNE 21. Kwantpetser washed. Have a great deal of washing on hand.

SAT. 25. We have an Indian now who I am trying to learn to milk. . .

SAT. [JULY] 2. Took up the carpet on my bed room floor & cleaned up my house, baked. . .

SUN. 3. Mr. Walker went to the river. Mr. E. to Seakwakin. Have felt concerned in view of my carelessness in regard to private devotions & resolved to make reading the scriptures & prayer the first duty in the morning. Feel concerned lest I do not endeavor to make known the way of salvation to my children as early as I ought. . .

TUES. 5. Washed & ironed a little & made things ready for Mr. W. . .

WED. 6 . . . Husband left about seven. . .[38]

THURS. 7 . . . Have traded [for] about three packs of small huckleberries. Have K. now mending shoes.

FRI. JULY 8 . . . Have just [done] nothing to day but trade or take care of berries. . .

MON 11 JULY. Frost last night, kill vines & make potatoe tops look rather sorry. Thought to sew pretty steadily to day but [found] a fallen down tub & spent several hours fixing it up, succeeded better than I expected to. It is a pretty little tub now & I am glad I did not throw away the old staves.

TUE. JULY 12. Myself & children went with Mr. E. to the fish weir. One would think they would never want for food to see them now. They seem not to waste any. . .

SAT. 16. JULY. Churned a lot of butter, scalded brine, cleaned

---

[37] Even though they were within a few miles of their homes, yet because of it being Sunday they remained all day in camp. Undoubtedly the missionaries also felt the necessity of setting an example for the natives.

[38] Elkanah found it necessary to return to Walla Walla for supplies.

house. Mrs. McDonald arrived about two P.M. . . & Gaudies wife & their children, in all 14.

SUN. 17. Mr. Eells has gone to the river. The company took breakfast with us.

MON. 18. Mr. W. arrived while we were at dinner. . .[39]

SAT. 23. Went with husband to the barrier almost six hours ride. Cyrus rode alone for the first time, tied but guiding his horse himself. . .

FRI. JULY 29. Feel tired & almost sick or discouraged. I see so much to do & so little prospect of being able to do it. Regret I am able to spend so little time in teaching the children. . .

MON. AUG. 1. Churned & began filling a large keg with butter. . .

MON. 8. Churned. Some half dozen Indians stood & watched me from the time I put the cream in the churn till the butter was salted.

TUES. 9. Washed. Kwantepetser wishes to return to live with us. We hardly know what to do about taking her.

WED. 10. A young man called whom I took for a gentleman [i.e., one of the traders of the Hudson's Bay Company] & treated accordingly, but found he was the man who has been held a sort of prisoner at C[olville] for some time past.

MON. 15. Washed. Cyrus seemed not as well as usual, get asleep on the floor several times.

TUES. 16. Cyrus still continues sick.

WED. 17. Delayed starting for C. as we had intended. C .still sick.

THURS. 18. Had concluded to start but just as we were getting ready noticed that C. had the mumps, so we gave up going till he is better.[40] The weather now is very warm.

WED. 24. Had concluded to start for Colvile but Dr. Whitman arrived early in the morning,[41] so we delayed a day longer.

THURS. AUG. 25, 1842. Left home in P.M. . .

SAT. 27. Reached Colvile about noon. Lodge in the room we occupied the first time we were at C.

---

[39] E.W. "I made the whole trip down in less than three days and one-half. Had considerable talking to do & some of it not of the most pleasantest kind. . . Spent Tuesday at the Dr's." It appears that the Mission at its June meeting voted to have Spalding and Whitman exchange stations. Both Spalding and Whitman objected to this decision, so the whole matter was reopened. Gray was adamant in demanding that the exchange be made. Walker was asked to talk over the question with Eells and send back their decision.

[40] The main childhood diseases, as mumps, chicken pox, and measles, were by this time common among the natives of the Oregon country and of course the children of the missionaries were likewise afflicted.

[41] E.W. "Soon after sunrise the Dr. made his appearance & took us by surprise. He came up on Mr. G. account. . . We had much conversation on the state of the Mission, especially the vote that was passed last spring recommending a change between Mr. Spalding & Dr. W." Walker and Eells agreed with Whitman and Spalding that the exchange should not be made. This decision led to Gray's withdrawal from the Mission the next month.

SUN. 28. Mr. W. gone to talk to the Indians. We seem to be doing very little for the Indians because we are inadequate to the work before us & now Mr. G[ray] is threatening to leave us. I hope if it is best he should leave, he will do it & if not he will see how it becomes him to do & be so.

MON. 29. Cool & a little showery. All goes pleasantly. Abigail loses her bonnet.

TUES. 30. Have not found the lost bonnet yet, fear it is stolen.   .   .

FRI. [SEPT.] 2. Reached home in safety about 1 P.M. Found a dinner ready for us. Abigail has the mumps. Wish I knew how to turn these visits to more & better account. It seems to me we do no good & get but little.

SAT. 10. Went to Spokane with husband & the children.   .   .

SUN. 11. A pleasant sabbath. The Fool's son had many inquiries to make about the priests. Nothing seems so destestable to me as papacy.

MON. SEPT. 12. Reach home about two P.M.   .   .

FRI. SEPT. 16. Had something of a headache, took a pill which made me rather ill all day.   .   .

SUN. 18. Mr. E. went to the river & Mr. Walker staid at home. I feel depressed. My children, especially Cyrus, is a heaviness to me particularly on the Sabbath day. It is as if he was almost possessed with some demon, he is so noisy. I do not know what to teach him first about his Maker.   .   .

MON. 19. Feel lonely, depressed.

TUES. SEPT. 20. The express we were looking for arrived, bringing letters from Dr. W. & Mr. Green, stating that the Board have concluded to recall Mr. Spalding, Smith & Gray & to discontinue the southern branch of this Mission. But as we have already written that the difficulties are settled & that we should wait a reply to the last letter. Mr. G. had already determined to leave & do not know as any one has any objections. Dr. W. desires Mr. Rogers, Walker & Eells to come to his place immediately.

WED. 21. Mr. W. & E. left about nine A.M. leaving the Chief in charge. In the evening Mrs. E. & myself had our maternal meeting, & also united in prayer for our husbands. I never felt more of a spirit of prayer nor greater freedom. I feel exceedingly distressed when I think of the affairs of our mission. How the reproach can ever be taken away, I know not. But I do hope Almighty God will devise some way to reveal himself in power & mercy. I do not know how we should feel toward those who have gone out from [the] mission, how we ought to treat them.   .   .

FRI. 30 SEPT. Have had our Indian girl sewing for me several days on shoes. Mungo arrived at sunset bringing word that Mr. W. & E. were at W., also Mr. Spalding & Gray, so I see not why they cannot attend to any business they please.

SAT. OCT. 1.   Mr. W. & [E.] unexpectedly arrived, having come in three days. They hastened their return on account of Mungo as he has been sent away by Dr. W. & they feared he would impose on us & get us into trouble as he no doubt would. Messrs. W. & E. had much trouble with Gray & Co. The Mission have concluded to send Dr. W. to the States to represent the Mission & obtain a reinforcement or settlers or do something.

WHITMAN LEAVES FOR THE EAST

The first immigration of American settlers to Oregon came in the summer of 1842 when a party of one hundred and twelve people with eighteen wagons, under the leadership of Dr. Elijah White, crossed the country. The wagons were left at Fort Hall and the party completed the journey on horseback. Dr. White arrived at Waiilatpu on September 14 or 15 and delivered to Whitman the expected letter from the Board. At the time Gray was in the Willamette Valley making arrangements to move his family there. Whitman at once sent word to Spalding, Walker, and Eells requesting that they hasten to Waiilatpu to decide what should be done. The following entries from Walker's diary throw much light on this important meeting:

TUESDAY [SEPT.] 20.   Just as we were about to sit down to breakfast the long looked for express came in which some letters from the Dr. & from Mr. Greene. It was stated in Mr. G's letters that it was decided that the southern part of this Mission was to be given up and all called home except the Dr. & he was to be connected with the northern branch. . .   The Dr. requested us to come down immediately. . .   We felt that we ought to go & our wives urged us on.

WED. 21.   Mr. E. seemed to talk as though if he were at home he would remain there. But I have not felt that we did wrong.

MOND. SEPT. 26.   Reached the station of Dr. W's about ten & found Mr. Spalding there. Did nothing of business until evening when we had rather a hot session discussing Mr. Gray's case.

By this time Gray had returned from the Willamette Valley with the news that he had secured a position with the Methodist Mission. He presented his resignation. Strange to say Eells and Spalding voted against accepting it; Whitman and Gray were in favor; Walker as the Moderator cast the deciding affirmative vote. The four remaining men of the Mission then turned their attention to Green's drastic order. They all felt that the action taken at their June meeting nullified the order of the Board until further facts could be presented. Whitman began to feel that the only solution to the impasse was for him to go

*East and make a personal appeal to the Board. Walker's comments
continue:*

WEDNESDAY 28. Rose this morning with the determination to
leave & found Mr. E. had the same view . . . as he felt that
nothing could be done. At breakfast the Dr. let out what was his
plan in view of the state of things. We persuaded them i.e.,
Spalding and Whitman to get together & talk matters over. I think
they felt some better afterwards. It was then the question was
submitted to us of the Dr.'s going home which we felt that it
was one of too much importance to be decided in a moment but
finally came to the conclusion that if he could put things at that
station in such a state that it would be safe, we would consent to
his going & with that left them & made a start for home.

*Before Walker and Eells left for Tshimakain, they and Spalding
signed the following: "Resolved, that if arrangements can be made to
continue the operations of this station that Dr. Whitman be at liberty
and advised to visit the United States as soon as practicable, to confer
with the committee of the A.B.C.F.M. in regards to the interests of
this Mission." Walker and Eells left with the understanding that Whitman was to wait for letters that they would write to Greene. Walker in
his diary indicated that he completed writing his letter on October 10
and Mary wrote that a packet of letters was sent by special messenger
to Whitman on the twelfth. However, Whitman became concerned
over the difficulties he would face while crossing the Rockies in the
late fall or early winter and left without the letters on October 3.*

*Beginning in 1864, Spalding became involved in a controversy with
the Roman Catholics, in which he set forth the theory that Whitman
rode East to save Oregon to the Union. Spalding said nothing about
dissensions within the Mission or about the fact that he had been
dismissed. The Whitman-saved-Oregon story rapidly gained nation-
wide acceptance.[42] Even though the theory was disproved by com-
petent critics in 1900, yet it has manifested an amazing tenacity to
survive. The story is still being repeated by some writers and is occasionally broadcast on radio and television programs. However, the
contemporary evidence as set forth in the Walker diaries is conclusive.
Whitman's primary purpose in going East was to save Spalding and
the Mission. And such was the opinion of the editor of the* Missionary
Herald *who, in his report of the Whitman massacre given in the July,
1848, issue, stated clearly: "He made a visit to the Atlantic States in
the spring of 1843, being called hither by the business of the mission."*

---

[42] A review of the extent and the literature of the Whitman controversy may
be found in Drury, *Whitman,* pp. 447 ff.

WED. 12. We sent off our letters for Dr. Whitman this morning. Have had [a] busy time the past week writing letters. . . Mr. Walker has written a long letter to Green. . .

THURS. 13. OCT. Mr. Eell's family left for Colvile.

FRI. 14. I feel constant distress & concern on account of our Mission. Sometimes feel that it will be given up. Fear all the time that I may have done wrong in some way myself. If in no other way, I fear I have too often thanked God that I was not like some other Missionaries. . .

TUES. 18 . . . The Chief's sons returned from Dr. W's., found no one at home.[43] Brought no letters so we know nothing.

WED. OCT. 19. We found Mr. E's house broken open & things stolen.[44]

THURS. 20. Mr. Eells & family returned. . .[45]

FRI. OCT. 21. Mr. Walker left for Colvile to carry Elizabeth. I sat up all night to get her ready & Mrs. E. & myself worked till after she was on her horse to get her things ready. Made out to get her in pretty good repair. I feel bad to part with her now tho I do not know how to keep her. I fear I have not done all I could to make her a good child. . . Mr. E's folks continue to miss this, that & the other thing. I hope we may be guided by wisdom & right feelings in regard to the thief.

SAT. 22 OCT. . . . A woman to whom I gave a few rags came to tell me her child was cold. How true it is that if you do any thing for an Indian they seemly expect you to do more. . .[46]

MON. 24. Kwantepetser came with the most part of the stolen goods. . .

TUES. 25. Mr. Walker returned from Colvile . . . brought a letter from Sister P[hebe]. It brings the cheering intelligence that many hard drinkers of my acquaintance have reformed. Also that brother Isaac has become hopefully pious & that he is more serious. . .

[43] Mrs. Whitman left Waiilatpu for The Dalles on Oct. 11, where she spent some time with the Rev. and Mrs. H. K. W. Perkins. In a letter to Mary, dated Nov. 5, Narcissa wrote: "I had made up my mind to spend the winter in our own dwelling but that week husband left a saucy Indian got into the house about midnight & tried to force himself into my bed room. John, Mr. McKinleys man was sleeping in the house but not very near. But I made a great noise & called as loud as I could & he took to his heels & ran." Coll. c.

[44] This was one of the most serious cases of stealing experienced by the missionaries during their nine years' residence at Tshimakain. As will be noted, most of the missing items were recovered.

[45] E.W. "I had a letter from McLean requesting that his daughter might be sent to him."

[46] Walker to Greene, March 27, 1844: "It seems to be a fixed opinion among them that if you give once, you are under obligation to continue giving, and to double the amount every time."

THURS. . . . The Old Chief came. Mr. W. has been out to the lodges talking with him. He does not manifest a very proper spirit and we think none of the people do. . .

SAT. 29. OCT. A few more of the stolen goods have been returned. . .

SUN. 30. Mr. Walker labored hard to convince the chief that he could [not be] saved by keeping the law but only by the atonement. . .

MON. 31. Mr. Walker & E. commenced making a book with the Old Chief as teacher.

TUES. Nov. 1. Received letters from below informing [us] that Dr. W. left for the States the 3 ult. consequently our letters were left behind. He took Mr. Lovejoy as a companion. We feel sorry he left so abruptly and [are] concerned about his station. . .

WED. 2. Mr. Walker had Indians help dig potatoes. . .

FRI. 4. Mr. W. & E. at the book. Chief for teacher. . C. is quite fond of learning to repeat & sing hymns but acts like a dunce when we try to teach him to read. Marcus . . . can climb & stand by things. . .

TUES. 8. The ox was killed. . .

WED. 9. Cleaned tripe & tried tallow. Have two pails full and a half. Mr. Walker & Eells not done with making the book. Old No-Horn has been lost these last two days, fear she will be quite done giving milk when we find her again. The Indians are about the house the whole time watching me. I scarcely do anything from morn till night without being seen by some of them. Some times I feel out of patience. I [feel] I cannot endure it any longer & then I think if I do not teach them in this way I never shall in any. . .

THURS. 10. Marcus requires a large share of my attention. Have been talking with Mr. E. & trying to have a fair understanding in regard to Sarah G.

FRI. 11. In the evening Mr. Walker cut up our beef. . .

MON. 14. Salted a keg of beef by the rule of 4 qts salt, 4 lbs. sugar & 4 ozs saltpeter to 100 lbs. The Old Chief came to assist about making the book. . .

THURS. 17. Mrs. E. teaching some girls to knit. She succed well.

FRI. 18. Had Soshenamalt to help me some. She made a pouch for Mr. W. & I fixed him a cap to ride in.

SAT. 19. Have done a good job of baking mince pies among other things. . . Mr. Walker finished his Indian book, ready for printing. . .

MON. 21. Mr. W. started about noon for Lapwai. I had occasion about sunset to give my children a little whipping upon which Miss Abigail ran off towards the lodges bawling & calling "father, father, come home, Mother whipped me." Cyrus inquired if his father had taken his tent with him. I told him no that he would sleep out of doors by a big fire, but he still expressed much concern. . . At supper he not only insisted on asking a blessing but on serving too & was frequently asking if he could pass me the butter & help me to berries. . .

TUES. 22. Washed & think I will not try to wash in the day time again very soon. Cyrus disobeyed in going into Mrs. Eell's house without permission. I tied him to the table leg. He was any how but contented with his situation & at last exclaimed, "I dont want to be tied. I think Indians tie dogs. When I went to the Chief's lodge, I think I saw his dog tied." A while since I kiss[ed] him after washing his face. He asked why I do so, adding "dogs kiss." . . . .

WED. 23 . . . Gary visits Mr. E.

THURS. 24. Mr. E. hunts the cattle & sends off the bull. Had to put a ring in his nose. . .

FRI. 25. Mr. E. went down to the Chief's encampment & sent off the package [of letters] in order to overtake Ellis. . .[47] Marcus is as uneasy as a child can be a great part of the time. Seldom sleeps more than half an hour by day light so that among them all they are almost more than I can comfortably manage. I can hardly cook my food & when it [is], I have a hard chance to eat it.

SAT. 26. Killed & dressed some chickens that had frozen their feet. Brought out the big rocking chair & fixed for Marcus a cradle & succeeded in making him sleep several hours, to pay for which I had his company till 8 this evening.

SUN. 27. Have been reflecting on the prospect before me. . . I can see no way that I can bestow that labor or attention on my family which it requires. In vain do I renew my courage & double my dilligence & retrench the hours of sleep. . . I was feeling much distressed in view of the weight of care, labor & responsibility that rests & must continue to rest upon me when the words of our Saviour occured to my mind, the spirit indeed is willing but the flesh is weak. I was led to hope that. . . God would look in compassion on my infirmity & . . . by his gracious Spirit supply what will be & is lacking on my part in the education of my children. . .[48]

28 MON. All the horses lost. Mr. E. with several Indians hunting them in morn. The first snow for the season.

[47] Mary's first reference to an important Nez Perce chief who, as a youth, spent about four years in the Red River mission school in Canada.

[48] Elkanah was at Lapwai on this day and was invited by Spalding to speak to the Nez Perces, using Lawyer as the interpreter. Commenting on this experience, he wrote in his diary: "I do not like to talk in this way as I do not know what he may say to them." Lawyer spoke both the Flathead and the Nez Perce tongues and had some knowledge of English.

TUES. 29. Had two girls sewing. Work as fast as I could all day & past 8 in the evening. Commenced washing, finished about midnight, rather too tired. Concluded to give up teaching Cyrus his alphabet & commenced with the Mother's primer. He is pleased with that & seems to understand. . .

WED. 30. Our girl helping sew. Feel the worse for my hard work yesterday. Our Maternal meet. should have been here. Got my hymn book out & looked for Mrs. E. in, but she did not come. Had a good season alone. . .

THURS. DEC. 1. Mr. E's lost horses found. We weighed our little boys. Edwin weighed 24½ lbs., Marcus 22½. . .

SAT. DEC. 3. Traded a nice bag of old Solomon, gave him seventeen loads for it, & a few feathers in it. . . I find my children occupy so much of my time that if their Maker should see fit to withhold from me any more till they require less of my time & attention, I think I shall be reconciled to such an allotment.

SUN. 4. The children obliged me to rise so early that [I] felt unfit for any thing all day. . .

WED. 7. Cyrus' [4th] birthday. Mr. E's family took dinner with us. After which we sang the Hymn commencing "My Soul know thou the Lord," followed with a prayer. . . At night he inquired if his birthday would be gone in the morning, said he did not like [it] to go away, but wanted it to stay always. I thought how often have I too sighed because the pleasures I tasted were so fleeting. May he so live that he will never wish his birthday had never been and may the day of death be better than that of his birth. We weighed him. Found his weight 43 lbs & Abigail's 31½. . . He is very tardy about minding, either loses or breakes all his toys.

FRI. 9. Finished one frock [for] Marcus & nearly another of some flannel. I colored [i.e. dyed them] myself [think] them very pretty.

SAT. 10. Mr. Walker returned bringing the first book ever printed in the Flathead.[49] He was obliged to set the type himself, tho he never set type before. There are misprints, but all things considered it looks pretty well, & consists of 16 pages. It is indeed to us a marvellous little book. The Mill at Waiilatpu is burnt, wheat & all.

SUN. 11. McPherson arrived from the Flathead country. I thought to have time for reading but most of the day was spent in conversation.

TUES. 13. The Eagle[50] arrives with an express from Mr. Spalding.

---

[49] This is one of the rarest of the eight items printed on the press at Lapwai. A copy is in the library of Pacific University, Forest Grove, Oregon, and another in Coll. c. See article by Myron Eells in *Washington Historian*, July, 1900, on "The first book written in the State of Washington."

[50] A Nez Perce sub-chief who often served as a messenger between mission stations.

Dr. White & company are there trying to regulate Indian affairs; [51] little hope they will now make us a visit. Tried to wash in the day but had to sit up & finish in the night.

Thurs. 15. Wrote a note to Mrs. Spalding. Marcus commenced running alone a step or two. In the evening stitched, pressed, trimmed 1½ dozen of the first book in Flathead.

19 Mon. Mr. Walker commenced teaching a school down in the Chief's encampment with eleven scholars. . .

Wed. 21. Ironed & press the rest of the books not yet stitched. Have of late many anxious thoughts about our mission. It grieves me to think [how] our brethren at the Islands feel towards us & about us as they seem to.

Sun. 25. Attended worship, left Marcus with Mrs. E. In the evening Mr. E's family came in to sing with us. . .

Tues. 27. Find I have taken cold in [a] decayed tooth & consequently have done little but tend upon it.

Wed. 28. Had little rest all night with my tooth.

Thurs. 29. Find my face much swollen, my tooth easier but not well. Took medicine & was rather sick all day.

Fri. 30. Feel much better, able to work most of the day & get my poor children washed & attended to a little as usual. I think sometimes what would become of them if their mother were taken away. I feel that I need to be sick occasionally to remind me of my mortality.

Sat. 31. It becomes me with feelings of devout gratitude to acknowledge the mercies of the past year. That our little family has not been lessened but increased & still all enjoy good or at least usual health. That we have been so bountifully fed & clothed from the same hand that feeds & clothes [the] raven & [the] lily.

1843 — A NEW AND BIGGER HOUSE

Big things were happening for Oregon during 1843 but Mary was too close to them to appreciate their true significance. In September, Whitman returned to Oregon at the head of an immigration of about one thousand people and two hundred wagons. He and his nephew Perrin joined the wagon train before it left the western frontier. At Fort Hall the Hudson's Bay factor urged the people to turn back. "It is impossible to take wagons over the Blue Mountains," he argued. "And without wagons it is not safe to take women and children." But Whitman, remembering how he and Spalding, in 1836, had taken their wagon to Fort Boise and how some mountain men, in 1840, had

---

[51] Hearing of the attempted assault on Mrs. Whitman and of the burning of Whitman's mill in October, Indian Agent White decided to visit the upper Columbia country. He was at Waiilatpu on December 1 and at Lapwai on the 3rd. White proposed a code of eleven laws to the Nez Perces, which were accepted by them. See Drury, *Spalding*, pp. 294 ff. tor a copy of these laws.

taken three wagons over the Blue Mountains, stoutly maintained that it was feasible for the wagon train to continue. So after leaving Fort Hall, Whitman was the acknowledged leader. The success of this first great immigration into Oregon was the magic key which unlocked the whole Pacific Northwest to the restless thousands on the western frontiers. Mary, however, failed to note its importance. Rather, she registered keen disappointment that the Doctor had not brought back a reinforcement. Little did any of the missionaries realize that the success of the 1843 immigration spelled the doom of their Mission.

Mary's diary continues to sparkle with comments on the flow of life about her. The first and only wedding ever held at Tshimakain during the mission period took place in the Walker home, after which Mary served "cake and cold water." She noted the difficulties that some mountain men in their employ had with native wives. During the year a number of material improvements were made on the mission premises. A well was dug, a barn was built, and on August 2 the Walkers moved into their new house which had been in the process of construction for over two years. The new house had more than seven hundred square feet of floor space, plus sleeping rooms in the low attic. This was more than twice the size of the first rude cabin which had been their home for more than four years. Now Mary could stretch out. She even had the luxury of a fireplace in her bedroom. Instead of a dirt roof the new house had a board roof. Mary still had to wait another two years before glass could be obtained for all of her windows.

During the year there was considerable sickness at Tshimakain. Myra Eells was often ill and this meant that Mary had to do extra work. The second Eells son arrived on October 7. Dr. Whitman had just returned from this eastern journey and was able to be present. In the fall Elkanah was called to Lapwai, where both of the Spaldings were seriously ill with scarlet fever. Elkanah contracted the disease and was very sick. In due time Cyrus also came down with it. Mary escaped.

This was a year of peace within the Mission. The trouble makers were gone. However, with the passing of time and with a fuller knowledge of the language and the customs of the people, the missionaries began to see more clearly the difficulties of their task. A whole tribe could not be transformed in a few years or even in a generation. As Elkanah and Mary were made more painfully aware during this year of the deep hold the medicine men and old superstitions had upon the minds of the people, they became more and more discouraged over the prospect of ever being able to do much good. The Christian forms of worship which the natives observed were but a thin veneer covering their age-old superstitions and practices.

On Christmas day a visitor came, the German botanist Karl Andreas Geyer. At first he was most welcome as he brought news of the outside world. But by presuming too much upon the hospitality of his hosts, Geyer outstayed his welcome.

SUN. JAN. 1. We observed the sacrament of the Lord's Supper. Found the season one of much profit & enjoyment. Tho I still desire earnestly a clearer view of the atonement. My mind seems obscured. O that I could overcome my slugishness in religion.

Another year dawns upon us. May God grant me a preparation of heart for whatever awaits tho it should be my own death or any of my family. . . May it please God this year to pour out his Spirit & convert many of the poor natives & may they be rescued in this way from false teachers. . .

WED. 4. Mr. E. & W. killed another young ox. There is about a foot of snow & it rains tonight. . .[1]

---

[1] E.W. for the 3rd: "Heard that they [i.e., the Indians] were going to play the medicine again at the Chief's. Felt somewhat tired about it. . . When will they learn not to trust in lying vanities?" Also for the 5th. "Had a considerable talk with the Old Chief about their medicine & was astonished that his belief in it was so strong. . . It does not seem quite right to keep silent [but] to come out boldly upon them, it seems to me, would do them no good." Previously, on January 27, 1841, Walker noted in his diary that the natives in their medicine ceremonies took up "hot stones in their hands." In a letter dated February 26, 1843, to Greene, Walker gave further details: "I presume that they attend worship in their lodges morning and evening, even when performing their heathen ceremonies. . . There can be no doubt that their system amounts to devil worship. They have given me to understand that it was, and that they pay it to appease him. . . Most of the evils they suffer in this life, they attribute to this evil spirit. . . Hence the necessity of their medicine men, who have power to destroy his evil influence upon them."

In 1847 J. M. Stanley, an artist, visited Tshimakain and painted portraits of several Spokane Indians including Big Star, whom he described as being "A Medicine Man of the Spokanes." In his commentary accompanying the picture, Stanley gave the following account of the practices of the medicine man:

"Whenever a person is sick, this tribe supposes that the spirit has left the body and hovers invisible in the air until it can be charmed or brought back through the agency of the medicine man. To accomplish this end, the patient is placed in a sitting posture, enveloped in a buffalo robe, or other covering, having only the top of the head exposed. The medicine man then commences dancing and singing around the patient, gesticulating mysteriously and often clutching in the air with his hands, as if in the act of catching something. The spirit is supposed to be attracted by the chant, and to hover near the aperture at the top of the lodge; and the dance is often continued for an hour before it can be caught. It is then pressed and rubbed as the medicine man pretends through the patient's skull, whose recovery, if not soon effected, he supposed to be thwarted by his having caught the spirit of some other person; and it then becomes necessary to undo his work by sitting it at liberty, and repeating the performance until the right spirit is caught. During my stay among the people much sickness prevailed and I was often kept awake all night by the wild chant and monotonous drum." Stanley,

SAT. 7. An express from Mr. Spalding's arrived. . . Mr. Little-john concludes to connect himself with our mission. Dr. White sent or ordered the express & a letter of advice to the members of the Mission. . .

THURS. 12. Marcus still sick. . . Paid off an Indian girl for footing stockings. Gave her two basins potatoes or a peck, a quart of flour & a knife & a piece of soap. But she complained bitterly because I paid her so little.

FRI. 13. Finished a gown for A. It takes me so long to finish every little job of sewing that I get most discouraged trying to do any thing.

SUN. 15. Our American cow has a calf.[2]

MON. 16. Salted a bag of beef. Washed in the morning.

TUE. 17 . . . Our ears are pained with hearing how much accord the Indians still pay to their superstitions. . .

WED. 18. Sat up all night to dip candles. Dipped 26 doz. . .[3]

FRI. 20. We went with all our children down to the Chief's. The weather clear & cold. . .[4]

SAT. 28. Cyrus done wearing frocks.

SUN. 29. Some six inches of snow or more have fallen within a day or two. . . Mr. E. took his family to worship on a horse sled. I have spent most of the day studying the scriptures.

MON. 30. Torteser returned bringing letters from below. I washed as usual in the evening.[5]

WED. FEB. 1 . . . Mr. W. is in trouble because Mr. E. don't do & talk to suit him.[6]

FRI. 3. Went to the Chiefs with Mr. Walker, took the children. . . The chief's old wife made a good fire to warm us. Took

---

Portraits of North American Indians, 70. The painting of Big Star was among those destroyed in the disastrous fire of January 24, 1865, at the Smithsonian Institution, Washington, D.C.

[2] E.W. "Went to the Chief's to address the people & found that he & his two wives were gone. . . The only thing which seems to engross their attention is what shall we eat & how shall we get it without labouring."

[3] E.W. "Confined to the house most of the afternoon to take care of the children to let Mrs. W. for dipping candles."

[4] E.W. for Sunday, the 22nd: "Found Mrs. W. reading newspapers when I returned both times from Indian worship & she said she had read nothing else all day." On Sunday, April 2, Elkanah wrote: "Think Mrs. W. spends too much of her Sabbaths in reading newspapers which as a general thing are not appropriate reading for the Sabbath day. They were never designed to be read on the Sabbath unless for a relaxation. No one who spends most of their time in reading papers, although of a religious character, on that holy day can have a very clear & exalted view of its sacredness & must suffer if not in time, they will in eternity."

[5] E.W. for the 31st: "Laid late this morning as Mrs. W. was up till past middle night washing."

[6] Elkanah reveals in his diary the fact that he and Eells were having some minor differences of opinion. On January 31 he wrote: "I have been brought into difficulty in listening to his remarks & suffering them to have influence with me."

off Cyrus' shoes & rubbed his feet & acted as motherly as anybody would. . .

FEB. TUES. 7 . . . Snow still continues to fall & the poor cattle come home every day almost in search of food. The Indians too begin to think about eating moss. . .[7]

THURS. 9. Have been thinking today that Satan does not consider this an unimportant field, if he did he would not give himself so much trouble about it. Neither has the Pope considered it so.

SUN. 12. Another snow storm. The snow is now very deep, piled to the eves of our little hut.[8]

MON. 13. The poor cattle, I fear, suffer much. They pick their living mostly in the water or along the banks. The horses live by digging. . .

SUN. 19. Have been reading Mirrors [of Portland, Maine] of 1840. How I would like to see those of '43 instead. Mrs. E. unwell again

TUES. 21. Cutting out shoes, I think for the last time this winter. It still continues to thaw. The Indians kill plenty of deer. . .

THURS. 23 . . . I still continue to have many thoughts in regard to our Mission. I feel that though one soul is not as valuable as two souls, yet for some reason God has seen fit to call us hither to labor & that he gives to some one tallent & to another two, places one in a field of extensive usefulness & another in a more limited sphere. True I may be deceived, yet my feeling is that God in his providence appointed to us our field of labor & that it becomes us to occupy it to the best of our abilities & not enquire why we were not sent elsewhere.

SUN. 26.[9] Mrs. E. is still distressingly ill. Washed to day. Have been reflecting on the Mercy of God to me. . .

TUES. Washed. Had Sarah & Edwin in our house some.

WED. MARCH 1. Cold weather yet & deep snow. Mrs. E. a little more comfortable. . .

THURS. 2. Cyrus has a kind of eruption, I do not know what. Abigail recently had the same.

FRI. 3. Mrs. E. still getting better. Mr. E. & W. drove their horses & sent them to the river where they can find better feed. . .

---

[7] In times of great necessity the Indians ate moss and fed it to their animals. Simpson, *An Overland Journey*, 88, wrote: "We found many large trees cut down, which, from their enormous size, must have cost great labor. . . We afterwards learned from the Indians that their object was to collect from the branches a moss having the appearance of horse hair which they used as food. By being boiled for three days and nights, this moss is reduced to a white and tastless pulp, and in this state it is eaten with the kammas."

[8] E.W. "Garry came in to day after some medicine for his boy who has been sick a long time."

[9] E.W. "The Indians get a plenty of deer & are as big & independent as they need to be."

SUN. 5. Five years since I bid farewell to home.[10]

MON. 6. Mrs. S. seems rather worse than better. Continues to vomit. Marcus & myself neither of us seem to get the better of our complaints. Find I am getting more feeble, conclude to wean Marcus. The cold weather continues severe. . .

WED. 8. Had two Indian girls to help me wash. They did nearly all. . . Mrs. E. seems no better. How much cause of gratitude have I; am usually blessed with good health. How much more have I than I deserve. . .

TUES. 14. Mr. W. walked to the Chiefs & back. The Indians inquired whether if Mrs. E. were dangerously ill, we would not apply to their medicine men? O! how pitiable is the condition of a mind bound in the chains of superstitions! Made some chicken broth which Mrs. E. has relished & ate as much as we dared give. She seems to be gaining now. . .

THURS. 16. Marcus birthday. He weighs only 24 lbs. not two lbs. more than he did three months since. . . Mr. W. to look for the cattle & found one of the Chief's cows dead. One of ours also is dead. It seems a pity they should starve. It was in consequence of their calves not being weaned. . .

MON. 20. Washed for Mrs. E. & myself, had two boys to help. Helped wash Mrs. E's floor & cleaned my shelves. Worked harder than usual but did not feel very much fatigued. Think my health improving since weaning my babe, as well as his.

TUES. 21. Ironed & finished making another suit for Cyrus. The Old Chief came, said he had opened & examined his dead cow, found she died in consequence of eating sticks.

WED. 22. The Chief came again & Mr. E. & W. commenced making another book. I baked 18 loaves of bread. A hard job for our old baker. What a handy thing an oven would be.

THURS. 23. Cut out a pair of leather pantaloons [for Elkanah] & set a girl making them. . .

FRI. 24 . . . I think I never saw a child whose mind was so constantly on the stretch as Cyrus. He is constantly making inquiries in regard to everything he can see or hear of. Wishes every word defined which he hears spoken that he does not understand. To day he stood at the door, halloing a while & then came in, wished to know what it was he heard in the mountain. We did not know at first to what he alluded, but he added, "Cyrus knows. We & the trees & every thing have a shadow & it is like that I think. My voice has a shadow." Seemed to be his idea.

---

[10] E.W. "The coldest night we have had for the winter. I pity the poor Indians that have no food & the poor beasts that have but little to eat." For the 6th: "Mrs. W. quite unwell to day so that I did the milking & cooked my own breakfast & supper."

In the evening Edwin E. came in & the four little ones sat all close together before the fire. When he [Cyrus] said "Now we are a group because there are plenty of us all close together. . .

MON. 27. The Chief's bull found drowned. . .

WED. 29. Mr. E. & W. hunting for a lost calf which they have found alive. They gave the Chief a live bull instead of his dead one & sold him the carcass of the dead one for three deer skins.

THURS. 30. The express arrived bringing the sad intelligence that Mr. Rogers & wife, Esq. [Nathaniel] Crocker, Mr. Leslie's youngest daughter & two Indians were drowned in the Wallamet the 1st inst. of Feb. They had reach[ed] in safety the end of voyage & were about to step from the boat. Dr. White who was with them had already stepped out when the boat gave a turn & was drawn into the suck of the fall & went over them. . .[11] Mr. Rogers was much esteemed by all & from his knowledge of the Nez Perce, we had anticipated much, altho he was not connected now with our Mission. . .

FRI. 31. Mr. McPherson arrived. Mr. E's family & ours all dined at our table. Mr. McP. has Charlotte along. Mr. Ogden has arrived at Colvile. A man has recently been murdered at New Caledonia. It seems Mr. McP. has been keeping house all winter. . .

APRIL, SAT. 1. Mr. McPherson was married to Miss C[harlotte] by Mr. E. in our house. We treated them with cake & cold water & the marriage passed off very passably.[12] Mr. E's family dined again at our table. Mr. Walker swaped horses & gave Mr. McP [some] Barnes notes.[13] They left after dinner. . .

To day is my birthday, 32. I can remember when my mother told her children she was 32. . . I hope I am better for having lived another year. . . I feel often to say with the Centurion, "Lord I am not worthy that thou should come under my roof but speak the word only." . .[14]

WED. 5. Cleared the bed room of mats[15] & white washed, Mr. W. & an Indian helping.

THURS. 6. Cleared the kitchen. . .

FRI. 7. The Chief & Big Star have come to make ground. Repaired the chimney & cleaned my bed room.

---

[11] Rogers, his wife, little child, and several others were swept over Willamette Falls on February 1, 1843.

[12] E.W. for 31st: "Mr. McP. . . had his intended wife with him. It was new to us as we had no intelligence that he had taken a wife. In the afternoon he spoke to me about being married. We thought some of doing it this evening but did not as we were delivered late about our chores." April 1: "Had the wedding in our house about eleven o'clock. Had cake but no wine."

[13] A reference to the well known Presbyterian minister and author of many Bible aids, Dr. Albert Barnes.

[14] Matt. 8:8.

[15] An important part of house cleaning was the removal of the old mats that lined the walls and ceiling and putting up new.

SAT. 8.   Had the Old Queen & her daughter helping me. The old woman whitewashed the kitchen & her daughter scoured all my tables, chairs, stools & shelves & then both together gave the room a faithful washing.

SUN. 9.   Glad to rest a little.

MON. 10.   Aired beding, had the door yard cleaned &c.   .   .

TUES. 11.   Cooked the last of our fresh beef.

WED. 12.   The Big Star's dog killed our only cock & three hens. Marcus taken sick.   ·.   .

FRI. 14.   Mr. W. sewing his wheat. Have given Marcus calomel & oil.   .   .

SUN. 16.   Edwin sick in the same way as Marcus.

MON. 17.   Think Marcus a little better. He begins to have an eruption if so it may be called as there is no pimple but only a curdly red appearance under the skin. When warm, very distinct, when cold scarcely discernable. Cyrus & Abigail [had] the same a short time since.   .   .[16]

TUES. 18.   Mr. W. left [for Colvile], not till near 11.   .   .   I have done little but take care of Marcus since he left.   .   .   Had a hard job milking because I could not ketch the calf. Feel very lonely this evening. Mr. W. has been gone so little of late that I have forgotten how to do without him. When I went out to milk all the children were awake. I left C. to rock M. A. got tired waiting, went way out in the garden & cried Mother a while & then came back when I came in. Marcus was asleep & A. sitting by him on a stool leaning on his chair partly noding & partly rocking her brother. Cyrus sleeping on the box & the room dark. I could not help pitying the poor things.   .   .

THURS. 20.   Ironed & cleared & cleaned up my bed room & did a small job of white washing & hearth fixing.   .   .   An Indian just now accosted me insultingly but suppose he [was] doing it in sport thinking I would not understand what he said.

FRI. 21.   Baked bread & mince pies. Finished whitewashing the kitchen. Just as I was finishing, Mr. Ermatinger with the express arrived. He brought word that Mr. Littlejohn's child, two years old, is drowned.   .   .[17]   He had much to communicate. We sat up till 12 at night. Mrs. Whitman has reached Walla Walla but fears to return to Waiilatpu as there is much talk of war among the Indians.   .   .[18]

---

[16] E.W. "Garry came in & he has promised us that he would come here & stay with us." The missionaries were eager to have Garry live in their vicinity to help them in translating the Scriptures.

[17] P. B. Littlejohn, one of the independent missionaries, entered Spalding's employ in January, 1843. His son, Leverett, was drowned in the mill race at Lapwai on March 29.

[18] Narcissa Whitman in a letter to Mary dated 11 April, 1843, wrote: "Nothing is talked of or has been for the whole winter but War! War! They say they [i.e., the Indians] have been told Doct W has gone home & is coming back next fall

SUN. 23. Only nine Indians at our place. . . Our little folks are all well again. . .

THURS. 27. Finished sowing onions. . . Mr. McKenzie arrived on his way to Colvile from the Flathead house.[19] Says the Indians are going to Waiilatpu to receive their laws and protect Mr. Spalding if necessary. . .[20]

SUN. 30. Another of our quiet sabbaths. No opportunity to benefit any but ourselves. . .

MAY, TUES. 2 . . . We have been for several days hourly expecting Mr. Ermatinger to return from Colvile but he does not appear. Mr. W. took calomel & ipecac which lays him up to day.

WED. 3. We had quite done looking for company when about noon Mr. Ermatinger & Mr. Ogden arrived. They dined & took tea with [us] & lodged in Mr. E's.

THURS. 4. Mr. Ermatinger . . . concluded to accompany Mr. Ogden to O[kanogan.] They left us in the morning & Mr. W. accompanied them to their first night's encampment. We enjoyed a pleasant visit except there was too much trifling conversation & Br. E's ego was quite too prominent. When a man of such extensive information is present, I regret to have the time occupied with trifles that might be filled up so usefully. After Com[pany] took leave, cleared up the storehouse & churned ten pounds of butter. Think my health improving. . .

MAY. SAT. 6. Found four hens that were setting; sure never going to hatch, but fortunately the eggs were not spoiled. . .

SUN. 7. Still another sabbath & no Indians about us.[21]

MON. 8. One Indian camped here to night, the only one we have

---

with 50 men to fight them. Dorion that came up with Doct White last fall has told them many things that has excited them greatly such as — there are troops coming into the mouth of the Columbia this spring. The Agent is coming up this spring with an armed force to take away their lands & compel them to adopt & enforce laws to regulate their own people & redress the wrongs of the whites." And also, "The Indians response to imagined threats said: 'We shall not fall alone. We shall notify all the Indians from the Rocky Mountains to the Coast & all join together to exterminate the whole white population. We shall not take the day for it but the night when they are all asleep." Coll. c.

[19] The location of this Hudson's Bay post among the Flatheads was not ascertained.

[20] Dr. White revisited Waiilatpu and Lapwai in May 1843. A big gathering was held at Waiilatpu on the 19th when between four and five hundred Nez Perces joined the Cayuses and the Walla Wallas. The Indians agreed to accept the laws but the attempted introduction of the white man's regulations brought complications. Since there was no enforcement agency set up beyond the voluntary cooperation of the chiefs, the laws were soon null and void.

[21] E.W. "Notwithstanding I love our English services, I want to have something to say to the natives when they stand so much in need of it & for that purpose I come here."

seen for some days. I do hope there will soon be some way opened for us to do more to benefit the Indians. . .

FRI. 12. Troubled about something. I did not wish to have my husband know, but hoping to relieve my mind told him. . .

SUN. 14. Still I feel sad about that something. My nerves are so much excited I can hardly eat or attend properly to many things. I feel ashamed & provoked with myself for thinking & feeling so much about a trifle, still I am unable to help it. I feel much perplexed in regard to what is best to be done. I have tried to cast my burden on the Lord but fear that sinful passions have the control of [my life.] If I could know what manner of spirit I am of, I should feel better. . .[22]

WED. 17 . . . Evening Mr. W. invited in Mr. E., had quite a talk with him, Feel some relief but said something I regret.[23]

MAY, THURS. 18. Slept little last night. Felt sadly this morning. But conclude my mind is probably more affected by my health than my health by my mind. Found my nerves in such a state as to occasion concern. Concluded to be bled. Found considerable relief from it. . .

FRI. 19. Rested pretty well last night but as soon as I began to stir in the morning, the faintness & distress at my stomach returned. . . I kept stirring till 3 P.M. & then tried to rest & read but could not feel comfortable, so went to work in the garden bringing water & watering plants which relieved me, also took some more ipecac. Just at night Garry came & his arrival seemed to exert a more salutary effect on my nerves. . .

SAT. 20. Rested very well last night. Feel better this morning. . . when once my nerves are unhinged, it was not easy to hinge them on again. I felt so much a horror of making difficulty. . .

22. MON. . . . Mr. Walker returned to day in the evening. Had a pleas[ant] time except that his horses came home before him so he had to borrow. . .[24]

THURS. 25. Plenty of Indians about. Showed Garry's wife how to make bread. . .[25]

SUN. 28 . . . Attended worship. Garry interpreted but seemed

[22] E.W. "Finished the fence around the field to day." During the winter months, Elkanah with some Indian help had been able to draw to his premises some timbers out of which he made his rail fences.

[23] E.W. "Had some conversation with [Mr. E.] in the evening, rather Mrs. W. did & [she] felt much better about things than I did. Mrs. W. in a very nervous state. I felt not well satisfied with all she said."

[24] Elkanah made an itinerating trip to the Bay over the week end. While there his two horses got loose and made the thirty-mile trip back to Tshimakain without him.

[25] E.W. "Commenced upon the second chapter of Matt. We have gone through five verses. . . Gary manifested some disposition to help about the work." Drury, *Walker*, Appendix 3, contains Walker's translation of the first four chapters of Matthew. Original in Coll. w.

embarrassed.[26] He does pretty well at teaching & learning. I hope we shall be able to obtain much help from him. But I fear we shall not have wisdom to manage him as we ought, & that Mr. W. & E. will not have patience enough to get along. I feel at a loss [to know] what to do with my children on Sunday. They are so restless. If I attempt to make them do as I would wish to have them, I cannot enjoy that rest I need myself. I do not know how much restraint it is desirable to impose. . .

TUES. 30.   Mr. Walker & Garry are getting on pretty well with the translating of the Commandments. . .

THURS. 1 JUNE.   A frosty night to finish May. Partly kill potato tops. . . Mr. W. & Garry went to Seakwakin. Mrs. Garry seemed not pleas[ed] about something. . .

SUN. 4.   A little frost. Gary so sleepy & stupid as not to be of much service.[27] The people seem more regardless of the Sabbath than formerly.

5.[28] MON. . . . Mr. McDonald's son Angus is dead. . . A poor foolish gambler at C. has shot himself. . .

WED. 7.   Transplanted some vines. Gave some of my squash plants to Mrs. E. We understand Gary intends to leave .Much as we need his assistance & anxious as we are to have him remain, we shall feel it a great relief to have him go. What is to become of us or our Mission, I do not know but I trust we shall learn to put our trust in God only. . .

THURS. 8.   Garry threatened to leave. Rode off a while & then came back, apparently better natured. . .

FRI. 9.   Mr. Walker left for the Bay. . .[29]

MON. 12.   Mr. W. returned from the Bay. A number of Bay Indians encamped near. I syringed out a boy's ear.

TUES. 13 . . .   Garry's wife went off with the Bay Indians to her mother. Garry also left.[30] Mr. E. had a long talk before he started. He

---

[26] E.W. "Had some talk with Garry . . . and it was finally decided that I should talk to him in English & he was to tell it to the people & we did. This is the first time I have talked to the Indians through an interpreter since I have been . . . at this place."

[27] E.W. "Had worship with the Indians & gave them part of the ten commandments in the forenoon. Had Garry sit near by me & when I did not go right to correct me."

[28] E.W. "Called Garry to worship & he did not come. He talked loud & long last night & his subject as near as I could understand it was showing the people the difference between the worship of us & the priests." For the 6th. "Do not like the appearance of Garry. Think he will not stay long."

[29] E.W. for Sunday, the 11th. "Laid late this morning & before I was up had a leg of venison given me. I told the one who gave it that I did not like to have things given me on the Sabbath. He replied that he did not give it me on the Sabbath, he gave it yesterday. I thought it showed his wit & said nothing more to him. Had worship with the people four times today & was quite tired at night."

[30] E.W. "Mr. Eells had a long conversation with him [i.e., Garry] and found

said the occasion of his leaving was not because he was displeased with us but because the people laughed at him & his heart was sad and evil. He evinced much remorse but no determination to break off his sins by righteousness. Surely unless the Almighty interferes in behalf of him or his people, swift destruction must overtake them. . .

JUNE, WED. 14 . . . The Indians brought us the first fresh salmon for the season. Several Indians who had started for the lower country returned on account of some disquietude among the Kayuses. . .

THURS. 15. The prospect before us in regard to the Indians seems to darken. I feel almost that we may as well not try to do any thing for them. . . The Old Chief came in to day. He had a long talk to make, telling how good he was & benevolent. I never saw him farther from goodness. What depraved hearts do they manifest.

SAT. 17. A fine rain again, caught abundance of washing water. Sewed some more turnip seeds. About 5 P.M. Mr. & Mrs. Littlejohn arrived from Clear Water. Mrs. L. extremely fatigued having had a fall from her horse & been drenched in the rain. . .

MON. 18. Still rainy. . . Washed. Mrs. Littlejohn helped me. She does thus far more work than she makes. . .

FRI. 23. Messrs W. & Littlejohn at work on the house. . .[31]

SUN. JUNE 25. Mr. W. & L. went to Seakwakin & Mr. E. to the river. I was somewhat disconcerted by an Indian entering the house. He came to my bedroom. I told him not to come in.[32]

MON. 26.[33] Washed. Traded [for] strawberries & huckleberries

---

that it was the people who drove him off, not being able to withstand their ridicule. Poor things, they know not what they do." This marked the end of the efforts of the missionaries to use Garry. Although he remained friendly, Garry rarely visited Tshimakain after this date. Garry's two wives were named Lucy and Nina. Jessett, *Chief Spokane Garry*, 84, identifies the one with him at this time as Lucy.

[31] With Littlejohn's help, Walker put in the gable ends of the roof on the new house on the 21st and the 22nd. In order to get greater insulation, he put mats and grass "under the boards" on the roof. Walker refers to the use of cedar shingles on the barn. Perhaps the use of the word "boards" actually refers to large board shingles. However, the reference may have been to overlapping boards laid parallel to the gable.

[32] See entry in Mary's diary for April 20 of this year. Note also that all three men were away when this incident took place. Not a single instance of molestation of the women occurred at any of the Mission stations even though the women were often left alone for days and even weeks. However, as here indicated, there are records of the women being insulted several times and at least twice, once with Mrs. Whitman and here with Mrs. Walker, of Indians attempting to enter their bedrooms at night.

[33] E.W. "We heard this morning that a white man was on his way to our place but who he was or his object in coming we could not learn." For the 27th: "Just at night the man came in & proved to be a New Englander, [Mr. Campbell.] who had been employed by the Methodists." Walker agreed to hire him to work on the house for "a dollar per day & his food & to cook it himself, till the end of October."

WED. 28. Mr. Walker engaged Mr. Campbell to work. Mrs. McDonald & family with Mr. McKenzie arrived about noon.

THURS. 29 . . . Had our Maternal meeting instead of yesterday. Mrs. McDonald & family being present. She dines with us but takes breakfast & supper in the other house.

FRI. 30. Considerable going on for this place. Mr. C. build chimney; [34] Mr. L. planing boards. . .

SAT. JULY 1. The Chief came in scolding because we did not keep the Indian horses out of his fields, & seemed any how but pleasant. Camped near.

SUN. 2. Mr. E. went to the river in the forenoon. Mr. W. spoke to the Indians. Mr. & Mrs. L. held a sabbath school with the children. Mr. W. preached in English in the afternoon. . . I think we have passed rather a pleasant & profitable sabbath. . .

MON. 3. Mrs. L. did most of the washing. I traded berries, cooked, bake some, got very tired. Monthly concert in the evening.

TUES. 4. Mr. E. & most of the children went to the river but got no salmon. Wish I could know how brothers, sisters, cousins & friends are spending the day. . . [35]

THURS. 6. Baked a dozen loaves of bread in the old baker. Hope some day I'll have an oven. Campbell is making the brick. . .

SUN. 9 . . . Have been arguing with Mr. L. He contends that if a parent does his duty, the salvation of the child is certain.

MON. 10 . . . An express arrived bringing letters from home & the S.I. The letters from the U.S.A. came by ship & were not so recent as the ones I received last fall. The British flag flies over the S.I. [36]

TUES. 11. Mr. W. left for C. . . About sick myself from fatigue & excitement in reading letters. Several boxes for our Mission were sunk in the Columbia [River] as well as our big kettle. . .

SUN. 16. Mr. W. went to the river & Mr. E. preached in English in our new house. . .

JULY SAT. 22. Things go on much as usual. . . Mr. C. has burned the brick-kiln. The weather is exceptionally hot. . .

TUES. 25. Ironed. Have green beans & potatoes every day. . .

---

[34] E.W. "Rode out with Mr. Campbell to see if we could find any clay to make brick. He concluded that that near the house would do." When the author visited the mission site in July 1960, he and Mr. Robert Seagle, the present owner of the premises, noted a cavity at the foot of the hill near the original building site from which the clay was probably dug. Walker in his diary tells of constructing a rude kiln in which some clay bricks were burnt. These were used for the oven and the fireplaces.

[35] The return of such popular holidays of that time as the Fourth of July and New Year's Day usually called to Mary's mind nostalgic memories of her home in Maine.

[36] The captain of a British frigate raised the flag of his country at Honolulu on February 25, 1843. However, the British government refused to endorse this action and the Hawaiians regained their sovereignty on July 31 of the same year.

Fri. 28 . . . A white man [came] around, named Adams.[37] His Indian wife is the mother of Mr. Ogden's eldest son.

Sat. 29. Campbell finished the chimney [in the kitchen.] Adams went [to] work with him. . .

Mon. 31. Washed. Campbell building the chimney in our bedroom.

Wed. Aug. 2. Ironed in the morning. Moved into the new house.[38]

Thurs. 3. Tried to heat the oven but can not make the flue draw. After a time succeeded in getting a good heat and baked some nice bread. Spent considerable part of the day trying to do something to relieve Mungo's wife who seems to be in a critical situation.

Fri. 4. The jugler or medicine men kept up their business till about midnight when they rested. I arose about two when they had again commenced. Went out to the lodge. When they saw me approaching they ceased. The woman remains the same. About 9 A.M. gave her cathoric pills. About noon tried to administer an injection but did not suceed well. After dinner gave more pills. But all seems to effect nothing. This evening they commenced their medicine again. I went out determined to induce them to stop, talked a long time, gave them my advice & then told them to do as they thought best, play or not play it. They have ceased but how the matter will end I know not. But hope all will be ordered in mercy.

Sat. 5. After a little time the medicine men commenced again, rather still at first but became louder as soon as the dead of the night came on. In the morning we were informed that a child was born. The safe delivery was all the result of their ridiculous jugling. . .

Mon. 7. Mr. & Mrs. Littlejohn & Mr. Walker left about ten A.M. for Clear Water. Campbell's woman came back in the night & insisted in being admitted to his house. . .[39]

Tues. 8 . . . That woman has not moved off, I fear the man is as much in fault as she. . .

Thurs. 10. Cleaned furniture & house. Kwantepetser came & helped me in the morning. Mungo came for his wife who is not able to return. . .

Fri. Aug. 11. Cleaning & preserving berries & ironing. . . Pleased at the course C[ampbell] appears to pursue with his Indian wife. . .[40]

Sun. 13. Get along very quietly in the new house. . .

Tues. 15. The men set about diging a well, dug near as deep as

---

[37] E.W. "Still another man from the mountains came in after employment." For the 31st. "Made a bargain with Adams to day & agreed to pay four pounds per month till the first of October & find him food enough for himself & wife."

[38] E.W. "Moved into our new house. Had a hard day of it. The Teacher's family came in for his daughter [Mungo's wife] to be confined."

[39] E.W. for August 1st. "Campbell sent off his woman because she was with child by an Indian." Evidently the Walkers let Campbell live in their old house.

[40] Mary evidently approved Campbell's decision not to take his wife back.

they could on account of its caving as they began on a small surface, but just as they were about concluding to abandon it as hopeless, Mr. E. was punching a hole in the bottom & perceived the water beginning to run in.[41]

WED. 16. They shored the well. Mr. C. gave his woman a severe horse whipping. But altho he cut gashes through her leather dress, skirt, & hide, yet before sunset she was back, teasing him again. . .

THURS. 17. Still looking rather anxiously for Mr. W. . .

FRI. 18 . . . That troublesome woman is encamped near the wheat field. Suppose she helps herself to corn & wheat as much as she likes. I hope she will not be suffered to do any harm. . .

SAT. 19. My dear husband reached home again. He waited several days for Mr. Spalding to return but did not see him after all.[42] I think C. will not succeed in throwing away his wife but that to get rid of her, he will take her again.

SUN. AUG. 20. Another quiet Sabbath. I sometimes think it is pleasant to be where we feel that we are dependent on God alone for security. Mr. W. had some talk with the woman & gave her some bread. He said she threatened to burn the house because she was mad but that she did not intend to do it.

MON. 21. Washed with water from the new well, find it soft, had Adam's wives taught to help me.

TUES. 22. Campbell's woman came round the house & told Mr. W. she wanted him to tell her husband to take her back. He told him what she said & so he yielded & took her back & that was like having a woman to get rid of her.

WED. 23. Adams left to day.[43] When his wife found that C. was going to keep his wife, she was for leaving at once. Her plan no doubt was to induce C. to set aside his wife & take her daughter, and she no doubt felt not a little vexed & mortified at her defeat so the thrown-away woman is again reinstated mistress of the old house. . .

FRI. SEPT. 1 . . . Commenced making a cap for Mr. Campbell yesterday & finished it to day. Adams returned saying he was the happiest man in the world having got rid of his wife. But before sunset

[41] The original well is still in use. After the mission period some one lined the well with cement.

[42] A few days after Walker left Lapwai to return to his home, Mrs. Spalding was taken seriously ill with scarlet fever. After his return, Walker began the construction of a log "barn & school house." The logs had already been assembled and with Indian help the building was soon up. On the 30th he wrote in his diary: "Finished the shingles to day & brought home eight hundred & twenty five." During the first part of September, he stored some hay in the barn. Thus for the first time some provision was made for the feeding of the animals during the winter months.

[43] E.W. "Adams came in while we were at breakfast & said he was going to leave me. . . His excuse was that the women would not agree."

wife came after him & took him a willing captive & he turned in with as contented & happy [spirit] seemingly as any man who had been separated from his wife a few days. . .

Sun. Sept. 3 . . . Mr. W. held two services in Indian and one in English, aside from herding horses an hour or two in the morning. His labors are too arduous. I feel concerned for him. . . Last night an old man came who said a daughter of his had lately hung herself because her [husband] scolded at her. He wished to know whether the husband should be killed. It seems to be an Indian rule if one gets vexed or commits suicide, to kill the one who vexed. . . An old woman came on account of the snake bitten son saying that the man by whom we sent certain articles yesterday refused to give to the sick an old rag designed to wrap his sore limb.

Mon. 4 . . . Just at night went to see the bitten boy who is brought near that we may do something for him. The flesh on most part of foot & ancle is falling off leaving bone & sinews exposed. It is a filthy state so that it is difficult to tell how much live flesh there is. I feel little courage to undertake to do anything for him.

Tues. 5. Dug eight hills potatoes. . . Went this forenoon to attend to the sick boy. Had him washed, tried to clean his wound with suds but to little purpose. Applied a poultice of charcoal & yeast.[44]

Sat. 9. Continue to apply the poultice to the boy's foot. But [in spite of all] I am able to do, I cannot clean it from filth & vermin. I give him salts to regulate his bowels. . . I have given him opium two nights past. To night an old man came in & complained that we did not administer powerful medicine. . . We have had the oven taken down & rebuilt, altered & enlarged it & it bakes pretty well now. . .

Sun. 10. Feel much discouraged. It seems almost in vain to hope to benefit this people. They seem determined on their own destruction. . . I feel that God will be just should we never see any fruit of our labors & should they all be left to perish. . . How much we need a strong hold [on God] in everyday trouble & darkness. I feel that we dwell as it were in a den of lions and except the Lord had shut their mouths, they had long ago devoured us.

Mon. 11.[45] The Indians concluded their own medicine was best & did not wish any more poultice, thinking it to be powerless. At night he sent desiring nothing but opium. I gave him a mild dose. . .

Tues. Sept. 12. We were awakened about midnight by a frantic wailing of the Indian woman. Before sunrise an old woman came to

---

[44] Undoubtedly gangrene had set in. Charcoal would absorb toxins and bad odors.

[45] E.W. "Succeeded well in hauling down the hay. Had three light loads & laid up a part of the gable ends of the barn." Here is another reference to a wagon at Tshimakain.

say the boy was dead. . . The friends, some of them, seem to think that an old Indian medicine man occasioned his death because he had a quarrel against his father. I think it fortunate that they took him off my hands so much before he died. . .

Evening — An express arrived from Mr. Spaldings stating that Mrs. Spalding was at the point of death & desiring Mr. Walker to come immediately.

WED. 13. Mr. W. left or sat out at about eight o'clock. . .

SAT. 16. Still I go on my old course. It is a great tax on my time & strength to feed so many. Have cut out two dresses to day. . .

MON. 18. Had Adams woman helping me cut pumpkins. . .

TUES. 19. Have been baking & choring about. . . Get so tired of being looked at the whole day that my patience almost deserts me some times. Told the father of the deceased boy my heart was not good because he was about me all the [time] & desired him not to come again till Mr. Walker's return.

SAT. 23. We still look in vain for Mr. W. Feel very anxious to hear from him, & from Mr. Spalding & from Dr. W. & to know what God will do with our Mission. It is sad to think what it is & what it probably might have been had all been engaged in hold[ing] up each other instead of pulling each other down. . .

TUES. 26. Received a letter informing that Dr. Whitman was expected to reach his station about this time. . .[46] As no rumor of Mrs. Spalding's death reaches us, we trust she may still be alive. . .

THURS. 28. P.M. Mr. Walker reached home. Left Mrs. Spalding convalescent altho when he arrived they supposed her dying. Mr. Spalding was himself sick but is better now. Dr. Whitman reached Clearwater on Monday last. Has brought no reinforcement but expects one next year. . .[47]

MON. OCT. 2. Dr. W. arrived in the night.

TUES. 3. Mr. Walker diging potatoes with the assistance of Indians. . .

THURS. 5. Mr. Walker set out for Waiilatpu. David Malin went with him. The Old Queen has gathered in the potatoe tops. I have put a window in the study, had oats threshed & filled a straw bed, corded a bedstead & made up a spare bed & Dr. W. is occupying it.

---

[46] Dr. Whitman, having heard of the serious illness of Mrs. Spalding, left the immigration and hastened on to Lapwai where he arrived on the 25th. Walker left the next day for his home.

[47] The September, 1843, issue of the *Missionary Herald*, pp. 356 ff., commented as follows on Whitman's visit to Boston: "After a long and toilsome journey, he reached Boston early in the spring; and upon hearing the representations he made, it was resolved to sustain the operations of the mission without any material change. . . Another object of Doct. Whitman, in making the above mentioned visit, was to procure additional laborers. He desired also to induce christian families to emigrate to settle in the vicinity of the different stations."

FRI. 6.   Dr. W. very uneasy, regrets he came soo soon.   .   .

SAT. OCT. 7.   Was called up about midnight to attend on Mrs. E. She was not so [sick] but what she rested & allowed us to [do so] considerable after day light. I came home, milk[ed], got breakfast & Dr. W. ate, then returned to attend on Mrs. E. Mr. E. came to take some breakfast. When he returned, he found his wife nicely in bed & was presented with a son.   .   .   As she & the babe both appeared well, Dr. W. concluded to leave immediately & had his horse about noon.[48]

SUN. 8.   Mr. E. went to attend worship but the Indians were off threshing wheat.   .   .

MON. 9.   Have accomplished a large washing.   .   .

SAT. 14.   An express brought letters from home, & Mirrors &c.   .   . I commenced writing a letter for home.   .   .

SUN. 15.   Quiet & lonely as ever.   .   .

FRI. 20.   Took up the hearth in the kitchen & laid down the [stones] to suit me better, while about it Mr. Walker arrived.   .   .

SUN. 22.   A part of the day reading DeSmet's book, sufficiently disgusted with the accounts he gives of Indian character & with the doctrines he teaches.   .   .[49]

MON. OCT. 23.   Mr. W. unwell, took calomel last night.   .   .   Many Indians about us.

FRI. 27.   Mr. W. better but not well yet. Milked & got kicked over & hurt me some.   .   .

MON. 30.   Mr. W. took down the chimney in our bed room as far as the mantle piece & rebuilt it as far as the roof. It draws well now. I washed in the evening.   .   .

WED. [Nov.] 8.[50]   Mr. W. unwell again. Received a note from or Mr. E. did from Dr. Whitman. He has got home from below with his wife. Mrs. Littlejohn reached Waiilatpu on Sat. & was confined on Wed. Nov. 1st. Mr. L. is to winter with the Dr. & to take the farm next summer. I hope things will go pleasantly, but I fear.

---

[48] Whitman had reason to be restless as he felt the importance of being at Waiilatpu when the main body of the immigrants would pass. According to Walker's diary, Walker with David Malin were detained somewhere after they left Tshimakain on the 5th. They met Whitman at the "Palouse crossing" and from there the three travelled together arriving at Waiilatpu "early Tuesday morning." The main body of the immigrants had already passed. On the 5th Walker wrote: "I was introduced to quite a number of interesting gentlemen with whom I had a pleasant interview."

[49] While passing through St. Louis, Whitman purchased a copy of DeSmet's *Letters and Sketches*, which had just been published. On p. 367 of this volume was the reference to Tshimakain quoted herein, page 221 note 63. Undoubtedly Whitman turned his copy of this volume over to the Walkers to read.

[50] On Nov. 6 Elkanah wrote in his diary: "Finished putting the roof on my barn & hen house." His diary contains no other entries until December 7 when he commented on his illness and added: "Although Dr. Whitman was sent for, he did not come which was a great disappointment to me."

THURS. 9. Had an Indian girl mending shoes yesterday & today. Mr. W. sick. To attend on him, the children, & the Indians takes nearly all my time so my sewing drags on heavily. I feel much concern in regard to our Mission, hope all will yet end well.

FRI. 10. Mr. Walker took calomel & jallop [51] which distressed him very much, exciting naucia. . .

SUN. 12. Mr. W. seemed to day [to be] under the operation of the medicine he took on Friday . . . towards night was bled which seemed to afford some relief. I find it difficult to keep the children at all quiet.

MON. Nov. 13. Mr. W. seems not much if any better. Conclude to send for Dr. Whitman. Old Solomon started about noon. We are quite uncertain what may be the kind of Mr. W's sickness. . . Complains much of his head. We fear he may be dangerously ill.

TUES. 14. Passed a sad lonely night last night. Mr. W. rested very little. . . He is very sick but I do not know whether to be alarmed or not. . .

THURS. 16. Mr. W. more restless. Seems to have more fever. He awaits very anxiously the arrival of Dr. W. Feel faint & exhausted with watching.

FRI. 17. Mr. W. rested better so that I had to be up only once, about two hours. He seems very low, sweats much of the time.

SAT. 18. Look in vain for Dr. W. . . Gave him a little wine to revive him & opium to make him rest.

TUES. 21. Solomon returned without the Dr. Neither his own nor his wife's health would admit of his coming. He sent medicine & directions. Mr. W. still appears to be getting a little better. . .

THURS. Nov. 23. Gave no medicine to day except quinine in the morning. No food seems to suit him except gruel & sour berries. Less disposed to sweat. Countenance brighter. . .

SAT. 25. Very cold & blustering. Mufflehead returned from [Colville.] Did not arrive till late in the evening. Mrs. McDonald sent a hen to me & another to Mrs. E. Mr. McD. sent wine, lime juice, rice & coffee to Mr. Walker. The wind beat down [the] chimney so that Mr. Walker had to do without [a] fire in his bedroom for several hours.

SUN. 26. The wind continued to blow till near sunset. It has taken all the time to tend fires & sweep up soot, etc. Have had an unpleasant day in some respects, no time to read. Feel much solicitude about Mr. Walker. . .

TUES. 28. Washed, had two Indians to help. Mr. W. quite patient till towards night. . .

[51] Jallop or Jalap was the dried root of a tuberous plant that grows in Mexico. It was used as a mild cathartic.

WED. 29. With the aid of a girl chinking the house with moss.[52] Find I cannot have exposure without inconvenience. . . Mr. W. seems to be recovering quite rapidly.

THURS. 30. Cleaned my buttery. The weather more moderate.

MON. [DEC.] 4. Had a new girl or rather woman to help me, find it requires patience to get along. Monthly concert in the evening. Feel tired. Have hard work to find time to eat. Scarcely sit down from morning to night.

TUES. 5. A pleasant day. Mr. W. walked to Mr. E's twice & rode on the sled once. May not our anticipation in regard to his health be disappointed. . .

THURS. 7.[53] Cyrus 5 years old. Mr. E's family took dinner with us. Mr. Walker eat with the family the first time for a month & rode out also on horseback.

FRI. 8. Had two girls sewing, one of them a young married woman. Fear she will not make much, she seems so heedless. Had to take out some of her work several times.

SAT. 9.[54] Mrs. E. & myself went to attend on an Indian woman. It was a case of preter natural labor & we succeeded better than we expected we could. We probably saved the life of the mother tho we could not that of the child. We were obliged to obtrude our services & on account of their distrust we hurried more.

MON. 11 . . . Swaped potatoes for bitter root. Near night heard that she stole the roots. Sent them back to the owner. Send an Indian down cellar to pick up a kettle of potatoes. Went out of the room, soon returned & caught Mufflehead stealing potatoes. The one in the cellar handing them to him & he puting them in his own [basket.] He looked much ashamed.

TUES. 12. The woman who stole [the] bitter [root] did not make her appearance. Took another in her stead.

WED. 13. Have risen for near a week past about four. Feel tired & sleepy. . .

SAT. 16. Warm showery weather. Mr. W. sized the window in the kitchen. He is able to over see the Indians, three of whom he now employs & do considerable light work himself.

SUN. 17. A lonely sabbath. Wish I were not so stupid. . .

---

[52] Evidently the spaces between the logs had not been properly filled in with mud or clay before this time. Chinking with moss was but a temporary expedient.

[53] E.W. "Cyrus is to day five years old. . . As have been our custom, we made a dinner & invited Mr. Eells & wife to dine with us. Sat down with the rest for the first time for more than a month."

[54] E.W. "Mrs. W. spent some time at the lodges over a woman that could not be delivered. After a little exertion they succeeded in delivering the child."

Wed. 20.[55] Mr. W. employs three Indians out of doors & to day I had two girls but find it too hard work to keep two busy. Told only one to come tomorrow. Would be glad to keep them all out of idleness if I could. . .

Mon. 25. A German botanist arrived. . .[56] Took supper with us.

Sat. 30. Mr. Geyer takes supper with us, breakfast & dinner at Mrs. Eells. . . The weather being cooler, we have killed beef again. Cyrus unwell for several days past. He manifests much thoughtfulness for a child. The other day he enquired why some of the Indians travelled on the sabbath. I told him because they did not remember the sabbath day & keep it holy. He enquired where then they would go when they died. I told him. Then said he, "I think plenty of Indians will go with me." I asked where? He said, "to the bad place." I asked him if he expected to go there. He said, "Why my heart is always bad & you tell me if I have a bad heart I will go to the bad place." He said he had asked God a great many times to make his heart good but he had not done it yet.

Sun. 31 . . . Mr. Walker unwell, taken ill in the night. Cyrus not appearing any better. . . We have great reason for gratitude in view of the mercies of the past year. Many mercies still continue to follow us.

1844 — LABOR AND TRIAL

The year beginning January 1, 1844, was a quiet, somewhat uneventful year for the Walkers at Tshimakain. Life had settled into a routine. Both Elkanah and Mary continued to be involved in the steady grind of hard physical labor. Both were at times discouraged at their appar-

---

[55] During these days Walker was busy hauling in fire wood. On the 21st he wrote: "I have been busy about the windows & have got them fixed pretty much to my liking. This house has more light in it now than we have had at any time since we have been in the country. The roof has leaked quite bad which has cost Mrs. W. considerable trouble. The school commenced to day." On the 22nd: "Made me a whip & made one important discovery. That the Yew tree is a very smart wood & will be very useful to us." The Western Yew which grows in that vicinity has the qualities of toughness and elasticity which make it a good wood for whips.

[56] E.W. "A white man came in to day saying he was a Botanist employed by Sir Wm. Drummond Stuart. He appears a well informed man. "See *Oregon Historical Quarterly,* June, 1940, with article by author on "Botanist in Oregon in 1843-44 for Kew Gardens, London." Walker may be mistaken in saying that Geyer was employed by Sir William. Geyer in a letter dated May 16, 1845 (quoted in the above mentioned article) stated that he traveled for a time with the Stewart (or Stuart) party but "left that party at the upper Colorado of the West." While at Tshimakain during the winter of 1843-44, Geyer made a drawing of the mission buildings. See illustration on page 185. This gives us the best conception of the premises that we have.

ent lack of progress in evangelizing the natives. Their fourth child, a son, was born on February 10. The birth took place about ten days earlier than was expected. When Dr. Whitman finally came, Mary met him at the door with her babe in her arms. The child soon developed a rupture in the groin, which gave his parents much concern. In April they journeyed to Waiilatpu to have the doctor see him. When they returned, the Walkers took with them the motherless, six-year old Emma Hobson who lived with them for a year. In addition to Mary's usual duties, she found it necessary to begin the education of both Cyrus and Emma.

The German botanist, Karl A. Geyer, wore out his welcome. On July 4, Elkanah had frankly to tell him that they could no longer entertain him. During the year, a number of material improvements were made in the home and on the premises. The Walkers took a heating stove back to Tshimakain with them when they returned from Waiilatpu in May. However, Elkanah delayed in putting up the pipe until the first part of October. Mary got some paint and painted the doors and wood-work of her house and all of her furniture. Elkanah built a log school-house for the Indians, which is also referred to as the Indian house or chapel. On July 13, Mary heard of the death of her mother, which had occurred on February 26 of the previous year. At the end of the year Elkanah wrote in his diary: "It has been a year of labor & trial but one of health to me & mine."

Mon. Jan. 1   .   .   .   Conclude Cyrus has scarlet fever.   .   .

Wed. 3.   Cyrus is very quiet, seemed to suffer but little.   .   .   I hope he is not to be taken away till he is prepared.   .   .

Fri. 5.   Salted our beef. Feel very lazy most of the time. Cyrus not as smart as yesterday. Gave him oil & a little calomel.   .   .   Still says he is not sick, only wishes to lay still, cannot walk but cant know why. I do not know whether we have reason to be alarmed or not. Hope he is not to be taken from us. Tho I feel that I too well deserve such a chastisement.   .   .

Sun. 7 [1]   .   .   .   Little or no change in Cyrus. As frequently of late, had an Indian to watch while we eat supper.   .   .

Tues. Jan. 9.   Cyrus seems a little better.   .   .   To night he took quite a little supper.   .   .

Wed. 10.   Sosphenamalt ironed & cast wickes for candles.

---

[1] E.W. "This is the first time I have had worship with the people for a long time. . . One of my [wood] choppers came in just at night & staid until the table was cleared off when he left, no doubt offended. It is hard not to feed them, but if one should feed them at such times, our house would be over run with them at meal time." During the winter months, the natives were often hungry. The missionaries found it easier to hire Indians to work for them during this season than during other months of the year. Wages were never paid in money but in food such as potatoes and other commodities.

THURS. 11. Cyrus seems better, eats considerable & wants me to help him play much of the time. S. helping me dip candles, dipped 26 doz. . .

TUES. 16.[2] Employed two girls again, one just to get rid of her. . .

THURS. 18 . . . The Teacher as we call [him,] here in the forenoon & evening. But Mr. Geyer engrossed most of the time relating his adventures.

FRI. 19.[3] Baked mince pies &c., got very tired. . .

FRI. 20. Cyrus seems better. Wants to eat a great part of the time. Finished making him a suit of clothes. . .

TUES. 23. Employed two girls washing. Feel at loss often [to know] what to do. It is very perplexing to deal with such characters. When we see them in fair, sunny weather of summer, idle or gambling, we feel vexed but when in consequence we see them starving in winter, how ought we to do?

WED. 24. Cyrus seems to be gaining tho not able to stand alone. Girls & I at work repairing shoes & stocktings. Commenced raining this afternoon. . .

MON. 29. Sosphenamalt did my washing & washed the floor & got done by noon, only I boiled the clothes, heat water & the like. Cyrus seems to improve. Walked a little with leading. . .

WED. JAN. 31.[4] Our Maternal fast day or should be. I dismissed my Indian girl & enjoyed a quiet day, only the children were rather troublesome. So I found little time for devotion. We were to have had our meeting but Mrs. E., I suppose, could not manage to attend. Cyrus commenced walking a few steps alone, was so pleased he told of it several times. . .

SAT. [FEB.] 3 . . . Partly made a broom of corn of our raising. . .

THURS. 8. Weather quite cool. I baked brown bread & pumpkin pies. Cyrus is beginning . . . to run from one house to the other alone.

FRI. 9. Pieced together a pair of pantaloons for a rug.

SAT. 10. Baked & did some couloring [i.e. dyeing], got very much fatigued so that with much difficulty I got supper. Washed & put my children to bed. Scarce succeeded in clearing the gable [room] when I became so ill I was obliged to call Mrs. E. We managed to get along the best way we could & about ten o'clock in the evening or a little

---

[2] E.W. "I went to the river. . . The people at that place are making medicine for snow."

[3] E.W. "A child died last night & they buried it without calling us to have worship. Taught the school." At this time the school was being conducted in Walker's old house.

[4] E.W. for the 30th. "Another horse has been killed to day [by wolves.]"

later, we were blessed with another son. A fine plump little fellow, weighs 8¼ lbs. . .[5]

TUES. 13. Rested tolerably well last night. Babe quiet. . . Not much pain. Took medicine & crawled off my bed on to the settee. . .

WED. 14 . . . To day am some better, dress myself & sit up considerable. . . I hope I shall soon recover as it makes it so hard for Mrs. E. The weather is fine & the children play out of doors much of the time. . .

SAT. 17.[6] Took supper with the family & helped wash & undress the children. . .

MON. 19. Babe slept well last night. . . Had Sosphenamalt & her brother to wash. Superintended myself & washed a little. S. got done about two o'clock, floor & all.

TUES. 20 . . . At noon went out to work in the kitchen, made mush, boiled wheat & fried doughnuts & cleaned my buttery a little. . .

THURS. 22. Baked. Dr. W. arrived in the evening. I met him at the door with my babe in my arms.

MON. 26.[7] Dr. W. left. Mr. Walker & Cyrus accompanied him to his first encampment. . .

SAT. MARCH 2.[8] Garry called on us this morning. Traded an ax. Baked fried cakes. . .

MON. 4. Adams & family, Mr. Geyer & Mr. E. left, good ridance to all.

TUES. 5.[9] Rode out on a sled. The first time I have rode out since

[5] E.W. "Mrs. Eells & myself had to manage the affair & we felt considerable anxiety about it but finally succeeded quite well. . ." This son, Joseph Elkanah, was graduated from his father's seminary at Bangor, Maine, in 1871. Ordained as a Congregational minister, he went out to China as a missionary under the American Board. He thus had the distinction of having been the first native born Oregonian to be a foreign missionary.

[6] E.W. "As I was cooking my breakfast & toasting some bread, an Indian came in & blew his nose upon it. It so vexed me that I told him he was like the hog which caused him to leave the house & as he was young I called him back to take his pay. After awhile he came, I paid him off. He asked if he was done working, I told him he was."

[7] E.W. "As the Dr. was called last night to attend an Indian woman & staid late, we did not get up very early this morning. It was about noon when we started & we were compelled to travel slow as the snow was very bad. . . Cyrus stood the ride well." Cyrus, then a little more than five years old, was riding his own horse.

[8] E.W. "Sold Garry an ax for five deer skins." The Walkers used the deer skins for moccasins and for some articles of clothing as pantaloons. In all probability Mary had a leather dress. Finely dressed deer skins were also used in place of window glass.

[9] E.W. "I harnessed up my team & gave the family a ride."

July except to see a sick woman in the winter. The 6th anniversary of our marriage.

SUN. 10. Mr. Eells babe was baptised by the name of Miron by Mr. Walker & ours by the name of Joseph Elkanah.[10] It was also the communion service. . .

TUES. 12 . . . Mr. Walker left this morning for C. Cyrus went with him. The cows ran away. It has been a windy evening & I feel extremely lonely.

FRI. MARCH 15. Warm pleasant weather. Work with all my might all day & a good part of the night. . .

TUES. 19 . . . We found it necessary to cook what fresh beef we have.

WED. 20. Set the watch with the sun. Observed the afternoon to be some ten minutes longer than the forenoon.

THURS. 21. Find my Indian maid has worked about 100 days. We have paid her a hundred & ten loads worth of [ammunition] aside from numerous little presents to amounts to ten or more. The Indians all moved off to day. . .

SAT. 23. Baked, rode out up the plain to see water coming. Mr. E. set fire to burn the dead grass. Cleaned my house myself. Find I am better able to do it than I feared I would be having put work of that kind so much upon my Indian girl. . .

TUE. 26. Dis[cover] in dressing my babe a rupture near the groin. . .

SUN. 30. We have been looking for Mr. McTavish but he does not come. Mr. Walker sowed peas. The water appeared in the well.

MON. APR. 1. My birthday, 33.

TUES. 2. Mr. W. helping Charles plough. . .[11]

THURS. 4 . . . Have fixed a truss for my babe. . .

SAT. 13.[12] Mr. McTavish arrived. Brings sad news from the Willamet. Two white men have died from wounds made by Indians.

[10] Both of the boys baptised this day became Congregational ministers. Myron Eells wrote the life of his father and many articles bearing on the history of the Mission.

[11] Elkanah in his diary makes frequent mention of the help he gave to the natives in plowing their fields and putting in their crops. For instance, on the 10th, he wrote: "I went & helped Big Star plough & we made out very well."

[12] E.W. "A letter from Dr. Whitman . . . brought distressing intelligence from the lower [Columbia] country. There has been some fighting between the Indians & whites. One Indian was killed & two whites were wounded so that they died of their wounds." The increasing influx of the whites brought many clashes with the natives. No further information is available about the event of which Whitman wrote. On May 11 Walker wrote in his diary: "We hear by reports that Mr. Spalding's life has been attempted by an Indian. . . I hope it is all a lie." These ominous incidents cast long shadows into the future.

SUN. 14.[13]   Mr. Mc. left & in the evening Mr. Geyer came.

MON. 15.   Conclude to go to Waiilatpu. Washed in the afternoon.

TUES. 16.[14]   Got ready & started. Crossed the river & encamped
. . .

SAT. 20.   Made a prosperous journed & reached Waiilatpu towards evening. Made the distance from Snake river to the Dr.'s in one day. Met a cordial reception from our friends.

MON. 22 —FRI. 26.   Had a little washing & ironing to do. Mrs. Littlejohn assists Mrs. Whitman when she needs. Mr. Walker assisted in ploughing, the farming business being not yet done.

SAT. 27.   Mr. Gilpin of Missouri arrived on his way to Mr. Spaldings. . .

SUN. 28.   We had a meeting. Mr. Walker administed the Lords Supper.

MON. 29.   Mr. Gilpin left for Mr. Spalding's. Some jar in the family about Perin's [Perrin Whitman] going with him.

TUES. 30.   We left W. about noon, encamped on the Tucia [Tucannon] about sunset. Cold & windy. . .

MON. [MAY] 6.   Reached home. Found all safe. . .

WED. 22.[15]   I have just been able after a long time to bring up my journal. We had a prosperous journey & considerably pleasant visit. Dr. Whitman did not think best to undertake to do anything for our babe. But thought he would soon outgrow his difficulty. Since we returned Mr. Walker assisted by Mr. Eells has made a front door & partly set up the stoves, made a cradle, & nine more shelves in the buttery. We brought home a little English girl with us [Emma Hobson]. She is considerable help. We find it very pleasant to have a little more house room. . . May the comforts with which we begin to be surrounded not turn away our hearts from the work of saving the heathen about us. I feel distress & sometimes [am] almost discouraged in view of the much which needs to be done & the little I can do. I

---

13 E.W.   "Mr. Mactavish & family left before I was up & I was glad to see them go if they must go on the Sabbath. Mr. Geyer came in this evening. It seems rather strange that most of the calls we have are . . . connected with the violation of the Holy Sabbath."

14 E.W.   "Mr. Chief Trader Manson came in to day on his way to Colvile & then to New Caledonia. I planted some more corn." From the repeated references to travelers, it is evident that Tshimakain was located on what was then one of the main roads of the Old Oregon country. The trail from the Flathead country passed on the north side of the Spokane River to Tshimakain Creek where it met the trail from Walla Walla.

15 E.W. for Sunday, the 19th.   "We were again disturbed to day by a party of Boatmen coming in on their way to Colville. . . I long to meet with the people of God in his house. Mr. E. & family came down just at night & we had a good sing which pleased the children very much."

cannot keep my house as nice as I wish to. . . . I have almost no time except on Sunday to read & I regret exceedingly that I find so little time to teach my children & as to doing [something] for the Indians, when can I expect to? When can I find time for private devotions. Weary & heavy laden may I cast my burden on him whose yoke is easy & whose burden is light. Remember O Lord that I am but dust & let my desires be accepted before thee.

FRI. 24.[16] Abigail four years old. The children made a little party in the dining room by themselves. . .

THURS. 20. The Teacher's family moved here on account of Kwantepetser who is evidently near her end, sick of consumption. Would I could have an evidence that she is prepared for death.

SAT. JUNE 1 . . . Went this afternoon to see the sick girl. Tried to converse with [her.] She said she thought she was not prepared to die.

SUN. 2.[17] Mr. Walker has been to Seakwakin. This evening I have been out to see K. who is in great distress & I fear may not live long. It would afford me great satisfaction to gain some evidence that she is prepared but it is so little I can converse in Indian.

MON. 3. Heard the medicine man had been sent for, went out & told [them that] I wished them not to have him play. He was not found at home so did not come.

TUES. 4. Went to see Kwantepetser, found her getting worse. Prayed with her, but was not able to converse.

THURS. JUNE 6. K. continued to grow worse, gave her such little medicine as we thought might make her more comfortable.

FRI. 7.[18] Went in the afternoon to see K. Found her dying.

SAT. 8.[19] She ceased to breath & was buried about noon. I gave them some advice in regard to burying & a garment. There is no wailing but the people conduct calmly tho they resorted a little to playing medicine, tho I had remonstrated against it. . .

FRI. 14. Mr. W. & Cyrus left for Mr. Spalding's about nine o'clock

SAT. 15. Employed three women to help me hoe & weed my garden. . .

SUN. 16. A quiet sabbath, not an Indian about us. Have been reading D'Aubigne's History of the Reformation.

---

[16] E.W. "All the Indians in the plain left today so that we are destitute of any Indians just now."

[17] E.W. "I started this morning for the camas ground. The flies are so bad that I found it very unpleasant. I think I felt for the poor wicked & ignorant creatures. I addressed them with more sympathy than common."

[18] E.W. "The girl is supposed to be in a dying state. They played the medicine last night, most all night, & say she is some better."

[19] E.W. "The girl died this morning & was buried. I followed Mr. E. in addressing them."

Mon. 17. Washed in haste to get done. Entrusted the babe to Emma. Crying he injured himself so that it was more than hurt before I could return. He knows enough to cry after me. When he feels tired, won't allow me to go out of sight.

Tues. 18. Churned, made a cheese (used deer rennet). . .[20]

Wed. 19. Ironed & baked. A fine shower of rain. Worked two hours in the garden. Sowed English turnips. Goudie's wife came yesterday to see Sarah. . .

Sat. 22. Mr. W. returned heavily laden with provisions. Mr. Geyer came with him. . .

Wed. 26. Churned, made cheese, ironed. Our Maternal meeting. Big Star brought us two salmon.

Thurs. 27. A refreshing rain. Mr. Geyer eats breakfast & dinner with us & supper at Mrs. E.'s. I think he is wholly composed of Indian rubber.

Fri. 28. McKenzie arrived. Wrote to Mrs. Whitman.

Thurs. July 4.[21] Got dinner ready. Mr. Geyer & the children were away, so we invited Mr. and Mrs. E. to dine with us.

Sun. 7.[22] Mr. W. gone to the river. We are tried on account of Geyer but do not know what to do, are determined to be rid of him soon.

Mon. 8.[23] Washed. Mr. W. told Mr. G. we could not entertain him longer. He took it patiently.

Tue. 9. Mr. W. went to Colvile Mr. G. went away to be gone a week.

Wed. 10.[24] Mr. W. returned. . .

Sat. 13. Succeed for once in geting the children in bed about sunset. . .

Thurs. 18. An express arrived bringing letters from home. Onc was from the Islands from Mrs. Whitney. It was a great satisfaction to me to receive it as I had feared she was displeased with some thing I had written. But it seems this was not the case. She writes she is expecting

---

[20] In order to make cheese, Mary had to use rennet, which is the mucous membrane lining of the fourth stomach of a suckling calf or sheep which is capable of curdling milk. Naturally the Walkers did not wish to slaughter one of their calves just to get some rennet. According to the manuscript by Ida Eells, "Mother Eells," in Coll. w., "Mrs. Walker thought that perhaps young deer's rennet would so. So after awhile an Indian brought one which we tried, and it did well."

[21] E.W. "I have become so worn out with our guest that I hardly know what to do. I hope he will soon leave us. We have come to the conclusion that we shall tell him to go soon if he does not leave without."

[22] E.W. "My patience is clean gone with Mr. Geyer."

[23] E.W. "After breakfast this morning I told Mr. G. that it was not consistent for us to entertain him any longer as our means were not given to support any but missionaries."

[24] Walker made the round trip to Colville, 140 miles, in two days. Just why there was need for such haste is not indicated in either diary.

her daughter to return from the States as an assistant missionary. So would I wish to see my children return to me should I be spared to see them of mature years.

Mr. Walker received a letter bringing joyful intelligence that his father at the eleventh hour has obtained an interest in the great salvation. Bless the Lord, oh our souls & forget not all his benefits.

A letter from sister Charlotte brings the news of my Mother's death which occured the 26 of February 1843. I had as I thought already buried my friends so that I imagined I should hardly reallize their death when it should occur, but I find this is not the case. I feel very sensibly the loss of my mother. I would adopt the words of Cowper, "My Mother — when I heard that thou was dead" &c. May I believe her spirit does indeed hover over her sorrowing child. . . Everything calls her to mind. The image of her is vividly impressed on my imagination. I think of so much I would have written her & altho I never expected to see her myself again, I had fondly hoped my children would. But she is gone. Such dreams all vanish. I am thankful we had such a mother to lose.

Had I been call[ed] to yield to the hand of death that friend who I considered best prepared, I would certainly have selected her. . . She had no preparation to make on the bed of death, for from her youth her lamp had ever been trimed & burning. . . May her mantle rest on each of her children. . .

SAT. 20. Mrs. McD. and suite arrived. Her little son, Samuel, suffering from fever & ague.

SUN. 21. We passed as quiet a sabbath as we could hope to under existing circumstances. Mrs. McD. gave her boy calomel.

MON. 22.[25] Mrs. McD. started about noon. Her little boy had a fit of ague just before she left. Mr. Geyer arrived in the morning & accompanied her. He has a letter from Dr. McLoughlin so that he will be off our hands now.

TUES. 23. Busy here & there. My thoughts often return to home

THURS. 25. Have been reading my mother's last letters to me & think of writing a tribute to her memory.

FRI. 26.[26] Commenced eating new potatoes of good size. . .

SAT. AUG. 10.[27] Mr. W. has two Indians helping him. They have

---

[25] E.W. "I was awaked this morning by the noise occasioned by Mrs. McD train & felt that they have conducted worse than the natives themselves. Soon after breakfast Mrs. McD left & I felt some relieved."

[26] E.W. "Went & hauled in my hay. . . I brought it home & put it in the barn.

[27] E.W. for the 7th. "Another birthday has come. I am now thirty nine years old. We invited Mr. and Mrs. E. with their family to dine with us. He did not come as we were rather late. The Indians gambling all day." There are several contemporary accounts of the widespread practice of gambling carried on by the Spokanes. The missionaries did what they could to curb the evil but without much success.

commenced on the well.[28] S. left yesterday. I gave her a due bill of 25 loads for pay. Several of the Indians have had their camas burned.[29] There is gambling going on in the camp. . .

Fri. August 16.   Wrote last evening to Mrs. Whitman, this morning to Mrs. Perkins. Mr. Geyer arrived yesterday from Colvile. I have been painting wash tubs. . .

Thurs. 22.   Mr. Geyer left. Painting oil cloths.

Fri. 23.   Find bed bugs have come to reside with us. Have commenced a war of extermination. The children disturb us much nights by coughing.[30]

Sun. 25.[31]   Went in the morning to administer to an Indian child.

Mon. 26.   The child still gives us much anxiety. This morning is partially relieved. She with our own children have so broken my rest for some nights that I feel nearly sick. Elkanah coughs much nights, also Abigail.

Wed. 28.   Spent the forenoon in trying to do what I could to relieve the sick girl. Found the bladder so distended as to fill all the lower cavity of the abdomen. Succeeded with some difficulty in using a catheter but it produced no effect unless perhaps by exhaustion to hasten death as she lived only about an hour after. She died without having the medicine played. The first instance I recollect.

Thurs. 29.   The [sixth] anniversary of our arrival in this country.

Fri. 30.   Painting doors. Mr. W. has completed the wood shed which looks well.

Sat. 31.   Painted Mr. E's front door.

Mon. Sept. 2.[32]   Washed & cleaned furniture, ready for painting.

Tues. 3.   Painted chairs, settee & stools. They look better than I expected they would.

Wed. 4.   Painted or finished painting our tables. Think they look nice. Baked & ironed. Mr. Walker has two Indians helping him. They are at work on the Indian house.

Thurs. 5.   Repaired the plastering in the kitchen & painted a part of the buttery.

Fri. 6.   Finished painting. Glad to see the end of a long job. Fix the hearth in our bed room better. . .

---

[28] Probably the well was being deepened.

[29] Since the Indians were frequently moving, they found it necessary to cache their supplies of camas roots for winter use. Sometimes a cache would be burned in a forest fire.

[30] E.W. "We drew in our corn this afternoon. Our children appear a little better with the whooping cough."

[31] E.W. "It is a grief to me that Mrs. W. is disposed to read so much that is not devotional on the Sabbath. I have thot that her view of the correctness of this day is very limited."

[32] E.W. "We heard Mr. E. nailing up his house this morning as soon as he could see well. They left [for Colville] in pretty good season & I went to work in the afternoon on the Indian house & laid the foundation."

SAT. 7. Mr. E's family returned from C. Received a present of pink gingham from Mrs. McD. Found I was getting behind hand about cleaning but hearing my girl S[oshenamalt] was come in, sent & got her to help me so I got through.

MON. 9 . . . Had my squashes harvested, about thirty besides little ones.

TUES. 10.[33] Sopermal, as the children call [her,] sewing. . .

MON. SEPT. 16. Soshenamalt did my washing. Repaired my riding dress. McKenzie arrived from W.W. but brought us no letters. Concluded to go to Colvile. Baked in the evening.

TUE. 17. Left home about noon. Met. Mr. Geyer of whom we took final leave.[34]

WED. 18. Encamped at the farm house.

THURS. 19. Reached Colvile in the forenoon. Had a cordial reception from our friends.

FRI. 20. Took an early breakfast & left for home having enjoyed a pleasant visit. Mr. McDonald's family expect to set out on their departure from the country on Sat.[35] We came on to a little this side of The Fool's.

SAT. 21. Reached home about two P.M. & found all safe. Had a pleasant journey. The children all behaved pretty well. Babe very little trouble.

MON. 23. Washed. Mr. Walker with 2 Indians dug our potatoes, the finest crop we have ever had. . .

WED. 25 . . . Mr. E. set out for Waiilatpu.

THURS. 26. Little Elkanah has been quite unwell ever since we returned from Colvile. Swept the chamber, got out & put up garden seeds. Indians mostly off. . .

WED. [OCT.] 2. Wish to be writing letters but cannot compose my mind. . .

THURS. 3 [36] . . . Exchanged potatoes for mountain berries.

SAT. 5 . . . Got my saturday chores done in good season. S. sewed in the forenoon. Mr. W. & the children rode out but did not meet Mr. E. . .

TUES. 8. Mr. E. returned from Waiilatpu.[37] About more immigrants are arriving across the Mts. . .[38]

---

[33] E.W. "I finished the second chap. of Matt."

[34] Geyer wrote in Mary's Autograph Album, now in Coll. WN., under date of March 1, 1844: "Through the whole dreary winter you entertained the stranger under the hospitable roof of your habitation in the wilderness — not like a stranger, but as a friend. He came to you with no other passport or recommendation than that of an honest face, yet he received your full attention and regards. . ."

[35] John Lee Lewes succeeded McDonald as Chief Factor of Fort Colvile.

[36] E.W. "I made a hole in the roof for the stove pipe." For the 4th: "Finished putting up the stove. Built a fire in it. We found it carries smoke well."

SAT. 12. Wrote to my sisters. . .

TUES. 15. We sent off our letters by the Teacher to Walla Walla. Filed away answered letters. . .

THURS. 17. Baked, ironed & sat up till a late hour to make a rag baby for Abigail. When I had finished it, I carried it to her bed. She took it & embraced it with as much fondness as ever [a] mother could a living child.

FRI. 18. Mr. Walker making a window in the dining room. . . Some Indians from Spokan encamped in the Indian house. . .

WED. 23. S. commenced wash[ing] again. Many of the Indians seem to be making their calculations to spend the winter here. Hope if they do, we shall be able to do more at teaching. Wish I had utensils for spinning & weaving. Commenced teaching Cyrus & Emma their geography & arithmetic. . .

THURS. 24. Cut out a dress for E[mma]. In the evening cleared up the clutter Mr. W. had made in my bed room & hunted bed bugs, found four. A young snow storm, the first we have had.

SAT. 26 . . . Mr. W. built a chimney in the Indian house.

MON. OCT. 28 [39] . . . Abigail struck Cyrus & he came in crying & complaining bitterly. I said she ought to be whipped. When she began to threaten to run away, I then sent Emma to get a stick when A. went out doors & began to cry as loud as she could. Soon she was hushed & Cyrus told me she was hid & he would not tell me where & he told her not to cry lest I should find her. I asked what she would do when it came night. He had not thought of that & began to pale & said he would not have A whipped. I told him I thought that was what he wanted. He said no. I asked what he did want done. He said nothing. I told him as it was him she hurt, if he did not want her punished, he might go & tell her. He ran & call[ed] her from her retreat. I told her she ought to kiss him for his kindness but she hesitated where[upon] he caught her & kissed her several times & evinced the greatest joy at her deliverance & so the matter ended.

---

[37] E.W. "About noon Mr. E. made his appearance & brought a letter from Mr. Greene which very much displeases me." Greene criticized Walker, who was the scribe of the Mission for a time, for not making a fuller report of conditions. The affairs of the Oregon Mission, which during 1837 and 1838 were given 234 and 138 column inches in the *Missionary Herald*, were barely mentioned during the years 1845-47 inclusive. Here is eloquent evidence that the Board was apologetic over the unhappy state of its Oregon work. On Oct. 9, Elkanah noted: "I did not do much to day but read & brood over the state of things in the Mission."

[38] The Oregon immigration of 1844 totaled about 1,500. Mary's entry seems to indicate that she intended to put in some figures later, but this was not done.

[39] E.W. "We commenced on the school house." Here Elkanah seems to indicate work on another building different from the "Indian house" already completed. It may be that this was but an addition of a room to the Indian house. The record is not clear.

WED. 30 [40] . . . We weighed our little boys. Miron & Elkanah weighed 20 lbs each. Edwin 33 & Marcus 32.

THURS. 31. Mr. Walker building the Indian meeting house. . . I am making a cap for Mr. Walker. . .

SAT. NOV. 2.[41] S. came & with her assistance, I succeeded in getting my work done but not in as good season as I could have wished. On which account as usual Mr. W. loaded me with reproaches so that my night's rest was far from being quiet.

SUN. 3. A pleasant day. We had worship in the new chapel tho it is not yet completed.[42] A good number of Indians present. DeSmidt passed here yesterday & encamped near. Simpleton went out to see him.

THURS. NOV. 7. Went out to see the Indian chapel & house & called at the Chief's lodge, who came in yesterday, found them eating. Some laping the kettle, some eating with spoons from a basket, some making bread with unwashed hands. There are seldom so many people here as at present. Hope we shall continue to have many about us & be able to do more at teaching them than formerly. And if nothing is too hard for God, I hope we shall see them turn & live. Our ears are annoyed by night by the song of gamblers & while Mr. W. is laboring all day to erect [a] building for them, a company of strong men are gambling at a little distance.

FRI. 8.[43] Partly cut a coat for Cyrus. Old Queen brought some meat. . .

SUN. 10.[44] A large assembly of Indians. . .

SUN. 17.[45] Did not attend worship. Have a cold & the damp air affects me considerably. . .

MON. 18. Mr. W. left in good season for Clear Water. . .[46]

---

[40] E.W. "We have been busy on the house all day . . . have finished laying up the walls. I had a long ride to night after the horses but could not find them."

[41] E.W. "Mr. DeSmet passed here to night." The Oregon Historical Society has an 1839 imprint of the Roman Catholic Rheims-Douay Bible with an inscription which shows that it was presented to Dr. Whitman by Father P. J. DeSmet. No date of the presentation is indicated.

[42] E.W. "We had worship in our new house & find it very comfortable." Walker completed putting in the chimney on the following Tuesday and on the 7th he wrote: "Put a roof on the Indian room."

[43] E.W. "Put the seats in the meeting house & had some wood sawed in the yard."

[44] E.W. "Our new house was pretty well filled & we found it more comfortable than a smokey lodge." Walker commenced a school in the new building on the following Tuesday with "ten scholars."

[45] E.W. "We had worship in our new house without any fire."

FRI. 22 . . . Have to keep the children in the house for the most part [of] the [day.] They make so much noise, it is almost enough to confuse me. Miss a school very much.

SUN. 24. Mr. — on his way to Colvile called. Brought a letter from Mr. Geyer who is about to depart from the country & one from Dr. Whitman who writes he has at last a school teacher & invites us to send Cyrus. . .[47]

THURS. 28. Finished a bonnet for Abigail. . .

SAT. 30. Finished Marcus bonnet & did up our sun bonnets. . . Baked biscuits on the stove. Looked in vain for Mr. Walker. . .

MON. [DEC.] 2. Two girls at work on bonnets for themselves.

TUES. 3. The two bonnets done, the Chiefs two wives also supplied with bonnets & Sillapal is to make herself one when she returns from Colvile.

WED. 4. The Big Star's daughter finished making her bonnet. Think they look pretty well. Mr. Walker reached home in the evening. He had been detained in crossing the Palouse river & narrowly escaped drowning. The grave was permitted to open its mouth but not to swallow him up. . .

SAT. 7.[48] Cyrus birthday. We observed it as a day of thanksgiving as it occurs so near the usual day of Thanksgiving in N.E. & in view of the many mercies we are permitted to enjoy. No death has yet occurred among us & we are all in health, have housing, food & clothing convenient for us. Mr. E's family took dinner with us & also Mr. McPherson & wife who arrived from the Flatheads. . .

TUES. 10 . . . One girl repairing cloaks, the other making drawers & mending shoes. Mr. W. & I are not well agreed about the way in which he should answer Mr. Greene. . .

THURS. 12. Mr. Walker shoring the well.

FRI. 13. Completed two more bonnets making ten in all, including three that were altered & repaired. . .

SAT. 14. The Indians finished shoring the well. . . In the afternoon rode out. . .

THURS. 19. Mr. W. went on the Mts. to look for ax helves. Sillapal came to make her hood. . .

---

[46] Walker went to Clearwater with some wheat to be ground into flour at Spalding's mill.

[47] The Whitmans having received the seven orphaned Sager children into their home in October of that year, found it necessary to open a school. Alanson Hinman, who also came with the 1844 immigration, was hired to be the teacher.

[48] E.W. "Mr. McP. gave me two bales of buffalo meat which is good." Possibly two bales constituted the load for a pack horse, which would mean from 200 to 250 pounds.

SUN. DEC. 22.[49]   Attended worship forenoon & afternoon.

TUES. 24.   Mr. E. & Sarah G. left for Colvile.   . .

THURS. 26.   Emma with Mrs. E. Cyrus had several spells of bawling because he had no one to help play. Abigail [then 4½ years old] washed breakfast dishes. Elkanah commenced walking alone.   . .

FRI. 27.   Finished the children's cloaks. Mr. E. returned from C.

SUN. 29.[50]   A restless night from pain in my back & limbs.   . .

MON. 30.   Had rather a restless night but have been getting better through the day & feel quite comfortable. Have taught one girl to knit & another another way of kniting mittens. The old blind woman came & I employed her to make some sinew thread.   . .   Try every day to do as much as I think my strength will admit but find always many things undone which I feel unwilling to leave undone at death. May I at the close of life find my work done, all done & well done & may I ever reallize that [that] which I omit today I may not live to finish.[51]

THURS. 31.[52]   Thanks to God for all his mercies, especially for the past seven years.

1845 — RUMBLINGS OF DISCONTENT

Mary wrote less in her diary for 1845 than for any other of the ten years under review. It was a quiet year at Tshimakain and throughout the Mission. Elkanah completed building another room to their home and now for the first time since they settled at Tshimakain, the Walkers had glass for all of their windows. The interior walls of their home were whitewashed. More imported tapa cloth from the Hawaiian

---

[49] E.W. "An express came in just at night from Colville with a request that Sarah might be allowed to go home & spend the Christmas." This is the first of two times that Elkanah used the word Christmas in his diary. Mary made no reference to this term. True to their Puritan background, the missionaries considered the observance of Christmas as being a Roman Catholic custom. The *Pacific Homestead* for December 21, 1911, carried an article by Cyrus Walker on "Christmas in Oregon Pioneer Days," in which he said: "As for me in earlier years, I knew no Christmas. . .   as I remember Christmas was not once named."

[50] E.W. "We have hung the door to the meeting house. . .   I have felt much down to day at the sad desolation [going] on all around us & no prospect seemly of being able to do any good to any one. . .   I fear I profess too much of a spirit to pray that fire might come down from heaven & destroy these idolitors."

[51] Mary's diary is sprinkled with choice pithy statements which speak so clearly of her philosophy of life. In the author's opinion, this is one of the best.

[52] E.W. "Mrs. Walker did not rest much better last night than the night before. I was up & built her a fire. . .   I set the Indians cutting lumber for a new room. We have all been permitted to see the last day of another year. It has been a year of labor & trial.   . ."

Islands replaced the rough Indian mats on the ceilings and more paint was applied to the woodwork and furniture. Never before was their home so comfortable and attractive.

The two families attended the Mission meeting at Waiilatpu in May, at which time Emma was taken back to join her father. The Walkers spent two weeks with the Spaldings at Lapwai in July. And in the latter part of November, shortly before his seventh birthday, Cyrus was taken by his father to Waiilatpu to attend the school for white children which the Whitmans were conducting. Harmony ruled among the missionaries. However, ominous rumblings of discontent and even threats from a few of the natives, especially from the Cayuses, were being noted. Whitman told his associates at the May Mission meeting that he was fearful that his people "intended taking his life."

WED. JAN. 1.   We dined with Mrs. E. with mingled emotions I hail the opening year. May I not hope ere it shall close to see some of these wretched people about us converted. May we have grace to do all in our power for them. Cyrus & Emma commenced reading the Bible. . .

SAT. 4.   Baked & salted three kegs of meat. . .

MON. 6.   Concert & fast. . .

TUES. 7.   Mr. W. left for Colvile. Washed, cleaned windows & put cloth [on the] windows in the chamber. A sunny day. The water appeared in the well.[1] Paid Chief's daughter a pair of leggings. She always gets the better of me.

WED. 8 . . .   Salted our meat for drying. This evening set three panes of glass. . .

FRI. 10.   Had S. clean house in the forenoon. Afternoon finished my shawl & repaired Mr. W. cap. Dont know [how] I shall get along when she leaves me. . .

MON. 13.   Was informed that Big Star's daughter, who has been working with me, was confined but her child died, probably from their not tying the umbillicus.

TUES. 14.   The above named woman came to our house about a quarter of a mile, bare foot on the frozen ground after sunset. I gave her some motherly advice & a piece of meat & lent her a pair of shoes to walk home in. We all went to Mr. Eells to attend worship in the evening. . .

FRI. 24 . . .   I have no Indian girl to help me. We have been looking for the express [to come] along. Think it may have given up the ship.

---

[1] The well often failed to give water in the late fall and early winter. By this time the winter rains and snows were renewing the supply.

SAT. 25.[2] Mr. W. moved the stairs. I baked & cleared away a little. Mr. E's American cow found dead just at night, so the Indians are supplied with food.

SUN. JAN. 26. We all attended worship. On returning Mr. E. found his house had been opened. He immediately informed the Indians, several went in search of the stolen goods, found them concealed at a short distance. The Thief was seen near driving horses. Mr. W. met & talked with him.

MON. 27. Elkanah sick. Our bed room partitioned off again. The girls' bed moved up stairs & ours in its place. Had a girl mend shoes a part of the day. . .

FRI. 31. Dipped 24 dozen candles.

SAT. FEB. 1. Baked & had my ironing done & house cleaned, chiefly by my Indian woman who is learning fast. . .

SUN. 2. We all went to meeting on a sled. . .

TUES. 4. Washed. Mr. [W.] metaphorsed [i.e., made over] a bedstead & door. Weekly concert as usual. . . Fitted up our bedroom a little this evening. How little time we bestow on Indians compared with what we do on ourselves.

SAT. 8. Glad when Saturday comes because then employ no Indian help. Baked mince pies for the first time this winter. Marcus quite ill.

SUN. 9. Marcus still unwell. Gave him some sumac-root which seemed to exhilarate him so he was frolicsome all day. I spend the day as a tale that is told. To what purpose do I live? . . .

THURS. 13. We received letters from Dr. Whitman's station. All there seems to be going on prosperously. I am glad to hear they are going on so steadily.

FRI. 14. Tired, have set up & worked till near midnight for many nights. Gave my Indian girl a spoon. . .

MON. 17. Very rainy in the forenoon. Mufflehead gave me a talk after making as much fuss as he could about pay.[3]

WED. 19. My Indian girl commenced working a rug.

THURS. 20. Got a good freeze on our beef last night.

FRI. 21.[4] More at leisure than I have been on any Friday since I can remember.

[2] E.W. "I concluded to commence at the alteration in the house. It is quite an undertaking but I do not dread it as I know the change will afford us so much comfort." He not only moved the stairway but also rebuilt the chimney.

[3] E.W. "I was hindered by an Indian who in the end abused Mrs. Walker. . . We have hunted all day but have not found the cow." For the 18th: "She was found without any calf." During these days Walker with Indian help was hauling logs to the premises and overseeing the sawing of them into boards.

[4] On this day Elkanah wrote a long letter to the *Christian Mirror* of Portland, Maine, a copy of which he put in his diary. In this letter he discussed the customs of the natives, their food, etc., and commented as follows about the trials of living with them: "If they should remain constantly about us the whole year, it would

SUN. 23.   We still find that [we] dwell where thieves break through & steal. May it lead us to seek the more earnestly to lay up treasure in heaven. . .   Things were taken from Mr. E's store house which was broken up. My riding horse is missing & we hear may have been stolen. May God grant to bring good out of evil. May these poor miserable Indians be roused to a sense of their situation before it is too late.

MON. 24.   The lost horse was found tho he had evidently been rode off. No Indians employed on account of the theft.

THURS.   Rode out. The plain bare. Fresh grass starting up.

FRI. 28.   Fixing curtains & clothes press. Girl working on rug.

SAT. MARCH 1, 1845.   Get on quietly through the day. Just at night, my girl came & wanted pay. I paid & dismissed her as she was expecting more than I had been calculating to give, don't know how I shall get along unless I have some one. . .

MON. 3.   Br. J.C. 32 years old. Would like to see how those brothers & sisters look, now they are getting so old. Washed & ironed. . .

TUES. 4.[5]   Garry made a visit at Mr. E's, having recently returned from California.

WED. 5.   The anniversary of our marriage. Surely goodness & mercy have followed us these seven years & we have not lacked ought. . .

SAT. 8 . . . Mr. W. has been putting up an addition to our house. I have made him a spencer. The Teacher has encamped here with his family, his daughter being sick. We are treating her for spine complaint. . .

THURS. 13.[6]   Mr. Fraser's family arrived.

FRI. MARCH 14.   Mr. F. unable to proceed on account of horses having strayed. . .

TUES. 18 . . . Many of the Indians are beginning to cultivate.

---

to all human view soon kill us. It is their leaving us for a part of the year that affords us time & opportunity to renew our strength & prepare for our labors anew. I fully coincide with the views expressed by a lady of this Mission, probably the most devoted of any one in the Mission, that they could not endure their labors if it were not for the respite they have in the summer season when the natives are absent after roots & fish." Perhaps the "lady" to whom he was referring was his wife.

[5] Sometime during the winter of 1844-45 a party of Spokane, Walla Walla, and Cayuse Indians went to Sutter's Fort in California for the purpose of trading furs and horses for cattle. Included in the group was Spokane Garry and the son of the Walla Walla Chief, Peupeumoxmox, who had been given the name of Elijah Hedding (after the Methodist Bishop Hedding). While at Sutter's Fort a dispute arose which resulted in the killing of Elijah by a white man. The party of Oregon Indians hastily returned without their cattle. The death of Elijah caused great excitement among the Indians at Walla Walla. This was a contributory factor of the discontent which climaxed in the Whitman massacre. Garry was able to give a first hand account of this incident to the Walkers.

[6] E.W. "Mr. Fraser & family came in. . . I heard some unpleasant news from below that the Indians there had threatened to kill Mr. McKinlay & the Dr."

The Old Chief has been to C. & purchased a plough & several hoes.

WED. 19.[7] Baked mince pies. . .

MON. 24. Washed. Had some women carry out our potatoes of which we have only ten or twelve bushels left. Moved the beef into the cellar of which we have three kegs. The Old Chief made us a call.

WED. 26. Maternal meeting. Dog killed another hen, the third we have lost recently. . .

FRI. 28. Cut out a cap for Marcus. Have been thinking how stagnant my thoughts are getting. I go the same round over & over till J seem almost ready to fall as if dizzy.

SAT. 29.[8] Mr. W. & Cyrus went down to the Barrier. . .

TUES. APR. 1. My birth day, 34 years old. . .

FRI. 4.[9] Mr. McTavish spends the night with us. We are informed Mrs. Spalding has a daughter born on the 2nd ult. Also that Emma Hobson's father wishes her sent to him. . .

TUES. 15.[10] The after express passed. Brought a line from Dr. W.[11] Had a woman to help wash. Sewing in the afternoon.

THURS. 17. Mr. W. went to Spokan & returned. I milked but found it fatigued me much. Worked a little in the garden. The wolves killed a calf for Mr. Eells. . .

WED. 23. Worked in the garden . . . sowed the beans & peas, but not the squashes. Just as I was done, Mrs. McPherson arrived. We scarce know what to do about going from home. . .

THURS. 25. Mr. E's family seem to hesitate about starting. We are determined not to go unless they do.

SAT. 26. Mr. E's folk seem to be making their calculations to start, so I think we shall all go.

---

[7] E.W. "I set three hands to threshing & about noon they finished all my wheat. I have a pretty good pile of it." Of course the threshing was done by the old-fashioned winnowing method.

[8] E.W. for the 30th. "A Catholic Indian making inquiries on the subject of crosses & beads. I told him what God required & that it was of no use or profit to worship any erected thing. . . The Indians standing by seemed to understand that the priests worship was the same as their former worship."

[9] E.W. "The express came along & we manage to have them stop all night. We had a pleasant time & learned that all was quiet in the civilized world."

[10] E.W. "The horses were near & a wolf was seen among them. I have been making fence." See Drury, *Diaries of Spalding and Smith*, for the several references it contains to wolves. Altho wolves preferred smaller animals, yet when desperately hungry two would sometimes jointly attack and kill a horse.

[11] Whitman in a letter dated March 5, 1845, to Walker, wrote: "You will get the news of the California affair from Garry. We are to have a great assembly of Indians at W.W. next week. . . We look for an agitation near us this spring. The Indians were all notified to meet DeSmet at Walla Walla when the grass is about five or six inches long. . . There are so many things involved in our situation in this country that I do not see we should be discontented. I feel that vast results have followed us, & that to leave now would be wrong." Original Coll. c.

THURS. MAY 1.[12]   Left home in care of old Solomon. Encamped at the river. Mr. E. returned home to take a farewell & fix things a little more secure.

FRI. 2.   We reached our usual encampment in good season. Mrs. McPherson accompanied us.

SAT. 3.   Encamped at Kaihakailu. Passed an encampment of Spokan Indians.

SUN. 4.   Rested according to the commandment.

MON. 5.   Designed to start early but Mr. E's horse was not to be found. We proceeded without him & sent our Indian to hunt. We had just stoped & were about to encamp when the Indian was seen coming with the horse. He stated that he found him at some distance with horses belonging to the Cordelane [Coeur d'Alene Indians.] Perhaps it was so & perhaps he was himself the thief. We packed up & went on.

WED. 7.   Crossed Snake River & encamped on Tusha. Encountered a gale just before we reached camp.

THURS. 8.   Reached Waiilatpu about noon in safety. Cold riding. Found all well & glad to see [us] apparently. Mr. Spalding arrived soon after with Eliza.[13]

FRI. 9.   The meeting was opened.

SAT. 10.   Quite a number of people called on their way to the States. . .   Considerable business was transacted.

SUN. 11.   A church meeting in the morning. Mr. Hinman was examined for admission to the church. Mr. Walker preached in the forenoon & Mr. Spalding administered baptism & the Lord's Supper. Mr. Hinman was baptized. Dr. Whitman had the five orphan [Sager] sisters & Mary Ann B[ridger] baptized.[14] At noon there was a sabbath school.

MON. 12 . . .   In the evening Mrs. F. found she had taken a severe cold from bathing & took medicine. Mr. Hinman had fits in the evening,[15] occasioned probably by excitement on the sabbath. . .

THURS. 15.   Waiting to have the truss made [for the baby.]

---

[12] The two families were leaving to attend the 1845 Mission meeting at Waiilatpu. Mary evidently wrote the entries for May 1-12 inclusive in retrospect and then a few days later made duplicate entries for the same period. Entries for this period herein given are selected from both accounts.

[13] All members of the Mission were present at this meeting except Mrs. Spalding.

[14] Entries of these baptisms appear in the record book of the First Presbyterian Church of Oregon. According to the minutes of the Church, a formal meeting of the members was held on May 10, at which time letters of dismissal were granted to the Rev. and Mrs. A. B. Smith and to Mr. and Mrs. W. H. Gray. Also, "At this meeting James Connor, a suspended member, not having shown repentance but otherwise incorrigibility was excommunicated from the visible church of God. His crimes are Sabbath breaking, fighting, neglect of worship, to which he has added polygamy & intent to fight duel & liquor vending."

[15] Possibly Hinman had epilepsy.

Fri. Mr. W. & E. have both had a talk of going to the Willamette with Dr. W. but conclude it is not best. Mr. Howard [16] has made the truss & a tuning fork for Cyrus. We left W. towards night & only went a little way.

Sat. 17. Went to Tusia. I dug a root which I mistook for camas & found it to be an emetic.

Sun. 18. Passed a very comfortable day.

Mon. 19. Had a weary ride to Snake river. Mrs. E. very much over-come or rather sick perhaps. Found Indians ready with several boats to take us across. It was sunset when we were over & ready to leave the river. We traveled by moon light to the island & encamped without pitching our tents. Mrs. McPherson was much fatigued. . .[17]

Fri. 23 . . . reached home safely in good season. Found all safe. The Chief with Solomon. Some of the plants in the garden had been killed & some not.

Sat. 24. Abigail's birthday, five years old. Had to use diligence to get things decent for sabbath.[18]

Sun. 25. Rainy, did not go to worship. The children went once, quite a number of Indians.

Mon. 26. Mrs. McPherson was delivered of a son about noon. . .

Note.[19] We had rather a pleasant visit to Waiilatpu. Formed some acquaintances with Mr. Hinman who was received [in]to our church. All the Mission were present except Mrs. Spalding. She, her husband says, is discouraged & he seems much so himself. Dr. Whitman enter-taining fears that his people intend taking his life. We think they will not do it but it is very trying to have them conduct as they do. They thus requite all the good the Dr. has tried to do them. He is now gone by this time to the Willamet, hope no evil will befall him. Emma Hobson, we left to go down with him to her father. I miss her work a little but her noise, fret, tease much more. The other children are much better contented with out her than they were with.

Sun. June 1, 1845. A quiet day. . . So rainy Mr. W. remained at home except that he went to the Chiefs & had one short service. Reading Heralds & newspapers. . .

[16] Howard was a blacksmith, perhaps a member of the 1844 immigration, who was then at the Whitman station. His son, James Haden, born Dec. 26, 1844, was among those baptized by Spalding on May 10.

[17] It seems amazing to us that Mrs. McPherson should make the 300 mile round-trip to Waiilatpu on horseback during the last days of her pregnancy. Perhaps she expected to be confined while at Waiilatpu, when she could have had the services of Dr. Whitman. In all probability she was a half-breed.

[18] Elkanah objected to his wife working past midnight on Saturday. She records several instances of having been rebuked when she happened to be busy into the early hours of Sunday morning.

[19] Mary inserted in her diary this summary of their trip to Waiilatpu after the last entry for May.

THURS. 5. We had our Maternal meeting as it has not been convenient before. I led. Collected a few plants for pressing & intend to collect one at least per day through the season. . .[20]

SUN. 8. Mr. W. went to Seakwakin. The people conducted with pleasing propriety. We went to Mr. E. to sing. . .

WED. 11 . . . Accomplished a job of painting. Traded roots,[21] passed away four pairs of leggins & an old garment.

THURS. 12. Ironed what I deem a years stock of colars & bosoms &c. . .

SAT. 14.[22] Employed a girl to tap shoes. . .

MON. 16. Washed or tried to, was much hindered by the people coming to trade roots. Traded some 30 or 40 loads worth. Soshenamalt came & tarried long enough to make a pair of shoes.

TUES. 17. Rose before sun, swept round the door step & ironed before breakfast. . . Mr. W. had four Indians helping build chimney & mend the wall of the new room. . .

MON. 23.[23] We left home about noon. Crossed the River & encamped. Was so much fatigued I could not sleep till near morning

FR. JUNE 27. We arrived at Clearwater. Had to wait a long time in the scorching sun for a boat. But at last we passed the river. Found our friends well & the wheat ready to harvest.

SUN. 29. The weather excessively hot. We sleep in our tents. We tarried at Mr. Spalding's two weeks. Dr. W. did not come as we expected, not having returned from the lower country.[24] The wheat was however stacked except a portion let on shares to Mr. Craig.

FRI. [JULY] 11. We set out for home. Mr. Spalding & family accompanied us. . .

SUN. 13. We spent at Polluse.

THURS. 17. We reached home safely. Mrs. Spalding had the misfortune to have her clothing &c wet on the way. We found all safe at home & things growing finely, dug new potatoes for supper.

---

[20] Here we note both Mary's interest in scientific subjects and Geyer's influence.

[21] Altho Mary does not indicate what kind of root she was getting, it was probably camas.

[22] E.W. "I had the thistles pulled up among the wheat. . . All things have been quiet among the Indians. I hope God will have mercy upon us and not suffer violence to fall upon us."

[23] The Walkers left this day for Lapwai. In retrospect Walker wrote in his diary: "The next Sabbath was so warm or rather hot that it seemed almost impossible to endure it. We were there two weeks & accomplished much labor. Mr. & Mrs. S. accompanied us home. . . Since that time up to this date, Saturday 26 of July, I have been very busy. We have fixed up the new room so that it is occupied. . . Mr. S. is & has been busy on the sash." Evidently Spalding with his skill in carpentry was working on the window sash preparatory to the placing of the glass.

[24] On this trip to the Willamette Valley, Dr. Whitman appeared before Probate Judge J. W. Nesmith in Oregon City on June 3, and was appointed the legal guardian of the Sager children.

SUN. 20. Messrs. Spalding & Walker went to the river.[25] Mr. Eells sick. His ill[ness] probably caused in part by the death of Mrs. E's riding horse. . .

TUES. 22 . . . Mr. W. purchased a horse & the man who sold him rode him off.

WED. 23. We all took dinner at Mr. Eells. . .

THURS.[26] 31. Mr. & Mrs. Spalding after much hesitancy conclude to remain till after the Sabbath on account [of] the hot weather. We seldom have so hot weather as for a week past.

SAT. AUG. 2. Making a bonnet for E[liza] Spalding.

SUN. 3. Mr. W. went to the river in the morning. In the afternoon we had the communion.

MON. 4. Mr. S. & family left a little past noon. They have three Indians & as many cows. The weather a little cooler. . .

TUES. 7.[27] Mr. Walker's birthday, 40 years old. Think he looks as young as he did 5 years ago. . .

SAT. 9 . . . My Indian girl works well, has partly made a bed tick & mended not a few stockings.

SUN. 10.[28] Think we never had warmer weather at this place, feel anxious to hear from Mr. Spalding's family. . .

THURS. 12.[29] Ironed. Cut out shoe taps. Paid my girl a shawl. Mrs. E. spent the P.M. with me. . .

THURS. 14. No small part of the day consumed in trading [choke] cherries. . .

TUES. 19. Mr. W. left about sunrise for Colvile. I washed. Mrs. McPherson ironed. . .

WEDNES. 20. Ironed. Get very tired when I have to milk. . .

FRI. 22. Mr. W. got home a little before noon. . . Mr. E. folks dined with us. Mr. W. brought the sad intelligence that four of Mr. McDonald's children died last winter of scarlet fever & were intered in one grave. . .

---

[25] The missionaries did not object to riding up to about ten miles on Sunday in order to conduct worship services for the natives.

[26] E.W. for Monday, 28. "We laid pretty late this morning but was up in time to get through with milking as soon as Mr. E's milk maid. I wish he would send her off as she is a pest to all of us. He seems to think that it is necessary for her to stay here [even] if it proves the curse of all the other children at the place." Very few references have been found to any milking done by Mrs. Eells.

[27] E.W. "Thus through the goodness of God I have been spared to another day when it was said 'A man child was born into the world'. Forty years God has borne with me & preserved me."

[28] E.W. for the 11th: "I hauled in what wheat I had down & then reap some more. I shall have my barn pretty well filled up I think when I get it all in." Walker & Eells had separate fields and separate barns. Each took care of his own animals.

[29] E.W. "I have been hard at the sickle all day & have cut down all my wheat."

SAT. 23.   Spent a good part of the day gathering & boiling green corn to dry.

SUN. 24.[30]   Mr. Eells had quite an ill turn. Imagined himself dying. We were not much startled.

MON. 25   . . .   This morning made a cheese   . . .   & Mr. E. has started for Waiilatpu.

THURS. 28.   Mr. E. turned back not feeling able to pursue his journey. Concluded his complaint is intermittent fever. He has an ill turn every other day. I commenced painting window sash.

SAT. 30.   Baked early. Finished painting sash. Washed children, cleaned house, picked over dry meat. Mr. W. left after dinner for Nathowa.[31] All Indian help gone & Mr. E. sick. Sarah got the cows.

SUN. 31.   June, July & Aug. have [been] without frost. The longest period I think without frost since we came to this country.   . .

MON. SEPT. 1.   Milked. Made cheese, washed   . . .   cooking, scolded &c as usual. Mr. W. returned about noon.

TUES. 2.[32]   Ironed, commenced setting glass.

FRI. 5.   Setting glass & not done yet. Got on slowly, have so much else to do.

SAT. 6.   Baked twice. Churned & cleaned house before dinner. I am glad to see so quiet an afternoon & thankful to find my health & strength according to my day.

FRI. 12.   Painting the window casings. Have been for days occupied in finishing the windows. Our house is wholy glassed tho to complete it, I had to set 47 squares of glass that was more or less injured, 12 of which I begged of our neighbor Mr. E.   . .

TUE. 16.[33]   Ironed & Mr. W. painted the walls of this part of the house & commenced on the new. I smoothed after.

WED. 17.   Worked hard washing over & smoothing.

THURS. 18.   Had a girl helping whitewash. Mr. E. & family left for Clearwater via Waiilatpu.

FRI. 19 [34]   . . .   Had an old woman whitewash & clean our room so we are better prepared to entertain company than we have been. Mr. Fraser sent some dresses, one as a present. It [will] have to be altered.   . .

---

[30] E.W.   "Mr. E. had an ill turn & said he was dying. I told him he was not. He soon recovered. It has been a lonely day. I have not read much as I was so much fatigued."

[31] Location unknown but according to Elkanah's diary, half a day's ride away.

[32] E.W.   "I have been to work on the windows."

[33] E.W.   "We commenced painting our house inside. I have been over most of it today alone. I had mud made for me & brought in."

[34] E.W.   "I had worship with the people this morning before sunrise & again at noon & at night. They seem devoid of all feeling on the subject of their soul's concerns but with help from on high I am determined that they shall have an opportunity to hear."

SUN. 21. We feared we should be interrupted by company but have not been but I can not say as much of vain & worldly thoughts.

MON. 22. Made cheese & sewed on the silk dress. . .[35]

SAT. 27.[36] Have got through with whitewashing this part of the house & got cleaned up & moved into our sleeping room again. I think I feel thankful for the success which has attended our labors of late. . .

WED. OCT. 1. Whitewashed the new room. I am now done with whitewashing, I hope, for a long time. Elkanah [the little child] set the house on fire with a broom. . .

FRI. 3.[37] Ironed & painted the new doors.

SAT. 4.[38] Mr. E. & family returned. We did not expect them so soon. Brought book, papers & letters. . .

MON. 6. Continued to read. Mrs. E. gave me about half the goods received in a cask from Blanford. . .

WED. 8.[39] Lined overhead in my bedroom with tapa which accomplishes a hard job of work on the house. It is six weeks since I began to paint sash & I have improved all the time I could spare in doing something on the house ever since. . .

MON. 13. Wrote to Mr. & Mrs. Caldwell, Carlisle. Mr. W. has been obliged to hunt cows the whole day. . .

FRI. 17.[40] We received a short call from Mr. Ogden. . .

SUN. 26.[41] Rather rainy. A large number of Indians. . .

---

[35] Mary's first reference to her having a silk dress. Perhaps this was a present from Mr. Fraser. See entry for Sept. 19.

[36] E.W. for the 26th: "Much against my will I cut out the door in the end of the living room & put in the door." Evidently Mary got what she wanted.

[37] E.W. "The place is clear of Indians save one. I am much fatigued & am rejoiced that my harvesting is all done."

[38] E.W. "I was not well pleased with Mr. Greene's letter to me." Elkanah was still very sensitive over what he considered to be unjustified criticism of him by the American Board.

[39] Coll. o. has a photostat of a letter Walker wrote to Greene, dated October 8, 1845, from which the following extracts are taken: "The feeling is deeply impressed upon me & also upon that of Mrs. Walker, that you have little, or no confidence in me — that every thing I say is looked upon with suspicion. You must be sensible that this state of feeling. . . makes my situation very unpleasant. . . I was rather inclined to despondency. At least the first year I was in the country, I was inclined to give up & go home. . . When the members of the Southern Branch of the mission, at least part of them, requested a meeting to discuss the propriety of selling out to the Methodists, what was the answer I gave? It was that we ought not to do it. . . when there seemed no hope I said if every other member of the mission left the field, I was determined to stay, & bark as long as I could — I do not like the language; but it is the language I used on the occasion."

[40] E.W. "Cyrus has done well with the cows today." Evidently Cyrus, not quite seven years old, was given the task of watching the cows for at least part of the day.

Mon. 27 . . . Mr. W. left for Colvile. . . Had the children take up the corn. . .

Fri. 31. Mr. Walker returned from C. The express has arrived from Canada but brings no letters for us. So I fear we shall not soon hear from home.

Mon. [Nov.] 10.[42] Mr. Walker left this morning for Clearwater. Took Mufflehead & Charles with him. . .

Wed. 12 . . . Many of the Indians are sick with colds & coughs & difficult respiration. I have given several of them saltpetre. They seem to find great relief from it. Simpleton came to night from a neighboring encampment to get some. Called it the medicine that resembles hail. . .

Thurs. 13 . . . Cyrus too sick to eat or play & Abigail but little better. A moon eclipse. The moon rose nearly totally eclipsed, at what time it ended we could not tell as it became cloudy. . .

Sat. 15. The children seem better but all sick enough to be very cross. I had hoped to commence on Cyrus clothing. . .

Sunday 16. Rainy in the forenoon, did not allow the children to attend worship. They are all half sick at least. It seems as if they would wear me out with their continual tease. I feel lonely & shall be glad to have husband come home again. . .

Wed. 19 . . . Finished Cyrus spencer. It looks comfortable well but does not set as well as I would like to see it. . .

Fri. 21. Mr. W. reached home about sunset.

Sat. 22. Mr. W. thinks to start on Tues to take Cyrus to Dr. Whitman's to attend school. A little snow storm. . .

Mon. 24. Rose early, made a pr. of pantaloons for Cyrus. Mrs. E. assisted me a little. She made him a spencer. I sat up nearly all night to sew, bake, etc.

Tues. 25. Mr. W. & Cyrus left about eleven A.M. I spent the day clearing up the clutter they left behind & in putting things in repair such as the well curb, &c. I salted the pork Mr. W. brought from Mr. Spalding's, baked the ribs & cleaned the head & feet & got very tired. . .

Fri. 28 . . . In the evening I churned & took up my older churning of butter & worked it over & mixed it with the new & made it up for the [winter.] Have now 28 balls to last me through the

---

[41] E.W. "Mr. Eells talked to the people in the forenoon. He had as large a congregation as I ever saw in that house. . . He needs, as well as myself, to improve in the use of the language." After seven years' residence among the natives, the missionaries were still struggling with the language barrier.

On this day Whitman wrote to Walker saying in part: "I do not feel as keenly perhaps on some of the points about the immigrants [as you do,] nor will I for I am here and the meeting of them is one important part of my duty." Coll. c.

[42] Walker went to Lapwai to help Spalding in the butchering of three hogs and took some of the meat back to Tshimakain.

winter. I had many little chores to do & sat up very late. Indeed I do not know as I have rested till midnight or past a night since Sunday. But I have got along. . .

Sun. 30. Had a long night's rest which refreshed me much. The morning was fine & I attended worship with the children. Have had a fire only in the bedroom. Have been reading Mothers Magazines . . .[43]

Tues. [Dec.] 2. Traded this morning with one of the Finleys.[44] Brought nine prs. of shoes & seven deer skins for which I paid a kettle, knife, spoon, fire steel, a few pins & needles, a shawl, an old coat of C's & an old dress of my own & a pice of Baize worth 20 loads. He seemed pleased with his trade & I am sure the skins & shoes are worth more than I gave for them & probably the things are worth more to him than he paid for them. . . In the evening Mungo arrived bringing letters from Dr. Whitman. One of them, the last of rather a disheartening character. He fears he must leave his people. . .[45]

Sat. 6. Night came & we began to despair of seeing Mr. Walker. I was beginning to feel sad & concerned but the sound of his footsteps at the door soon relieved my anxiety & . . . I thanked God once more for his goodness.

Sun. 7. Cyrus' birthday. He is seven years old & has just commenced attending school. He was sick on the way down but was pretty well when his father left him.[46] I have been reading Heralds to day not quite a year old. . .

---

[43] Some copies of the *Mothers Magazines,* with Mary's signature, are in Coll. Wn.

[44] Note comment about the Finleys under "List of Persons."

[45] On Nov. 25, 1845, Whitman wrote a letter to Walker from which the following extracts are taken: "I write. . . to inform you that I have given the Indians from now to next spring to consider whether I shall leave them or not." Whitman reported having had a talk with Young Chief (also called Tawatowe or Tauitau) who accused the whites of "having a design to obtain their country & property" and that the whites were "being prepared with poison and infection to accomplish their purpose." Young Chief also referred to the death of some relatives "as the result of diseases which Americans placed among them" and of the death in California of Elijah Hedding. "I told them," wrote Whitman, "I was in ignorance of any such causes in operation and that I was not aware that I myself was. . . accountable for such base things as they might have been told." In reply Whitman was told: "It is not to be expected that you would confess it even were it true." Whitman warned them that such talk "would remove all restraint from the reckless and that I would have no assurance but that I might be killed on the most slight or sudden occasion." Coll. c.

[46] Walker in his diary for the 28th wrote: "He [Cyrus] vomited at the Palouse & complained of being sleepy but made out to ride. . . He would eat no supper." On the 29th: "I had a restless night as I did not dare to let the fire go down. . . Cyrus rested better than I expected. He vomited in the night. He was quite bright this morning & said he could ride."

WED. 10.[47]   Have made a pr. of pants for Cyrus out of a pr. of his fathers old ones & glad I am they are done for it makes me sick to think of doing tailor's work. . .

THURS. 11.   Got through with a two weeks wash quite easy & in good season. Had quite a sun-shiny day which is a great rarity. . .

FRI. 12 . . . Looked over some letters Mr. W. has been writing. Abigail set her fathers newspapers on fire & one was entirely consumed.

SUN. 14.[48]   A cloudy day but the house of worship was well filled & Mr. W. thinks the people seemed attentive. . .

MON. 15 . . . Mr. E. had a cow calve but the wolves kill the calf. Teacher here in the evening. Mr. W. translating.

TUES. 16.   Mr. W. & E. slaughtered an ox. I mended the broken ear of a kettle. . .

WED. 17.   Tried out the tallow, salted the beef & cast 23 dozen of wickes. I trust I am thankful for the success that attends our labors.

THURS. DEC. 18.   Dipped 24 doz. candles, get done just [at] dark

SUN. 21.   Cold enough to freeze in the buttery all day. . .

THURS. 25.   Very rainy. Ironed & sewed a little. Feel discouraged. I see so much that needs to be done immediately.

SAT. DEC. 27.   The business in hand yesterday & to day has been repairing Mr. W's old blue coat. Very rainy. We have a calf. . .

WED. 31.   The close of another year. A year of health & prosperity, but as [a] Mission we seem to have effected little. Oh! that it would please God to open the eyes of this people. . .

1846 — GROWING SENSE OF FUTILITY

This year was one of the quietest that the Walkers spent at Tshi-makain. No Mission meeting was held during the year; Elkanah had but few business trips to make; and the family made but one excursion and that was to Fort Colville in September. Cyrus returned from the school at Waiilatpu in April, being escorted back by his teacher Andrew Rodgers, who remained as a visitor at Tshimakain for a few weeks. Walker's fifth child, Jeremiah, arrived on March 7 and for the second time Dr. Whitman was unable to attend the mother.

Since the missionaries received no salaries from the American Board and were supposed to make their respective establishments in Oregon self-supporting, this meant that both Elkanah and Mary had to con-

---

[47] E.W. for the 9th: "Mr. Eells commenced the school with seven. I hardly know what we ought to do under such circumstances." The small and irregular attendance was most discouraging.

[48] E.W. "We were up [in] pretty good season & had breakfast & worship by candle light. They [i.e., the natives] gave good attention although the truth was aimed at their superstitions."

tinue spending most of their time and energy in those routine duties necessary to maintain a home in the wilderness. Elkanah remained faithful in conducting religious services for the natives whenever possible, and was also able to do some more work translating the Gospel according to Matthew into the Flathead tongue. Mary's time was almost entirely taken by her household duties and her children. She had some opportunity to carry on her ministry of healing with the natives by handing out some simple remedies.

During this year the Walkers had problems of discipline in regard to their children which come to parents everywhere. There is the pathetic story of how they tried to break the will of their little two-year old boy, Elkanah, when he refused to say please. Mary quickly repented the harshness of their course. Soon after Cyrus' return from school, his parents heard of some incident which involved him and some girls. We are not told the exact nature of what happened but it apparently involved some childish curiosity about sex. The affair precipitated serious problems at Tshimakain when, for a short time, Cushing and Myra Eells did not want their little boys to have any association with the Walker children.

Both Elkanah and Mary had a growing sense of futility when they saw so few results in the evangelization of the natives after so much sacrifice and labor. For the first time during this year they began to consider the advisability of leaving the field. However, such a course would involve a loss of face. It seemed contrary to the Biblical injunction that once you put your hand to the plow, there should be no turning back. A high sense of duty kept them at their post. Before the year closed, both Elkanah and Mary were commenting on the severity of an early winter. By the middle of December the ground at Tshimakain had a layer of snow about two and a half feet deep. This was the winter in which the Donner party was trapped in the snows of the Sierras, and this was the winter that took such a heavy toll of horses and cattle owned by the Indians in the Oregon country. The suffering and material loss of the Indians contributed to the growing discontent that came to the tragic climax in the Whitman massacre of the following year.

THURS. JAN. 1. Mr. Eells family dined with us. . .

FRI. 2. Mending, mending old garments.

SAT. JAN. 3. Have milked for several days past which has helped to hinder my needle. . . I feel lazy enough, have to summon all my fortitude to do anything. . .

MON. 5. We observed the concert & fast. Old Jezebal,[1] as we call her, went to Mrs. Eells & cried & made great profession of penitence but we think it all hyprocricy. . .

---

[1] No further identification is known.

WED. 7.[2]   Mr. W. not being about much, I had to milk & do some other out door work. Cut a pair of aprons for A., made one & commenced on the other.

THURS. JAN. 8.   Baked in the forenoon. Mr. Pelley & others called in passing. . .

SAT. 10.   Repaired some garments & made a broom. . .

TUES. 13.   S[oshenamalt] did not come to day. Understand the medicine was played in her father's lodge last night, so I suppose she could not sleep. . .

FRI. 16.   S. mended shoes, sifted meal & made diapers. I hung up beef to dry; look to sundry things, read & sewed a little. . .

MON. 19 . . . Mr. W. & E. translating this evening. . .

THURS. 22.   Mr. W. made a small table. . .

FRI. 23 . . . I painted the table Mr. W. made yesterday. . .

SUN. 25.   Warm rainy weather. The time with me pass tediously away. I trust I am in some measure thankful for the many mercies I enjoy, tho often tempted to fret.

MON. 26.   S. commenced on a rug & I on a Merino dress for myself. . .

SAT. JAN. 31.   Baked twice & fried cakes. Despairing of cold weather concluded to bake a lot of beef. S. washed potatoes, children, & floors. . .

SUN. FEB. 1 . . . A little snow last night & to day has been fair, to night it freezes. . .

MON. 2.   By morning the cold passed away. . . I [had] a man to pound & S. to rub. So I got out my washing about noon without doing much of it myself. . .

TUES. 3.   Got my ironing done. Found S. was making such shiftless work on her rug that I put it by. . .

FRI. 6 . . . Mr. Walker made a couple of small stools, moved his saddles &c from the store house to the old house & moved the meat kegs. I have worked most of the day cleaning & brushing. Have painted five stools & our bed room hearth. . .

SAT. 7.   Baked twice. Mr. W. went to the river hoping to meet Dr. W. but instead an Indian arrived bringing letters to inform us he can not come on account of lameness.[3] We feel exceedingly disappointed.

---

[2] E.W. "The teacher came to inquire after my health tonight. It is more probable that he came after something to eat."

[3] On February 3, 1846, Whitman wrote to Walker: "My horse fell with me early in December & hurt my knee joint. . ." Therefore he was unable to make the long horseback trip to Tshimakain. Regarding Mrs. Walker's approaching confinement, he wrote: "Let nature have its unobstructed course which is all the physician aims at as far as possible." On the same day Mrs. Whitman wrote to Mary: "I entirely forgot to send the apple trees as you desired by Mr. Walker — I was very sorry for it for you can have them as well as not. You will be pleased to hear that Cyrus is doing well both in school and out. . . We all love him and feel it is a privalege to have him in our family." Both letters are in Coll. c.

SUN. 8. I have become quite composed in my feelings. Feel that in God's hands I am safe. But without him there is no security. . .

TUES. 10. Elkanah's birthday.[4] The weather for a day or two cold enough to freeze meat. S. ironed & mended stockings. I was part of the day sick & part well. Made a comb case in the eve. . .

THURS. 12. Paid S. by giving her a quilt. She went home apparently pleased & satisfied. But [in the] afternoon, her old mother came & said her daughter wanted me to give her a little more of something no matter what. I doubted whether the old creature did not come of her own mind so I told her Mr. Walker told me I had paid her too much already & I would not give her more at present. . .

SAT. 14. Baked, boiled & parboiled most of our fresh beef. S. came to bring the skins she had been smoking. I paid her a slip, apron, &c. I proposed to her to wash the floor but she declined. So I did it myself. Got through with my days work quite comfortably. A hen which stole her nest hatches only one chicken. . .

TUES. 17. Ironed. S. returned to work again. . .

WED. 18. Boiled meat & vegetables for supper, the first boiled dish we have had for the winter. . .

SAT. 21 . . . Made a doll for Abigail. . .

SUN. 22. The day passed heavily. Quite unwell part of the afternoon. Feel quite too impatient. . .

WED. 25 . . . The coldest day we have had this winter. The wind blowed so yesterday & to day, we could not have fire in our bed room. Bread, milk, &c. in the buttery frozen hard. To night we are able to have a fire in our bed room. . .

FRI. 27. The cold weather gone & raining sweetly as ever. Mr. Pelley & party, we hear, are at the river. At work on my rug. . .

SAT. 28. Our American cow which was lost yesterday was found but had lost her calf. I baked in the forenoon, washed children & floor in the afternoon. Mr. P. took supper with us. We received a letter from Dr. Whitman who is still lame but was on a visit to W.W. as Mr. McKinley is about to leave. It rains to night sweetly as ever. . .

SUN. MARCH 1, 1846.[5] So rainy the travellers were obliged to remain quiet. Mr. Pelley took breakfast with [us] & lunch at noon. We had an English service. Several of the men attended.

MON. 2 . . . Mr. P. moved camp in the morning. . .

TUES. 3 . . . Another calf so Mr. W. has three cows to attend to & milk. Mr. E's workman gambled last night & lost all he had. . .

WED. 4. Rather unwell all day. Made out to iron & sift some meal & mend a little. . . The frogs are singing & the Indians gambling.

---

[4] All references to Elkanah in Mary's diary are to their son born on February 10, 1844.

[5] E.W. "Mr. Pelley is a well informed man and as gentlemanly in his manner as any one I have seen in the country."

THURS. 5. Eight years ago to day was married, & left my father's [house.] God has been gracious thus far. May his mercy still follow us. . . Feel the need of a physician very much. . .

FRI. 6 . . . Feel rather dejected. Would give a great deal to see a physician.

SAT. 7. Took a portion of salts before retiring, was restless all night. Somewhat indisposed through the day. About the middle of the afternoon became worse & was delivered of a son about sunset. I think I never felt more gratitude & joy. After a month of solicitude & suspence to find myself so safe & comfortable to see another so fine a son. His father calls his name Jeremiah after his father. . .

SUN. MARCH 8. Mrs. E. staid with me all night. I took no medicine except a little camphor. Rested considerable. Have a tolerably comfortable day. . .

MON. 9 . . . Plenty of milk for my babe & sound nipples. A comfort I never knew before.

TUES. 10. Dressed myself & sat up a considerable part of the [day.] All seems going right. I am so glad not to have trouble with my breasts & nipples. . .

THURS. 12. I arose early & assisted Mr. W. in making a fire cake for breakfast. Dressed my babe for the first time. Changed my clothes, swept my room, read some & sewed some. . . The old blind woman came & knocked a long time at the door but could not gain admission. . .

SAT. 14. Resumed my seat at the table. Assisted some about baking &c. Did not get quite so tired as yesterday. . .

MON. 16.[6] Marcus's birthday, four years old. He knows his alphabet pretty well. Can spell most monosyllables & many disyllables. . . Mr. E's children came down & partook with ours a little collation [i.e., a light supper.] I have cooked & washed dishes & sewed a little. Mrs. E. took my washing. . .

WED. 18. Mr. W. building a back-house. I fried some pancakes, swept the kitchen, worked about the house a good part of the day. . . Had to extinguish the fire in our room on account of the wind.

THURS. 19. Mrs. E. & Sarah came down & helped churn & washed the floors.

FRI. 20.[7] Seven years ago to day we arrived at this place. I walked

---

[6] E.W. "I have had some calls for seed which I could not supply." Evidently the natives were showing a greater interest in cultivating the soil than ever before.

[7] E.W. "I have been to work on the backhouse. . . This is the seventh anniversary of our coming to this place with our families. Seven long years we have been here & what have we done. But little what we ought to have done & might if we had been of the right spirit. We have been here just one year of Sabbaths."

to day as far as the hen house. One hen we found dead & two cocks we killed. . .

SUN. 22.[8] My babe & c[hildren] have not allowed me time to read enough to hurt me. Mr. McKenzie passed on his way to Colvile.

MON. 23.[9] Had [an Indian] to help me wash. Mrs. E. assisted a little too. . .

THURS. 26. Mr. Walker away ploughing for Charles. The gentleman who goes to the Flatheads called to take some things that were stored here. The mother of Soshenamalt has tried my patience some to day. Old Solomon made me a call. Brought green clay. . .

SAT. 28. Baked in the morning. . . Weighed the children: Abigail weighed 51, Marcus 41, Elkanah 28 & Jeremiah 10¾ lbs. . .

MON. MARCH 30, 1846.[10] Had a boy to help in the forenoon but babe was worisome & along in the afternoon Mrs. E. & Sarah came down & helped me out of the suds.

TUES. 31. About ten o'clock in the morning Elkanah asked for some sugar. I told him to say "please sugar," but he refused but continued to cry, "I want some sugar." I thought best to try the rod which I continued to do with increasing severity till his father came when I delivered him to him, and he followed the same course till noon when the child became so much exhausted that we concluded to let him sleep but he did not seem to yield at all. He slept till three or four in the afternoon but sighed deeply for a long time. When he awoke seemed refreshed & pleasant. We thought not to allow food or drink tell he should say please some, but if he asked for milk & we told him to say "please milk," he would say "I dont want to say please," or "I dont want milk." When night came, we allowed him to rest. In the morning, Apr. 1st, we again tried to compel him to yield but he was still firm. We used the rod till we feared to longer. We tried to tempt him with food & drink but to no effect altho he had taken not a drop of any thing for more than 24 hours. . .[11] It was affecting to witnes the joy he evinced. We kept him in bed all day & still tried to induce him to say please, but to no purpose.

WED. APRIL 1. My birthday, 35 years old. I think I should long remember it.

THURS. 2 . . . We concluded to release our poor little boy.

---

[8] E.W. "I have been dull all day. I am so worn out that I can hardly take care of myself. I should like to go off somewhere if I could leave home."

[9] E.W. "I felt Mondayish enough to day."

[10] E.W. "An Indian came in last night for seed & came this morning. I told him as he came in on the Sabbath I should give him none. Quite a number of people left to day for Spokane to eat Buffalo meat."

[11] At this point the page in the original document is damaged so that the full entry cannot be transcribed. Evidently the parents relented and gave the child some food. See Mary's entry for September 13, 1840, when Cyrus refused to say please. He was also about two years old at the time.

After he was dressed he wanted, he said, to go out & see the bright sun. At breakfast he several times said please when he wanted any thing without being told. I regret the course we pursued tho I do not perceive that he is injured by it except for the time but less severity would I think have been just as well. I often fear being guilty of the very thing for which I punish my child. . .

THURS. APR. 9, 1846.   I have been so busy by day & so drowsy by night that I have not been able to write in my journal for a week past. During that time I have had S. my Indian woman to assist me part of the time. . .   To day just as we were done dinner, three gentlemen arrived, Mr. Lane of the H.B.C. & the two English officers that Mr. Ogden accompanied across the Rocky Mts. last summer. Mr. Eells family came down & we enjoyed a social dinner together. Mr. Walker has gone with them to their night's encampment. Dr. W. sent word that Cyrus & Mr. Rogers would be along soon.

FRI. 10 . . .   About sunset Mr. Rogers [12] & Cyrus came. He was much interested in seeing his new br. The children were almost crazy with joy to see each other. Cyrus did not stop to take off his cloak before he told me the flowers [13] were already blooming at Dr. Whitman's.

SAT. 11.   Baked & went my accustomed round. Mr. Rogers thinks to remain awhile with us. . .

MON. 13 . . .   Cyrus has been so disobedient that I had to send him up stairs awhile. . .

TUES. 14 [14] . . .   Mr. Rogers set out my apple trees. . .[15]

FRI. 17.   Tried in vain to write in the day time, sat up & wrote by night to Father & sisters. . .

MON. 20.[16]   Commenced a letter to Mr. Caldwell. . .

---

[12] Andrew Rodgers, who arrived at the Whitman station in the fall of 1845, remained there until the time of the massacre, when he was one of the victims. Writing to Mrs. Walker on November 2, 1846, Mrs. Whitman said: "Mr. Rodgers acts as our minister and maintains the station with considerable ministerial dignity." He was taken under the care of the Mission as a candidate for the ministry and was carrying on his theological studies at the time of his death. Original letter is in Coll. w.

[13] Mary makes no mention in her diary of raising flowers. Near the Robert Seagle house on the site of the Tshimakain mission today is a lilac bush or tree of great age. It might have been planted during the mission period.

[14] E.W. "I have been hauling manure all alone. Some [Indians] have moved off & I wish the rest would go soon."

[15] Rodgers took with him to Tshimakain some apple trees about which Mrs. Whitman had previously written. Two very old apple trees are still alive and bearing fruit on the Tshimakain mission site.

[16] E.W. for the 19th: "The after express came along with a letter to me from Mr. Ogden with some numbers of the Oregon Spectator." The first number of the Oregon Spectator, the first newspaper to be published in Oregon, was dated February 5, 1846.

SUN. 26. The Lord's supper administered by Mr. Walker, he also preached. Our babe was baptized by Mr. Eells by the name of Jeremiah. I have felt very stupid all day. The cares of my family so engross my mind that I have no room to think of anything else. I feel at times scarce courage enough to try to live, because the prospect is of only an increase in care from year to year for years to come. Still I trust to find strength equal to my day. . .

WED. 29. Set out woodbine. . .[17]

SAT. [MAY] 2.[18] Churned & baked. Got along pretty well with my work altho there are so many things that need to be done, I hardly know what to do first. . .

WED. 6 . . . I rode out with my babe for the first time. Abigail rode alone on my saddle. . .

SAT. 9. Took down my bed curtains, scalded the cracks & attended to matters of like importance. Churned & was a long time about it.

SUN. 10. We had an English service at our house. Mr. E. read a sermon. I have been reading the Mirrors of '43. . .

WED. 13.[19] Made a cheese. Rode out & gathered some plants to press. . .

SUN. 17. We had a meeting. Mr. Rogers had a sabbath school for the children. . .

TUES. 19. Mr. E's family left for Mr. Spalding's. I made a cheese & ironed. . .

SAT. 23. Abigail's birthday, 6 years old.[20] Made a cheese & baked pies & plum pudding. Hung up buffalo tongues to dry. . .

WED. 27. Ironed, churned & mended a little. The Indians are returning from popo.

THURS. 28. Made a cheese. Several Indian women were in who were much interested in seeing it. McKay passed on his way to W.W. . .

FRI. 29.[21] The Indians have been calling all day to get medicine & trade popo. I grudged to spend so much time but wished for some roots & did not like to disoblige the people. Some of the people were not pleased & talked rather insultingly to Mr. W. which has an un-

---

[17] In those days it was customary to plant woodbine near an outhouse to cover it.

[18] According to Elkanah's diary, he and Rodgers were busy these days building rail fences.

[19] E.W. "Mrs. W. & myself rode out in the afternoon. It has been a most lovely day."

[20] Actually Abigail's birthday fell on the 24th, which was a Sunday. Undoubtedly the parents felt it was more appropriate to observe the occasion on the day before.

[21] E.W. "Some more have come in to day & there has been much trading & scolding. I got so out of patience that I said that I would either stop the trading or leave the place." The Indians were always inclined to barter and Elkanah became impatient with the haggling.

pleasant effect on him & as usual when things go wrong to trace the cause to my management. . .

SAT. 30 . . . The Indians very quiet & Mr. W. is getting to feel better. . .

MON. JUNE 1. Had an Indian to pound. Got done washing in good season. Went out to see several sick people. Gathered plants to press. . .

THURS. 4. Had a little time to sew each day. The weather so warm I have done without a petticoat. . .

WED. 10 . . . Mr. & Mrs. E. returned. Did not make much of a visit at Mr. Spaldings after all. On reaching the Dr.'s were surprised to find that they supposed we were so much at variance that we could not live together any longer. They were full of trouble & wished an explanation. They also had other painful intelligence to communicate in relation to Cyrus & their children & Sarah G. & Emma H. . .[22]

FRI. 12 . . . Talked with Cyrus & with Mrs. E. about him. I find my fears were but too well founded. But Dr. Whitman & Mr. E. family still seem to feel that Sarah has not been a chief cause. They evidently feel that he has injured her rather than she him. Mr. E. is now unwilling that his children would associate at all with ours. My feelings are exceedingly tried on the subject. I can endure to be treated with contempt myself better than to see my children. While conversing with Mr. E., my children came in & as soon as Mr. E. found they were there, he called Edwin into the bed room with him.

SAT. 13.[23] Mr. & Mrs. E. came down & we talked over our troubles. But whether they will be better or worse, I do not know. I do not feel as well satisfied as I had hoped. Mr. E. did not admit that he had ever done wrong about any thing. Neither did he give any encouragement that he would do better. Mr. Walker thinks best to give up his contemplated visit to Willamette & let Mr. Rogers go instead.

SUN. 14. Mr. Walker dropped a note to Mr. & Mrs. E. proposing to over look all that is past & in future when any thing unpleasant shall happen to speak of it immediately. . . I lay [awake] all night thinking. I do not know what course to persue with our children. They

[22] On September 11, 1846, Mrs. Whitman wrote to Mrs. Walker suggesting that both Cyrus and Abigail be sent to the school. Regarding the incident of the previous year, she wrote: "I hope you will not suffer your mind to be influenced by what I wrote you in my last to deter you from sending them — for I feel with regard to my own children that I am better prepared to keep watch over and instruct them than I was last winter from the fact of knowing their previous acts. . . they did not understand the evil nature of such acts before. . . for in ignorance they all did what they did and I feel to rejoice that we were permited to come to the knowledge of it before going any further." Coll. c.

[23] E.W. "It has been an eventful day here. I fear great consequences are suspended on the events of this day. We have had a long & hard talk with Mr. & Mrs. Eells. . . If one or the other of us will leave, I shall make no objection."

need much more care than I can possibly bestow. . . I hope Providence will dispose of me as is best even if it be to remove me from this place & even to another world. I fear to pray to forgive my trespasses as I forgive others. I would rather say forgive *not* as I forgive others.

MON. 15. Baked biscuit for Mr. Rogers & fitted him off. Mr. Walker went to the river with him & while he was absent I broke Elkanah's truss.

TUES. 16.[24] Mr. Walker left for Colvile. I set out cabbage plants

THURS. 18. The Indian children constantly coming to sell strawberries. Baked those I had purchased & made some cake.

FRI. 19. Mr. W. returned. . . E's truss fits him well. I have to hear the children read myself now, find it hard work.

SAT. 20. Mr. E's family to dinner with us. . .

MON. 22. Frost again last night. Mr. Walker planted over his corn to day. I washed with only Cyrus help.[25] I feel much anxiety on account of the affairs of the Mission & particularly in regard to ourselves. May Providence make the path of duty plain. . .

TUES. 23 . . . In the evening we had a long interview with Mr. & Mrs. Eells & I trust were all able to come to a better understanding & state of feeling. . .

FRI. 26. Finished leather pants for Marcus. Had salmon for dinner, the first time this season.

SAT. 27. Baked & churned 14 lbs. of butter in about five minutes

SUN. 28.[26] Mr. Walker went to Seakwakin & Mr. E. to the river. Few of the people attended worship. I have been reading old letters. My mind dwells much on our late difficulties. I do not know whom to blame most, myself or others. I see much to regret. I feel provoked with myself that I did not adopt a more decided course in relation to Sarah. . .

TUES. 30. Soshenamalt had a daughter born. . .

FRI. [JULY] 3. My father's birthday, if living 61 years old. A frost last night. Had a long talk with Mrs. Eells. Feel somewhat better than I did before I talked.

SAT. 4.[27] Rainy. Our children went to dinner with Mr. Eell's.

SUN. 5.[28] Mr. Walker went to the River.

---

[24] Elkanah found it necessary to make a special trip to Colville to get the truss repaired.

[25] Cyrus Walker reminisced in the article he wrote for the December 21, 1911, issue of the *Pacific Homestead*. Of his childhood, he wrote: "My playmates were Indian boys. My choicest diversion was to roam through the nearby pine woods, bow & arrows in hand, hunting birds and squirrels. So earnest was my insistence that my father kept me supplied with these Indian weapons of hunting and warfare."

[26] E.W. "Found so few disposed to attend worship that I felt almost discouraged."

MON. 6.   The Indians are taking several hundred salmon a day.   .   .

TUES. 7.   Mr. W. winnowing wheat. Has about ten bushels.   .   .

FRI. JULY 10.[29]   Have to exert myself to get dinner in season when I teach the children. Thought to sew a little but had berries to trade & to work a while in the garden.   .   .

SUN. 12.   Spent considerable time in singing. Went with the children to Mr. E's. Feel better in some respect [than I] think I did a few weeks ago, especially toward our associates.   .   .

WED. 15.   Traded several bushels of sepet or whurtleberries.   .   .

FRI. 17.   Mr. Walker irrigating the garden. The Indians continue to bring berries.

SAT. 18 [30]   .   .   .   I have a great many lonely feelings, a great many things I want to say but no body to say things to. If I knew where I could go to find a welcome, I would not be long in starting.   .   .

TUES. 21.   Trading berries & hunting bugs up stairs as well as in the bed room. The thoughts of my heart trouble [me] very much these days but I cannot tell why.   .   .

SUN. 26.[31]   Mr. Walker at the Barrier. The people so noisy he could not sleep on account of them.   .   .

WED. 29 [32]   .   .   .   The fire consumed several bags of the Indians camas. I finished ironing, scalt bugs & mended a little.   .   .

SUNDAY [AUG.] 2.[33]   Mr. E. at the Barrier. An unpleasant camp of people at this place, who have little regard for the Sabbath.

MONDAY 3.[34]   The Indians who were about us yesterday gave us

---

[27] E.W.   "I had to whip A. to day for looking into Mr. Eells' window."

[28] E.W.   "They turned out well to worship to day so that I was much encouraged."

[29] E.W.   "I have been busy all day on my wheat & potatoes.   .   .   I have much more than I expected. There are eighteen large bushels. It will fill my barn pretty well."

[30] E.W.   "I want to go some where but can think of no place that will suit me. I feel quite lonely & quite lost to know what to do."

[31] E.W.   "I had but little sleep last night on account of the noise of the dogs & people." For the next day he wrote: "Notwithstanding the fleas & muskeetoes & horses, I had a good nights rest, but was very tired this morning.   .   .   I reached home before Mrs. W. had been to breakfast."

[32] E.W.   "The [forest] fire is raging near us. Some camas has been burned up. The children had their ride today."

[33] E.W.   "There has been coming & going all day. The traveling on the Sabbath among this people is increasing. It has been a lonely day to me. It seems that I can not endure to stay here any longer. With my feelings it is almost impossible for me to do the people any good."

[34] E.W.   "The Indians who were here gave considerable trouble before they left. They beset Mrs. Eells. I was absent at the time or I expect they would not have conducted quite so bad. One of them climbed upon the house & talked very bad to Mrs. W. but on seeing me coming, he got down."

some trouble & probably pilferred a little. . . I washed & hunted bugs again, found several. . .

WED. 5. Made a shirt for Marcus, besides my other work. It is the first cotton shirt I have had occasion to make since I have been in the country except infant shirts.

THURS. 6 35 . . . My health is better this summer than usual. Cyrus is pretty good about work but seldom meddles with a book unless he is compelled to. Abigail does better in some respects, but she hardly knows how to spend time to study her spelling lesson. She is so anxious to be painting or drawing. Marcus learns easy but is so lazy. . .

FRI. AUG. 7. Mr. Walker 41 years old. Mr. E's family dined with us. . .

SUN. 9. Quite a house full of Indians. I attended the worship forenoon & afternoon. . .

SAT. 15. W. & Marcus left to spend the sabbath on the road to Colvile. . .

THURS. 20. Mr. W. returned. Marcus stood the journey well. Mr. W. had a pleasant visit. Mr. & Mrs. Lewis made us various presents. . .

SUNDAY 23. Read English or rather Scotch newspapers a part of the day, only one year old.

TUES. 25. Mending, mending, day after day, stitch, stitch. Mrs. E. took a vest to make for Mr. Walker. I have so many things that I do not know how to leave undone that I feel almost distracted. . .

FRI. 28.36 Find nearly every woolen garment in the house covered with nits. Do not know of what but conclude they must be those of flies. . .

SUNDAY 30. Wish I could write of duties better done to God & man.

MON. 31. Washed & scalded bedsteads once more. Mr. E. went for soda, took Edwin with him. Mrs. E. took tea with us.

TUES. SEPT. 1 37 . . . Mrs. E. dined & spent the afternoon with us. She is making clothes for Mr. Walker. Abigail goes to sleep with her.

WED. 2 . . . Mr. E. returns. . . Have hard work to get my childrens lessons out of them. Cyrus learns any thing better than books. . .

---

35 E.W. "The Indians have been quiet & have gone out of sight to gamble. Quite a number proceed off & among them the gamblers & I am always glad to see them go."

36 E.W. for the 27th: "I have been rather miserable this two or three days past & feel often as though I must leave. I cannot feel satisfied that it is my duty to stay here for I can see no prospect of any good coming out of it."

37 E.W. "I got two Indians to thrash to day. The one-eyed man & Mufflehead."

Mon. 7.   Busy all day repairing or rather altering my silk dress.

Fri. 11 . . . Churned, baked, & packed up & did many other things.[38] Had Mrs. E. help me some besides. She has made her vests & a pair of pantaloons for Mr. Walker. . . I have borrowed a quilt of her to give to Mrs. Lewis. . .

Sat. 12.   Left home in the morning. . .

Tues. 15.   Reached Colvile before noon. Met with a kind reception. . .

Wed. 16, Sept. 1846.   Spent the day mostly in sewing for Mrs. Lewis.

Thurs. 17.   Left Colvile after dinner. Mr. Lewis came out a few miles with us. They made us a present of a mirror, four cups & saucers, a merino dress, crape hankerchief, combs, Indian baskets, &c. We encamped at the farm house. . .

Sat. 19.   Reached home at seven, found all safe except the dogs had killed several hens. Simpleton was here, had brought letters, two were from home. One from sister C[harlotte] of March 5, 1845 & from I.T. and C. of Oct. & Nov.[39] My Father's family were all prosperous. . .

Tues. 22.[40]   Mr. E. left for Waiilatpu, took Edwin along. I wrote to Mrs. Whitman & Spalding. . .

Sunday 27 . . . I feel much at loss to know what we ought to do with our children. Dr. Whitman invites us to send them there to attend school. But we have thought best not to send them. They learn so much that has to be unlearned. And at home they learn so little of any thing. I hope we shall be led to do what is best. It is encouraging to me to know that my friends [41] live where there are good schools & I hope they will have the ability & disposition to assist [us] in the education of our children. I feel the desire to see some of my friends & intend when I write again to invite some of them to come over to see us. . .

---

[38] The Walkers were getting ready to go to Colville.

[39] The original letter from Mary's brother Isaac Thompson Richardson and her sister Charlotte was given to the author by Mary's son, Samuel, in the summer of 1939. The cover bore the address: "Mrs. Mary R. Walker, Care Rev. Mr. Walker (Missionary Station of the A.B.C.F.M.) Tshimakain, Oregon Territory." The author in turn presented the letter to the Eastern Washington State Historical Society of Spokane. The letter carried much family news. Isaac wrote: "Should you visit Baldwin now, it would hardly seem like the same place you left eight years since. It is so much changed and altered. Since our mother's death, it has seemed no more like the same old home where we used to all gather around the family alter." This letter is unusual because it was placed in an envelope. Most of the letters of that time were so folded that part of the back page carried the address.

[40] E.W. for the 20th: "I am now determined not to send our children to the Drs. to attend school."

[41] No doubt a reference to some of the missionaries of the American Board at work in the Hawaiian Islands, among whom would have been Mrs. Samuel Whitney with whom Mary had been carrying on a correspondence.

FRI. OCT. 2. Mr. E. returned. Brought three apples. They grew on Dr. Whitman's trees, are very nice. The first any of our children except Cyrus have seen since they were old enough to remember. Mr. E. also brought home a box of clothing &c from Holden.[42] Cyrus saw some of the things & came home & cried heartily because the people in the States send so much to Mr. E's folks & nothing to us. We also received several letters and eleven months reading of newspapers & periodicals.

MON. 5. Mr. W. finished diging potatoes. I received a portion of the clothing from Mrs. E's box, among other things a dress that wanted fixing a little which I attended to. . .

THURS. 8. We looked for Dr. & Mr. Spalding but they did not come. Fear we shall be disappointed again. . .[43]

FRI. 9. Baked &c. Looked in vain for Dr. W. & Mr. Spalding. . .

TUES. 13. Frederick Lewis came from Colvile. . .

MON. 26. Mr. W. left for Colvile, carried wheat to mill. After he left I set about taking up the chamber floor which I found to be rather an unwomanly job.

TUES. 27. Finished the chamber floor, put mats down under it. . .

SAT. 31. Mr. W. returned, the express not arrived from across the mountains yet. Mr. W. brought a valuable present of a shawl, broadcloth, &c. from Mrs. Lewis. . .

FRI. [Nov.] 6. Mr. Walker was very successful in fixing the kitchen fireplace. He expected he would have to take down the whole chimney, but he went to work with a [. . . ?] shaved out enough bricks to make a good draught & it now draws as well as a chimney needs to. How easily a great difficulty is sometimes removed when we go rightly to work. May we be guided aright in regard to some other difficulties. . .

MON. 9.[44] Mr. W. left about ten A.M. for Waiilatpu. This afternoon I dug out the mud hearth in our further room & built a brick one. Washed that floor & several others. Good weather for traveling.

TUES. 10. In the forenoon mended a shawl and made C. a kite. P.M. stitched newspapers,[45] evening repaired E's toys & divers garments & read some. . .

[42] Blanford (see entry for October 6, 1845,) and Holden, Massachusetts, were towns connected with Mrs. Eells' early life. Evidently groups of people in these places had been sending missionary barrels to the Eells family.

[43] The 1846 Mission meeting was to have met at Tshimakain. In a letter to Walker dated November 6, Whitman explained that he was detained because there was so much illness among the immigrants of that year. Original letter in Coll. C.

[44] E.W. "I started this day for Waiilatpu with the intention of getting some corn meal."

[45] Any kind of reading matter was so prized in the Walker home that even old

SAT. 14. Baked. Calcined some soda & think to make soap. Made some good pies by adding sepet [46] to pumpkin, prepared & baked in other respects as usual. Washed my floor quite clean with soda soap.

MON. 16 . . . An express from Dr. Whitman arrived. They are urgent that we should send our children to school. I am some in doubt what we ought to do. . .

WED. 18. Cut a pr. of leather pants for Cyrus. Read Oregon Spectator in the evening. They are full of talk about rail roads &c. across the Mts.[47] I trust the country will not long remain what it has been for thousands of years.

FRI. 20. Mr. Walker returned from Dr's. but his visit did not turn out just as I had hoped. . . Am sorry he went, had no talk with the Dr. of any importance. . .

TUES. 24 . . . Have had a great many evil thoughts towards the members of the Mission as well as towards myself. . . I wish I had a little more of that charity which suffereth long & is kind & thinketh no evil. My bad feelings are rather subsiding & I hope better ones will succeed them. . .

WED. 25. Our Maternal meeting. Mrs. E. led. Just at its close a letter from Mr. Lewis informed us of the arrival of the long expected express. They have been detained by sickness. The measles & influenza are very mortal on the east side of the Mts. 100 have died at Red. River.[48]

THURS. Nov. 26. Forenoon went as my forenoons all go, I know not where. . .

MON. 30. Got through with my two weeks wash once more. Cyrus read aloud most of the forenoon. The children are all doing well at present & I am glad we did not send them away. . .

WED. DEC. 2. Not so stormy as for several days past. . .

---

newspapers were kept for rereading. Mary made some of the notebooks she used for her diary by folding and stitching folio size sheets of paper together. In a few cases she even improvised a binding made out of deer skin. Now she was preserving her newspapers in the same way.

[46] See entry for July 15, 1846.

[47] The September 3, 1846, issue of the *Spectator* carried an editorial on "Rail Road to Oregon." The editor wrote: "We believe in the practicability and utility of the construction of a railroad, running . . . westward through the South Pass, to terminate either at the Dalls, or . . . at Puget Sound." He prophesied that such would come in "less than ten years."

[48] It has often been stated that the epidemic of measles which decimated the inland Oregon tribes in the fall of 1847 was introduced by the immigration of that year. A more likely theory is that this epidemic here referred to by Mary was the source of the infection which reached Oregon the next year. Walker, in his diary for this date, says that the express was delayed "on account of sickness of the crew." The constant flow of fur traders and Indians back and forth across the mountains could easily have introduced this virulent form of measles into Oregon before the arrival of the 1847 immigration.

Sat. 5.[49] Cold weather as we could wish to see. The ground has a good mantle of snow.

Mon. 7. Cyrus 8 years old. Mr. E's family took supper with us.

Mon. Dec. 14. Washed. So much snow I put no clothes out doors to dry.

Tues. 15. The snow increases every day. Almost warm enough to rain. . .

Sun. 20.[50] So stormy the children & I remained at home except Cyrus. . .

Wed. 23. Cast wicks & dipped twenty four doz. candles. . .

Thurs. 31. And so another year is ending & its account is sealed up. Pardon O! God the sin with which it is full that it rise not up to my shame & consternation in a coming judgment. Thanks to God for his goodness & mercy for it cannot be told. Oh! could I be where nine years ago I was sitting to see the year die by my father's fireside with my own sisters. The poor foolish Indians are playing their medicine to find their lost spirits. When will they care for their lost souls?

1847 — MASSACRE AT WAIILATPU

The last year of the Oregon Mission of the American Board was marked by tragedy and death. The year opened with the country gripped with the severest weather ever noted. The winter did not release its icy grip on the Spokane country until the first part of April. The loss of livestock by both the whites at Fort Colville and the natives was very heavy. Fortunately the missionaries had filled their barns with fodder and their animals were for the most part spared.

The 1847 Mission meeting was held in June at Tshimakain. All members were present except Mrs. Spalding. At this time the Mission voted to buy the Methodist station at The Dalles. Dr. Whitman was eager for the Walkers to take over this work but after Walker made a trip to investigate, he decided against the move. Mary takes up a new hobby, that of taxidermy, somewhat to the displeasure of her husband. Two artists visited Tshimakain in the fall, Paul Kane and John Mix Stanley. The latter painted portraits of Elkanah and of Abigail. In October Elkanah made a trip to Waiilatpu and returned with an immigrant woman of that year, Mrs. Marquis, who was to help Mary in her home. Another baby was expected the latter part of December.

---

[49] E.W. "It was exceedingly cold this morning. . . I finished banking up the house."

[50] E.W. "I got up this morning & found it stormy & that it had stormed considerable during the night. It has snowed most of the day. . . Some of the cows have been about to day. The silly things will not stay away." No doubt the cows were wanting to be fed. By this time the Donner party was completely marooned by the deep snow in Truckee Pass. Rumors of their fate reached the Walkers on April 3, 1847.

The measles epidemic struck the Spokane country in the fall and the children of both the Walkers and the Eells came down with the disease.

A number of factors combined in the fall of 1847 to precipitate the Whitman massacre. There was a general feeling of unrest among the Indians which can be traced back to 1843, when the first great immigration entered the country. The death of Elijah Hedding in California, in the winter of 1844-45; the ever increasing annual immigrations of white people; the growing conviction that Dr. Whitman was more interested in ministering to the whites than he was in helping the natives; the rivalries growing out of the conflicting claims of the Protestant and Roman Catholic missionaries; the devastating effects of the measles epidemic of the fall of 1847; and finally the lies of the half-breeds who said that Whitman was poisoning the Indians in order to get their lands and their horses, all combined to incite a few hot-heads among the Cayuses to take matters into their own hands. The Whitman station was the focal point of trouble as it was the first outpost on the Oregon trail west of the Blue Mountains.

Bravely the Whitmans stayed at their post in spite of repeated warnings. What else could they do? Where were they to flee and what was to become of nearly sixty immigrants who planned to spend the winter at Waiilatpu if they left? The massacre which began November 29 took the lives of fourteen, including Dr. and Mrs. Whitman. With this tragedy the Oregon Mission of the American Board came to an end.

Mr. Stanley and Old Solomon left Tshimakain for Waiilatpu on October 23. Dr. Whitman was to have returned with Old Solomon to attend Mrs. Walker. Old Solomon returned alone on December 9 with a letter from Stanley, telling of the dreadful news. Mary's diary for the remainder of December describes in poignant phrases the fear and suspense of those days. Her sixth child and her fifth son was born on the last day of the year.

FRI. JAN. 1.[1]   I made some proposals in the morning in regard to private devotions with which the children seemed pleased. Cyrus said he had prayed already while in bed. We took dinner with Mr. E's folks. . .

SUN. 3.[2]   Between the Indian services had a meeting & partook [of] the Lord's supper. . .

---

[1] E.W. "We dined to day at Mr. Eells. I did not enjoy it very well. As soon as dinner was done he left & went off after the cows which of course was a signal for me to leave & come home. I made me a good fire & enjoyed myself all alone. . . Our animals look bad."

[2] E.W. "It has snowed most all day. We went to Indian worship quite early this morning & only few attended. . . It seems as though most of the people's horses must die & put them on foot."

SAT. 9.[3] The past week the Indian who stole our knife came back with it. But he told lies about it. But still we were glad to find that he was not at ease while it was in his possession. . .

WED. 13.[4] Many of the Indians horses & some cattle have died. We have lost none yet. . . I have more thoughts than I used to have as to whether it will be duty to spend my days here. Kwilkwilharhun's wife has made 13 prs. of moccasins & I have paid 45 loads worth of ammunition.[5]

SUN. 17. A cold windy night last night. Mr. E. lost an old cow which being exposed to the wind chilled to death. . . Messrs. W. & E. went down to feed their horses, found them all well. To night perhaps as cold as we have ever experienced in Oregon.

MONDAY 18.[6] Too cold to write or do any thing else. Cut shoes out.

WED. 20. My shoemaker brought home some shoes which he had taken the liberty to trim rather too much. How hard it is for an Indian to be honest. Cut out a pair of leather pantaloons for Marcus & a pair of shoes & a pair of gloves for myself.

THURS. 21.[7] Last night & to day another foot of snow added. Mr. W. went with four Indians & brought home his horses & most of the cattle. The Indians expect to lose most of theirs. . .

---

[3] E.W. for the 6th: "I thought much of the poor suffering brutes. . . I heard last night & also this morning that the Old Chief had asked the people to come & make rain. I fear that should there be a thaw it will be ascribed to their medicine." For the 7th: "I heard that in all 20 horses have died. If the weather continues as it now is it seems as if all must die. I heard also that a medicine man has been murdered just below us." And for the 8th: "In the afternoon I took an Indian with me & went and cut down some trees for the cows. . . It is unusually cold and all their medicine does not seem to make it very warm." The killing of the medicine man is significant. It sometimes happened that the natives killed a medicine man who failed to work a cure or a miracle. In the eyes of the Indians, Dr. Whitman was a white medicine man who failed to cure those sick with measles.

[4] E.W. "It has thawed some. . . The animals are continually dying at the river. . . The Thief played the medicine for rain last night."

[5] Coll. w. has a letter of Mrs. Eells to "Sister Rogers" dated April 20, 1847, in which Mrs. Eells expressed her thanks for a donation of shoes for her children. She wrote that the gift "was certainly very valuable in this country where the snow lies on the ground four or five months a year. They usually wear moccasins & are obliged to stay in the house or have wet feet. . . Both Mr. W's children & ours have stayed in the house with their mothers most of the time. The extent of their pleasure walks was from one house to the other or to the barn & to the water."

[6] E.W. "Last night is allowed to be the coldest we ever experienced in this country. But we get along pretty well ourselves. We laid warm. When I got up this morning there was no fire to be found. I tried several matches, & they would not ignite on account of the cold until I held one down to the hearth. It was a long time in making fire but after I did get it going, I had a good one & I made out to get the house warm."

[7] E.W. "Unless there is a change in the weather, all the horses in the place must die." For the 22nd: "My horses will not eat pine bows very well."

ELKANAH WALKER

ABIGAIL BOUTWELL WALKER

From paintings by John Mix Stanley who visited Tshimakain in November 1847, a few weeks before the Whitman massacre. See page 304. Courtesy of Yale University Library, and Washington State University, Pullman.

KETTLE FALLS BELOW FORT COLVILLE, PAINTED BY PAUL KANE

Kane, in *Wanderings of an Artist*, wrote: "These are the highest in the Columbia River. They are about one thousand yards across, and eighteen feet high. The immense body of water tumbling amongst the broken rocks renders them exceedingly picturesque and grand." Mary Walker's diary, April 25, 1839, commented: "One of the grandest spectacles I have ever seen." Shown are the Indians' two methods of taking salmon: spearing and by wicker baskets. The falls are now covered by waters backed up by the great Coulee Dam.

INDIAN CAMP AT KETTLE FALLS, PAINTED BY PAUL KANE

Kane wrote: "The village has a population of about five hundred souls. . . . The lodges are formed of mats of rushes stretched on poles. A flooring is made of sticks, raised three or four feet from the ground, leaving a space beneath it entirely open, and forming a cool, airy, and shady place in which to hang their salmon to dry."

Illustrations on this and the opposite page, courtesy of the royal Ontario Museum, Toronto.

MON. 25. Got done washing in good season. Sit up late mending. When shall I ever get done mending? . . .

THURS. 28. Had a woman make leather pantaloons for Marcus. Paid her a spoon. The weather is quite moderate.

SAT. 30. Cut hair, cleaned house &c. Got through in season to escape what I so often get — a lecture on sabbath breaking. . .

MON. FEB. 1, 1847. Quite cold last night. One poor horse got stiff with cold. . .

FRI. 5.[8] We have moderate weather with a little more snow. Fear that horses are dying all about. . .

TUES. 9.[9] Fitted a pr. of gloves. . . Cold again. Poor horses of Indians, fear all will perish.

WED. 10. Elkanah three years old. Mr. E's boys came to eat tarts & play with our boys. Jeremiah begins to walk considerably. . .

FRI. 11. Baked this forenoon. Have had [a] girl helping make gloves this week. We finished five prs. to day. Abigail sewed hers herself. Yesterday I worked all day repairing & covering books with deer skin. Cover about twelve with skin & as many more with paper. The weather is moderate & the snow settles now. . .

SUN. 21. Several of the children have what seems to be chicken pox. . .

WED. 24. We had our meeting at Mr. E's. Yesterday their house took fire again, the second time this winter. . .

FRI. 26.[10] Winter is still reluctant to leave us. Many of the Indians have lost their last horse. Ours are all alive yet. . .

SAT. 27. Bake some mince pies, the first I have made this winter.

MON. MARCH 1, 1847. Had Sillapal sewing on shoes. The Indian who went to Colvile returned with letters from Mr. Lewes. The company have lost about 200 horses, have upwards of 20 left. All the Indian horses are dead. An Indian girl was frozen to death in the snow. Scarcely any of the servants of the Co. have escaped without some frozen member, toe, finger, or something.

TUES. 2.[11] Cut out three prs. of drawers for Mr. Walker. . .

---

[8] E.W. "My horses came up last night & I did not give them any thing to eat as I find that if I fed them they would come again." Walker had a limited amount of fodder so was unable to supply all the food the animals needed. They still had to do some foraging for themselves.

[9] E.W. "I cut down a tree for the cows." Perhaps for the sake of the moss. Regarding his horses, he wrote: "They came up tonight looking pretty bad. I have fed them a little." For the 12th: "I think I never saw the snow so deep as it is at present."

[10] E.W. "I have overhauled my fodder to day & find that I have about 250 bundles of straw with 100 or more of untrashed oats . . . and the same of wheat. I fear I shall come short. I will do the best I can with what I have got."

[11] E.W. "I had a visit to day from Garry. He promised to take some letters for me to Walla Walla. I have paid him ten loads of ammunition."

WED. 3 . . . In the morning fitted off Garry . . Sillapal sewed yesterday & to day. I gave her leggings for her work & soap for which I asked quills for shoes. Mr. W's poorest horse payed the debt of nature to night.

FRI. MARCH 5. The anniversary of our marriage & of my departure from my father's house. . . The weather windy, has thawed some today.

SAT. 6. A very windy day, snow drifting into all the out houses.

SUN. 7 . . . Mr. W. found two of Mr. E's cows dead this morning.

MON. 8. Still so cold. Mr. W. was not willing I should wash. Potatoes freeze badly in the cellar tho covered.

TUES. 9. Washed & dried my clothes out doors on the fence. The coldest wash day I have had this winter.

WED. 10. More snow. Weather a little more moderate. The poor Indians have scarcely a horse left & except the days are shortened, we fear ours must go next. . .

SUN. 14. Mild weather. American cow lost her calf in the creek

TUES. 16. Marcus five years old. . . Mr. E's boys came to eat cake & ice cream [12] with ours.

WED. 17. Warm rainy day.

* FRI. MARCH 19.[13] Mrs. E. finished Mr. Walker's frock coat. It sets well. She & her family took dinner with us.

SAT. 20.[14] Worked a part of the day on a frock for Elkanah. Mr. Walker has lost another cow. The weather warm & the snow decreasing tho an inch or so fell this morning. . .

TUES. 30.[15] Sweeping & cleaning all day. . .

WED. 31. In the morning went with the children to the Indian lodges. Found most of the women dressing skins. We took dinner with Mr. E's. . .

THURS. APRIL 1, 1847. My birthday, 36. Baked. Mrs. E. & children dined with us. The Colvile cow that we have fed all winter fell into the water & mud & died in consequence. . .

---

[12] The first and only reference to ice cream noted by the author in any of the writings of the missionaries.

[13] For the significance of the asterisk, see footnote 41, page 215. Mary's sixth child, another son, was born on December 31.

[14] E.W. "Eight years ago to day we took up our residence here & what have we accomplished? We are like the fishermen, we have labored all night & taken nothing."

[15] On this day Mrs. Whitman wrote to Mrs. Walker about the Mission meeting scheduled for Tshimakain in June. She wrote: "I would go if I could, and shall be tempted to try to . . . if I could ride native fashion. But I do not know how, neither do I think I can learn." Coll. c. Even the prevailing custom of the native women seemingly did not induce the missionary women to change from the use of the sidesaddle to riding astride.

SAT. 3 . . . The Colvile express passed by with which we sent our Vancouver bill & received a letter from Mr. Ogden. He writes very few of the Immigrants [the Donner party] had arrived when he wrote Jan. 6. Many were dead & children whose parents were dead were left to die at the encampment. Those who remain were suffering beyond description. What has been the cause of their suffering & delay we were not informed.

SUN. 4. We have now about one foot of snow in the plain. Considerable bare ground on the side hills. The cattle & horses need great care to keep them out of snow banks & mire. . .

MON. APR. 5 . . . The horse that was taken from the ditch in the morning of yesterday was found in again at night, left him in, this morning he was out & feeding.[16]

TUES. 6.[17] Have been working most of the day mending as usual. To day Mr. E. had a cow to pull out of the mud which he supposes had been in several days. . .

FRI. 9. The yearly spring express passed. Believe the name of the gentleman in charge was Low. We received several letters. . . Another letter was from Dr. Whitman at Vancouver.[18] One from Mrs. Whitney, S.I. Mr. Low & party came much of the way on snowshoes. . .

TUES. 13.[19] The after express passed being sooner than we expected. I had no letter ready as I expected. . .

SAT. 17 . . . The weather warm & the snow rapidly disappearing.

SUN. APRIL 18. Attended the Indian services to day for the first time this spring. Have read several tracts to day & have been trying to examine myself whether I am in the faith or not. Was much affected by a sense of my sinfulness, ingratitude & unfaithfulness, as also of my fellow laborers. It seems to me if Christ had sent us out saying, "See that ye fall not out by the way," but instead of regarding his charge, we had been continually quarreling & grieving our Lord by our disobedience. . .

---

[16] Both horses and cattle were forced to enter the small streams in order to feed on rushes and other water plants. The melting snow turned the edges of these streams into quagmires in which the animals sometimes got stuck.

[17] In a letter to her mother dated April 6, 1847, Mrs. Eells wrote: "The last Sab. in March was the first time since the 17th of Jan. that our meeting house has been open for worship & then Mr. E. went to it on snowshoes. The Indians . . . are now very miserable, as they express themselves, having no horses & do not know of half a dozen horses in all this region belonging to them & only two or three horned cattle. The Old Chief says he had over 50 horned cattle, now has two." Original in Coll. w.

[18] E.W. "I am not well pleased with the manner the Dr. writes. He seems to speak as though he was the Chief Factor & that we were clerks under him."

[19] E.W. for the 10th: "It is pleasant to ride on the bare ground again."

MON. 19 . . . Teacher's daughter had a child born. Her father was enraged & drove her off & threatened to shoot himself. . .

FRI. 23 . . . Mr. W. commenced ploughing. . .

SUN. 25.[20] In the evening Mungo arrived [with] letters. We sat up late to read them, & laid awake the rest of the night to think. My sisters write in fine spirits & seem to be prospering. I wish all my brothers were good men. May our Mother's prayers be heard in their behalf. . .

WED. 28 . . . I know not what to think — ought we to remain where we are or ought we to leave? My desire is that by some means our path of duty may be made plain. . .

FRI. 30. Had a little time to sew. Mr. W. sowing wheat & planting potatoes. We sell seed to the Indians this year. . .

SAT. MAY FIRST, 1847. Had a little time to sew besides cutting hair & washing children.

MONDAY. 3.[21] Washed & hunted bugs. . .

TUES. 4. Sowed garden seeds & filled a feather bed. . .

SAT. 8. Sewed most of the day & for once accomplished more than I expected to. . .

MON. 10.[22] Washed. . . Got very tired. Mr. Eells left for Waiilatpu. . .

FRI. 14. Was quite ill for an hour this morning. I wish I could know what manner of spirit I am of & what our motives are in remaining where we are. . . In regard to the Indians, I have almost no hope. See nothing that can be done for them that is likely to be of permanent benefit. . .

TUES. 18. Made a cheese & cut a pr. of leather pantaloons for Mr. W. & four prs. of shoes.

WED. 19.[23] Mrs. E. finished a spencer for Marcus & took dinner with us. . .

SUN. 23. Abigail 7 years old. Can get her Sunday lesson without much help. . .

THURS. 27. When S. came, had her wash the kitchen. In the after-

---

[20] E.W. for the 26th: "Last night after I had got to bed, we had a package of letters come. I thought at first I would not get up but Mrs. W. urged me to do it & I got up & read all that came. It was late before we went to bed & after I did I could not sleep."

[21] E.W. for the 2nd: "I have felt . . . that it was not my duty to leave. I do not know what others may think but I am persuaded of one thing that I dare not now say let us go."

[22] E.W. "I wrote a short letter to Dr. Whitman before breakfast. We had considerable discussion about what should become of this station." Evidently Dr. Whitman had already proposed that one of the families at Tshimakain move to The Dalles if the proposed transfer of this station from the Methodists were effected.

[23] E.W. "I have felt uneasy all day. I cannot set myself to work for I do not know what to do."

noon Mr. E. reached home & Mr. Rogers. Mrs. Whitman & Catherine [Sager] came with him. We went up to Mrs. E's to supper. . .

SAT. 29.[24] Cleaned some. Churned & ironed. . . Mrs. W. took tea with us.

SUN. MAY 30. Our minds are much agitated by the intelligence we have recently received. But our minds are made up, let others do as they may, we will remain where we are at present. . .

MON. 31.[25] S. washed for me mostly. I cleaned house &c. In the afternoon we had a meeting. Catherine prayed. Made a very sensible prayer with less embarrassment than I would wish to see & in the evening I heard her praying with the children in the wood house.

TUES. JUNE 1, 1847 . . . Mrs. W. took dinner & supper with us. In the afternoon we talked over the disagreeable matters. I feel better about some things & not so well about others.

WED. 2. Mrs. W. came to dinner but returned immediately. We had our Maternal meeting. After it some more talk on the subject of yesterday. Mrs. W. seemed not to feel pleasantly. I began to be somewhat excited. We were about to close when the Dr. arrived & Mr. Spalding. . .

THURS. 3.[26] After I got my work done up, went to call on the Dr. & his wife. The Dr. received me in so cordial and friendly a manner & seemed so much satisfied with the freedom with which I expressed myself that I felt much relieved. Mr. S. dined at Mr. E's & Dr. & wife with us. The meeting was opened after dinner. After business there was a conference and prayer meeting. . .

FRI. JUNE 4, 1847.[27] I baked in the morning. All the Mission dined with us. The business before the meeting to day has been the propriety of our leaving this station & going to the Dalles. The Mission expressed a unanimous wish that we should go & Mr. W. concluded to harken, so that it is considered as decided that we go. Much feeling was

---

[24] E.W. "After breakfast had some more letters handed me, particularly a copy of one Dr. Whitman sent to the Messrs. Wilson & Brewer [of the Methodist Mission] in regard to our occupying their station. It has made me feel all day that I wished I was out of the mission."

[25] E.W. "I went a short distance with Mr. Eells this morning & had some talk with him that made me feel some better. I did not know what were his feelings as well as I do now." By this time Walker had learned that the other members of the Mission felt that if The Dalles station were to be occupied it would have to be by the Walker family.

[26] E.W. "All things I see disturb me & make me feel quite unhappy. I do not know what to think. The Dr. asked me to take a walk with him. We had some conversation on our difficulties & did not get much excited. He opened the subject to me of my going to the Dalles. I told him that he should not think of my going there."

[27] E.W. "I . . . told the members I was willing to go see the station & if I could make such arrangements as suited me & that if proper arrangements could be made to make Mr. Eells comfortable, I would go & try it."

manifested on the occasion. We find it very trying to our feelings to think of separating or of leaving these people.

SAT. 5. Baked again in the morning. Had all the Mission to dine.

SUN. 6. Mr. Walker preached. Mr. S. administered the sacrament. . . Towards evening we had the monthly concert. Mr. W. led & I was much gratified with the remarks he made. . .

MON. 7. Prepared food for the journey. Our company took a late dinner & left afterwards. We think our meeting on the whole pleasant & useful.

TUES. 8. Prepared for Mr. Walker's journey.

WED. 9. Mr. Walker left early for the Dalls. . . After Mr. W. was off, set to work to put the house in order, swept the chambers &c. Worked some time in the garden. The Indians have been coming all day to trade little messes of roots, &c. Mrs. E. seems almost beside her self. . .

SUN. 13. Have felt stupid & drowsy most of the day. . . Have felt much dissatisfied with myself to think how little I possess the spirit of Christ, how little strive to please God & do good to man. I am also perplexed to know what duty is about some things. . .

TUES. 15. We took dinner with Mr. E's family. Mrs. E. gave Abigail a nice Dunstable straw bonnet, a pr. of slippers & a dress. I got Kanteken to shoot some ducks, two old & four young, gave half to Mr. E's family.

WED. 16. McCay called. I wrote a few lines to Mr. Walker. . .[28]

SAT. 19. Baked, mended, bathed children &c as usual. Have not been very well these few days past. Think I made myself sick by eating corn bread with too much soda in it. . .

SUN. 20 . . . Some Indians came & brought a letter from Mr. W. . . Muskettoes very troublesome. . .

SAT. 26. Spent a part of the forenoon in taking up a portion of the hearth, laying [it] to suit me better. The afternoon cleaning house & children & I wish I could add [my] heart too.

SUN. 27. A long lonely day. Never felt more desirous to see my husband once more. . .

TUES. 29. Repaired my old brown silk bonnet. Traded 26 qts of berries. . .

WED. 30 . . . Mr. Walker reached home, took us by surprise as we did not think of seeing him yet for a week. Was glad to see him tho.

THURS. JULY 1, 1847.[29] Baked. Mr. E's family took dinner with us.

---

[28] The original letter of Mary to Elkanah and one from Elkanah to Mary, dated June 14 at Waiilatpu, are in Coll. WN.

[29] E.W. "During the time from the last date of my journal [June 8] to the above date has been an eventful period in my life. I have traveled more than six

Mr. Walker thinks he shall not go to the Dalles. So I shall not be obliged to endure the fatigue of a journey thither. I hope we shall [be] led to do right. . .

SUN. JULY 4.[30] Our Nation's birthday. I wish I could see or hear even from some of those dear ones with whom in former days I spent such days. I hope my brothers & sisters will all find companions whom they will love as much as I do mine & be as much beloved, as I believe I am. I feel that it is a kind Father in heaven who has brought us to each others embrace & given us one soul as well as one body. . . It seems to me we shall eternally praise him for having given us a foretaste of heaven in the affection we cherish in each other. I esteem it the greatest of all the blessings I enjoy that I have a husband who is, instead of being a dead weight sinking me down, always as it were lifting me heavenward. I wish I could be as great a help to him. I never understood so well before why the sacred writer should select the marriage relationship as a type of Christ & his church. But what other emblem could have been chosen so appropriate?

MON. 5. Had a large wash but just as I was commencing. Providence placed a smart boy in the door who did all the pounding & drawing. In the evening concert, Mr. W. has decided that it is his duty to remain here rather than remove to the Dalls. It will I am sure subject me to much less fatigue. I hope the question will be decided in that manner, think it will meet the Divine approbation. . .

THURS. 8, 1847. A severe frost last night. Trading berries all day. Paid away a new & an old shirt, two hkfs., one pr. leggins, two knives & a lot of beads — 6 loads of ammunition, in all more than a hundred loads worth of berries.

FRI. 9.[31] Paid for berries, 60 loads worth or more. . . Made gooseberry preserves. . .

---

hundred miles on horse back & done a great deal of other business but which I fear will not amount to much. . . My feelings with all at this Station has undergone a cordial change." Since Eells was evidently not warm to the proposed move of the Walker family, Elkanah felt an increased affection for his associate.

[30] E.W. for the 2nd: "We had much conversation yesterday & to day about my Dalls [journey.] Just at night Mrs. Walker said that my going to the Dalls would be at the peril of her life. That at once decided me." Mr. and Mrs. Eells concurred. "We were all fully decided that we should stay here another winter. The importance of this station has much increased in my estimation. . . We are in a language spoken by more people than any other language this side of the mountains." Walker also felt that the southern tribes would suffer extinction because of the "lordly whiteman" whereas the northern Indians would be spared.

[31] E.W. "I wrote a letter to Dr. Whitman . . . saying that I could not think of moving this season at least." Of course Whitman was greatly disappointed as negotiations with the Methodists had proceeded too far to be cancelled. The station was turned over to Dr. Whitman on September 7. Whitman hired Mr. and Mrs. Alanson Hinman to take charge of the secular affairs. Perrin Whitman was also sent there and thus he was spared being included among the victims of the Whitman massacre.

318

Mon. 12. Washed. Had only the children to help me, got my clothes out about noon & worked all the afternoon cleaning the windows &c. . .

Tues. 13 . . . Simpleton came for medicine & to trade berries. Let him have an old shirt. Soshenamalt came & traded a pr. of leggins for berries. Some half dozen women came who had been for sour berries of which I traded about two bushels. Paid at about the rate of 15 loads for ten qt. pail full. Paid two handkerchiefs, one yard calico, one pr. leggings, one old half shawl, one old shirt [of] Cyrus & one [of] Elkanah, & an awl, a few beads, a bit of soap, some needles & thread. . .

Thurs. 15 . . . A partridge for dinner. Weather very cool. Paid 6 loads . . . for sepet & three quarters of a yd of calico for ten qts of service berries. . .

Sat. 17. Baked in the forenoon & dress a fowl for Sunday. . . Towards night Mr. Hinman arrived via Dr. W's. . . His business to procur the printing press of the mission. . .[32]

Mon. 19. Mr. H's guide forsook him & he left alone for Mr. Spalding's. Mr. E. & Edwin left for Dr. Whitman's.

Tues. 20. Weather warm. Musketooes plenty. Washed, had only the children to help. Got rather fatigued. . . Sillapal brought the [leather] dress she has been making & I paid her a knife for what she has done more on it.

Wed. 21. Baked. Soshenamalt brought berries enough dry & fresh to come to 50 loads which in addition to the former 50 purchases a blanket.

Thurs. 22. Spent a good part of the forenoon hunting for moths of which I found not a few. Churned & put down the butter for winter.

Fri. July 23. Ironed, & traded some berries & deal out as needed almost every day some doses of medicine.

Sat. 24. Got my house cleaning done before noon. Took the small children with Mrs. E. to the creek to bathe. Something which occured had me to reflect seriously on what should be the standard of Christian decency. . .

Tues. 27 . . . Traded about 50 loads worth of sepet & gooseberries. Had a talk about bathing & decency with Mrs. Eells.

Wednes. 28 . . . Have got poisoned as I did last year & year before which makes me half sick. Soshenamalt was crossing a stream & she & her babe were thrown, the horse falling on the babe which was so nearly drowned as not to breathe for some time after it was recovered from the water. . .

[32] The Mission at its June meeting voted to turn over the mission press to Hinman, who was to take it to the Willamette Valley where he intended to start a religious paper. The press happened to be at the Dalles station at the time of the Whitman massacre and thus escaped the destruction which followed that event.

FRI. 30. Mr. E. returned from Waiilatpu. Mr. W. received a rather severe letter from Dr. W. & a very kind one from Mr. Greene. . . I received one from Mr. Caldwell. . .

MON. [AUG.] 2. Mr. W., Cyrus & Marcus set off for Colvile. After they were gone I commenced winowing berries. Winowed about three bushels of service berries, 40 qts. of sepet & 16 of sour berries. Cleaned up the chamber & hunted all about it for moths, found a few. . .

TUES. AUG. 3 . . . Purchased a trout & a trout & salmon skin. Spent half the afternoon stuffing or fixing them.

WED. 4. Purchased a couple of trout skins & 12 qts. of sour berries & a few thorn [berries]. . . Bought a mocking bird.

THURS. 5. Stuffed a sparrow skin & bought a rattlesnake skin ready stuffed except it wanted fixing a little nicer. Mr. W. returned from Colvile, got only one bag of flour. Brought a present of shoes from Mrs. Lewis.

FRI. 6. Purchased a duck skin & stuffed it, also a crossbill. . . Mr. W. got out of sorts not liking my new trade of dressing birds &c.

SAT. 7. Had a talk in the morning with Mr. W. Got permission to pursue collecting a few objects in Natural History. Mr. Walker's birthday, 42 years. A quiet day. Went with A. to the creek to bathe, got much fatigued. . .

TUES. 10 . . . purchased a few stuffed skins. But think I will wait till I can procure arsenic before I collect more. . .

THURS. 12 . . . McCay with his family camped here on their way to the lower country. . .

SAT. 14 [33] . . . I went the usual tedious rounds of Saturday duties. Got much fatigued. Sometimes wish there was a way to live easier.

SUNDAY 15. Quiet as Sabbath always is with us. Read some & pray little. What a miserable Christian I am. . .

WED. 18. Bought four partridges. Mending. . .

SAT. 21. Washed floors before breakfast. Baked after. In the afternoon skinned & stuffed a small bird. . .

TUES. 24 . . . Purchased a bushel of thorn berries & a peck of cherries & three ducks. . .

WEDNES. 25 . . . Our Maternal meeting, I led. Spent the rest of the P.M. in skinning a crane. Think I will not undertake another very soon.

FRI. AUG. 27, 1847.[34] Baked, & partly pressed out the juice from thorn berries boiled the night before. . .

---

[33] E.W. "Mr. Eells & family took dinner with us to day. We had a chicken pie made out of partridge."

[34] E.W. "It is very smoky so that we cannot see but a short distance. . . I sent the Indians hauling in wheat & they have got in 300 bundles & it is in fine order."

SAT. 28. Finished the job commenced yesterday. Obtained about four gallons of thorn berry syrup for vinegar. . .

MON. 30. Had Mufflehead's daughter to pound & had great ado to pay her, she would take nothing I could offer her. Messrs. Walker & Eells tearing down their old houses. I took Mrs. E's washing & she took Mr. W's coat to repair.

TUES. 31. My woman came again this morning & I finally paid her a bit [of] striped cotton worth three loads but she did not seem pleased & I hope I shall remember not to employ her again very soon.

WED. SEPT. 1, 1847. Mr. W. started to go after soda. After he left I commenced washing & putting the house to right, but before I got through Mr. Lewes & family . . . arrived so I had to stir myself, get dinner &c. the best way I could. . .

THURS. 2. Was very tired but slept well & got rested. Baked. Had plum pudding, boiled beef, potatoes, onions, & squash & fried trout. Mrs. L. takes tea with Mrs. E. I have spent the forenoon washing floors & dishes. Feel much fatigued. We have in all 12 to feed, 5 only come to the table. We are so nearly out of flour that it is difficult getting along. Hope Mr. W. will get home by tomorrow.[35]

FRI. 3.[36] Mr. W. returned. I skinned a small hawk. . .

SUN. 5. Our visitors all went to Indian worship with us. We also have a sabbath school which they attend.

MON. 6. Our visitors took their departure in the morning. . .

TUES. 7. I skined a big hawk Mr. E. shot on Saturday. Mr. Paul Kane & Frederic Lewes arrived. . .

THURS. 9.[37] Mr. K. took dinner & supper with Mr. E. . .

SAT. 11. Messrs. K. & L. left.[38] I think Mr. K. is a clever artist but

---

[35] This marks the end of one of Mary's notebooks. The next volume which contains her entries to October 11, 1848, has the notation "Copied by J. E. Walker, Nov. 1896." It is possible that this is the imperfect transcription which the author used in the writing of his *Elkanah and Mary Walker.*

[36] E.W. "We arrived home late in the afternoon. Found the Leweses here. We were refused boats to cross in. This is the first time that any of my people have done the like." The refusal of some of the natives to permit Walker to use one of their boats in crossing the Spokane River reveals an ugly spirit.

[37] E.W. "Finished winnowing up my wheat & found I had five bushels & one half. . . I employed Big Star some to day to put all my corn fodder under cover. The Indians report that there has been fighting at the Dalls between the whites and natives & two were killed on each side."

[38] Paul Kane in his *Wanderings of an Artist,* pp. 214-15, wrote: "Each of the missionaries has a comfortable log-house, situated in the midst of a fertile plain, and, with their wives and children, seem to be happily located. . . The Spokan Indians are a small tribe. . . They all seemed to treat the missionaries with great affection and respect; but as to their success in making converts, I must speak with great diffidence, as I was not sufficiently acquainted with the language to examine them, even had I wished to do so; I have no doubt that a great number have been baptized. . . No influence, however, seems to be able to make agriculturists of them, as they still pursue their hunting and fishing, evincing the

an ungodly man of not much learning. He gave me considerable information about birds. . .

Mon. 13.   Spent [day] in preparing Mr. W. to go to Colvile.

Tues. 14.   Mr. W. left in the morning. . . Milked in the evening. . .

Thurs. 16 . . . We received a letter yesterday from Mr. Rodgers stating that there is a very large immigration this year & much sickness & death has occurred among them.

Wed. 22.   As ever busy mending. Rode out for the first time this year. I have been wishing to ride all summer but could not find time.

Fri. 24.[39]   Sewed nearly half the day on pantaloons.

Sat. 25.   Mr. W. left about noon for Spokane. Cyrus broke a pane of glass & I mended it. . .

Sun. 26.   Fair weather. Mr. E. read a sermon. No Indians here.

Mon. 27.   Finished at last the pantaloons I began so many weeks ago to repair. Husband returned about noon. . .

Mon. [Oct.] 4.   Mr. W. & Cyrus left for Waiilatpu. . .

Fri. 8 [40] . . . S[oshenamalt] left about noon. We finished Abigail's dress & commenced mine. . . Came nearer detecting S. in theft than ever before. . .

Sun. 10.   The children got their lessons pretty well in catechism. I have read Mirrors all day. . .

Fri. 15.   Mr. W. returned from Dr.'s brought a woman [Mrs. Marquis] with him. I hope she will prove useful.

Sat. 16.   Have been looking over some Mirrors & have found the death of my eldest brother.[41] But of the circumstances of his death, I know nothing. I feel disconsolate. I fear the little religion he professed would prove but little preparation for a death bed. May the dispensation be rightly improved by those of us who survive. I hope my younger brothers may have profited. . .

Sun. 17.   Have felt very sensibly the loss of my brother. The sight of the word brings him vividly before my mind. Could I but know

greatest dislike to anything like manual labour." Two of Kane's paintings made at Fort Colville are reproduced in this volume. After leaving Tshimakain, Kane went to Waiilatpu where he painted the likeness of Tilaukait and Tomahas who soon after were the leaders in the Whitman massacre. Kane described their countenances as being "the most savage I ever beheld."

[39] E.W. "I received a letter to day from the Chief Factor Ogden giving me the recent information. The Romanish Mission has received a large reinforcement in men & women. This information had considerable effect upon me."

[40] E.W. "Reach the Drs. this morning before they had been to breakfast. . . I had some pleasant intercourse with the people." Elkanah met some of the members of the 1847 immigration. Cyrus did not stay at Waiillatpu but returned with his father.

[41] Joseph Carpenter Richardson, who was five years younger than Mary, died September 26, 1846.

that he now strikes a harp of gold. Mr. E. read a very appropriate discourse from the text — "Cease ye from man whose breath is in his nostrils &c." [Isaiah 2:22] But I find myself inclined to depend on something else rather than on God. My heart is full of idols. In trouble I am prone to cast myself into the arms of my husband rather than my Saviour. . .

Mon. 18. We finished our letters & sent them off by an Indian to Colvile. . . Mr. W. had his potatoes dug.

Tues. 19. Washed, had S. to assist Mrs. Marquis. Find it the sorest trial that ever was to give up my work to any one else. Sometimes . . . repent trying to have help. . .

Thurs. 21 . . . took care of garden sauce. Mr. W. hurt by a rock falling on his leg . .

Sun. 24. Attended Indian worship. Found the walk to the meeting house rather long. Towards night Mr. Stanley arrived with our letters from the U.S.A. He came by way of Okanogan. I received a letter from each of my sisters. The account of my brother J.C.'s death is exceedingly interesting & consoling. He was cheerful & resigned, enjoying an unwavering hope of a blessed immortality. . .

Mon. 25. Slept but little last night. Could not avoid thinking of home. I am informed also of the death of Uncle Ephriam Richardson & Grandmother Richardson, for her I was named. She died . . . at the age of 94. . .

Tues. 26. Tried to get along & not work hard & let Mrs. [Marquis] bake but did not succeed very well.

Wed. 27. Mr. Stanley was to have left but being a little rainy concluded to remain to day. So [he] set to work to paint a likeness of Abigail. . .

Thurs. 28. Mr. Stanley left for Colvile. . . Mr. W. & myself spent a part of the evening at Mr. Eells.

Sat. Oct. 30.[42] Chored around in the forenoon, sewed in the afternoon. Towards night baked.

Sun. 31 . . . Mrs. [Marquis had] a headache all day because we had tea instead of coffee for breakfast.

Mon. Nov. 1.[43] Mr. W. left for Colvile. . .

Wed. 3. Spent most of the day arranging dried plants. Find my collection becoming large.

Thurs. 4. Baked & cut a dress for A. A priest dined at Mr. E's.[44]

Fri. 5 . . . It has snowed most of the day, some 8 inches deep. The news from below distressing. . .

---

[42] During these days Elkanah made several references in his diary to the presence of measles among the Spokanes.

[43] E.W. "I started this morning for Colville with fourteen animals, three Indians & nine packs."

[44] The identity of this priest is not known.

SUN. 7 . . . Mr. E. children have measles.

MON. 8. The weather still cold so that we have to cover the potatoes, the house not being banked up. . . Abigail & Jeremiah unwell, apparently [they] too have measles coming on. Feel concerned about husband but hope for the best. The cows have been missing several days so that old American is dry I suppose. We are picking up our last fragments of meat & have to beg milk of Mrs. E.

TUES. Nov. 9 . . . Mr. W. & Mr. Stanley arrived. . . They had on the whole a prosperous journey. . . My woman acts very tired. . .

FRI. 12. Salted beef & dipped 24 doz candles. Abigail has the measles.

SAT. 13. Worked about house all day. Mrs. M. ironed & washed dishes. Got Soshenamalt to wash floors. Baked & got dinner myself.

SUN. 14. Very rainy. Have been disconcerted all day with the movements of my woman, such as screaming &c. Think I shall be obliged to say something.[45]

MON. 15 . . . Had S. to help us wash. Did most of the house work myself. . . Mr. S[tanley] painting Indians.[46]

THURS. 18. Mr. S. finished Abigail's likeness. Cyrus beginning to have measles perhaps.

FRI. 19. Marcus & Elkanah not well to night. My patience gets more thread bare. Not very well this afternoon. Mr. S. painting a likeness of Mr. Walker.

SAT. 20. Toiling about as usual. Patience tried as ever with my help. Cyrus sick with measles.

SUN. 21. Many Indians & calling for medicine. . .

MON. 22.[47] Baking in the forenoon, in the afternoon sat & looked to see Mr. Stanley paint a likeness of an Indian girl. Think I learned considerable. . . Mr. S. also finished Mr. Walker's likeness.

TUES. 23. Fixed up food &c. for Mr. Stanley. One guide failed & he at last had to take Old Solomon. . . Mr. S. left after dinner. We have had a very pleasant visit from him. Cyrus, Marcus, & Elkanah quite sick with measles. Many of the poor Indians seem to suffer much. I have been trying to color [i.e., dye] red today & by some means or other have become much fatigued.

WED. 24. Had a woman to help wash. Waiting & tending on my

---

[45] E.W. "Mrs. Walker talked some to our helper this morning about her conduct. It was an unpleasant talk but I hope it will do her good."

[46] A collection of 151 of Stanley's paintings was on display in the Smithsonian Institution, Washington, D.C. at the time of the disastrous fire of January 24, 1865. All but five were destroyed, including pictures painted of the Spokane Indians and Stanley's conception of the Whitman massacre. Stanley had intended to paint the portraits of both Dr. and Mrs. Whitman during his visit at Waiilatpu.

[47] E.W. "I finished setting for my profile. It is a good likeness."

sick children. Finishing or doing over the coloring I was about yesterday with better success. Cleaned the buttery a little; washed the things I had been coloring & made toast for supper. . . Some of the poor little Indian children are crying nearly all night.

THURS. 25. Stirred about a good deal waiting on the children & Indians, & bound up about 100 pieces of [dried] salmon. Had Mrs. M. clean the further room.

FRI. . . . The children all seem doing well. . .

SUN. 28. Think I took some cold or worked too hard yesterday. Have felt out of tune all day.

Monday, November 29, 1847, was the tragic day at Waiilatpu when the Whitman massacre began. The Walkers and the Eells did not learn the terrible news until Old Solomon returned on December 9.

MON. 29. Washing day.

TUES. 30. Mr. W. went to the river with Mr. E. . .

WED. DEC. 1. In the forenoon emptied a keg of linseed oil. Find we have more than I supposed. Painted several shawls. This afternoon cut some aprons & a shawl for Mrs. M. . .

THURS. 2. At work on a rug. Mrs. wiped up the floor without being told.

FRI. 3. I walked as far as Mr. E's. Dealt out food & medicine to Indians as usual. Worked on my rug & fitted work for Mrs. M. Find her about half as smart as Soshenamalt.

SAT. 4. Have stirred about most of the day. Helped get breakfast, bake, wash floors &c. . . We have had no weather for some time as cold as we often have in June.

SUN. DEC. 5.[48] Our children are all able to attend the Sabbath School. . . Many of the Indians continue sick.

MON. 6. The ground this morning frozen. The sun & stars have made their appearance once more. . .

TUES. 7. Cyrus 9 years old. Mr. E. family took supper with us. I baked a dozen mince pies. Work about full enough to get tired. . . We make Cyrus' birthday our annual thanksgiving. And in reviewing all the way in which we have been led, we find numberless subjects for gratitude, even our afflictions have been full of mercy. I think of home & of former merry meetings of my brothers & sisters around the parental hearth but how is that circle now broken. Instead of our parents & grandparents, it is we & our children. . .

WED. 8. Had. S. at work on shoes. Took me all day to wait & tend on others & call on Mrs. Eells. . .

---

[48] E.W. "Many are sick still & all constantly calling for medicine. . . Some I have sent empty away & some I have sent medicine."

THURS. DEC. 9.[49]   We were hoping to have Dr. Whitman to supper with us to night. But about sunset Old Solomon arrived bringing the sad intelligence that Dr. & Mrs. Whitman, Mr. Rodgers, John & Francis Sager & others have been murdered by the Indians. Mr. Stanley was apprised of it . . . & went to Walla Walla instead of Waiilatpu or he too might have been killed. May God have compassion on those that survive & stay the hand of the ruthless savages. We are safe only under the Divine protection. May we trust only in God.[50]

SUN. DEC. 12.[51]   We are still the spared monuments of divine protection. And this seems [to be] our only security. . . I wish I felt as anxious in regard to the souls as the bodies of men. We feel very anxious to know what may have been the fate of those who were not murdered — whether they are rescued or are perishing with cold & hunger. We also have fears that we may share the fate of others. I

[49] E.W. "Solomon returned to day & brought most horrid intelligence. The Dr. & wife, Mr. Rogers, John & Francis Sager, three or four more men were killed on the 29th of last month by the Indians at that place. Mr. Eells also returned with sad intelligence from Spokane. The people are dying off in all directions. O what will be the end of these things."

Stanley's original letter dated from Fort Walla Walla on December 2 is in Coll. c. After giving such information as he knew about the massacre, he added: "I am informed that a party of Indians started to Mr. Spauldings to complete their horrid butchery — also to the Dalles."

In his reminiscences of these days, Edwin Eells, who was more than six years old at the time, wrote: "Among my earliest recollections, which are very vivid, was his [i.e., Solomon's] arrival at our home. . . my father had gone away to . . . an Indian village seven or eight miles distant, and my mother and her two little boys were alone. Mr. Walker's residence was a short distance from ours. In the afternoon we were visiting them. We children were having a great deal of fun and were very noisy. We were riding the stools which we called our horses and pack others in imitation of our fathers when going on a journey. We were in the height of our fun when this Indian arrived.

There was nothing unusual for an Indian to come but this one brought a letter. We all stopped playing and gathered around Mr. Walker to hear the news. When he broke the seal and glanced at the page before taking in the full import of its contents, his face blanched and he turned so pale that we all became frightened. He then read in trembling accents how Dr. & Mrs. Whitman, Mr. Rodgers . . . and many other men had been killed by the Cayuse Indians and that the women and children had been taken prisoners. It seems as though a black cloud of horror settled down upon us. . . Of the two families, there was one courageous and one timid in each. My father was a brave man but mother was very timid. Mr. Walker was timid & Mrs. Walker was brave." Original ms., Coll. w.

[50] Walker for the 10th: "We did not rest much last night & have felt miserably all day. The people seem to be of one mind about the affair that has occurred at Waiilatpu & say they will defend us to the last. . . We find our situation very precarious for we know not what these Indians may be left to do. . . we are anxious for more intelligence, yet we almost dread to receive it."

[51] E.W. "I wrote a letter last evening to Mr. Lewes, we having concluded to send an Indian off after the Sabbath."

am thankful that we are able to maintain so much composure. I have felt but little concern in regard to my approaching confinement. Feel that all will be well even tho they slay me, I think I can trust in him. But my sense of eternal things seems dull. I do not see what I should expect to be preserved when more faithful servants are cut off. Perhaps in mercy they are taken away from the evil to come.

MON. 13.[52] Washing day as usual & fair weather.

WED. 15. Flathead party [i.e., the express] passed.

THURS. 16 [53] . . . A number of Indians continue sick. The Indian sent to Colvile returned to day, brought a very kind letter from Mr. Lewes, invited us to C. in case of alarm. Many of the Indians at C. are dying. Six died the day before he wrote. I am still working on my rug.

FRI. 17.[54] Mrs. M. finished her shawl. . . A dog killed a hen last night so now we have only six left. A number of our Indians remain sick. The news of the late murder excites general indignation. The Halfbreeds offer to come to assist us in case we are molested & the Indians say they [i.e., the Cayuses] must kill them first before they can us. I feel confident that God is able to protect us & that Indians can have no power at all against us unless it be given them of God. If it is best we should die, why should we desire to live. God's time is best.

SAT. 18.[55] Worked about house most of the forenoon. Did most of the baking myself. This afternoon finished my rug. Think [it] a nice one.

SUN. 19.[56] Sick Indians, some dying, some calling for medicine. . .

---

[52] E.W. "I had many calls to day & had considerable talk with three of the principal men. They all assured me that we had nothing at present to fear from the Indians below, that they will not come without sending here & sounding [out] the Old Chief."

[53] E.W. "We received this evening a very kind & sympathetic letter from Mr. Lewes inviting us all to come to his place if we had any certain intelligence of an attack from the Indians from below."

[54] E.W. "I am anxious to hear and dread the intelligence that we may receive. I am rather puzzled if Mr. Spalding is alive that we have no intelligence & then if he is dead, it seems we should hear from Mr. McBean." At this time McBean was in charge of Ft. Walla Walla.

[55] E.W. "We have received no intelligence from any quarter to day. . . We should have seen the Old Chief to learn what his feelings are in view of what has been done. It looks rather strange that he does not come to see us & give us his assurance if he feels disposed to lend us any help if danger comes."

[56] E.W. "I had not a very quiet night. . . The people turned out well to day. The house was well filled. . . There were present in the afternoon 62 besides our own families. I read a translation which seemed to interest them much . . . made more translation from the New Testament."

Have felt much distress in view of the late murders. See no way that looks promising. But I will still hope in God. . . My own stupid heart is after all what most troubles me.

MON. 20. Washing day. . .

TUES. 21. Continue to deal out medicine to Indians. Hear nothing from the south as yet. Simpleton called to night; willing as he says to defend us at loss of life.

FRI. DEC. 24 . . . I have been at work, what time I could get, since Mon. on another rug which I have finished.

SAT. 25.[57] Helped iron, mended a dress, cleaned my room, chored about most all day.

SUN. 26. Some Spokan Indians called, as they said to quiet our fears.

MON. 27. Did not wash as Mrs. [Marquis] had so bad a cold.

WED. 29.[58] A little snow down. . . I had more ado to get the house clear of Indians.

THURS. 30 . . . I washed dishes, baked & got dinner. . . This evening was so unwell as to call Mrs. E., who spent the evening & returned.

FRI. 31. As soon as Mrs. E. returned home, my illness came on again & I had soon to call her again. Our business went on more tardily than common. However, about breakfast time perhaps 8 in the morning, I was delivered of another son.[59] A fine little boy, weight 9 lbs. Every thing went safely & favorably as could be expected & we feel our cause for gratitude is unbounded. I hope our unprofitable lives may yet be prolonged to look after our children for I hardly know what other good we can hope to do in the world. I fear our labors for the Indians must soon cease or if prolonged will only hasten that certain destruction which ere long seems to await [them.] The hope of our seeing them much better than they now are, fondly as I would wish to cherish [it,] is all hope against hope.

---

[57] E.W. "This has been Christmas day. We made no account of it except the children went up to Mr. Eells in the afternoon & had a small repast of cakes &c. . . I have felt down hearted & long to hear what is the result of things below. I am sometimes half inclined to feel vexed that no one from the people is inclined to take letters down."

[58] E.W. "I have felt lonely all day. . . It is just one month to day since the dreadful work was done at Waiilatpu & how little we have heard about it." On this day Ogden succeeded in rescuing the fifty-one survivors of the Whitman massacre. Spalding and his family were escorted to Walla Walla by a band of friendly Nez Perces, arriving there on January 1.

[59] The six children born to Mrs. Walker during the nine-year period, December 7, 1838-December 31, 1847, were on the average spaced about twenty-two months apart.

1848 — SANCTUARY AT FORT COLVILLE

For years Elkanah and Mary Walker had been fighting off feelings of frustration as they realized their apparent failure to Christianize and civilize the Spokanes. At first they felt that any suggestion of deserting the field was a temptation of the devil. The hand of Providence had brought them together and had led them to that needy place. What would their friends, the Mission Board, and their Lord think if they gave up? On the other hand, the tenacity with which the natives clung to their old superstitions, their seeming inability to understand the simplest facts of Christian doctrine, and their exasperating slowness in adopting the white man's ways of making a living from agriculture, were discouraging. Any consistent program of education was impossible with a people always on the move. Moreover, Elkanah and Mary had children who needed to be in a school. Even before the dreadful news of the Whitman massacre had reached them, Elkanah and Mary were beginning to be more and more receptive to the idea of leaving the Mission. The massacre decisively answered this question for them, although the realization of the fact that they would have to move was painful. Elkanah with characteristic caution did some cultivating that spring at Tshimakain, and as late as the last part of April sowed his wheat and planted his potatoes.

Five months passed before the two missionary families and their eight little children were escorted by soldiers from the Spokane country to Fort Walla Walla. This period was divided into two equal parts. During the first two-and-a-half months the missionaries remained at Tshimakain through nerve-racking days and sleepless nights, when dreadful rumors reached their ears of the intentions of hostile Indians to kill them. Could they depend on the loyalty and the ability of the Spokanes to protect them? Chief Factor Lewes, at Colville, assured them of the protection of the Fort and finally during the first part of March, after another alarming report of danger, urged the men to bring their families to the Fort at once. They arrived on March 18, where the women and children remained until June 1, when all left for the lower country. The two men shuttled back and forth between the Fort and Tshimakain.

In the meantime several hundred Oregon Volunteers had arrived in the Cayuse country to punish the murderers. The Cayuses fled to the mountains. All efforts of theirs to induce the Nez Perces and the Spokanes to join them in warring on the whites failed. Finally the officers in command of the white troops felt that it was safe to evacuate the missionary families from the Spokane country and sent a detachment of soldiers to escort them. The Walkers and the Eells left Col-

ville on June 1, and on June 3 they passed Tshimakain. With heavy hearts they said goodby to the beautiful little plain nestled against the pine-covered hills, which had been their home for over nine years. The Indians among whom the missionaries had lived were dismayed with the news that they were leaving, and begged them to return when things became calm again.

On Saturday, June 10, the mission party with the soldier escort reached Waiilatpu. Here they had planned to camp over Sunday before going on to Fort Walla Walla. Writing to Greene on July 8, Walker told of their painful observations: "The native fields were all grown up to weeds, their fences broken down. The bones & hair of the Missionary & wife with others had been scattered by the wolves . . . I will not attempt to describe my feelings." Little Elkanah, then a few months more than four years old, saw his mother pick up some of Mrs. Whitman's golden hair and show it to Mrs. Eells. The incident imprinted a memory on his mind that he never forgot. The spectacle was so depressing that the party moved on to camp at another site. "The shortest time was sufficient," wrote Walker to Greene. They arrived at Fort Walla Walla on Monday, June 12, and soon after left by boat for Oregon City.

Thus 1848 was a year of transition. Not only were the Walkers obliged to move from Tshimakain to the Willamette Valley but also to change from one type of work to another. Their days as missionaries to the Spokane Indians were over. Now they were just another immigrant family trying to establish a home and gain a livelihood in one of the growing white communities of Oregon. At Tshimakain they had become largely self-supporting with only a few hundred dollars paid each year by the American Board for supplies. With no financial reserves and no promise of work of any kind, both the Walkers and the Eells faced an uncertain future. They soon entered into a new and wonderful world. No longer were they alone: they were a part of a rapidly growing community of Americans. Their children could go to a school. And Mary could go shopping — a delightful experience.

SAT. JAN. 1.[1]   We are permitted under circumstances of great mercy to commence another year. We look forward with great anxiety. We feel much concern in regard to persons & affairs at the other stations as we can hear nothing.

---

[1] E.W.   "I rode out in the afternoon & met the Old Chief. He did not appear very well, quite down & out, not disposed to say much. . . He said that if he was well he would go to that place [i.e. to the Cayuses] & see what the intentions of the Indians were. I wish he would go as he would be the best I think of any one here."

Sun. 2.[2] Felt so well I dressed & sat up most of the day. Can hardly realize that I have been confined. Surely God is pleased to deal kindly with me.

Mon. 3. Our annual fast. Do not feel quite so well to day, the weather not so pleasant. Did not rest very well last night; got to thinking of the recent murder. . . I feel anxious to know what turn events are taking. How distant must be the reign of peace, universal peace, over this world, this wicked world, be. . . Our little son, whom we call John, is very well & quiet.

Tues. 4. Washing day. S. helped Mrs. M. wash. A fair but cold day. I fried cakes for dinner & sat up & kep busy about one thing or another all day.

Wed. 5. Got up & dressed when others of the family did. . . Made my bed & dressed my babe myself. Have been as far as the buttery many times to day. Took dinner at the table. Feel rather tired to night.

Thurs. 6 [3] . . . Mr. W. received a letter from Mr. Lewes. The Indians at C. are still dying. . .

Fri. Jan. 7, 1848. I know not what may be on the morrow, but he who has kept us hitherto is able still [to] keep [us.]. . . I have hardly felt as well to day as I did a day or two since. . . I made a firecake for breakfast but found it rather hard work. Have sewed some but find my hand tremulous.

Sat. 8. Babe continues quiet. I feel pretty well but not strong. . .

Sun. 9. Dressed the children & with their help got breakfast nearly ready by the time my help was up. . . Have read some but do not feel much inclination to read. My mind is so anxious & distracted.

Mon. 10 [4] . . . Sun. night after we had retired to rest, the Old

[2] E.W. "The Old Chief did not attend worship to day either time. He gave as his excuse that his eyes troubled him." At this time Old Chief is reported to have been blind in one eye and with but little vision in the other. He was unable to find anyone willing to venture a trip to Walla Walla. Even the Spokane Indians were afraid of the Cayuses.

[3] Lewes wrote to Walker on January 2 from Fort Colville: "Since my last to you I have little or no good news to impart to you from this place. Sickness unabated in its virulence continues to rage around me. The mortality among the poor Indians has been distressingly great, up to this date including six at the Fools, 83 men, women, and children have paid their last debt, and I am grieved to say that many more undoubtedly will be yet added to this list, for many, many are still very low, with little or no hopes of their recovery." Original Coll. H.

[4] Eells in his Reminiscences for April 14, 1883, (Coll. w.) explained that during the winter of 1847-48 about sixty of the Spokane Indians were in the lower Columbia country, and added: "The Cayuse adroitly fabricated the statement that when intelligence of the Wai-i-lat-pu tragedy was received by Americans in the Willamette, they combined and killed all the Indians from this region there sojourning." Such a false rumor, intended to arouse the Spokanes, was carried to Walker by Old Chief on Sunday evening. Walker wrote in his diary that if such a report were true, "We should be likely to fall a victim to the rage of the people

Chief came with a report which is likely to cause much excitement but not likely to be true. I helped some about baking & sewed some & kept busy about nothing.

Tues. 11.   Mr. W. writing letters to send off an express. They have engaged two Indians to go but they could not find their horses. Our fears are some what excited but we hope in God for deliverance. . . It is rather trying to feel that we are liable to be murdered at any hour. We washed to day. . .

Wed. Jan. 12.[5]   Two Indians started for Walla Walla. I have worked & waited & tended all day . . . till I feel miserably tired & discouraged. All looks dark, look where I will. . .

Thurs. 13.   Last night very windy. Indians, some of them, could not sleep because they thought they heard disturbances at our house, at least they said so. . .

Fri. 14.   We took dinner & spent the afternoon with Mr. E's folks. In the evening felt refreshed & rested by my walk & visit. We received a call by Mr. W's request from Dumont, a half breed, who resides between here & Colvile. He thinks we need have no apprehensions from hostile Indians at present. We made him a present or rather paid him for his call & for hunting horses a while since.[6]

Sat. 15.[7]   Baking &c. Stirred about most all day & got tired. Mrs. M. afflicted with tooth ache. I dare not say I regret she ever came here but it does seem to me it will be a great relief if I ever get rid of her. We are still in ignorance what may have been the fate of our friends at the other stations. We have made our horses as secure as we well

---

around us." However, he assured the Old Chief that such a thing could not happen. Walker also noted on the 10th: "We have been advised by the Indians to use great caution & not to admit any into our houses in the night or early in the morning."

[5] E.W. "I spent most of the afternoon In fix[ing] my house, making it more secure. . . We shut up our best horses to night in accordance with the advice of the chief." In a letter to Greene describing the events of these days, Walker, on April 3, wrote: "Our Indians were more alarmed for our safety than I have ever seen them this winter." He reported that Old Chief advised them to darken their windows at night and to lock their doors securely.

[6] It is possible that the three half-breeds, Dumont and the two Finley brothers, had once been in the employ of the Hudson's Bay Company. They and their families had settled near the encampment of the Spokane sub-chief, called The Fool, in the vicinity of what is now Chewelah, Washington. During these tense days both the Walkers and the Eells were more generous in handing out food and presents to Old Chief, the half-breeds, and others than ever before.

[7] E.W. "I had considerable talk with Dumont during the evening. He went to the Indian house to sleep, as he had two boys with him. I did not like to take them all in the house. He came this morning & took breakfast with us & so did the boys. They were the most awkward of any I have seen, not knowing how to use a knife & fork at table but ate with their fingers. I gave him two milk pans & let him have a small kettle & an old pair of pantaloons. He gave me two dollars." Here is a rare reference to a cash transaction.

can. And I hope if called to drink the cup which they have drunk, we shall be able. Yet we can but pray if it be possible it may pass from us.

Sun. 16.[8] [The day] passed away too much in idle thoughts & worldly cares.

Mon. 17.[9] Had S. to help wash & clean house. . . Mr. W. received another letter from Mr. Lewes.

Tues. Jan. 18.[10] An Indian report reached us that the Governor had been up to Walla Walla, sent up for Mr. Spalding who came down escorted by 30 Nez Perces who received presents & returned by way of Waiilatpu. Mr. S. went down the river & 10 Cayuses set off to way lay him.

Thurs. 20.[11] An express from W. Walla arrived bringing letters. On the receipt of the intelligence of the murder at Waiilatpu, Mr. Ogden came up & after three weeks succeeded in rescuing all the captives. He has taken them all down in boats. Mr. S. & family also. The dead were ordered buried by the Catholic [priest,] who also as-

---

[8] E.W. "The people turned out pretty well to day, better than common. I chose for my subject Matt. X:28. [And fear not them which kill the body, but are not able to kill the soul: but rather fear him which is able to destroy both soul and body in hell.] The people gave good attention. If they were interested I think they heard something that they needed. I drove in the horses near night & put in four of my best & biggest horses."

[9] E.W. "All was quiet about us through the night. . . I received a long letter tonight from Mr. Lewes as kind as any one we have received. The number of deaths at Colvile among the natives is immense. Mr. L. makes them 94 while the Indians report is 127. Intelligence comes in to day from the Bay, the number of deaths there is considerable. How many I did not learn. The same feeling seems to exist there as at all the other places, that is to go & fight the Indians at Waiilatpu."

[10] E.W. "Another report has reached us to night which is of a very favorable kind. At the last moment Mr. Spalding was alive & the Dalls station had not been molested. This report will be likely to have a favorable effect on the minds of the Indians to counteract the other report."

[11] E.W. "We were thrown into a state of excitement by letters from below, especially by one from Mr. Spalding. Spalding, writing from Fort Walla Walla on January 1, just after his arrival, said: "I caution you to pack up privately to prevent the Indians from plundering. . . Let me *repeat*. Make no proposition to your Indians in regard to your remaining or leaving, or promise to return, and by all means secure the assistance of Mr. Lewis or the Canadians [perhaps a reference to Dumont and the Finleys] in transporting your effects to Colville, where I *advise* you as you *value your lives* [to remove] as soon as the circumstances of your families will admit." Original Coll. w. Upon the receipt of this letter, Walker and Eells called on Old Chief, who strenuously objected to the missionaries moving to the Fort. Writing to Spalding on January 24, Walker explained the Chief's attitude by saying: "He said he should be held in desolation by all the people in the country and made a laughing stock to all if we went away as they would say he could not protect his teachers." After some discussion, it was decided that Walker should go to Fort Colville to get the advice of Lewes.

sisted Mr. Spalding to make his escape, who reached home from the Utilla where he was at the time in six days having suffered much from cold & hunger. He found his family under the protection of the friendly Nez Perces in great anxiety on his account. . . Mr. S. arrived at Walla Walla under a large escort of his friendly Indians. E[liza,] his daughter, was among the prisoners.

FRI. 21. On Thursday evening, Messrs. Walker & Eells had a talk with Old Chief on the safety of our remaining here. He insisted strongly on our remaining. . . Mr. W. concluded to set out for Colvile. Left home about noon, took Mufflehead with him.

SAT. 22. The Indians sent to W.W. returned having accomplished little except to bring back uncertain reports. They say the Kayuses talk of coming here or sending word to our Chief to destroy us if the whites make war on them. May God grant wisdom to those to [whom] it belongs to take vengence.

SUN. JAN. 23. A lonely anxious day. Our way is so dark & I feel so uncertain what duty is. It seems almost as bad as death to think of leaving this place. I hope the path of duty may be made plain & that we shall cheerfully walk in it, let it lead whither it may. Forsake us not O God & suffer us not to forsake thee.

MON. 24.[12] Washing day. Had S. to help. In the evening commenced a letter home. . .

WED. 26.[13] Mr. W. returned from Colvile. Concludes [not] to remove [from] this place yet, but if we must go, Mr. Lewes is to send us an escort.

THURS. 27. Writing a letter to my Father's family. Mrs. M. sick with tooth-ache. . .

SUN. 30.[14] Find it difficult to put my attention on anything but murder & its consequences that I can not improve my Sabbath to much profit.

MON. 31. An ox killed. I helped clean tripe. Mrs. M. still afflicted with toothache.

TUES. FEB. 1st. Had S. to help wash. Worked about house all day myself. S. washed the floors. Think she [is] better help than my other.

---

[12] E.W. at Fort Colville: "I spent most of this day in writing . . . three long letters, one to Mr. Spalding, one to Mr. Stanley & one to Mr. Ogden." Only the letter to Spalding is known to be extant.

[13] E.W. "Spent the night with Dumont & was treated as well as I could expect at such a place & under such circumstances. I had on the whole a very comfortable night." According to Eells, in his Reminiscences, Walker brought back word that Lewes advised the missionaries to remain at Tshimakain as long as possible. "If you shall be convinced of real danger," he said, "then come to my Fort and I will protect you equally with myself and family."

[14] E.W. "I feel at times much depressed & hardly know what to do. I fear at times unless some relief does come, I shall sink down in despair."

WED. FEB. 2, 1848.[15] Salted beef. Mended a little. Heard a toad sing. . .

SAT. 5.[16] Have been cleaning tripe, trying tallow, diping candles, boiling feet, &c. Have S. to work two days & have felt so tired & sleepy at night I could not write my journal. Yesterday dipped 17 doz. candles in the morning. We had our preparatory meeting, but I feel that I need something more than a meeting to prepare me for the communion or any thing else. My mind is so cumbered with a deluge of little corroding cares that all I can think about is what shall we eat & what shall we drink and where withall shall be we clothed. My leanness! My leanness! Mrs. M. has been sick for some days. Think she works full as smart when she is sick a little.

---

[15] E.W. "I had a visit from my teacher this morning with several others. His object was to let me know that there was some feeling among the people about poison." And the next day he wrote: "The impression is so strongly fixed in the minds of the people in all quarters that the whites are poisoning them." On the 4th: "I have felt this day or two past that if we could retire a short time the excitement would be more likely to die away. I made this remark but I found that Mr. Eells had no confidence in any place of retreat. His views & mine do not coincide. He has less confidence in the protection we should have at Colvile than I do."

[16] E.W. "I went to the Old Chief's in the afternoon. . . while I was there. . . there was another report. . . The account of the story was that three persons, Indians from this region, what people not known, had been killed, that the Cayuses had offered [Old Chief] 60 horses, 40 cows, the property of the Mission if he would join them & that the whites had offered him 100 horses & the same number of cows to join them. He had as yet refused them both wishing to know whether his people had been killed & by whom. There is much reason to suppose that there is no truth in it as the reports do not agree. Every thing seems to be to keep the people in a state of excitement."

Among the paintings made by Stanley of Spokane Indians was one of Old Chief whose Indian name, according to Stanley, was "Se-lim-coom-clu-lock or Raven Chief." This was one of the paintings destroyed in the Smithsonian fire of 1865. In the explanatory note describing this picture when it was on display in 1850, Stanley wrote: ". . . he had adopted the white man's religion, and had used his influence to promote Christianity among his people. Shortly after the butchery at the Wailetpu Mission, a rumor reached the Spokanes that the Cayuses were coming to murder the families of Messrs. Walker and Eels, missionaries located among them at Tshimakine. The Old Chief collected his people and with their lodges surrounded the Mission declaring the Cayuses should first murder them. In the meantime Messrs. Walker and Eels prepared themselves by barricading their houses to resist the fate of their co-laborers to the last extremity. At this exciting moment, a report reached the Spokanes that a number of their people residing in the Willamette valley had been killed by the Americans in retaliation for the Wailetpu massacre. The young warriors collected for the purpose of protecting Messrs. Walker and Eells from the hands of the murderous Cayuses, now became clamorous and were with great difficulty restrained from spilling their blood themselves. The Old Chief told them the rumor might be false, and by his influence and good sense, the lives of these pious laborers in the cause of Christianity were spared." Stanley, *Portraits of North American Indians*, 69.

SUN. 6.[17] The care of my babe &c occupied me all the forenoon & much of the afternoon. . . Messrs. E. & W. had two services with the Indians. We then had an English service at which our babe was baptized by the name of John Richardson. The Lord's Supper was administered by Mr. Eells. I did not enjoy the occasion much because I felt it was wrong to be so private. Very few of our Indians have ever had an opportunity of witnessing the administration of baptism or the Lords Supper. . . Three Indians came just as we were done worship.

MON. 7 [18] . . . Concert in the evening.

TUES. 8 [19] . . . We have many rumors, but I am not much moved.

WEDNES. 9.[20] Repairing old garments.

THURS. 10.[21] Elkanah's birthday. Edwin & Miron came down to play in the forenoon & eat dinner. E. dressed in pantaloons & Jeremiah

---

[17] E.W. "Just as we closed [the English service] three Indians from Spokan rode up. I let them into the house but I was much grieved that they should come on the Sabbath & Mr. Eells told them so. They did not stop long saying as they went out that our hearts were not good."

[18] E.W. "Soon after breakfast, I was sent for to go to the chiefs to hear what they had to say & to hear the news. . . The people want [that] we should get guns &c. from Colvile to keep them ready in case the Cayuses should come. I think that will be impossible as there are only a few there. They made one advice, that was that it might be well for us to send our families to Colvile so that we could be with the people in traveling about."

[19] E.W. "We had another report, said to come from one of the Finleys [i.e. Nicholas] who has been sometime in the Cayuses. The report is that the Indians are collecting from all parts & that the whites are determined to make a grand sweep of the natives of the whole land, that the Americans are coming to fight the Company as well as the Indians & that he had come up to get his friends to go down & join the Cayuses. . . How much of this is true we cannot tell." If Walker had known that Nicholas Finley was one of the ringleaders of the Whitman massacre, he would have had additional cause to be alarmed. Much of the unrest which came during the following days may be traced back to Nicholas, who was then visiting his two brothers.

[20] E.W. "I have been most anxious about the coming of Nicholas. I fear he has some evil design against us. Our Indians are much moved, more I think than we are. I have tried to compose myself but without effect. I have had much talk with the Chief but he does not offer me much consolation. The idea that he has [come] after his brothers & the people to join the Cayuses makes it very evident that he is deeply implicated with them. . . One thing very certain that if his brothers & the Spokanes join him, we are placed in a very precarious situation."

[21] E.W. "I have suffered more from excitement to day than at any previous time this winter. I have been at the Chiefs once or twice. He does not seem well pleased with the movements of things. I have been expecting the half-breeds all day but they have not made their appearance. . . The report is to night that all the Spokans are going to join the Cayuses . . . but it seems that it was modified & that the Chief at Spokane had sent a word to our Chief to remain here & take care of us."

in drawers for the first [time.]. . . We continue to hear rumors. Mr. and Mrs. E. seem much excited but I have so much confidence in God that I am afraid to fear. My feeling is that he has not brought us out into this wilderness to slay us. I feel rather anxious to know what he does intend to do with us. It seems to me he will yet bring us out to the light. . . When I lose sight of God, I begin to be fearful & like Peter begin to sink. It seems to me that like him I am walking on water. I seem to stand firmly yet cannot perceive what sustains.

SAT. 12.[22] An express from Colvile. Mr. Lewes alarmed about us in consequence of Indian rumors. We are much perplexed to know what to do. We fear to go, we fear to stay. . .

SUN. 13 [23] . . . This afternoon another express from Colvile arrived. Affairs there have taken a serious turn. The men are under arms & in alarm for themselves & us. May a gracious Providence interpose to prevent all mischief.

MON. 24.[24] Still no harm comes nigh our dwelling. . .

TUES. FEB. 15, 1848.[25] Spent the afternoon & evening contriving & making a foundation to Mrs. Lewes' bonnet.

WEDNES. 16. Got along pretty well with my bonnet. Indian reports favorable. . .

THURS. 17.[26] Reports continue favorable. Finish one bonnet.

FRI. 18 . . . I am thankful Mrs. Lewes' bonnet is done. It suits me better than I expected.

SUN. 20.[27] Another letter from Mr. Lewes. He has also sent a Canadian [Thomas Roy] to remain a while.

[22] E.W. "My state of excitement continued & I have felt most miserably the fore part of the day. . . . In the afternoon a letter came from Mr. Lewes that was quite satisfactory repeating his offer of assistance."

[23] E.W. "After we had finished our Indian service, I received another letter from Mr. Chief Factor Lewes stating that things at that place had taken a very serious turn & that they had been under arms ever since three o'clock that morning." Walker and Eells considered the possibility of taking their families to the Fort and then returning to travel with the people. This was what the Old Chief had advised.

[24] E.W. "The people are anxious to know what course we are going to pursue & seem well satisfied with the idea of our taking our families to Colvile until the strain is over."

[25] E.W. "Some Indians from above came in to day & reported that none of the Spokans was induced to follow Nicholas. If this is really the case, it is encouraging."

[26] E.W. "This morning I had some talk with the Big Star & the Spokane Chief who was present. I did not like all the Big Star said. He seemed [to feel] that if we left they would be laughed at because they were not able to defend us." As a result of this attitude, the two men decided to postpone moving their families to the Fort.

[27] E.W. "I felt quite comfortable last night & this morning until I heard what the Big Star did. I then felt that our situation was quite critical. I see no way in which we can remain here with any comfort to ourselves or use to the people if

Mon. 21. Washing. Mrs. E's folks attending on the Old Chief. Feel alarmed lest they shall be killed for not saving him.

Tues. 22.[28] Busy on bonnets. . .

Wed. 23. Sent off two bonnets [to Mrs. Lewes] by Torteser. Our Mother's meeting. . .

Sun. 27. Atended Indian worship for the first time this winter. Left babe at home.

Mon. 28. Washing as usual. . .

March Wednes. 1. Some things go pleasantly & some not. The weed [29] & our housekeeper are sources of trouble. In the afternoon showed S. how to skin a bird. The one I dressed was a wood duck. The Indian told me they make their nests in hollow trees. After the job of hatching, they take them on their backs to the water & there rear them. . .

Fri. 2 . . . Indian reports more favorable, still I fear we may yet be obliged to remove. . . Mr. E. bled Mrs. M. How glad I should be if she were with her own folks again. . .

Mon. 6.[30] One of the Finleys arrived from the seat of war. There had been one engagement. More than 300 Americans, 200 half breeds, 200 or 300 Kayuses were waring. 100 Nez Perces on their way to join the Americans. I hope matters may be brought to a speedy close and the land again enjoy rest. . .

Thurs. 9 [31] . . . William Peone mother called. Wishes for garden seed. I feel anxious & low spirited.

---

they are going to make slaves of us or that they will rule us by threats. . . They seem much excited if any thing is said against their medicine . . . I did not like the talk of the Indians. . . They say it is better for us to die here than move off. This is a most dark & trying thing to me at least."

[28] E.W. "I cannot get it out of my mind the remarks which some of the Indians say, that it is better for us to die here than to move." For the 23rd: "The remark shows that they have no regard or compassion for us & would willingly see us sacrificed to gain their own point. . . I wrote to Mr. Lewes this morning."

[29] Another reference to Elkanah's use of chewing tobacco.

[30] The soldiers had a skirmish with the Cayuses on February 24 in which a Cayuse chief was killed and Five Crows was wounded. Five Crows, or Hezekiah, was the only Cayuse who had been received into the membership of the Mission church. He had not taken an active part in the Whitman massacre. Commenting on the news of the battle, Walker wrote in his diary: "They had heard that a battle had been fought between the whites & Indians & the latter were worsted. Some of the chiefs tried to make peace but the young men would not listen." The news of the success of the white troops had a subduing effect upon the Spokanes.

[31] E.W. "In the afternoon Baptist Peone came in on his way to Colvile. He gave some new ideas about the fight. They all seem to lay the blame on the young men among the Cayuses because peace was not made. . . What we hear does not tend much to quiet our fears." Peone may have informed Walker that the defeated Cayuses were moving northward. The Palouse Indians were inclined to join the Cayuses. There was a possibility that the warring parties might move into the Spokane country.

FRI. 10.[32] S. & I made a hood for Jeremiah & a petticoat. Thomas Roy left for Colvile this morning. It is a tedious long winter. May a kind Providence send us some good news soon. . .

SUN. 12.[33] I attended Indian worship & sabbath school. While at school Frederick Lewes and Thomas Roy arrived. Mr. Lewes seems rather afraid to have us remain here longer. I feel exceedingly perplexed & bound in spirit & altogether in doubt what course to pursue. Oh that the path of duty may be made plain. I feel exceedingly troubled.

MON. 13.[34] We concluded that it is best to remove to Colvile for a while at least. Wash.

TUES. 14. S. ironing & fixing shoes. Mrs. M. baking & I packing. Feel very sad about leaving, but feel on the whole it is safest.

WED. 15. We left home about noon. Perhaps to return no more. It commenced raining just as we left. Mrs. E. quite ill. It rained most of the afternoon & evening so we got a good sponging. But the weather being warm, we did not suffer much.

THURS. 16. Marcus' birthday. A little stormy all day but we got on pretty well & at night encamped at the half-breeds. Found a dry floor & a good fire more comfortable than mudy ground to encamp on.

FRI. 17. The weather pleasant & we came as far as the [farm house of the Fort.] Encamped in our tents. . .

SAT. MARCH 18. We reached Colvile about noon, where we re-

32 E.W. "The boys left about noon with the cattle." At this time Walker and Eells owned twenty head. They evidently felt that it was best to move some if not all of them to the half-breeds or possibly to Fort Colvile. Thomas Roy seems to have been given this responsibility.

33 A second skirmish between the American troops and the combined forces of the Cayuse and Palouse Indians took place on the Tucannon on March 12 and 13. Lewes may have learned of the probability of such an engagement and was fearful that the conflict would spread to the Spokane country. Hence his advice for the missionaries to move to the Fort at once. Walker wrote that day in his diary: "My opinion is that we had better go. . . Mrs. Walker does not see how she can make the move."

34 E.W. "Nothing was said about leaving until late this morning. I did not find Mr. Eells folks so ready to make the move as I anticipated. . . In the evening we had another [talk] which ended in our deciding to leave on Wednesday. . . The people will not object to our going there with our families." Eells, in his Reminiscences, makes the following comment: "Mr. Walker was constitutionally very timid, Mrs. Eells less so. Personally Mrs. Walker had strong nerves. Her six children increased her caution. . . I was not convinced of reason to apprehend real danger. . . I invited a second meeting on the same evening, and signified my willingness to prepare to leave on the Monday following, the 20th, being the ninth anniversary of the arrival of our families at that place. No! said Mr. Walker, we will pack up tomorrow and start the next day. It was done. In falling rain the move was made. So joyous were the timid that discomfort of weather was not named. At night an encampment in snow was made without murmur."

ceived a cordial welcome. Tho I regret the necessity of making so much trouble.

Sun. 19. We had no publick worship, only a sabbath S. for the children.

Mon. 20.[35] Mr. W. & Mr. E. & Edwin returned. Mr. W. was inclined to tarry another night but Mr. E. would not consent. Mr. W. was not pleased either with the idea of Edwin's returning. I spent the day looking over & arranging things. But feel anxious to be at home again, altho I fear it is not best for us ever to return. I still feel at loss to know what duty requires. But I hope light may soon dawn on our path. I feel that we deserve chastisement, yet I hope in the mercy of God. . . Help Lord for vain is the help of man. . .

Wed. 22.[36] We washed & cleaned our room & the furniture.

Fri. 24. Busy about many things.

Sat. 25.[37] An Indian has arrived from the lower country, says about twenty people from this place have died of sickness the past winter in the Wallamet. . . I had some flour, butter & grease brought to my room, baked some firecakes. Boiled roots & berries. We get along quite comfortably. Fear I do not keep my children as close as I ought. Wrote to Mr. W.[38]

Sun. 26.[39] Mrs. L[ewes.] & her children came in to attend our morning worship. . .

---

[35] E.W. "I tried hard to have Mr. Eells stop another day . . . but he would not consent. We started about noon & rode very fast." For the 21st: "Reached home before sunset & found all safe."

[36] E.W. "I have had much company to day. Dumont came in about noon. I have asked & he has consented to stay two nights." For the 23rd: "It seemed good to get into a soft bed again. . . Ploughed a pretty good piece to day in the garden." Elkanah wrote to Mary from Tshimakain on March 22 (original in Coll. Wn.) saying in part: "The house looks lonely & I feel quite alone. I shall I suppose remain in our house what time I stay here. I think that is Mr. Eells wish for each to take up his abode in his own house." The implication is that he preferred that the two stay together.

[37] E.W. "Last night was the first night that I have slept alone in our house. I had a good night's rest & was not disturbed at all."

[38] Mary's newsy letter is in Coll. Wn. The following are quotations: "Mrs. M. is as smart & active as ever. Makes her appearance in my room by the time I get through my tedious round of morning duties. . . The poor soul would relish a cup of coffee as much as you would a quid of that *detestable* —— ." "All things go on as well as I could expect & I think Mr. Lewes does all he consistently can for us." "Mrs. E. appears to great disadvantage in Mr. Lewes' presence. She is all of a titter & [I] suppose feels much as you do in the pulpit." "Abigail stole off with the other girls to take a sunday walk without her bonnet & lost a nice shell side comb. I hope it will teach us all to remember the sabbath day next time."

[39] E.W. "I felt uneasy all day. . . Soon after the second worship, I heard a yell in the woods & soon saw people running. . . At first I did not know whether they were friends or foes but soon found that they were friends & had come to our relief, they having had some information as led them to suppose that we were already cut off by the Cayuses." Walker later learned that Old Chief,

Tues. March 28, 1848.   Messrs. Walker & Eells arrived just at night having reason to fear the Kayuses were lurking about the station. They left it on Monday morning & fled for their lives. I fear they are not out of danger yet. . .

Thurs. 30.   Mr. Walker concludes to remain at Colvile & Mr. E. proceed to visit the Old Chief by way of our place.

Fri. 31.   Last night considerable disturbance in the fort on account of strange Indians reported to have been seen about the place. This afternoon three Indians came from our Old Chief bringing considerable news. Much of it rather favorable. Our house was safe yesterday.

Sat. April 1.⁴⁰   My birthday. I am 37. In view of all the goodness & mercy which have followed me thus, I will trust in the Lord & hope for the future.

Sun. 2 . . .   "All is well," the guard calls out. Yes all is well, I trust. But it does not seem well to see the Sabbath so little observed. It has been a cold blustering day to day. Gary & one of the chief's sons arrived. . .

Tue. 4 . . .   Mr. W. & T. Roy set out for Tshimakain. . .

Wednes. 5.   E. sick all night so I got little rest. I applied a . . . plaster to prevent inflamation. This morning used injection & about noon succeeded in reducing it. He kept vomiting all night. To day Goudie tightened the spring of the truss. . .

Thurs. 6.⁴¹   I commenced writing letters. Mr. Frazer arrived from New Caledonia & Mr. Simpson from the Flatheads. Mr. S. saw Mr. Walker this morning. He was not able to proceed on the journey yesterday being sick. The Finlays have gone to bring off their brother from the Kayuses. Ellis, the Nez Perce chief, is dead & all his family. . .

Sat. 8 . . .   Mr. W. returned in safety tho I did not expect to see him. Mr. E. came as far as the Halfbreed's & has returned again. . .   The Finleys turned back & did not go for their brother. Old Solomon returned to the Bighead [Old Chief] in safety. But the Kayuses sent word they should pay no attention to his message.⁴² We

who was camping with some of his people in the Palouse country, received information which led him to believe that the Cayuses had sent some of their warriors to Tshimakain to kill the missionaries there. Old Chief then sent some of his men to protect the two families. The incident caused Walker and Eells to take extra precautions. "At night," Walker wrote in his diary, "all our animals are yarded & a watch kept." They decided to return to the Fort.

⁴⁰ E.W. "According to my request I was placed on the guard. I had the first guard."

⁴¹ E.W. "Reached our place in pretty good season & found Mr. Eells & all with him safe. We decided to pack up & make a good start in the morning. I went to work & packed up fast as I could having Dumont & Roy to help me."

⁴² Old Solomon had been sent to the Cayuses with a message from the Spokane Chiefs not to molest the missionaries at Tshimakain. However the threat of any such attack was diminishing as the American troops forced the Cayuses to retreat into the Blue Mountains.

are anxious & afraid to hear what will come next. Mr. Lewes is concerned for the fate of Mr. Low.

SUN. 9. All is well. . .

WEDNESDAY 12 . . . We took a long walk after dinner down by the river. The stone is stratified. I should think a felspatic rock, very nice for building. It is very brittle.

WED. APR. 12.[43] Mr. Eells returned to night. His account of things does not increase my anxiety to return to Tshimakain again.

THURS. 13.[44] Mr. Low arrived. Came by land, had no trouble with Indians. We received letters from the Islands but none from the States. Dr. Armstrong is dead. . . The war makes slow progress. They succeeded in recovering property but not in killing the murderers. . .

FRI. 14. Read newspapers till dinner. . .

SAT. 15 . . . Iron after dinner, cutting hair & bathing children.

SUN. 16.[45] We had worship in the dining room. Mr. W. baptized Michel Ogden.

MON. 17. Washing. Mr. E. left for the Barrier. . .

THURS. 20. The boats arrived. Mrs. Ermatinger & daughter . . . called at our rooms in P.M.

FRI. 21 . . . Mrs. Ermatinger concludes not to go on at present. Thinks the journey too much. . .

SUN. 23.[46] We had an English service in Mr. E. room. Mr. E. preached.

MON. APR. 24, 1848. The boats left. We all went down to see them start. . . In the afternoon Messrs. Walker & Eells left for the station again. . .

WED. 26.[47] Accomplished very little. Our Maternal meeting, I led. We invited none to attend but ourselves.

THURS. 27. Made some butter for the table. Washed the rest of the day. Got rather out of patience with poor Mrs. M. & spoke full cross enough.

---

[43] E.W. "Mr. Eells came in to night & did not give a very favorable account of the conduct of the Indians."

[44] E.W. "The intelligence from the army is not very cheering." The elusive tactics of the hostile Indians made a decisive battle impossible for the soldiers.

[45] E.W. "I have felt some anxiety about baptizing Michel. I should much prefer to perform the ceremony according to our practice but I know it will be more pleasing to all to perform it according to the Episcopal rite." Michel was an adult son of Peter Skeene Ogden, who had been a frequent visitor at Tshimakain.

[46] Bishop Modeste Demers was one of the passengers on the express boats which arrived on the previous Thursday. E.W. wrote in his diary for Sunday: "They had wine on the table, the first time since we have been here. . . After the service by the Bishop, the day was spent in playing cards & so forth."

[47] E.W. "Reached our place in pretty good season & found that there had been some pilfering among the people. I did not feel very safe." For the 27th: "Commence ploughing & nearly finished." For the 28th: "Planted my potatoes & finished putting seed into the ground." This was the end of any cultivation by either of the missionaries at Tshimakain.

FRI. 28 . . . Baked some bread & cakes in the oven. The bread not being put in in season may not [be] done in season, so I [am] told. . . The remark was made, "I never saw warm rocks for dinner before." . .

SUN. 30. The fort has been as busy as if it were a week day. An Indian hung himself, but Michel Ogden & others cut him down before he was dead. . .

WEDNES. [MAY] 3. Mr. Walker returned.[48] Think we may perhaps be able to return home again soon.

THURS. 4 . . . I have found a good way to bake bread in a kettle. . .

SUN. 7. A report that the Americans are [on] this side Snake river. I spent most of the day reading. . .

MON. 8. Washing & some other chores. Mrs. M. reading a romance all day. The children neglected. . .

THURS. 11. Mr. E. does not come yet. . .

SUN. 14.[49] Nothing special. Read Mothers Magazines. Had a Sabbath school. Mr. Walker preached in the room. . .

TUES. 16 [50] . . . Mr. E. returned having received a letter from the American camp. . .

WED. 17. Mr. E. left for Tshimakain again. May God preserve both him & the station & grant us patience. . .

SAT. 20 . . . Mufflehead came with letters from our place. One was from Mr. Lee the commander in chief. 500 men were once [at] Dr's station; the army to cross Snake river the past week.

SUN. 21 . . . Had the rump of a reindeer [caribou] for dinner.

MON. 22. Mufflehead left with letters for our place. . .

TUES. 23. Abigail 8 years old, gave her a testament. . .

FRI. 26.[51] Mr. E. returned to this place.

[48] Elkanah shuttled back and forth between Tshimakain and Colvile five times during the spring of 1848. After the women and children were taken to the Fort, Walker spent no more time at the mission site than was necessary. Eells remained at Tshimakain most of the time and was in contact with the officers in command of the Oregon Volunteers.

[49] E.W. "I felt as though I ought to have some service with the men & spoke to Mr. Lewes about it. He had no objection so I called them in & preached to them my sermon on the worth of the soul. Some few attended & paid good attention."

[50] E.W. "About noon Mr. Eells came in with much important intelligence. It was manifest that the Palouses were anxious to make peace with the whites. He brought a good letter from Lt. Waters [Col. James Waters] manifesting much sympathy for us & profering us aid if we needed."

[51] E.W. "Soon after noon Mr. Eells came in thinking it best for him to leave as he could do nothing more as our people had met the troops." Eells, in his Reminiscences, wrote: "At that post [Fort Colville] the two missionary families had been enjoying generous hospitality during ten weeks lacking one day. I had been there ten nights. The saddle had supported my body by day and my head

SAT. 27. Did a few odd jobs such as covering books. . . No prospect of our being able to return to Tshimakain yet.

SUN. 28.[52] An express to inform us that an escort has arrived at our place to conduct us to the Valley. We conclude it will be our duty to go.

MON. 29 MAY.[53] Messrs. Eells & Walker left for Tshimakain. I washed.

---

by night. According to my estimate I had traveled fourteen hundred miles." Eells was writing in retrospect and included the full period the two families were at Fort Colville.

[52] E.W. "While we were at dinner, an Indian came in with letters from the commanders of the Army, one announcing that a party were on their way to escort us out of the country if we wished to go, with the advice of Col. Lee that we had better improve the opportunity. We have found it necessary to say much that was in ordinary cases inconsistent with the sacredness of the day. We have made arrangements to start to our place in the morning to meet the party who is expecting to be at our place to day. I feel myself wholly unfit for such a journey. . . It seems a great & important undertaking to move & to leave our people to the influence of the Romanists."

[53] E.W. "We left this morning before sunrise for our place which we reached [when the] sun [was still] three hours high & met the party who had come to our protection." For the 30th: "We left to day for Colville about noon." And for the 31st: "Reached Colvile & commenced preparation for starting on our long journey."

Farewell to Tshimakain

Mary made no entries in her diary after May 29 until the summary statement of July 3 which follows. However Elkanah was fairly regular in keeping up his diary for June and a detailed account of the evacuation of the missionary party from the Spokane country was written by one of the officers of the escorting company of Oregon Volunteers. This was published over the pseudonym "Rambler" in the July 13, 1848, issue of the *Oregon Spectator*. Also Eells, in a letter to Greene dated July 17, 1848, and in his Reminiscences, gives us further details of the departure from Tshimakain and of the trip to the Willamette Valley.

The rescue company of sixty volunteers under the command of Major J. Magone arrived at the mission site on Monday afternoon, May 29. Of this Rambler wrote:

> We came in sight of one of nature's 'most sweet and peaceful scenes' that I ever beheld — a perfectly level prairie valley, of the richest soil and vegetation — about 10 miles long and 3 wide; at the southeast corner of which stood the neat little buildings and pleasure gardens of the mission — the whole surrounded by lofty pines, covering the hills, which gave it the appearance of a grand amphitheater. Near the houses and gardens, at the foot of a lofty hill, nature pours forth of her sweetest fountains which, in the language of the natives is called "Tshimakain," hence the name of the mission. [Footnote Chimerkine.] We had just arrived, and unfurled our banner from the top of the house, when Messrs. Eels & Walker, with young Mr. Lewes, having heard we were coming, came from Colvile. It was a meeting of joy.

Major Magone, reporting to Colonel Waters, wrote: "They gave us, one and all, a hearty welcome to their once happy home; after the usual preliminaries were over, Rev. Mr. Eells unlocked his door, and I found myself at once in a house which would do honor even to Oregon City." Walker and Eells were soon satisfied with arrangements and indicated their readiness to return to Fort Colville the next day to get their families. They turned their premises over to the soldiers and furnished them with an abundance of provisions.

The two men were back at the Fort on Wednesday, May 31, and the next day the mission party of five adults, counting Mrs. Marquis, eight children, and a pack train of ten or twelve animals loaded with the belongings they wished to take with them to the Willamette Valley, left for Tshimakain. They arrived at the station at eleven o'clock Saturday morning, where they tarried for about two hours. By this time the natives in that vicinity had heard that their missionaries were leaving. They gathered at the mission to bid their friends farewell. Rambler wrote: "They asked many questions concerning the length of their absence, and on being told that when all things became calm again, their teachers would return, they seemed much better satisfied." Major Magone reported that "Several shed tears on bidding them adieu."

In his letter to Greene, Eells wrote concerning the deposition of their twenty head of cattle:

> One [was] loaned to Cornelius [Old Chief.] Three have been furnished to the Army for food. Seven sold, for which orders on the H.H.B. Co., have been received. Two exchanged for horses, & the remaining seven are to be driven to Colvile where they will remain in safe keeping till further arrangements shall be made respecting them.

Regarding other items, Eells wrote: "The more important part of two sets of harness, two ploughs, & six sickles have been loaned to our people. The crops now growing they are to harvest, & if we shall not return before snow shall fall, they will be at liberty to appropriate them to their use." Many of the articles used within the homes were likewise given away. The remainder of the moveable property which the missionaries considered worth saving was turned over to young Lewes to be taken by pack train to Fort Colville. The Hudson's Bay Company may have purchased some of these items and some may later have been sent down the Columbia by boat.

The hour of departure came. Joseph Elkanah, then a little more than four years old, years later recorded his memories of how they traveled:

> Cyrus had me on behind him, Marcus rode behind Abbie, father carried Jeremiah in front of him, while one of the volunteers was detailed to help mother carry the babe, John R. Edwin Eells rode alone while Myron rode with his father.[1]

We can only imagine the emotions of Elkanah and Mary Walker and of Cushing and Myra Eells as they bade farewell to their first homes, the place where five Walker and two Eells children were born,

---

[1] A copy of the recollections of Joseph Elkanah Walker is in Coll. Wn.

and where they had spent nine of the best years of their lives in such devoted self-sacrificing service for the natives. Of the four adults, only Cushing Eells is known to have revisited the site. For the other three, it was goodby forever. As the long caravan left the plain for a camping site on the south side of the Spokane River, a company of the Indians mounted their horses and followed.

The soldiers, aware of the unwillingness of the missionaries to travel on Sunday, remained in camp on June 4. Rambler reported that two "Divine services" were conducted in camp that Sunday and that he was greatly moved when he heard "the soft and plaintive" voices of the women raised in song. In his letter to Greene, Eells added: "There was another service with the Natives. . . Solemn thoughts crowd upon my mind. This is the termination of my labors for a time, perhaps forever, [with this people."]

For Wednesday, June 7, Rambler wrote:

Passed the day quite agreeably in the company of Madame Walker, conversing on the natural history of the region, character of the natives, their manners and customs, volcanic eruptions, tertiary, or igneous and aqueous formations. An intelligent and virtuous woman, her price is far above rubies." Encamped on the Palouse river.

The caravan crossed the Snake River the next day and arrived at ruined and desolate Waiilatpu on Saturday about one P.M. The place called up too many painful recollections for them to tarry. Rambler wrote:

'Twas a very sad and trying scene to them to witness the mouldering ruins of the former habitation of their worthy brother and sister. They rested but an hour or two, and went out a few miles and encamped till Monday.

The mission party with some of the volunteers arrived at The Dalles on Saturday, June 17. It was then decided that Walker with the women and children would continue their journey by boat while Eells with the volunteers and the pack animals would take the Barlow route across the Cascades. The boat party reached Oregon City on June 22. Eells arrived two days later. Among the first to welcome the mission families to the Willamette Valley was the artist, John Mix Stanley,[2] who was the first to inform them of the Whitman massacre.

[2] Stanley revisited Tshimakain in 1853 as a member of the Stevens Expedition which was exploring a route for a railroad. At that time Stanley made a drawing of the mission premises, see p. 189, Drury, *Elkanah and Mary Walker*. There is no recognizable likeness in the buildings of this drawing and the one made by Geyer nine years earlier. The original cabins had been torn down in August, 1847; another house was burned some time before the summer of 1851; and by 1853

On Monday, July 3, 1848, Mary resumed her diary. Before beginning the entries which told of her new life in the Willamette Valley, she wrote the following brief summary of the events of the previous five weeks:

It is a month since I have had time to look at my journal. We left Colvile the first of June. Reached the Station Sat. afternoon [June 3], stopped two hours, passed the Spokan & encamped. We did not move on Sunday but I was obliged to work most of the day as it threatened to rain. We left the Spokan on Monday & reached the ruins of Waiilatpu on Sat. [June 10.] Passed on & encamped near. Rested the Sabbath day & went on again on Monday. On Sat. reached Wascopen, [The Dalles,] concluding to take boats. Left Sunday evening there being too much wind to sail by day. We went down only a few miles & encamped in the dark among rocks, & slept without tents. On Sunday John quite sick. The next day better.

We had a prosperous journey but were delayed some by wind. I was much interested in the scenery of the Columbia. So different from our Snake R. I almost fancied myself on the old Mississippi again.

As Mary and her family proceeded by boat down the Columbia, her memory leaped back to the time when she and Elkanah, as newlyweds, started out for Oregon and of the boat trip they took down the Ohio and up the Mississippi to St. Louis. Thus the last entry in Mary's diary for the mission period links up the end with its beginning. Even as ten years earlier, she and her husband as missionaries were embarking on a great venture of faith into the wilderness of Oregon, so now she, her husband, and six little children were starting life anew as pioneers in the white settlements of a new Oregon.

FIFTY YEARS IN THE WILLAMETTE VALLEY

Mary Walker spent nearly sixty years of her life in Oregon, ten years as a member of the Oregon Mission of the American Board and nearly fifty years in the Willamette Valley. Although it is not within the scope of this work to present a biography of Mary, a brief summary of the main events of this latter period is in order.[3]

other buildings had been erected on the site, perhaps by the half-breeds who probably moved in after the missionaries left. Walker, in a letter to his wife written from Cascade City on June 1, 1851, (original Coll. WN.) said: "I hear also that our house at Tshimakain has been burned up." However, Stevens, in his *Report of Explorations*, pp. 147-48, states that in 1853 "The house occupied by Walker is still standing, but Eel's house has burned down." The identification was no doubt made by Stanley.

[3] For further information regarding these fifty years see McKee, *Mary Richardson Walker: Her Book*, and Drury, *Elkanah and Mary Walker*.

Mary continued to write in her diary but gradually with less regularity. Her entries for the first weeks of their residence at Oregon City reveal what was to the whole Walker family a tremendous change in their manner of living. They were now in a community of white people. They attended the First Congregational Church of Oregon City where Dr. George Atkinson, the father of Oregon Congregationalism, preached. What a thrill to be worshipping with a congregation of English speaking people again! Mary made note of the fact that on such occasions as going to church she could wear her silk dress. Instead of bartering with the Indians, she could go shopping. Her children could go to school and play with white companions of their own age. But evidently there were some adjustments that had to be made in these relationships for Mary noted in her diary for August 5: "Cyrus got bruised & his shirt torn by a bad boy." On July 23, 1850, she wrote: "Had a ride in a chaise for the first time since I left Maine." The Walkers were back in civilization again.

Financially, Elkanah and Mary had a most difficult time for several years. Elkanah found a house in Oregon City which he rented for a short time for thirteen dollars a month. Neighbors lent furniture. Elkanah purchased a wagon on credit and with the two horses he had brought with him from Tshimakain turned to trucking. Fortunately for him, the gold rush to California was just beginning and labor was in demand. The American Board permitted him to keep such little property as he had brought out of the Mission and there is some evidence that the Board also helped out in a modest way with a cash supplement. But for the most part Elkanah had to turn to manual work to make a living for his family.

The Walkers moved to Forest Grove in October, 1849, where they spent the rest of their lives. Here Elkanah purchased a donation land claim of a square mile from one who had become infected with the gold fever. A good portion of this claim is now occupied by the present city of Forest Grove. Here he began farming again and at the same time was active in preaching. He was once described by his son Joseph Elkanah as "half-farmer, half-preacher." In June 1858 Elkanah received an appointment from the American Home Missionary Society with a stipend of three hundred dollars a year, which was later increased to six hundred dollars. For many years he served Congregational churches in Forest Grove and vicinity. Walker was a member of the first Board of Trustees of Whitman College in 1860, and was one of the organizers of Pacific University at Forest Grove. He gave land to this institution on which the first building was erected, and served as a trustee from 1866 until the time of his death.

In the meantime Mary with her characteristic energy threw herself into the work of her home, her church, and her community. In January, 1849, she organized a Maternal Association.[4] Even with six little

4 Original record book is in the archives of Pacific University.

children to take care of, she ventured in September, 1848, to adopt an orphan baby. The child died soon afterwards. The seventh Walker child, another boy, was born at Forest Grove on February 3, 1850. They called him Levi Chamberlain, after a prominent missionary in the Hawaiian Islands. In the spring of 1852, Mary's younger brother, Samuel, who was seventeen years old when she left for Oregon, visited the Walkers. He was the only member of her family to call on them in her Oregon home. Samuel later settled in California. When Mary's eighth child, and another son, arrived on May 2, 1852, she named him Samuel after her brother. This was the Samuel Walker whom the author knew who turned over to him so much source material used in the preparation of this work.[5]

During the Civil War, three of Mary's sons, Cyrus, Marcus, and John, enlisted in the First Regiment of Oregon Volunteers. Cyrus became a first lieutenant. On September 14, 1863, Abigail became the wife of James Anderson Karr who took his bride to Hoquiam, Washington. They became the parents of seven sons and five daughters, several of whom made notable records for themselves in business and professional circles. One of the daughters, Ruth Karr McKee, served as a regent of the University of Washington, 1917-26, and was honored by having a residence hall named after her. In 1945 Mrs. McKee published a fine interpretative study of her grandmother under the title *Mary Richardson Walker: Her Book.*

Several of the descendants of Elkanah and Mary were missionaries. The Reverend Joseph Elkanah Walker went to China in 1872, under the American Board, where he served for about fifty years. A daughter of his, Josephine, also was a missionary in China under the same Board. Another granddaughter of Elkanah and Mary, Nellie May, a daughter of Samuel Walker, went out to China in 1926 and in 1935 was transferred to South Africa. Thus a member of the third generation went where her grandparents originally planned to go. Two of the daughters of Levi Chamberlain Walker, holding doctorates from Cornell University, Dr. Elda Walker and Dr. Leva Walker, were members of the faculty of the University of Nebraska for many years teaching botany.

The first of the family to pass away was Jeremiah, who died at Forest Grove on January 26, 1870, in his twenty-fourth year. On May 13, 1895, John Richardson, who was born at Tshimakain shortly after the Whitman massacre, died. He was the second of Mary's children to pass away before her death.

---

[5] The author received an apple box full of books and documents from Samuel Walker in the summer of 1939, shortly before his house with all of the contents was burned. This collection was turned over to the library of Washington State University, Pullman.

MARY WALKER AND HER FAMILY BEFORE HER FOREST GROVE HOME ABOUT 1896 Mrs. Walker is seated. Her six sons and one daughter, left to right are: Joseph Elkanah (ordained a Congregational minister, and went to China as a missionary in 1872); John Richardson; Cyrus Hamlin; Marcus Whitman; Abigail Boutwell (who became Mrs. James A. Karr); Levi Chamberlain; and Samuel Thompson. Jeremiah is not shown as he died in 1870.

ABIGAIL AND CYRUS WALKER
Daughter and son of Mary Walker. A photograph taken
about 1855, and reproduced here by courtesy of the
Oregon Historical Society, owner of the original.

Walker continued to chew tobacco for about seven years after the family settled in the Willamette Valley, much to the annoyance of his wife. But there came a time when he gave up the habit. In a letter written to the author by Samuel Walker on September 5, 1935, the incident is thus described:

Time and time again he tried to quit; but the Drs. told him it was of no use. When he was about 50 he read the last chapter of Revelation at morning prayers. About ten o'clock he came in and asked mother to fix him some kind of tonic to carry him till noon. She told him she "could not bolster him up as long as he used tobacco" and quoted the verse "He that is filthy let him be filthy still." (Rev. 22:11). He took his tobacco from his pocket and gave it to her saying: "Keep that till I call for it."

Mary laid the plug on the shelf behind the kitchen stove where it remained for years. He never used it again.

The Spokane Indians made repeated requests for their missionaries to return. At first the unsettled condition of the country was a sufficient reason for not going back. After two years of wandering, always fearful of the soldiers and never daring to return to their old camping grounds on the Walla Walla, the Cayuses finally decided to deliver up five of their number, who were the most guilty, for the welfare of the tribe. These included Tiloukaikt and Tomahas. The five were tried at Oregon City. All were found guilty and were hanged on June 3, 1850. The half-breeds, including Nicholas Finley and Joe Lewis who were also involved in the crime, were never apprehended.

After all this was over, the Spokanes still begged their former teachers to return. The January, 1852, issue of the *Missionary Herald* reported:

Last year a large party of Spokans traveled about four hundred miles to request the Superintendent of Indian Affairs to furnish them a missionary. They said they had not forgotten the instruction of Messrs. Walker and Eells; but they must soon forget what they had heard unless these brethren or others should become their teachers. While encamped near Oregon City, they prayed in their tents, morning and evening, with much apparent devotion.

However, both Elkanah and Mary felt that the needs of their growing family made any such move inadvisable. Eells remembers Mary as saying: "O that the Indians might live, but my Isaacs must be cared for." For several years after the Whitman massacre the American Board kept the Oregon Mission on its list of activities. Finally, in the January, 1853, issue of the *Missionary Herald,* the announcement was made that "It has not seemed expedient for the Board to resume operations in Oregon." So the Mission was officially closed.

Cushing Eells revisited Tshimakain in 1862 for the first time after his departure in 1848. He was warmly welcomed and found many evidences of the natives following the teachings that he and Walker had so assiduously tried to inculcate. In the spring of 1873, Spokane Garry invited Spalding, then at Lapwai, to visit the Spokanes and "to baptize my people." Spalding responded and baptized 253 adults and 81 children that summer.[6] He thus laid the foundations for the two Presbyterian churches still in existence among the Spokanes. William Threemountains, who as a boy had been given instruction in the Walker home, was one of the active leaders in the newly formed church. In the summer of 1875 when the Reverend Henry T. Cowley, a Presbyterian missionary, was ministering to the Spokanes, Eells returned to this people and took part in a communion service when 108 partook. Although the Walkers and the Eells in great patience carried on their work for nearly nine years without the satisfaction of ever seeing a single convert join the Mission church, still the seed had been sown and in due time it brought forth a harvest.

The American Board put in a claim to the government in November, 1857, for $20,000 for "damages sustained among the Spokanes."[7] However, there is no evidence that this claim was ever allowed. The mission site passed into private hands and it is now known as Walker's Prairie, rather than by the original name Tshimakain.

In May 1871, shortly after the completion of the transcontinental railroad, Elkanah and Mary returned to their old homes in Maine. They went by steamer from Portland, Oregon, to San Francisco, where they boarded the train. No record has been found of their travel experiences or of their feelings as they crossed the plains on the Union Pacific, which paralleled somewhat the old Oregon Trail over which they had ridden on horseback thirty-three years earlier. They arrived at Bangor Theological Seminary in time to attend the graduating exercises of their son, Joseph Elkanah. They spent several months in the East visiting relatives and friends. Two of Mary's family, Charlotte and Daniel, were still living in Maine. On their return trip, they visited Mary's cousin, Daniel Thompson, in Chicago. They returned to their Forest Grove home in November.

---

[6] For further details about the great revival that swept through the Nez Perce and Spokane tribes following Spalding's return in 1871 see Drury, *Spalding;* and Drury, *A Tepee in his Front Yard.* In the summer of 1949 the author interviewed, at Wellpinit, Washington, a Spokane Indian nearly 100 years old, who claimed that he had been baptized by Spalding at a spring near Cheney in the summer of 1873. He was probably the last survivor of those baptized by the veteran missionary.

[7] Original letter from L. S. Pomeroy, Secretary of ABCFM, Office Indian Affairs, Washington, D.C.

Elkanah Walker died at Forest Grove on November 21, 1877. The next day Mary wrote in her diary: "I seemed to hear the Savior say: Woman, behold thy sons. Thank God for them." The funeral services were held in the local Congregational Church with Dr. George H. Atkinson of Portland in charge. Burial was made in Union Cemetery at Forest Grove. Several entries in Mary's diary reveal the depth of her grief. "It seemed as though I can't live without my husband," she wrote on December 18. "It is so lonely to be a widow." And on the twenty-eighth, she confided: "I feel so lonely. Think of so many things I want to tell Mr. Walker. I realize more and more how much more I loved him than any one else." Mary survived her husband by over twenty years.

EPILOGUE

Only once did Mary return to the Walla Walla Valley after her departure from it in 1848. That was in 1888, when Whitman College sponsored the observance of the fiftieth anniversary of the arrival of the reinforcement of 1838 in Oregon. Myron Eells accompanied her to Walla Walla, that she might take part in the commemorative event. Cushing Eells was also present and his son Myron was the speaker.

One by one the members of the mission band of twelve passed away. The Whitmans were killed on November 29, 1847. Eliza Spalding died in 1851, Sarah Smith in 1855, and Henry H. Spalding in 1874. After the passing of Elkanah Walker in 1877, the next to go was Myra Eells in 1878. Mary Gray died in 1881, A. B. Smith in 1886, and W. H. Gray in 1889. That left only Cushing Eells and Mary Walker. When Eells died in 1893, Mary Walker remained as the sole survivor. Her end came on Sunday morning, December 5, 1897, at the age of eighty-six years, eight months, and four days. Surviving her were five sons, one daughter, twenty-five grandchildren, and six great-grandchildren. Her funeral service was held on December 7 — which was the fifty-ninth birthday of Cyrus — with the Reverend Myron Eells in charge. Previously Myron had conducted the funeral services for both his father and his mother. In his remarks at Mary's funeral, Myron pointed out the fact that the average life span of the twelve who went out to Oregon in 1836 and 1838 was sixty-five years and five months, "longer than the average of most who stay at home." The tragic end of the Whitmans brought down the average for the group.

Mary Walker's remains were laid beside those of her husband in the Forest Grove cemetery. Each grave was marked with a small headstone with their respective initials. A seven-foot monument was erected between the two graves. On the side facing Mary's grave is her name with the dates of her birth and death, and a similar inscription on the other side for Elkanah. On the front of the monument is the following inscription:

MISSIONARIES OF THE A.B.C.F.M.
Surely goodness and mercy have followed
me all the days of my life

On October 29, 1908, the Washington State Historical Society and the Congregational Churches of the State dedicated a granite monument at Tshimakain to the memory of Elkanah and Mary Walker and of Cushing and Myra Eells. The names of the children born to the two couples while they lived at Tshimakain are inscribed on the monument. In the fall of 1938 the monument was moved to the edge of the highway and rededicated on Sunday, September 18, with appropriate ceremonies by the Eastern Washington State Historical Society. A Daughters of the American Revolution chapter at Longview, Washington, has taken the name Mary Richardson Walker Chapter. It is hoped that the day will soon come when the beautiful and historic site of the Tshimakain mission may become one of the parks of the state of Washington.

Bibliography

Bibliography

ALLEN, Miss A.J. Ten Years in Oregon: Travels and Adventures of Doctor Elijah White and Lady. (Ithaca, 1848).

ATKINSON, Nancy. Biography of Rev. G. H. Atkinson. (Portland, 1893).

ATKINSON, George and Eells, Myron. Funeral Service in Memory of Mrs. M. F. Eells. (Portland, 1878).

BAGLEY, Clarence B. Early Catholic Missions in Old Oregon. (Seattle, 1932) 2 vols.

BROSNAN, Cornelius J. Jason Lee, Prophet of the New Oregon. (New York, 1932).

CANNON, Miles. Waiilatpu. (Boise, 1915).

CLARKE, Samuel A. Pioneer Days of Oregon History. (Portland, 1905) 2 vols.

DELANEY, Matilda Sager. A Survivor's Recollections of the Whitman Massacre. (Spokane, ca. 1920).

DESMET, Pierre Jean. Oregon Missions and Travels (New York, 1847). New Indian Sketches (New York, n.d.). Letters and Sketches (Philadelphia, 1843).

DEVOTO, Bernard. Across the Wide Missouri. (Cambridge, 1957).

DOUTHIT, Mary Osborn. Souvenir of Western Women. (Portland, 1905).

DRURY, Clifford M. Henry Harmon Spalding, Pioneer of Old Oregon. (Caldwell, Idaho, 1936).

—— Marcus Whitman, M.D., Pioneer and Martyr. (Caldwell, 1937).

—— Elkanah and Mary Walker, Pioneers among the Spokanes. (Caldwell, Idaho, 1940).

—— A Tepee in His Front Yard. (Portland, 1949).

—— The Diaries and Letters of Henry H. Spalding and Asa Bowen Smith, relating to the Nez Perce Mission, 1838-1842. (Glendale, 1958).

EELLS, Myron. Father Eells. (Boston, 1894).

—— Marcus Whitman, Pathfinder and Patriot. (Seattle, 1909).

—— Memorial of Mrs. Mary R. Walker. (n.p., n.d.).

ELLIOTT, T.C. Coming of the White Women, being five reprints from the Oregon Historical Society's Quarterly, 1936-37, rearranged and bound. (Portland, 1937).

EVANS, Elwood. History of the Pacific Northwest, Oregon and Washington. (Portland, ca. 1889) 2 vols.

FARNHAM, Thomas J. Travels across the Great Western Prairies. (Cleveland, 1906).

GRAY, William Henry. A History of Oregon. (Portland, 1870).

HENDERSON, Paul C. Landmarks on the Oregon Trail. (New York, 1953).

HINES, Gustavus. Life on the Plains of the Pacific: Oregon: its history. (Buffalo, 1850).

—— Wild Life in Oregon. (Arlington ed.).

HULBERT, Archer Butler, and Dorothy P. Marcus Whitman, Crusader. 3 vols. from Overland to the Pacific Series. (Denver, 1936-41).

IRVING, Washington. The Adventures of Captain Bonneville. (New York, 1851).

—— Astoria. (New York, n.d.).

JESSETT, Thomas E. Reports and Letters of Herbert Beaver. (Portland, 1959).

JOHANSEN, Dorothy O. Robert Newell's Memoranda. (Portland, 1959).

JONES, Nard. The Great Command. (Boston, 1959).

KANE, Paul. Wanderings of an Artist. (Toronto, 1925).

KELLY, Charles and Howe, Maurice L. Miles Goodyear, First Citizen of Utah. (Salt Lake City, 1937).

LANDERHOLM, Carl. (Trans.) Notices & Voyages of the Famed Quebec Mission to the Pacific Northwest, 1838-1847. (Portland, 1956).

LEWIS, William A. and Murakami, Naojiro. Ranald MacDonald. (Spokane, 1923).

MARSHALL, William I. The Acquisition of Oregon. (Seattle, 1911). 2 vols.

McBETH, Kate. The Nez Perces since Lewis and Clark. (New York, 1908).

McKEE, Ruth Karr. Mary Richardson Walker: Her Book. (Caldwell, Idaho, 1945).

MINUTES OF THE SYNOD OF WASHINGTON, (Presbyterian) 1906. This contains the records of the old Mission church.

MISSIONARY ALBUM. (Honolulu, 1937).

NICHOLS, Mrs. Marie Leona. The Mantle of Elias; the Story of Fathers Blanchet and Demers in early Oregon. (Portland, ca. 1941).

NIXON, Oliver W. How Marcus Whitman saved Oregon. (Chicago, 1895).

—— Whitman's Ride through Savage Lands. (Chicago, 1895).

PALMER, Joel. Journals of Travels. (Cleveland, 1906).

PARKER, Samuel. Journal of an Exploring Tour Beyond the Rocky Mountains. (Ithaca, 1838).

RAPPORTS sur les Missions du Diocese de Quebec, 1839-42.
RICHARDSON, Marvin M. The Whitman Mission. (Walla Walla, 1940).
Ross, Marvin C. The West of Alfred Jacob Miller. (Norman, Okla., 1951).
RUSSELL, Osborne. Journal of a Trapper. (Portland, 1955).
SAUNDERS, Mrs. Mary. The Whitman Massacre, a true story by a Survivor. (Oakland, 1916).
SCREIBEIS, Charles D. Pioneer Education in the Pacific Northwest. (Portland, ca. 1936).
SIMPSON, Sir George. An Overland Journey round the World. (Philadelphia, 1847).
STANLEY, John Mix. Portraits of North American Indians. (Smithsonian Institution, Washington, 1850).
STEVENS, Isaac I. Narrative and Final Report of Explorations. (Washington, 1860).
TEIT, J.A. The Salishan Tribes of the Western Plateaus in 45th Annual Report of the Bureau of American Ethnology, 1927-28. (Washington, 1930).
U.S. SENATE EXEC. DOC. No. 37. 41 Cong. 3rd session, ser. no. 1440. (This was compiled by Spalding.)
VICTOR, Frances Fuller. The Early Indian Wars of Oregon. (Salem, 1894).
—— River of the West. (Hartford, 1870).
WARREN, Eliza Spalding. Memoirs of the West. (Portland, 1916).
WILKES, Charles. Narrative of the U.S. Exploring Expedition. (Philadelphia, 1845).

PERIODICALS

Baptist Missionary Magazine
Chicago Advance
Christian Advocate and Zion City Herald (New York)
Christian Mirror (Portland, Me.)
Chronicle Express (Penn Yan, N.Y.)
Friend of Temperance and Seamen (Honolulu)
Frontier (Montana)
Kansas Historical Collection
Ladies Home Journal
Missionary Herald

Mother's Magazine
New England Magazine
New York Westerners
Oregon Historical Quarterly
Oregon Spectator
Oregonian and Indians Advocate
Pacific Homestead
Pacific Northwest Quarterly
St. Louis Observer
Transactions of the Oregon Pioneer Association
Washington Historian
Walla Walla Statesman

REFERENCE TO THE MANUSCRIPT MATERIAL used may be found in "Sources and Acknowledgments."

Index

Index

Page numbers for volume II refer to this volume; for references to volume I, see the Bison Books edition, titled *Where Wagons Could Go: Narcissa Whitman and Eliza Spalding*.